VIETNAM;
HONOR AND SACRIFICE

Gerry Feld

Copyright © by Gerry Feld 2020

ISBN Soft Cover: 978-0-578-58480-5
ISBN eBooks: 978-0-578-58483-6

All rights reserved. No part of this book may be reproduced or transmitted in any form or by any means electronic, or mechanical, including photocopying, recording, or by any information storage and retrieval system, without permission from the copyright owner.

Vietnam; Honor and Sacrifice is purely a work of fiction. Names, characters, places and incidents are the product of the author's imagination or are used fictitiously. Any resemblance to any actual person living or dead, or events and locales is entirely coincidental.

All Cover designs and art work created by K. Tarrier
Editing and Proof Reading: Lori Hawkins
Interior design and layout: Roseanna M White

Published by Ingram/Spark Content Group
Global Head Quarters in La Vergne, Tn. U.S.A.

Printed in the U.S.A.

OTHER TITLES BY GERRY FELD

A Journey into War, Published 2017
A Soldier's Final Journey, Published 2019

CONTENTS

PREFACE 7
Acknowledgments 9
Chapter 1: A Brutal War 11
Chapter 2: An Earlier Life 19
Chapter 3: An Explosive Decision... 32
Chapter 4: Military Life Begins... 57
Chapter 5: Medi-vac Training 93
Chapter 6: Return to Glendale 104
Chapter 7: Welcome to Vietnam 121
Chapter 8: Cambodia 134
Chapter 9: War knows no Boundaries 155
Chapter 10: Dissension in the Ranks 172
Chapter 11: Mackenzie's Second Thoughts 192
Chapter 12: The Move North 201
Chapter 13: Viet Cong 220
Chapter 14: The Mekong Delta 240
Chapter 15: A New Crew 269
Chapter 16: Babies and Brothers 285
Chapter 17: Unrest Back Home 298
Chapter 18: The War Within 303
Chapter 19: Chicago Burns 325
Chapter 20: Show Down 335
Chapter 21: Washington D.C. 345
Chapter 22: The Dirty Streets of Saigon 373
Chapter 23: Golgotha 382
Chapter 24: Grief in Glendale 410
Chapter 25: A Solemn Good Bye 427
Epilogue 441
Author's Notes 447
Facts About the Vietnam Memorial Wall 449

PREFACE

Welcome to my third book, *Vietnam; Honor and Sacrifice*. Having lived through this tumultuous period in America's history, it was interesting to take a look back. As the war has been over for forty-four years, memories become a little less clear, and we begin to wonder if what we believed back then is still valid today. Of course, now we have the benefit of hindsight, written history, and eye witness testimony on every aspect of the conflict.

Anti-war protests, coupled with racial unrest, tore apart colleges, cities, neighborhoods and families. The war not only brought down the Presidency of Lyndon Johnson, but it helped deliver the crushing defeat of Vice President Hubert Humphrey by Richard Nixon. However, Nixon's 'peace with honor' theory became bogged down in the Paris Peace Meetings, while North Vietnamese Forces began an all-out push to destroy all resistance in the South and reunite the country.

Film of the final evacuation from Saigon of the United States Diplomatic Corps and final U.S. Military Forces in the South was chilling. Watching the helicopters departing from the roof of the U.S. Embassy in Saigon in 1975, is painful to watch.

Casualties in the war were staggering, with the United States losing 58,220 men and women. However, it is estimated another 3,250,000 people on both sides of the conflict were killed. It will never be known how many combatants and civilians were wounded, many of them horribly scarred for life, physically and mentally.

My story does not take on the history of that war, right or wrong; nor do I wish to impress upon the reader my beliefs, doubts, criticisms or overall concept of the war. I did serve in the Army and National Guard during that period of time, but was never in Vietnam myself.

This book is considered historical fiction, based on many historical facts, dates, locations, and interviews I completed with both Veteran's and civilians over the years. I hope this story entices readers to learn more about the Vietnam War, and decide for themselves what history's final verdict should be. Many Americans never realized medics in Vietnam carried weapons to protect themselves and their patients. But through gripping interviews I came to realize how important it was for them to be armed.

To all those who fought the good fight, and for those who never came home, may God bless you all.

ACKNOWLEDGMENTS

I wish to thank all the Vietnam Veterans I spoke with over the years who gave me insight and ideas for my story. Your memories were riveting.

Getting my story from computer to book form would not have been possible without the professional help of three outstanding professionals. Lori Hawkins provided the proofreading and editing, Roseanna M. White completed typesetting and internal design, and K. Tarrier came up with all the art work for the cover. Lori and Roseanna worked with me on, *A Soldier's Final Journey*, so it was great to have their professional talents available once again.

As with all my books, I have to thank my wife JoAnn, for her complete support as a sounding board, adviser, and critic, and for keeping me focused and moving. Without her understanding and patience, these projects would never have taken place.

CHAPTER 1
A BRUTAL WAR

As another night of rocket and mortar rounds continued raining destruction down on the sprawling American base at Binh Thuy in South Vietnam, Army medic Tom Kenrude worked feverishly to assist the horribly wounded soldiers. It seemed impossible that anyone could get accustomed to dealing with such horrendous injuries day after day, but Tom and his fellow medics applied their skills to saving as many lives as possible in this hellish world.

Night after brutal night, their uniforms, faces and arms would be caked in blood and mud as they performed countless feats of heroism that would never get recorded in any history of this war. Of course, there were victims they were not able to treat. Many were either dead or dying as the over worked medics arrived at their sides. For the dying, all the medics could do was hold their hand, or attempt to comfort them for a brief moment, as they slipped from life into death. Tom always spent just a moment more, saying a prayer over the soldier's body before rushing on to his next victim.

While growing up in Glendale, Minnesota, Tom listened every Sunday as their minister preached about heaven and hell. He understood the concept well and hoped one day he could achieve heaven and strive to lead a good life. But the minister back home was never able to drive home the concept of hell as Tom was seeing it now in Vietnam. Death came in so many ugly and brutal ways it was impossible to fathom. Since arriving in country, Tom had heard the crying and the pleading of so many young men as they neared death's door. He was sure these brave young men would wind up in heaven, since they had already experienced hell here on earth in Vietnam. The shear brutality of the fighting was enough to make the toughest Ranger or Green Beret age well past their years.

Many of them had lost sight of true humanity a long time ago, and now killed at times for pure vengeance. Every line of hate, respect and kindness had long since been crossed, as the brutality of this war continued unabated. No one person should ever experience what these men had witnessed in their young lives, or what they had been forced to do in order to survive one more minute. But this was Vietnam, a country all its own, with a torrid, humid climate that could sap the strength out of the most well-conditioned soldier.

The mountains and valleys were covered by a triple canopy jungle, where death awaited anyone who chose to enter its domain. Rice patties and small primitive farms occupied the flat lands where poor inhabitants scratched out a living, just as their ancestors had thousands of years before. Severe poverty, lack of proper nutrition and many types of jungle illnesses combined to make the inhabitants appear to be sickly and weak, as they struggled each day just to survive.

Many young people attempted to escape the poverty of the farms, seeking out new lives in cities such as Saigon or Hue, only to fall victim to crime, prostitution, or death. One thing local inhabitants learned long ago, was not to trust any politician who proclaimed the government would make their lives better. Corruption and wealth was the name of the game in Saigon, until the next charismatic strong man could build an army of followers necessary to topple the existing government.

Most rural farmers had no idea who was in power in Saigon, and more importantly, didn't really care. After all, their government never did anything to improve their lot in life.

For the average American soldier, they were fighting three distinct enemies, and sometimes it was impossible to tell them apart. There was the established North Vietnamese Army; The Viet Cong, made up of North Vietnamese soldiers, farmers and South Vietnamese sympathizers, a guerrilla force that never fought by any established rules of war; and finally, the South Vietnamese Army, led by corrupt and cowardly leaders, that often played one side against the other.

Making matters worse, Russia and Communist China backed North Vietnam's inspirational communist leader Ho Chi Minh, with every type of war material he required.

The Viet Cong was not your typical enemy, by far. They fought tougher, more aggressively and were more savage than most soldiers could ever imagine. At times it appeared just killing the enemy wasn't nearly enough for them. They relished opportunities to torture the living and mutilate the bodies of the dead, in order to spread fear among South Vietnamese citizens and the American Army. They had no qualms about torturing the men, women or children of their own country, delivering a terrifying message to villagers throughout the south.

Making victory appear still more elusive, borders did not matter to the Viet Cong. They crossed into Cambodia, Laos or Thailand to regroup, rearm, or to seek sanctuary from American forces. No code of conduct or established rules of warfare applied to these jungle butchers, including or perhaps even especially, those of the Geneva Convention.

No matter how hard they tried, American military planners were never able to fully train their soldiers for the horrors of what they would experience when they touched down in Vietnam. Basically, most Americans leaving boot camp had still been trained to fight an all-out war with Russia on the European Continent, not the steamy treacherous jungles of South East Asia.

As most young men heading off to Vietnam in the mid 1960's, Tom Kenrude had grown up listening to his father and uncle talk about combat in World War Two and Korea, but what was happening in Vietnam was nothing like anything he had ever heard about. Here in Vietnam there were no front lines that could be used to mark progress in the war. Here, the front was where ever you were standing at any given moment.

This had been a terribly rough day for the medics from A-Company of the 571st Medical Evacuation Unit. Two of their choppers had been brought down by heavy enemy ground fire, costing the lives of a pilot, co-pilot and two medics. If there was one thing every medic in Vietnam had learned by this time, it was that the red cross emblem on your helmet or chopper was a big fat target for every enemy soldier. Although some medical staff had carried a sidearm in World War Two and Korea, just about every medic in Vietnam carried their sidearm and an M-16 rifle.

As dusk settled over Binh Thuy, heavy storm clouds from the South China Sea rolled inland, dumping copious amounts of rain onto an already wet, humid land. Although every G.I. was used to the heavy drenching rains that accompanied the monsoon season, tonight they were an added nuisance to the men of A-Company. Regrettably, several of their barracks had been recipients of Viet Cong rockets during tonight's attack. Every man tore through the rubble in the driving rain, searching for any remnants of their personal belongings.

After pitching a section of sheet metal to the side, Tom found the charred remains of his two wooden foot lockers. Desperately, he searched for his stash of photos and letters from his beautiful wife Mackenzie. Like most soldiers, these were the keepsakes that meant the difference between utter depression and mental stability, as they endured this dreadful war in this depressing country.

Sadly, all Tom could find in the rubble was a slightly singed photo of Mackenzie with her mother in front of their church in Glendale, which was taken when he was on leave. All the letters and small items she had sent him were gone, reduced to just so much soggy ash. Angrily, Tom threw a charred piece of his foot locker onto the ground as a tear rolled down his cheek. Tilting his head back, he allowed the cool falling rain to wash over his face. After several moments he walked over to Craig Summerville who was still searching for his belongings among the rain soaked muck that covered what was left of the wooden floor.

"Finding anything?" Tom asked, approaching his good friend.

"Nope. Everything was destroyed. But I guess I can have Brenda send new photos. Just six more months in this God forsaken country and I can finally get the hell out of here," Craig mumbled as he shook his head with disgust.

For the next hour, Tom and Craig helped several other men retrieve remnants of their belongings before everyone decided to call it quits. There was simply nothing left to save.

After getting everybody situated with dry clothing from the supply depot, Craig suggested they get something warm to eat as the night chill was getting into his bones.

The atmosphere in the company mess was rather somber tonight, as everyone knew somebody that had been killed in the last twenty-four hours.

While sipping his hot coffee, Tom looked over at Sgt. Trudell, a battle hardened airborne soldier most of the men had experienced the pleasure or sometimes displeasure to meet.

"Tell me, Sarg. This is your third tour over here, does it ever get any easier, or do you just become accustomed to all this crap?"

Placing his fork on his empty tray, Sgt. Trudell looked intently toward Tom.

"I guess it depends on who you are and why the hell you're here. My wife left me after my second tour. She didn't like the change in me, and my temper outbursts. So screw it, I came back for a third tour just to keep my mind occupied. So to me, I just don't give a damn about the gooks, the politicians back home, or what happens around here as long as my belly is full, I get my pay check, and no one expects me to be their therapist, counselor or best buddy."

"I've seen enough guys get killed, maimed or torn to shreds to not get emotional about any of it anymore. When this tour is up, I'm out of this man's Army for good. So Mr. Kenrude, I don't need to get accustomed to anything or anyone. All I need to do is get through this day without getting my ass blown away and I'm good to go. Everybody and everything else can just go straight to hell as far as I'm concerned. Sorry if I left you hanging or couldn't analyze your probing question for you. But when I leave here, I'm moving down to Mexico where I can live on a beach and get drunk whenever I want, and just plain screw the world."

Without saying another word, the angry sergeant picked up his helmet, walking off toward the door.

After a moment of sheer silence, Tom turned toward the men he was seated with.

"Wow. That caught me totally off guard. I was seriously expecting some words of wisdom from him. He and I have talked several times since I arrived, and I've never experienced an outburst like that."

Moe Ashton shook his head as he took a fork full of potatoes from his tray. "Well, losing your wife and spending three tours in this hell hole surrounded by constant death has to have a devastating effect on your nerves and soul after a while."

The men finished their evening meal in relative silence, each man contemplating on what Sgt. Trudell had just said, while wondering how the war would affect them.

All the medics who lost their quarters in the rocket attack were temporarily housed in the hospital as space allowed. After writing a letter to Mackenzie and explaining all that happened over the last twenty-four hours, Tom laid down on his bunk staring up at the ceiling. Numerous thoughts drifted in and out of his mind before finally drifting off into a fitful sleep, dominated by the reoccurring violent dreams that haunted him night after night.

The following morning, Tom strolled out to the flight line well before their mission was scheduled for departure. For the first time in weeks, he carried his M-16 along with him. After storing it just inside the sliding door, he pulled his sidearm from its holster to make sure he had chambered a round. Re-holstering his weapon, Tom walked down the flight line, pondering the wretched dreams he experienced throughout the long dark night. Returning to the 'Galloping Ghost,' Tom sat down on the door sill, waiting for the rest of the crew to arrive. Carefully, he pulled the brittle flame singed photo of Mackenzie and her mother from the pocket of his flak jacket. Running his finger across Mackenzie's face, he felt a knot growing in his stomach. After staring at the photo for several seconds, he took a deep breath as he struggled to fight back the tears that were slowly welling up in his eyes. He missed his beautiful young bride beyond explanation.

Looking upward, he closed his eyes, praying, "Dear Lord, please bring me home to her. I love her with all my heart and want to spend the rest of my life with her. If it's your will that I do not make it home, please take care of her and allow her to find peace in your abiding love and mercy."

As the rest of the crew approached the 'Galloping Ghost,' Tom carefully slid the damaged photo back into his vest. Standing up, he stepped back into the chopper where he settled down into the small seat he occupied on the way to a mission.

All along the flight line, soldiers laden with weaponry and heavy packs boarded Huey helicopters. They were destined for dangerous landing zones in a mountain valley known to be occupied by a regiment of North Vietnamese Regular Army troops. No doubt they would be backed up by an untold number of Viet Cong forces ready to pounce on them from well concealed positions. Although American air power had been striking at the enemy since dawn, everyone realized the enemy would hunker down in fortified underground bunkers and tunnels, to exit only when American ground forces arrived in force. The fighting would be ferocious, as the enemy would spring forward from countless spider holes dotting the surrounding hills.

Today, men would die and others would come to grips with their worst fears. Today men would be called upon to perform unexplainable feats of heroism. Today, they would all be bloodied.

No one could predict the outcome of the coming battle that lay just over the next mountain range. The only certainty was, that by days end God will have welcomed many brave warriors home.

CHAPTER 2
AN EARLIER LIFE

The rolling hills, punctuated with stands of natural forest and plentiful lakes of southwest Minnesota, was an adventure land to any child growing up in the middle of the twentieth century. There was plenty of room to roam, explore and create daily adventures. The clean clear waters of nearby Eagle Lake drew kids and families for picnics, fishing or a great day of swimming, all summer long.

As the land around Glendale, Minnesota contained a dark rich soil, farmers were able to grow healthy abundant crops to feed the region and a hungry nation. Glendale, situated southeast of Eagle Lake, had been a thriving, growing community, with a rich heritage since it was founded in the late 1800's. As America grew, so did Glendale. Since the town was located along a rail line and two main highways, new commerce of every type expanded into the region. Many of the large farms around Kandiyohi County, such as Kenrude Farms Inc., turned to cash cropping as the large milling companies in Minneapolis and Chicago were always anxious to buy their products. Several large grain distributors, such as Field Sweet Products, owned by August Godfrey, built huge grain terminals along the rail line to handle their produce.

Kenrude Farms began as a small family business, operated by Alex and Nancy Kenrude. Having two strong healthy sons, Steve and Mike, they were sure the farm would be in good hands for many years to come. However, those dreams were seriously tested by World War Two, as their boys were sent off to war.

With both son's returning, Kenrude Farms grew by leaps and bounds, becoming one of the largest farming operations in Kandiyohi County. Regrettably, their oldest son Steve was recalled to fight in the Korean Conflict, once again testing the faith of the Kenrude family.

After a brutal tour of combat, Steve returned, turning his entire life back into running Kenrude Farms, Inc., while enjoying his wife Karen and children Abigail and Tom. However, the one thing his loving wife wanted more than anything upon his return was another child, so in 1953, Peter Allen Kenrude arrived, a welcomed addition to the growing Kenrude clan.

Steve and Karen watched with delight as their children grew in strength and wisdom. Everyone in Glendale said Tom was a spitting image of his father, tall in stature and broad at the shoulders. His mother was quick to add that he also had the stubbornness and tenacity of all the other Kenrude males. The worst thing you could say to Tom, was that he did not have what it took to complete some objective. He would go out of his way to prove you wrong, and most often did.

By the time he was in high school, he was an accomplished athlete in every sport he attempted, with football being his favorite. Playing defensive back, there was not a running back or quarterback in their conference that did not know who Tom Kenrude was. By his senior year, coaches from all the major colleges in the Midwest were seriously courting him.

However, sports were not what ruled Tom's life. More than anything, he wanted to become a doctor, and realized his time would be best spent in the library not on the gridiron. Getting into the premed program at the University of Minnesota, was not a problem with his academic abilities. Besides, Mackenzie Bishop, his girlfriend who was one year younger, was also planning to attend the same university to become a nurse, like his aunt Christine.

Having Mackenzie close by as they worked through their studies was the perfect recipe. There was no doubt in anyone's mind that the two love struck students would be married once both of them completed their degrees. When Mackenzie followed Tom to the university a year later, they were excited to hear her dorm room was just a little over a block away, allowing them to get together for meals or long study periods in the library.

As Tom entered his senior year, he applied for, and was accepted into the University of Minnesota Medical School. Nothing could have pleased his parents and Mackenzie more.

The summer between college and med school, Tom returned to the family farm to help out and give his mind a much needed rest. Of course, he always found time to see Mackenzie, who was also home for the summer and working part time in the Glendale Hospital as a nurse's aide.

One Sunday late in August, Tom and Mackenzie spent the afternoon at Eagle Lake having a nice relaxing day, before the rigors of school took them over once again. As Mackenzie was smelling one of the small flowers that grew along the shore line, she looked over at Tom.

"Have you followed the war in Vietnam at all? It appears we keep getting ourselves further entrenched all the time. It really bothers me how many boys are being sent over there."

Tom nodded his head as he placed his arm around her.

"Sure. I've definitely been paying attention to it. The evening news is full of reports from Saigon and Washington every day. Dad says it almost sounds like Korea all over again, but worse. It really scares the hell out of him."

Mackenzie placed her head on his shoulder. "You have a deferment from the draft, right?"

"Yeah, it's all taken care of. Having a deferment for medical school is not a problem as long as you have the grades to back it up," Tom replied, as he kissed Mackenzie on the forehead.

"That's good, because I don't want you over there getting shot at. Your dad and mine spent more than enough time at war for several generations to come. Besides, we need good doctors," Mackenzie said with a smile.

Tom took a deep breath. "That's all I've ever wanted to do. Mom used to get so crazy when I would bring home an injured animal and nurse it back to health. She would always say I was going to get bit, or catch some sort of disease. But I never got bit and I never caught any strange diseases, and hey, I only lost one patient in all those years!" Tom laughed at the memories.

"But I can't imagine what it would be like to work on combat injuries. They're so traumatic and many times you wouldn't have a good starting point. Everything would be compounded by shock, loss of blood and exposure to so much infection and contamination. Those doctors over there must fly by the seat of their pants at times as they diagnose and begin treatment. I can't even imagine what they must go through."

Raising her head from Tom's shoulder, Mackenzie gave Tom a serious look. "So you have given serious thought to Vietnam then."

"Sure, sweetheart. Anyone in med school would have to think about it when you listen to the war reports, and see videos of paramedics rescuing the wounded. I don't know how you couldn't," Tom replied, looking intently into Mackenzie's eyes.

"Yeah, I understand. I guess it would be the same as the hospital after that bus crash a few weeks ago. They set up a triage post near the emergency room to decide which patients needed help the quickest. I thought about that all night. About how to make that decision. How you let one person suffer somewhat, while deciding someone else is worse. I guess you're right, things like that will affect me more as I get into nursing school. I never gave it much thought, I guess," Mackenzie replied, as she gently stroked Tom's back.

Once school started in the fall, Tom and Mackenzie saw much less of each other, as their studies and time in the hospital filled the hours. Just finding time to sleep was a big deal for Tom. Most often he spent twelve to sixteen hours a day in classes, making rounds at the hospital with doctors, or reading case studies and writing reports. Mackenzie became accustomed to Tom falling asleep when they were together, but she really didn't mind.

When the year ended, Tom signed on at the University Hospital for the summer to assist in the emergency room. Not only was he learning every day, but they paid him a small wage, money he badly needed. Although Mackenzie went home for the summer, she continued working as a nurse's aide in the Glendale Hospital, gaining much needed experience.

One Sunday as Tom waited to start his shift in the emergency room, he was watching a special news story on television regarding the war. He was mesmerized as he watched combat medics treat wounded soldiers and load them on choppers for evacuation to a hospital. Although he had heard much about combat from his father, he had never seen actual close up video footage of what the weapons of war could do to a human body. Tom sat forward in his chair in disbelief as the camera panned over a long row of rubber body bags, waiting to be loaded on a chopper. He wondered how he would react in a combat situation when life and death was on the line. He wondered what it would be like to have to decide who would live and die in a matter of seconds. He wondered if he had what it took to be that man. Little did he know that within the next hour, what he was about to witness would decide his fate in life.

At two-thirty in the morning as Tom was stocking the supply cabinet, Dr. Stride came running up to him.

"Kenrude, we have three men coming in from Camp Ripley, the National Guard Base in Northern Minnesota. They were caught in some sort of an explosion, one has a radical amputation, he is right on the edge. We can triage them when they hit the door."

Moments later, several National Guard medics rushed into the emergency with three seriously injured men. Dr. Stride pulled the sheet back on the first man. "First degree burns over his face and arms. Get him to the burn unit immediately." After checking over the second soldier he called out. "Shrapnel of several types over fifty percent of his body with serious abdominal injuries, get him down to the O.R. Quick."

Dr. Stride shook his head after looking over the third man, "Radical amputation, left arm below the elbow, he's in shock. Kenrude, begin an IV of ringers. His dog tags state he's type O-pos, get two liters up here right now or we're going to lose him!"

One of the nurses wheeled the man into the first treatment area to begin prepping for surgery as a second nurse brought in two bags of ringer's solution and the blood Dr. Stride ordered.

As Tom prepared to start an IV, the soldier opened his eyes and looked directly at him.

"Doc, am I going to die, Can you fix my arm?"

Tom forced a smile as he finished starting the IV. "I haven't lost a patient yet, Sergeant, and I don't intend to start now. We'll do all we can for your arm. Are you in a lot of pain?" Tom inquired.

"Naw, they shot me up with morphine just before the chopper sat down. I'm actually feeling sleepy," he replied, fighting to keep his eyes open.

"Good, that's good." Tom replied. "Go ahead. Close your eyes and relax. Once we get the transfusion started you'll be on your way to surgery."

Tom barely finished starting the blood flow into his good arm when Dr. Stride threw back the curtain, "How's he doing, Kenrude?"

"He's passed out from the morphine they gave him on the chopper. His vitals are sketchy and his breathing has become more labored in the last few minutes. I cleaned the edge of the amputation, and took out a few pieces of wood and metal debris," Tom replied, feeling like he was actually making a difference for the first time in his young life.

"Alright, that's good. Roll him down to the O.R. bay and get back here quick," Dr. Stride directed, patting Tom on the back.

Tom had barely started rolling the Sergeant down the hall when he went into cardiac arrest. Spinning the gurney around, Tom ran as fast as he could back into treatment room one as he yelled, "Cardiac arrest, he's gone into Cardiac arrest!"

Without being told, Tom jumped up onto the gurney to begin CPR as one of the nurses began using a bag to inflate the Sergeant's lungs. Dr. Stride came running into the room pointing at another nurse. "I need a thousand milligrams of adrenaline now!"

As the nurse handed Dr. Stride the needle, Tom stopped CPR, allowing the doctor a clear shot at the sergeant's heart. As soon as the injection was administered, Dr. Stride yelled, "Continue CPR!"

After Tom completed two more rounds of compression's without any changes to the sergeant's situation Dr. Stride said, "Paddle him!

With the paddles ready to go, Dr. Stride yelled, "Clear!" as Tom jumped down from the gurney.

The doctor looked over at the heart monitor and shook his head. "Turn it up to four hundred."

When the nurse told him it was ready to go, Dr. Stride yelled "Clear!" and hit the sergeant's chest with the paddles. He stood quietly for a moment as he watched the monitor. Slowly the heart began to come back with a very erratic heartbeat, before continuing back toward a normal rhythm.

Dr. Stride had just put the paddles down when the sergeant began to convulse. Shaking his head he yelled out, "Get me a shot of epinephrine, we need to end this quick or he's not going to make it."

However before he could administer the injection, the sergeant quit convulsing and began to breathe normally. The nurses quickly began attaching leads for the heart monitor. Dr. Stride watched the monitor as he said, "Come on Sarg. You can do this you're a fighter. Come on Sarg., keep it going. Yeah, that's what we need, you are doing great!"

After several minutes Dr. Stride smiled. "Alright he's back in normal sinus-rhythm, with a heart rate of 80 bpm. Let's give him about five minutes before we move him down to the operating room. They are aware of what's going on, so they are ready for him."

After monitoring his condition for several minutes Dr. Stride looked at Tom. "Go ahead, take him down to the operating room, he should be good to go."

The operating staff was waiting for the sergeant when Tom wheeled the gurney into the surgery alcove. As the nurses began prepping him for surgery, Tom walked up to a doctor that was looking over the sergeant's file.

"What can you do for him, doctor?" Tom inquired as he watched the nurses.

The doctor looked at Tom shaking his head. "Well Kenrude, about all we can do for him is to remove all the debris that is still in the arm, then cut it back so we have a nice area to work with. Then we will sew the skin back over the end of the stump. When we are finished, we will watch him real close to make sure he is getting circulation in the stump. If he does, were in good shape. If he does not, we may need to do a revision."

"What do you mean by a revision?" Tom asked, pretty much guessing what the doctor was about to explain.

"Well, if we do not have blood flow the tissue will die. So if we can't get good blood flow, we will have to take off more of the sergeants arm to a point where we are satisfied we can maintain good circulation, but we would like to save the elbow. Whichever way it goes, once we are satisfied everything is good, we will place a type of bandage on the arm that will help the stump heal properly so he can be fitted with a prosthesis. After that, his recovery is all up to him. How he handles his injury and what he wants to do with the rest of his life is all up to how he deals with it. In all reality, that is the real tough part."

After patting Tom on the shoulder the doctor smiled. "Well, I need to get ready to help inside, but be assured, Kenrude. We will do all we can for him."

Around 0400 Tom walked down to the surgical recovery area. He walked up to one of the nurses he knew. "How is Sgt. Alton doing?"

Sheila Anderson looked up at the heart monitor. "Everything looks fine. He's asleep right now, as the morphine and sedative we gave him is pretty much in control."

Tom nodded his head. "Did they have to do a revision?"

"Yes, they had to cut off about two more inches and start over. His arm was really in bad shape. But now he will be able to get a prosthesis to fit well. But that will be a while before they can think about that, there is a lot of healing that will need to take place.

By 0700 the day staff was beginning to arrive in the emergency room. It had been a long ten hour shift, and Tom was dead tired. He couldn't wait to get back to his dorm room and hit the bed. But first he needed to see how Sergeant Alton was doing. Walking up to the surgical desk, Tom could see the young soldier was awake. He slowly entered the room and approached the bed, not sure what kind of a reception he was going to receive, since the sergeant had inquired about saving his arm when he first arrived.

Tom was just about to speak when the Sergeant turned his head to the side and looked up. "You're the guy I first talked to when I arrived. I guess my arm was beyond saving."

Nodding his head Tom was not sure what to say at first. "Yeah there was nothing the doctors could do, but get your arm ready for a prosthesis. I'm sorry."

A tear rolled down Sgt. Alton's face, "That has been made quite clear to me. I just wonder what my wife will think when she gets here, I wonder if she will still want me in her life? There are a lot more questions than answers right now."

Tom looked intently at the worried soldier. "I don't believe your wife will think any less of you. She will understand you may need to make some adjustments, but you will be able to lead a pretty normal life, she will get that. Don't worry about that, Sergeant."

When the doctor arrived to check on Sgt. Alton, Tom wished him the best and told him he would stop back, although he now realized these type of injuries affected more than just the soldier.

Tom visited him several times before he was discharged. The last time he saw the sergeant he was sitting on the edge of the bed talking to his wife. As Tom entered the room, sergeant Alton looked at his wife.

"Would you mind stepping out and giving me a couple moments with this guy?"

After his wife departed, the sergeant smiled at Tom. "I want to thank you for helping me the night I came in here, and all those times you came up to see me. It really meant a lot. I served a tour in Vietnam in the regular Army. I saw several men lose arms and legs and wondered how they would go on with their lives.Now, here I am in the same boat. Never thought this could happen being in the National Guard. I thought I was far away from all the real danger when I came home. But with my wife's help, I'll make it. They're sending me to Walter Reed Medical Center in Washington to work on getting a prosthetic arm fit properly. I'm guess it will be a long process learning how to use it. But at least I'm alive, and can still play with my daughter. I think the biggest thing in this entire ordeal was the encouragement I received from all the staff here is those first few days after the explosion. That's what pushed me over the top and made me want to go on.

So Tom, remember as you go on into the medical world, those first few minutes, and for sure the next few days, they are crucial to an amputee. Be there for them, and never allow yourself to get negative over what you're seeing. The patient will read your mind in a quick hurry. Your humor in the E.R. that night was like a shot of adrenaline to me."

"You mentioned you were in Vietnam, What was it like?" Tom nervously inquired.

"Nothing you want to deal with. It is an ugly war that makes no sense, and men are dying for no real good reason. Don't do what I think is on your mind, Tom. You don't need to go over there and get involved. It will only take from you and give you nothing back!" Sergeant Alton replied as he looked sternly at Tom.

Tom knew it was time to change the subject so he smiled at the sergeant. "Thanks for your kind words on how I helped you, I will always remember them and I appreciate it very much. I learned a lot from you too about being a doctor. Now go to Washington and get that arm, you have a family that needs you."

After shaking hands Tom turned to leave, but Sgt. Alton called out, "Stay the hell out of Vietnam, Doc. You don't belong there!"

That evening as Tom watched the news coverage about Vietnam, he began having a nagging feeling that he needed to go over there and help our young men. He tried hard to shake the feeling, although it kept reoccurring nearly every day. His ordeal in the emergency room that night watching Dr. Stride triage the men, and making quick life and death decisions was exactly what Tom wanted to do. He understood Vietnam was calling him, but this was not something he and Mackenzie had ever discussed, and he knew his parents would be dead set against such an idea. Yet the feelings were there, and he knew he would need to come to terms with it in the near future.

The balance of the summer passed quickly, with Tom learning more each passing day. He spent the Labor Day weekend back home with his family, attempting to get some rest before returning to school. He and Mackenzie spent several afternoons swimming in Eagle Lake with his sister Abby and brother Peter. His mother always packed a nice lunch for them to eat.

On Labor Day, the Kenrude clan gathered at Alex and Nancy's house for the traditional fall family barbecue. It was a great time for the family to catch up and have some fun. It was a tradition Tom had enjoyed since he was a child. Sharing it with Mackenzie and her family now made the party much more exciting for him.

Nevertheless, this year the gaiety of the event was overshadowed by the news of Dan Sims being killed in Vietnam. Dan was two year older than Tom, and had been one of the best players on the Glendale Amateur Baseball Team for several years. He joined the Navy right out of high school, and reenlisted after his four years were up. According to his mother, the river boat he was serving on struck some type of mine in the Mekong River and exploded.

Although Tom tried hard to put the death of his friend in the back of his mind and enjoy the barbecue, he couldn't quite let go of it. He wondered how he died, if he suffered, or if he was killed outright, or was there something he could have done as a medic to save Dan's life. Once again Vietnam was on the forefront in his mind and it wasn't letting go.

Each day Tom had heard about the casualties in the war on the evening news, but this time it was more personal. Dan was the third young man from the Glendale area to be killed in South East Asia and his death kept bringing up the same question in Tom's mind over and over. *Could I have done something to save him, could I make a difference, are there men there that need me.*

Although Tom tried not to show it, Mackenzie could tell Dan's death was bothering him a lot. Taking a short stroll through the orchard she looked up at him.

"Tell me what's going on in that beautiful brain of yours. Does it have anything to do with Dan?"

Tom knew he could never hide anything from Mackenzie, she always read him like a book. "Yeah, Dan's death has really hit me hard. It just doesn't seem right somehow. I know there is nothing I can do to change it, or bring him back. I don't know, Mac, it just got into my head bad."

Stopping suddenly, Mackenzie turned toward Tom. "You know I'm always here for you. Whatever bothers you, bothers me, whatever you need or want, I will do my best to get it for you. Always and forever."

After giving Mackenzie a hug and a kiss, they turned to walk back toward the house. But what was on his mind was nothing Mackenzie could fix, nor was it anything she would ever want to deal with, but more and more he knew the time was coming they would need to have the conversation.

CHAPTER 3
AN EXPLOSIVE DECISION

Tom sat quietly in the back corner of the university library, paging through the latest edition of Newsweek Magazine. He stopped paging as he came upon a story regarding America's involvement in the escalating war in Vietnam. The photos of helicopters picking up wounded soldiers from the battlefield left him mesmerized.

Setting the magazine down, he walked over toward the large windows that looked out over the plaza. He stared out the rain streaked window, watching students scurrying about as they attempted to dodge puddles on their way to class. The dark skies and heavy rain sweeping over the campus was a perfect match for the turmoil that haunted his soul. He was just one month away from completing his second year of medical school, but the longing in his heart to graduate and become a doctor was nowhere to be found.

Somehow all his dreams had evaporated, leaving him with a feeling of abandonment and despair. Somewhere out in that cold rain-soaked world there was a mountain waiting to be climbed, a river to be forged, and a life ready to be lived, by someone who had the willingness and determination to take hold of the reins. Yet, how could he justify throwing away six years of school and all his dreams, only to start over again with no real plan in sight.

Sure, back in Glendale there would always be the family farm to fall back on to if he needed work, but that wasn't the vision he and Mackenzie had shared for so long. After several more minutes of thought, he returned to his chair, once more picking up the magazine he had left open to the story about Vietnam.

He was about half way through the article when Mackenzie came dashing up beside him. After giving him a kiss on the cheek, she dropped down on the couch beside him. "I got it, Honey. I got an 'A' on my procedural final. Wow, I never thought that was possible. I'm so excited, and really glad Professor Maxner decided to give his test last week. Now I can concentrate on my last two exams."

"That's great. I knew you could do it." Tom replied smiling at his excited girlfriend.

"I take it you must be feeling ready for your test this afternoon, if you have time to read a magazine, I mean." Mackenzie questioned as she stared at Tom.

Tom smiled at the pretty blonde he cared so much for. "I've always heard what a tough grader Maxner can be. You must have really aced it!"

Mackenzie smiled slightly as she searched her boyfriend's face for some sign of what was going on in his head.

"You didn't answer me, though. Are you ready for your test this afternoon?"

Tom nodded his head. "Yeah, I'm ready. I have been for a few days."

Not saying a word, Mackenzie picked up the Newsweek magazine Tom had set on the table.

"Hmm, Vietnam. Does anyone know where it's actually located? I mean, are we really supposed to be involved? Isn't it just a civil war like we had?" Mackenzie stated as she felt a strange feeling in her heart.

Reaching over, Tom took the magazine from Mackenzie's hands. "Vietnam is in Southeast Asia. It used to be called French Indo China. The French ruled the area for years. They attempted to reassert their dominance after World War Two, but were unsuccessful. Since then, North Vietnam, under the leadership of the dedicated communist Ho-Chi-Minh, has been attempting to force communist rule on the South. So, it really is more than a civil war. Both President Kennedy and President Johnson stated that if South Vietnam falls, all of Southeast Asia will fall under Communist Chinese control."

As Mackenzie unwrapped a stick of gum, she looked intently at her boyfriend. "It sounds like you really have done some research on the war. So do you agree with the president?"

"Well, I don't have all the intelligence he has on the war, but it appears to make sense in some respects. President Eisenhower was already concerned about the situation when he was in office. I feel like if the General who won the war in Europe is concerned, there might just be something to it." Closing the magazine, Tom let out a big sigh.

As Mackenzie gently stroked his neck, she inquired, "You're still having doubts about finishing medical school, aren't you? Do you have any idea how that would affect your folks? I mean, what kind of plans do you have? What would you tell them?"

Tom looked into Mackenzie's emerald eyes for a moment without saying a word. Then nodding his head slightly, he explained.

"Yes sweetheart, I'm still considering it. I understand this is not what we talked about or dreamed of for so long. But I just don't know if I can do this for two more years. Something is missing in my life, I mean there is a void that school isn't filling anymore, but it's so damn hard to explain." Tom explained shaking his head.

Trembling inside Mackenzie searched for words before she responded. "Is it me Tom, have you lost your feelings for me? Are you tired of our relationship? Or is it putting too many demands on your life? If that's the problem just tell me, and I'll walk away." As she finished speaking tears rolled down her soft cheeks.

Instantly, Tom turned toward her, gently wiping the tears from her face. "No sweetheart, it's not you, and it never could be. I don't want to be without you. Not ever. You are the best thing that ever happened to me, and you always have been. You have filled that part of my life completely, and no one could ever touch my heart like you. I just feel like I need to be doing something more important than sitting in school for two more years. It may sound crazy, but it feels like God has another plan for me, but I just haven't figured it out yet."

Relieved by Tom's response, Mackenzie drew in a deep breath. "You know I would follow you anywhere. I could live in a mud hut in the middle of the Congo, as long as you are there."

For the first time that morning Tom had to laugh. "A mud hut! Do they come with a double garage and air conditioning?"

They both laughed for a moment before Mackenzie continued. "I know you don't want to work on the family farm. You have made that quite clear many times. Is there something you have in mind that you really want to do?"

Nervously, Tom picked up the Newsweek magazine, opening it to the page with the photos of helicopter rescues. "It says the Army is drastically short of highly trained medics to work on rescue choppers."

Mackenzie sat straight up on the couch. "Thomas Kenrude, are you crazy? Your mom and dad—their heads will explode! There is no way they'll accept that decision. Your mom will lock you in the basement, then bar the windows before she'll ever see you in the army. When you think of all she went through with your dad, there's no way she'll go for that. Do you actually understand the kind of problems this will create in your family? My God, Tom!"

After several seconds of thought, Tom took hold of Mackenzie's hands. "Mud hut aside, be honest with me about your feelings. I really need to know. Will you accept that decision? Can you back me on this?"

The last thing Mackenzie ever wanted to do was hurt Tom's feelings or anger him, but she had to be truthful. "This is the mud hut issue, sweetheart, and it scares the hell out of me. There are a thousand other things

I think you could be doing, including working on the farm, or staying in school. But, I'm not angry with you, I never could be. I just don't want to see you get hurt, or worse, and I know I'll be just as scared as your mother. However, all that being said, I will follow you to the ends of the earth and back. I will always support your decisions, even though I'm not so sure I agree with this particular one."

Tom stood up and walked back to the window for a few moments before he spoke again. "No matter how my folks feel about this, I simply have to do it. As long as I know you'll be there for me, then I know everything will be alright."

As Mackenzie joined Tom by the window, she placed her arms around him. "Have you decided when you're going to enlist? Are we going to talk to your folks first, or are you going to lay it on them after the fact?"

Tom shook his head. "First off, I wasn't going to enlist until I knew where you were at with it. That was the most important thing. Then with your blessing, I planned to enlist and then tell the family. That way it's a done deal and they'll have to accept it. Actually, I was thinking about seeing the recruiter after your last class today. Will you go with me?"

This was a question Mackenzie never expected to be asked, and it made her feel uncomfortable. After watching several more students racing through the driving rain she turned toward Tom.

"Yes, I'll go with you. If we're going to share our lives together forever, I should be there for this important decision. But there is one thing you better keep in mind, Tom. You said that once it's a done deal your folks would have to accept it. They won't, I promise you they won't! You best be prepared for the fury of hell to come down upon you, and it will not be pretty."

After looking up at the clock, Tom smiled. "I guess we better be off to class."

Finishing her last class of the day, Mackenzie met Tom at a small coffee shop just off campus. They had to take a bus to the recruiting office, as all the military recruiters had moved away from the campus due to the rioting against the war.

After a half hour bus ride, they arrived at the Army Recruiting Center in Minneapolis. A tall forty-something sergeant greeted them as they entered the office.

"Good afternoon, my name is Staff Sergeant Spooner. What can I assist you with?"

With reality staring him in the face, Tom suddenly felt apprehensive. After taking a deep breath, he picked up a brochure from a cabinet that depicted soldiers jumping out of helicopters. Laying it on the recruiter's desk, Tom explained. "I have two years of medical school completed, but I'm in need of a serious break. I am considering enlisting in the Army. My father served in World War Two and Korea. I'm very proud of his service and what he accomplished. However, I know that neither he nor my mother will agree with this decision. I would like to be a combat medic so I can help wounded troops in battle."

Sgt. Spooner looked intently at Tom. "The army is in desperate need of men with your qualifications. With our helicopter rescue system, medics are more essential on the battlefield than ever before. Although your skills are already well above what most of our medics have, we would still require you to go through basic training, as well as our advanced medic training, so you'll understand how you're to operate under combat conditions. I won't lie to you though, it's really tough work, and it has plenty of risks. But what you would be doing is assuring that our soldiers would have a better chance of survival when they are wounded."

Mackenzie looked intently at the recruiter. "How many years would Tom have to sign up for?"

Sgt. Spooner smiled back at the pretty blonde sitting across the desk from him. "It would be a three year commitment, Miss. But he would get thirty days leave a year to come home and see you."

As Tom continued flipping through the pamphlet, he inquired. "Where would I end up after training?"

"That is a real good question, son," Sgt. Spooner stated, as he leaned forward placing his arms on the desk. "You have to understand that the needs of the Army come first. You can put in for any place you'd like to go, but to be brutally honest, your first stop could very well be Vietnam. But remember, your tour of combat would only be one year, unless you choose to extend for another tour."

Tom looked over at Mackenzie as he digested everything he had just been told. "Are you comfortable with all of this?"

Mackenzie placed her hand on top of Tom's. "Like I said before, I will support you one hundred percent in whatever you decide to do. You are my future, honey. I'll never walk away from you."

After hearing Mackenzie's reassuring words Tom nodded his head. "Alright Sergeant, get out the paper work, I'm ready to enlist."

With the completion of all the enlistment forms, the recruiter set up a date and a time for Tom to take his physical the following week at the Federal Building in Minneapolis.

As the young couple walked toward the bus stop, Mackenzie inquired. "When do you plan to tell your folks? I would like to be there to support you?"

Laughing loudly, Tom placed his arm around his girlfriend's waist, pulling her close to him. He then placed both his arms around her, kissing her on the nose. "You seriously want to attend the execution of Thomas Steven Kenrude for the crime of treason against the family? Actually, I hoped you wanted to be there, but I wasn't going to pressure you. I know we've been joking about it, but it really is going to be rough. My mom is going to be really angry."

Mackenzie had to laugh a little before she responded. "To be honest, I knew all of that, but I feel I should be there, since I had some influence on your decision. We can get through this together."

The following week, Tom reported for his physical at the Federal Building, along with about three hundred other young men. It was a long day of tests and questions before he finally met with a doctor who reviewed his file. After studying every notation, he placed the file down on the desk in front of him. "Well Mr. Kenrude, you have passed. Before I send you next door to be sworn in, I have a question that I'm required to ask you. Are you enlisting of your own free will, or are you being coerced? If you're enlisting on your own without any mental reservations, sign the form I have placed in front of you and we are finished."

Without saying a word, Tom signed the document before sliding it back across the desk to the doctor. After placing the form in the file, the doctor stood up and left the room. Seconds later a corporal walked in, directing Tom to follow him. Entering a large room down the hall they joined a group of about thirty men who were seated on metal folding chairs. Just as Tom sat down, a Captain entered from a side door. After completing a roll call, he told everyone to stand up and raise their right hands. With the swearing in ceremony completed, the captain looked over a sheet of paper on the podium.

"Alright, you men who are scheduled to leave for basic training today can head downstairs. The rest of you can head home and await your orders. Good luck, gentlemen."

Per Tom's request, the recruiter worked diligently to get the orders for basic training approved so he could have them prior to the day classes ended for the year. As Tom cleaned out his dorm, he stuffed them into an envelope with his school papers, so his parents would not find them accidentally.

The day classes ended, Steve and Karen arrived on campus with a large enclosed trailer to haul Tom's and Mackenzie's belongings back home. After everything was loaded, Mackenzie slid into Tom's car.

"So when are you going to unload the bomb on your folks? To be honest, I'm really scared about what's going to happen. I've known your folks forever, and I know this is going to anger them beyond words."

Tom was quiet for a moment, as he contemplated everything Mackenzie had said. "Well sweetheart, I leave for basic training in three weeks, so I can't wait forever to tell them what's going on, and the sooner the better. I kind of figured that Sunday would be a good day to tell them. Mom has already asked you, Uncle Mike and Aunt Glenda to come over for dinner, so I guess after everything is cleaned up and put away, that might be the best time to lay my cards on the table."

Heavy clouds blanketed the sky above Glendale as a light but steady rain kept everyone indoors that Sunday. Tom's sister and brother were playing Monopoly with their Aunt Christine in the dining room, as the rest of the family talked in the living room. Tom was unsure how to start the conversation, until his Aunt Glenda spoke up.

"Well Tom, how did your school year end? Are you looking forward to going back again in the fall?"

In all honesty, Tom was not ready for what he knew was about to come. But the door was open now, and he needed to step forward. Before speaking, he looked over at Mackenzie to get some sort of a reassuring sign. With a slight smile, she nodded her head and said.

"Go for it, sweetheart."

"Well Glenda, there won't be a next year at the university for me. I decided to quit the program."

Karen, his mother, bolted from her chair and stared at Tom. "Tell me you're not serious. Why on earth would you do that without talking to us first? What are your plans, have you even given any of this much thought?"

Swallowing hard, Tom looked at his parents. "I've given it a lot of thought, actually. And I've enlisted in the Army, I'm going to be a combat medic."

"No!" Karen screamed. "That's not an option, Thomas Kenrude. Not in this house, never again." Looking over at Mackenzie, she yelled, "Did you know anything about this? Did you know what your boyfriend, my son, was going to do?"

Standing up, Mackenzie nodded her head. "Yes, Mrs. Kenrude, we discussed it at length before he made the decision to enlist."

"Discussed it at length? My God, what's wrong with you, girl? You're letting the man you claim to love go into the Army where he could be killed? What's wrong with you? I prefer you leave my house right now! Get out, I mean it!"

Steve took hold of his wife's arm. "Now Karen, slow down, we need to hear this out. I'm no happier then you are, but we're not throwing anyone out of this house."

Karen pulled away from her husband. "No, I want her out of my house. She undermined my feelings and allowed my son to join the Army. I'll not tolerate that. No, not in my home!"

Wishing to avoid any more of Karen's rage, Mackenzie picked up her purse and began to leave. But before she could make it to the door, Tom took her by the arm.

"Mom, if she goes, I go. That's the way it is!"

Catching everyone off guard, Karen glared at her son for a moment before replying. "Your father and uncle wanted to build a business, a legacy they could hand down to their sons. Steve was taken back when you chose to become a doctor, but he accepted your decision. But this, joining the army, is just not acceptable. It's a slap in the face to both of us. So, if you wish to join Mackenzie in leaving that's just fine, you both can go. In fact please go, get out of my house, and don't worry about coming back before you leave for the Army, I don't want you here."

Nancy and Glenda took hold of Tom and Mackenzie, keeping them from leaving the house, as Christine and Steve held on to Karen, who was shaking with anger.

"Son, you should have spoken to us before you made that choice, you have no idea what you're getting yourself into. I just don't understand why you did this," Steve explained as he fought to remain calm.

Alex slowly walked up to Tom. "Why Thomas, why? Everyone in this room loves you, Can you explain to us why you made this terrible decision?"

Mackenzie put her arm around her boyfriend as she whispered in his ear. "Be brave my love, be brave."

Before Tom could speak, Karen called out. "Don't you tell my son what to say. You just stay out of it." Karen screamed, as tears rolled down her face.

"No one is putting words in my mouth, Mother. No one is telling me what to say. Mackenzie appears to be the only one in this room that understands my feelings, and is ready to accept them. So Mom, you need to lay off of her, or I'll leave and never come back, and that's a promise! Is that what you want?" Tom called out angrily.

"You will tone down your voice when you address your mother, young man. That attitude doesn't cut it in this house," Steve demanded, as he glared at his eldest son.

Tom shook his head. "Sure it was fine for you to enlist back in World War Two. There were speeches and hoopla, and it was all for the greater good. Then you went off to Korea and left a family behind and we all missed the hell out of you. Uncle Mike ran away to join the Army, but a visit from Grandma and Grandpa just smoothed everything over. Sorry to say, there was little doubt in my mind that this was the kind of reception I was going to get, no matter when or how I told you our plans. So I had to do it when I thought the time was right. I couldn't go back to school next year, my heart just isn't in it anymore. I wanted to do something good and bold, something I could be proud of. I want to make a real difference. We have men dying in Vietnam, because they don't have enough qualified medics to treat them before they're sent to the hospital. Can you imagine how much good I can do with my education? Dad, you of all people should be able to understand. What's wrong with all of you?"

Back under control, but breathing heavily, Karen approached her eldest son. "But baby, you could be killed or go missing. Then what do we do?"

Tom nodded his head in agreement. "True, but Uncle Mike was almost killed right here on the farm. Tell me, Mom, what's the difference?"

Angered by his response, Karen took hold of him and began shaking him as she yelled, "But you're my baby. I gave you life, I nurtured you, and I'll not throw all that away. I did not raise you to become a sacrifice for this country!" As she began sobbing uncontrollably, she pulled Tom into her arms. No one in the room said a word for several minutes, as they all were focused on Karen.

Finally Tom continued, "Mother, you've forgotten that I'm older than Dad and Uncle Mike were when they enlisted. I understand the risks, and I know what's important to me and Mac. I could have gone right after school ended, and sent you a letter from Fort Leonard Wood to let you know where I was. Now I'm thinking that's exactly what I should have done. I know you're upset, but this response has been totally unfair to me and Mac. Especially Mac." As he slowly pushed his mother away, he took Mackenzie by the hand. "Let's get out of here, I'm tired of this crap."

Immediately, Mike and Glenda blocked the door to the porch. With a reassuring smile, Mike held out his hand. "Congratulations, and good luck, soldier."

Glenda took hold of Mackenzie wrapping her in her arms as she continued to cry. "Honey you're always welcome in our home. Whenever you need to talk, you just call me, do you understand."

Karen stood quietly for a moment as she glared at Glenda and Mike. "He is my son. My son! How dare you interfere and undermine my feelings in my home."

Glenda walked up to Karen looking compassionately at her sister-in-law. "Honey, we aren't undermining you, your feelings or your desires. We just want them to know we'll be there for them. There is nothing wrong with that, we are all family here."

Karen shook her head. "No, you're wrong. My son has no business enlisting in the army and you have no right to let him think any differently. If you can't understand that then the four of you can go. In fact, it might be best for all of us if you just plain leave."

Shocked by Karen's last outburst, Alex walked up to his daughter-in-law. Placing his huge hands on her shoulders, he looked into her tear filled eyes.

"Karen we have loved you forever and we always will. We were so happy when Steve asked you to be his wife. But right now honey, you're out of control. We fought hard to keep Mike out of World War Two. Regardless of all the lectures and threats we made, he still wound up in that damn war. He was just a boy, Tommy here is a full grown man, capable of making his own decisions and deciding what is right for him. You may not like the fact that he talked it over with Mackenzie, but again, she is his choice for a life mate, just as you were with Steven. No parent ever likes every decision their children make, but we have to allow them to live the life they feel is right for them. It would be nice if we could put our children in a box under our beds where they would always be safe and near to us, but that's just not possible."

Karen turned her head to look at Steve. "Where are you at with all of this?"

Before speaking, he looked over at Tom and Mackenzie for a moment. Turning back toward his distraught wife he shook his head.

"I was angry when Tom first told us. There is no one in this room that understands war and combat better than I do. I would do anything to keep my son out of war, because I understand the cost. However, what Dad just said is right. Tom is a man, and he's old enough to know what he wants, and it's apparent that he and Mac have discussed it as adults. Honey, while

I still don't like is, I respect his desire to serve, and I'm willing to give our son my blessings."

Karen forced a stiff smile as she nodded her head. Looking up at Alex, she whispered, "I'm okay, Dad, I really am. Thank you."

Slowly Alex dropped his hands from Karen's shoulders, as he stepped back toward Nancy without saying a word.

After several seconds, Karen walked slowly up to Tom and Mackenzie. Placing her arms around her son, she looked up into his eyes. "Can you forgive me, son?"

Without hesitation, Tom crushed his mother into his strong arms as he kissed her on the cheek. "Mom, there's nothing to forgive. You were just letting me know how much you love me."

Karen shook her head slightly. "Just promise me you'll be safe and come home to us. I want you and Mac to give me lots of grand-babies, and I still want you to be a doctor someday."

Karen then took hold of Mackenzie's hand. "I know what it's like to send your man off to war. Believe me, I understand what's in your heart. And sweetheart you need to know that Steve and I really do love you, and will always be here for you, just as Mike and Glenda will. This will always be your home, no matter what, do you understand? I'm so sorry for the way I treated you."

Mackenzie wiped the tears from her face as she looked at Karen. "I love you guys, too. You don't have to be sorry, I understand your pain, I honestly do. I want nothing more than to be a part of this marvelous family. I love your son so very much."

Slowly, Karen let go of Mackenzie as she looked over at Mike and Glenda.

"My gosh, after all we've been through, how do I apologize to you guys? You've been like a brother and sister to me."

Glenda laughed as she took Karen by the hands. "Honey, you and I are cut from the same piece of cloth. We're as good as twins, so you never need to apologize to me. What sisters never have a spat now and then? You and I will get through this together like we have every other storm that has rocked our boat. But what's more important, now we have Mac to add to the famous Kenrude women. You, me, Nancy, Christine, and Mac are forever one. There is nothing we can't deal with, no storm that we can't weather together."

Slowly, peace returned to the Kenrude home as everyone sought to put what happened behind them.

As the gathering broke up, Tom drove Mackenzie home. As he walked her to the door, he took her in his arms. "Still want to be a member of the Kenrude family after tonight?"

Mackenzie laughed as she looked intently into his eyes. "Actually, more than ever. Your family dynamics are incredible. The strength everyone displayed tonight was remarkable. So, yes silly boy, I still want to be part of the Kenrude clan."

Tom smiled as he nodded his head. "Will you be busy around one o'clock tomorrow afternoon?"

"No, why? What's going on?" Mackenzie inquired.

"Good, I'll pick you up. I have something I want to show you before I leave," Tom explained with a smile.

The following morning, Tom kissed his mother on the cheek before heading out the door. "Don't wait lunch for me. I'll be back later this afternoon, I have some things to get done."

At one o'clock, Tom drove up to the Bishop home, where Mackenzie was sitting on the front steps waiting for him. As he pulled to a stop, she came running out to the car. "Are you taking me out to lunch? I'm starving," she exclaimed, as she slid into the car.

"Well, I suppose we can add that to the list of things we need to get done," Tom exclaimed as he pulled away from the house.

"List? What list, Mr. Kenrude?" Mackenzie asked, as she kissed him on the cheek.

"Patience my dear. Have patience and you'll find out," Tom replied as he drove out of Glendale.

Arriving at the field road just south of his grandparent's farm, he pulled off the main road, driving toward the end of the trail near Eagle Lake. Turning off the ignition, he took Mac by the hand, helping her out of the car.

"What are we doing here? I thought you had a list of things to get done this afternoon?" Mackenzie inquired as she brushed some hair from her face.

"I do, and the first thing on my list begins right here. Follow me," Tom replied.

As they walked out by the rocks, Tom picked several wildflowers that always grew in the area. He handed them to Mackenzie. "Have a seat, sweetheart."

Not sure what to think of Tom's demeanor, she sat down on one of the rocks. "I always loved this place. Your mom told me she used to come here with your dad a lot when they were dating. She loved these wildflowers, too."

Without saying a word, Tom knelt down in front of Mackenzie. Reaching into his shirt pocket, he pulled out a diamond ring. "Mackenzie Diane Bishop, you're everything I want in this world. You really are my dream come true. Will you do me the honor of becoming my wife?"

As tears flowed down her face, Mackenzie grabbed Tom, pulling him up from his knee and kissed him. "Yes. Thomas Steven Kenrude, I would love nothing more than to be your wife."

After kissing her once more, Tom slid the ring onto her finger.

Mackenzie studied the ring for several moments. I never thought I would own anything this beautiful in my entire life. What did this cost you?"

Tom laughed. "That, my dear, is the only thing I will withhold from you forever. All that matters is that you love it."

"I do love it, and I love you with all my heart," Mackenzie responded.

The rest of the afternoon was spent visiting everyone in the family, and giving them the news. When Tom arrived home late that evening, Steve was having a cup of coffee at the kitchen table. "I'm happy as hell for you, son. But I would like to talk to you about a few things. Since you plan to marry when you come home on leave, where will Mac live when your leave is over?"

"If I'm stationed stateside, she will come with me. We'll get an apartment and live off base if we need to. If I go overseas right away, she'll stay with her folks until she gets out of school. We both know things could be a bit tough at first, but we'll make it happen," Tom explained, not sure what kind of a response he was going to get.

Karen had been listening as she folded laundry. "You're taking on a lot of responsibility, with a whole lot of unknowns. Do you guys think you can handle everything?"

Tom smiled as he nodded his head. "Yeah, we do, Mom. We're ready for whatever comes along. We can discuss it and figure it out like we always do. We'll be just fine."

Placing his cup on the table, Steve smiled at his son. "You know what? I believe you. I think you two have a good sense for working through the difficulties of life. You two will do alright."

The happy couple spent as much time as they could during the days before Tom left for basic training. They talked of wedding plans, and just enjoyed spending time together. Glenda and Karen dove into the details of the wedding, knowing they only had about four months to get everything worked out before Tom's leave. As angry as Karen had been the night Tom made his announcement, she was now filled with happiness as she planned her first child's wedding. There was no detail that was going to be overlooked.

Mackenzie's mother was becoming a bit perturbed with her daughter's inaction over finding the right wedding dress. She knew there was a possibility that it may have to be ordered, and time was simply running out. After a tremendous amount of coaxing, she finally convinced Mackenzie to go shopping for her dress at Gloria's Bridal Apparel in Willmar. After nearly half an hour of looking over dresses and catalogs, Mackenzie spoke up.

"None of these are right, Mother. I should have said something earlier, but I wasn't sure how you would react. What I really want, is to be married in your wedding dress. I've looked at it so many times, and I just love it. What do you think of that idea?"

Gloria looked over at Edna, who was not sure how to respond to her daughter's request. "The two of you are about the same height and weight. Whatever would need to be done to the dress, could easily be handled right here in my shop, Edna. It would probably be an easy conversion."

Edna walked around the shop for a moment looking at dresses before responding. "Honey, there are some gorgeous dresses here that you could treasure forever. Are you sure this is what you really want?"

Mackenzie smiled at her mother. "You were such a beautiful bride. I want to look just like you did on your wedding day. Yes, that's the dress I want to wear."

With tears rolling down her cheeks, Edna nodded her head. "I would be honored if you would wear my dress. Nothing would please me more."

Mackenzie and her mother hugged as Gloria looked on before commenting. "If you can get the dress in here for a fitting over the next few days, I can guarantee it will be ready long before your wedding day. And it will be a whole lot cheaper than buying a new gown."

Mackenzie and her mother happily departed the shop, knowing the situation over the proper wedding dress was now completely solved.

Throughout all the wedding planning and conversation regarding Tom's departure date, Peter, Tom's younger brother felt completely left out. Two days before Tom was to leave, he observed Peter sitting in the back of their father's pickup, with Bosco, their dog, laying on his lap. Walking over to the truck, Tom called out.

"What's going on Pete? You've been pretty quiet the last few days. Is there anything wrong?"

Startled to hear Tom approach, Peter flinched. After giving Tom a slight smile, he turned away as he began giving Bosco a good rub down. "I guess I kind of feel left out of everything that's going on around here. Mom and all the girls are planning your wedding, and you and Dad have been having heart to heart talks. Nobody seems to care that I'm around, so I'm just trying to keep out of the way."

Tom felt bad for his younger brother, as what he had just said was close to accurate. Reaching out Tom rubbed Peter's head. "You want to go with me on the dirt bike down to the lake? Just you me and Bosco?"

Without saying a word, Peter scrambled out of the truck with Bosco at his side. Moments later Tom and Peter bounded toward Eagle Lake on the red Honda dirt bike, with Bosco raising a commotion as he followed along behind.

Arriving at the rocks, Peter jumped from one rock to the next until he was on the biggest one, several yards from shore. As Tom sat down on the huge rock, Peter looked up at him.

"Tom, do you know what you're getting yourself into? I watch the news almost every night with Dad, and I read the news magazines at school. Vietnam is a dangerous place! Are you ready for whatever happens if you get over there?"

Tom nodded his head. "Yeah Pete, Mackenzie and I gave that a whole lot of thought. From everything Dad and Uncle Mike talked about, I know that war is no picnic. And I have heard a lot of horror stories about the Viet Cong, but I need to do my part. I just can't sit back and allow all those other guys to fight, while I sit in school protected by a deferment, with skills that would really make a difference. It just doesn't seem right to me. I know Mom and Dad have not totally accepted it, but they'll have to eventually."

Pete gave Tom an accepting look before replying. "Why the Army? Don't you think the Navy or Air Force would have been a lot safer?"

"Yeah maybe. But it's the Army and Marines that do the heavy ground fighting. I want to experience the war the way Dad and Uncle Mike did, down there in the trenches. Plus, that's where the medics are needed the most. So it just made sense to me." Tom explained.

Pete watched Bosco chasing butterflies for a moment before turning back toward his brother. "So are you going to finish medical school when you return?"

"Yeah, I sure am. I'm not sure if I want to be a doctor in the city, or whether I want to come to Glendale or Willmar. But I'll have lots of time to think about it."

Peter shook his head in agreement. "Did Dad or Mom feel bad when you weren't going to come home and work on the farm?"

"Sure, we talked about that a lot, little brother. But I told Dad he had you and Uncle Mike's boys to keep the operation running and in the family for a long time. I told him he could spare one doctor," Tom explained, as he tossed a small rock into the lake.

"Therein lies the problem, Tom. I don't want to be a farmer either. It seems fine for Matt and Greg, they eat it up like candy. But it's not what I want." Looking up toward the sky, he pointed toward the contrail of a jet flying toward the west. "I want to join the Air Force or Navy and fly jets. I'd like to be a fighter pilot, Tom."

Taken back by Peter's response, Tom was speechless for a moment. "A fighter pilot! You're worried about Vietnam for me, and you want to strap yourself into a flying bomb? Next thing you're going to tell me is you want to be tossed off the deck of a carrier out in the middle of the ocean, thousands of miles from shore."

Peter laughed for a second. "That's right big brother, I want to be a fighter pilot. Sure it's breaking the Kenrude tradition of being a ground pounder, but that's what I want to do. Don't tell Mom or Dad, but Charlie Conrad took me up in his bi-plane about a month ago. I biked out to the airfield one day after school just to take a look around. I do that once in a while and no one knows. I just give Mom an excuse as to why I'm late."

Smiling Peter continued, "Anyway, one day Charlie was getting ready to take the Lame Duck up for a spin, that's what he calls his plane. So I was giving him some grief, and we were having fun. Then he asked if Mom and Dad would be alright if I went up with him. I told him they would be fine with it, so up we went. Tom, it was so exhilarating, and I've never felt so free in my life. We flitted back and forth through some low clouds, and dove low here over the lake, and did some twists and turns. I felt like I touched the face of God, and he opened up his arms to me, telling me to come back again. After we landed, I asked Charlie if he would teach me how to fly his plane. He told me I could fly with him anytime, but he wouldn't train me for a year or so. He wants me to be a bit older."

Tom smiled at his younger brother. "Pete, you're growing up way too fast. But I understand exactly what you're saying. When I watch the news and see the choppers flying around, that's exactly what I need to be doing. I want to ride into combat, patch up the wounded, and ferry them back to the hospital. So you actually do understand what's going on inside me?"

Peter gave Tom a wide smile. "Yeah, I do big brother. You need to promise me this conversation is just between you and me. Mom would raise a fit if she knew what I wanted to do. Although I do admit, you might have cracked that glass ceiling a bit for me. I'll never forget the day you and Mac told them what your plans were. I never thought our Mom could get that angry. She actually scared me for a few minutes there."

Tom laughed as he shook his head. "Scared you? Damn, little brother, you should have been on the receiving end of that explosion. It was like a tidal wave and a volcano coming at me all at once. There was a moment when I thought she would throw us out, and we would never rectify anything. I really felt bad for Mac, and it's hard to believe they're such good friends now."

As the sun began to set across the lake, Pete placed his hand on Tom's shoulder. "Just don't take any foolish chances if you get over to Vietnam. I need a big brother to share my feelings with."

Tears welled up in Tom's eyes as he grabbed his little brother to give him a hug. "As I need you, Pete. As I need you."

After chasing down Bosco, the three of them headed back home, leaving Eagle Lake in a cloud of dust behind them.

The morning before Tom was to leave, he drove his precious dirt bike back over to Eagle Lake to be alone. Climbing up on the rocks, he tossed several small stones into the water. His attention was suddenly shifted to the corn field, as a doe and her two fawns walked clear of the field, standing perfectly still for several moments. Feeling all was safe, the mother pushed her two children down toward the water's edge for a drink. Tom had to laugh as he watched one of the fawns splashing its front hooves in the water. After taking a long drink, the mother deer backed away from her offspring, allowing them to splash and run around in the cool clear water.

"I guess kids are kids no matter the species," Tom said quietly, as he watched the mom finally coax her two little ones back into the safety of the corn field.

For a moment Tom sat quietly, as he gazed about the beautiful lake his family enjoyed so much. He was happy his great grandfather had purchased the land back in the late 1800's. Looking skyward he began to pray.

"Dear God, I'm not sure what I've gotten myself into here. I feel I made the right decision, yet I'm afraid of what could happen to me in Vietnam. I joined because I want to make a difference in this world, and to help our men at their very worst time. But more than anything, I really want to come home and spend the rest of my life with Mackenzie. You know how much I love her. She is all that really matters in my life. I realize there are no guarantees, so I'm not going to ask you for one. Just give me the strength to do my job to the best of my ability, and never let the men down when they need me. And please, just bring me back to Mackenzie."

With that said, Tom stood up from the rocks as he pitched one more stone towards the middle of the lake with all his might. As he walked back to his dirt bike, he noticed Bosco laying in the tall cool grass. "Hey boy, I didn't know you followed me out here. Want to play? I'm ready if you are."

Immediately, the dog jumped to its feet, running up to him. Finding a nice stick near the corn field, Tom threw it towards the rocks. Bosco took off like a missile scooping up the stick as it bounced. After running in circles a few times, he brought it back, laying it at Tom's feet.

The two friends played pitch and retrieve for several minutes. Finally Tom threw the stick out into the lake. Bosco ran to the rocks where he stopped, and stared at the stick for several moments. Turning his head to face Tom, he yipped and whined as the stick floated farther out.

"What's the matter boy, you aren't going to be brave today? Come on, go get it!"

However, Bosco was not in the mood to get wet. After looking at the stick one more time, he ran to the dirt bike, waiting for his master to arrive. Tom enjoyed the ride home, as Bosco ran alongside, barking the entire way.

That evening, Karen, Glenda, Christine and Mackenzie put on a major feast for the family as it was Tom's last night home. Tom truly enjoyed the good humor and practical jokes everyone was playing on him. It was a wonderful night, and one he would remember for a long time to come.

Early the next morning, Steve, Karen and Tom picked up Mackenzie and her mother Edna, and drove to the Minneapolis Airport. Tom found it difficult as he realized he would not see the woman he loved for several months. However those sad feelings were dampened somewhat, as he knew the next time they were together, she would become his wife.

After checking in and arriving at his gate, there was only about ten minutes left before boarding. Turning to his father, Tom stated boldly, "I'll make you proud, Dad. I'll do my best and give it all I've got. Thanks for everything, Dad."

Steve choked back tears as he shook his son's hand. "I have no doubt about it, son. I know you'll do your best. Just be damn careful."

Turning toward his mother, who was already crying, Tom said softly, "I love you, Mom. And I'll miss you very much. Help Pete take care of Bosco, you know how that foolish dog is when I'm not around. And thank you for all you have done for me. I know you're scared for me, but I'm a Kenrude, I can take care of myself. You and Dad taught me what it takes to be a man and be responsible."

Karen crushed her son in her arms as she wept. Regaining her composure somewhat, she smiled, "I'll always love you my sweet child. Never do anything foolish, but show the army that the Kenrude's still count. Most of all, come home. You have a beautiful bride waiting for you, and I want grand-babies, lots and lots of grand-babies."

Tom laughed as he stroked his mother's long blonde hair. "We'll give you a house full, Mom. You may have to tell us to stop."

Next in line was Mackenzie's mother. She took hold of Tom, giving him a huge hug. "Son, you're part of our family now. My daughter is going to be your wife, and I'm so anxious for the two of you to be a family. We're proud as hell of you. Be safe, be smart, and come home to us." Edna said softly, as she kissed him on the cheek. Looking over at her daughter she added. "Go to her, she is your future now."

Tom placed his arms around Mackenzie and smiled. "I will miss you so much. I love you with all my heart, Mac. Take care of yourself, and study hard. I'll be home for the wedding before you know it."

Mackenzie smiled as tears ran down her cheeks. "Mr. Kenrude, you best come home to me, as I can't wait to be your wife. We're going to have a wonderful life together, be it in a house or that mud hut!"

Tom laughed as he tightened his grip on her waist and kissed her. After releasing her he kissed her one more time on the cheek. "I'll write as soon as I can. You'll always be in my dreams."

Mackenzie reached into her pocket, retrieving a silver cross on a long chain. "I had Reverend Carmichael bless this for you. Wear it every day, it will keep you safe."

Tom slid the silver chain over his head, allowing the cross to drop down inside his shirt. "I'll wear it forever, sweetheart. It's there for life."

Mackenzie smiled as she hugged Tom one more time and kissed him on the cheek. "I love you, Tom Kenrude. Never forget that."

After kissing Mackenzie one more time, he was about to say something to his family when they announced last call for boarding. Giving everyone a wave, Tom walked slowly down the jetway to his waiting plane.

His family walked over to the large glass windows, to watch as the plane was backed away from the gate. After the pilot ran up the engines for a moment, the aircraft slowly began to slowly lumber down the taxiway toward the runway. Several minutes later, Flight 458 took to the skies above Minneapolis, disappearing as it banked hard toward the south.

Mackenzie felt very depressed, as she watched the small dot in the sky getting ever smaller. She wanted him back, but that was just not possible.

Karen tried hard to be strong, as she watched the aircraft disappear into the morning sky. She wished she could have found a way to keep him at home forever. But in the end, she understood that every mother has to leave her children make their own decisions, like it or not.

Steve knew full well what his son was about to face when he arrived at Fort Leonard Wood. He knew it would catch Tom completely off guard as it did most recruits, but it would toughen him up for what was to come, as he moved on with his enlistment.

The ride back to Glendale was almost too quiet for Mackenzie. No matter what was said by Karen, Steve, or her mother, she still felt the Kenrude's continued to harbor animosity toward her over supporting Tom's decision. There was nothing she could do to change their opinions. All she could hope for today, was some type of forgiveness in the future, but it appeared to her, it was not coming any time soon.

CHAPTER 4
MILITARY LIFE BEGINS

Tom attempted to sleep during the short flight to St. Louis, as his nerves had kept him awake most of the night. A light mist was falling over Lambert International Airport as the aircraft rolled up to the passenger jetway at Gate 23.

He was yawning as a flight attendant tapped him on the shoulder. "I wanted to make sure you were awake, as you were sleeping the last time I walked down the aisle. I didn't want to wake you as you were sleeping so soundly."

Tom smiled up at the cheerful woman. "Yeah I needed the sleep, thanks. I think this is going to be the roughest and longest day of my life. Hope I'm prepared for it."

"I assume you're headed to Fort Leonard Wood, as are the other young men on this plane," she replied nodding her head.

"Yes ma'am. You know, my girlfriend and I talked this over several times before I enlisted. It always seemed like the right decision. But right now, I'm not so sure. Maybe it's just nerves," Tom replied, knowing he was getting more nervous by the minute.

The flight attendant smiled while placing her hand on Tom's shoulder. "Do you have any idea how many times I've heard those same words when I fly down here to St. Louis?"

Tom laughed as he shook his head. "I probably can't count that high."

As the aircraft rolled to a stop, Tom rose from his seat, pulling his small bag from the overhead compartment. After thanking the flight attendant for the conversation, he followed the passengers toward the door.

Inside the terminal, he followed the signs toward the baggage collection area, where the recruiter had told him he would find representatives from the fort. He knew he was in the right place, as he observed a long line of young men waiting to talk to several soldiers near a counter. When it was his turn, he handed a lieutenant his orders. After making a notation on a clip board, the lieutenant returned the orders saying, "Head outside, bus 512 or 513. It will be about a two hour ride."

Climbing aboard bus 513, Tom sat down in a seat near a window. Seconds later, another recruit with a shaved head sat down next to him.

"Darnel, Eddie Darnel. I'm from Wichita, Kansas. Where you from?"

Tom smiled at the nervous man as they shook hands.

"Tom Kenrude, from Glendale, Minnesota."

Eddie forced a smile. "Damn, I'm nervous. I keep thinking, "What the hell did I get myself into? I enlisted, how about you?"

"Me too." Tom replied. "I quit college, so I knew I would be drafted right away. So here I am, just like you."

"Quit college! What the hell did you do that for? I'm right out of high school and wish I could have been smart enough to get into college. I just wasn't smart enough to get the grades required to stay in school." Eddie replied, as he stared intently at Tom.

"It's a damn long story, Eddie. Something I'm still contemplating right now, and I guess I will for the rest of the time I'm in," Tom explained, as the bus began pulling away from the terminal.

Within minutes, Tom fell back to sleep as the cool air from the air conditioning soothed his weary head. He was just waking up when Eddie shook his shoulder.

"We're here, Kenrude. You better be prepared when we stop and that door opens up. They're going to skin us alive," Eddie remarked, as his jitters began once again.

Tom laughed. "Come on, Eddie. It won't be that bad. They may yell a lot, but no one is going to skin you. You have my word on it."

Nodding his head, Eddie looked at Tom. "Will you stay with me if we can? It would be nice to know someone for the first few days."

"I don't know if that's possible. But if we can, sure, I'll hang with you. Maybe we can go through the reception station together, that would be good." Tom agreed, although he was unsure of what was to come, yet he remembered the story about his dad and Harry Jensen making it through training together, but that was 1942.

As the bus door opened, a drill instructor climbed aboard. "Alright, listen up. You'll depart this bus and go to the building to your right. You'll keep your mouths shut, and proceed to the tables in front of you in three lines. When you're checked in, you'll be told where to go. Now get your sorry butts off my damn bus. Do it now, ladies!"

The men moved at break neck speed as they departed. Tom followed Eddie out the door and into the large building. There had to be nearly three hundred men going through the reception process. Tom watched Eddie get registered and depart out a door to their left. As Tom approached the table, he handed the clerk his orders. It took the man several minutes to make notations on several forms before looking up. "You were in Medical School?"

"Yes sir," Tom replied.

Shaking his head, the man looked back at Tom. "You should have graduated and then enlisted. You could be an officer, what kind of a dumb ass are you?" With that, the man handed Tom his papers, instructing him to exit to the left.

Walking outside, a drill instructor grabbed him by the arm. "Where in the hell are you going, troop? Did you look at your paperwork at all or can't you read." Pulling the papers from Tom's hand, he looked them over quickly. "To your left, by the wall with the rest of the crybabies."

As Tom walked up toward the group of men, he observed Eddie leaning against the wall. "Nice to see you, Kenrude. We made it," Eddie commented, before a large drill sergeant approached.

"Alright ladies, form into four columns. If you can't count, or figure that out, I'm here to help you sorry sons a bitches," the sergeant screamed as he shook his head in disgust.

In seconds, the men formed into four equal columns and froze into position.

"Very pretty, ladies. In fact, I'm about to cry. Now keep your mouths shut and follow me. By the way, in case any of you get lost, you can now tell whoever finds you that you belong to Sgt. Wallace. Now, keep up and don't hurt yourselves," Sgt. Wallace yelled, as he began walking out onto the road. They walked about half a mile before turning into an alley that led to a court yard. At the west end of the courtyard was an orderly room, where drill instructors stood on an elevated wooden sidewalk in front of the building. The other three sides of the courtyard were occupied by older wooden barracks. Sgt. Wallace marched them right up to the orderly room before he ordered them to halt.

The tallest of the drill sergeants walked up to the steps leading down from the walkway.

"Good Lord Sgt. Wallace, did you bring me the cast members of the latest Nancy Drew mystery? These certainly can't be new recruits. If they're supposed to be soldiers, will you please return them at once? I personally promised LBJ we would give him tough combat soldiers. There's nothing we can do with shit like this."

Sgt. Wallace turned to the platoon. "Well, you heard the man, you've been rejected. I guess I'll take you back to the reception building, put you on a damn bus for home, and write rejected on your miserable foreheads. Platoon, right face."

Just as the men turned, the tall sergeant called out. "Oh, what the hell, Sarg. If their mommies were willing to give them up so easily, who are we to break their little hearts? Put them in barracks 27, and get them out of my sight. I'll break out a new case of Pablum and diapers so we're ready."

"Yes, senior drill instructor, it will be done," Sgt. Wallace called out with a smile on his face.

After lining up the men in front of barracks 27, Sgt. Wallace paced back and forth for a moment. "Alright, listen up. First and second squads are on the main floor, third and fourth go up to the second floor. Go put your ditty bags on a bunk, put your name on the card at the end of your bunk, and get your foul smelling asses back out here."

It took merely minutes for the nervous men to complete the task and fall back outside where Sgt. Wallace and one more drill instructor awaited them.

"Outstanding, gentlemen. Just plain outstanding. Believe it or not, you just broke the fort record for the slowest bunch of recruits in the history of this base. My grandma is slow, but she's 101. What the hell is your damn excuse?"

Sgt. Wallace led the men down the street to another courtyard, where many other men were waiting in several lines.

"Alright listen up. First thing we're going to do is make you look pretty. You'll get in line and enter the barber shop to get a nice military haircut. Then you will proceed to the building on my right, and get in line, so we can make your dog tags. When that's done, fall back into place right here, and God help you if you get lost, now move!"

As the men entered the barbershop, there were several drill instructors pointing the men to the next open chair. Tom had to laugh to himself as each barber would point to a chart on the wall asking each man which of the hair styles he preferred. No matter what the new soldier requested, they all received buzz cuts.

A recruit from another training platoon with exceptionally long hair, and a small beard drew the attention of every D.I. in the shop. One of the instructors bowed down to him inquiring, "Which hair cut do *you* want Jesus? Or, are your angels going to come and give you a respectable hair cut we can work with? Well, what is it going to be my Lord?"

The soldier never said a word. He just sat erect in the chair, attempting to avoid eye contact with the man that was just inches from his face.

"Cat got your tongue, Jesus? Do you need some assistance here? You best tell me what the hell you want?" The instructor screamed even louder as he pushed his hat into the man's forehead.

"Take it off, take it all off," the new soldier called out, his voice shaking with rage. "I want my head shaved if that's fine with you, drill instructor."

"Well now, Jesus has spoken, I'll be damned." Smiling at the barber the instructor yelled, "Give the man what he wants. Make his head as smooth as my new baby's ass."

Tom was more than happy to get out of the barber shop and get his dog tags. The chances of screwing up in front of a drill instructor in there were more than he could count.

After everyone was finished, they were marched down to a large warehouse, where they were issued all their clothing and footwear. The day finally ended as they packed up all their civilian clothing, boxing it up for shipment home.

While the men were storing their new clothing in their lockers, Sgt. Wallace came in the barracks. "Listen up. Lights out will be in thirty minutes. Every one of you will be in your bunks with your mouths shut. Any screwing around, and you'll all pay the price for it. That's how it will be the entire time you are in reception. Now get your shit done and get in your racks."

At 2100hrs. Sgt. Wallace flipped off the lights. "Good night, ladies. Sleep well, and I'll see you all in the morning."

Everything was quiet in the barracks for about twenty minutes, before Eddie Darnel began to tell jokes and stories about his childhood. He had everyone in the barracks laughing and asking questions, which just added to the tumult. Suddenly the door flew open as all the lights went on. A young buck sergeant stood in the entry way wearing a rain coat. Slowly, he walked to the middle of the barracks.

"I'm Sergeant Pike, your babysitter for the night. I hear you want to joke and laugh. Well, that's fine with me. But I think this is the wrong venue for such a fun filled adventure. So roll out of your racks, file outside into the bleachers on the far side of the courtyard in your underwear. You want to bullshit, that's fine with me, and we can bullshit all night long. I got nothing but time, and you won't need a shower in the morning. Now move your asses."

The men ran from the barracks wearing only their underwear and T-Shirts, into the cool rainy night. When they were all assembled standing in the bleachers, Sgt. Pike called out. "No, no, gentlemen, I want you to feel at home. Take a seat so you'll be more comfortable." With everyone seated, the Sergeant paced back and forth for a few moments. "Now, where the hell was I. Oh yeah, I remember now. So my aunt Tilly on my mother's side came for Christmas last year. She's a nice lady for all intentions, except that she has a pretty dark beard about five inches long that she likes to braid."

Instantly, one of the men laughed out loud. Sgt. Pike stopped in his tracks, glaring at the men. "You think my Aunt Tilly is a joke? Are you laughing at my family? Who the hell do you think you are? Get off the bleachers and run around the courtyard, do it now! All of you."

After the men made three laps, Sgt. Pike stopped the cold and shivering recruits.

"Now that I have your attention gentlemen, maybe we can get some sleep around here. Get inside, lights out in ten."

The barracks was like a tomb when the men returned, not only that night, but the remainder of the time they spent at the reception center.

The last day of reception, the men were given varying work details around the base. Some filled sand bags, others unloaded trucks down in the warehouses, while others carried out groceries from the commissary for the wives of the men stationed at the fort. Tom spent the day unloading food trucks at the central distribution warehouse. It did have its benefits, as the Warrant Officer in-charge allowed them coffee breaks while giving them cookies from a broken case.

After the last men were delivered back to the barracks that evening, Sgt. Wallace performed a roll call. When he arrived at the name of Stimson, Arnold J., nobody responded. Three more times he called out the name with the same results. Looking over the bewildered men, he inquired. "Who worked with Stimson today?"

Eddie Darnel stepped forward. "He worked down at clothing issue. They gave him a job in the back room bundling up cardboard boxes. That's the last time I saw him."

"Good enough Darnel, you can step back, we'll take it from here," the sergeant responded.

After evening chow, the men packed their duffel bags in preparation to be moved to their basic training companies the following day.

Just before lights out, Sgt. Wallace came into the barracks. "Alright, listen up. We could find no trace of Stimson. It would appear he has gone AWOL. That's a serious matter, particularly in times of war. The Army will find him, and take all necessary legal action against him. I highly recommend that if any of you know anything about this, you come forward now, or you can be charged as an accomplice." He waited several moments for a reply, but no one came forward. Nodding his head, he continued. "I'll take that none of you know anything. And that is what I'll report to the base Provost Marshall, and the JAG officer who will handle this case. As I'm going to be busy in the morning, I will not be seeing you off. So I wish you all the best of luck in basic training. Keep your noses clean, and your mouths shut, and you will do alright."

As he began leaving the barracks he made one more stop. "If Stimson should get in touch with any of you, it's in your best interest and his to turn him in. Don't let that chicken-shit haul you down with him. Lights out in fifteen gentlemen, and I want a quiet barracks."

At 0700 the following morning, buses and trucks filled the courtyard, ready to deliver the men to their assigned companies. Tom was loaded on a deuce and a half with twenty other men, and was told they were going to have just a short ride."

Arriving at basic training site A-5-2, which stood for A-Company, 5th Battalion, 2nd Basic Combat Training Brigade. As the men unloaded, they could see drill instructors busy chasing down recruits that arrived earlier, who were not following directions. It appeared to be total bedlam, though it may well have been organized bedlam, but to a new recruit, it scared the hell out of them just the same. Before Tom could place both feet on the ground, a D.I. grabbed him by the arm.

"Are your legs paralyzed, son?" he inquired.

"No, drill instructor, they work just fine," Tom explained.

"Then why the hell aren't they moving. Get your sorry ass over to that sidewalk and follow everyone else. Or did you want me to requisition a gold cart and a chauffeur and give you a ride?" The D.I. was screaming in Tom's face as he pulled him down the last step of the bus.

Grabbing his duffel bag, Tom ran as fast as he could, passing several other men. When he decided to cut across the grass to get farther up the line, two drill instructors called out.

"Recruit, get the hell off of my grass," the shortest of the two D.I.'s called out. "The only living bodies allowed on that grass are goats, sheep and cows. Which one are you?"

Tom stopped where he was, responding, "None of the above, Drill Sergeant."

The smiling D.I. walked up to Tom, pulling his duffel bag away from him.

"Well I see your name is Kenrude. So Kenrude, get down on your knees and eat some grass and I want to hear you moo like a cow. Can you do that for us?"

"I'd rather not, Drill Sergeant!" Tom yelled out.

"Oh, you'd rather not. Hmm. You see that presents a problem, Kenrude. That was not a request. That was an order. Now get your ass down there," the D.I. exclaimed, giving Tom a push toward the ground.

Immediately, Tom began to move about on his hands and knees, pretending to graze on the long grass. Knowing what was coming next if he didn't make a sound, he began mooing several times as he moved about."

By this time, three more D.I.'s came over to watch the show. They all applauded and cheered to Tom's antics.

"Now there is a contented recruit," one of the sergeants called out.

After a few moments, the D.I. that forced him to get down in the grass, walked over to Tom. "Alright Kenrude, you can get up. Here's your bag. Fall in with third platoon over to your left, and just so you know, my name is Sgt. Dixon. I'll be your D.I. throughout basic. I've got your number, just keep that in mind. Screw up, and I'll be there to make you wish you hadn't. You got that, Kenrude!"

"Yes, Drill Sergeant!" Tom called out, as he stood up, physically shaking in front of the determined man.

"Alright then, as long as we have an understanding, we're good to go. Get off my turf and fall into third squad of the third platoon. You should be able to see that row is short one man, and that is your sorry ass, so go fill the position so we can get this show on the road!"

Tom ran over to the empty position as Sgt. Dixon walked to the front of the platoon. He stood at attention with the rest of the men, although he was seething inside. He had never been so humiliated in his entire life, and it hurt his pride. Every man in the company had seen the pathetic performance, and would surely remember when it came to dealing with him. He knew in his mind, he would have to do something to change the way everyone thought about him. It may take time, but he had eight weeks to come up with something.

As Sgt. Dixon walked over to confer with another drill instructor, Tom heard a voice speaking to him from the fourth squad.

"Hey Kenrude, this is Darnel. Looks like we made it together again. Don't let that stunt they pulled get you down. You'll do just fine. A lot of the guys are pissed about what they did to you. You're not alone, so hang in there buddy."

Tom acknowledged Eddie's comments by a slight nod of his head. He did not want Sgt. Dixon to catch him responding, as it would just heap more grief upon him and Eddie both.

When Sgt. Dixon returned to the platoon, their senior drill instructor of the company, Sgt. Kendrick stepped from the barracks door.

"Oh bull crap!" he exclaimed. "I personally promised General Westmoreland we would send him troops capable of winning that damn war in Vietnam. You mean to tell me we have to make soldiers out of this trash. Damn! Where are all the heroes in America? Is this all that's left?"

All the drill instructors laughed as Sgt. Kendrick walked back and forth in front of the company. "Well alright. If this is what we have to work with, we can make it happen. Sergeants, take charge of your platoons and get them settled. Then we go for our first run at 1430. Heaven help the first son-of-a-bitch that falls out of position on that run. He'll wish to God he had never been born!"

During that first run, Sgt. Nixon ran beside the platoon yelling, "Who wants to fall out, who wants to have some cookies and hot chocolate. Just say the word and we can deal with that."

No one from third platoon fell out of formation during the run, although many were gasping for air when they came to a stop back in front of the barracks.

Sgt. Nixon walked up to a man in the first squad. "What's your name, soldier?"

"Pvt. Sammy Brooks, Sergeant?" he replied, as Sgt. Nixon bounced his Smokey Bear type hat off his forehead.

"So, Private Brooks. Where is your sorry ass from?" Sgt. Dixon inquired.

"South side of Chicago, Sergeant," Brooks replied, with a nervous voice.

"South side of Chicago? Did you learn to run like that trying to flee from the police after stealing cars, or angry fathers that caught you messing with their daughters?" Sgt. Dixon screamed

Glaring angrily at Sgt. Dixon, he replied, "Neither, Drill Sergeant. I was all state running back at Lincoln Park High School two years in a row. If my mom could have afforded it, I would be in college instead of here. But it is what it is, and if you ever want to test my speed against what you think you've got, feel free to bring it on."

Angered by the response from Brooks, Sgt. Dixon pulled him from the squad, pushing him to the ground. "Well then, let's see how good you are at push-ups. I want your sorry ass to pump out one hundred real nice push-ups. Now hit it, Brooks!"

Brooks went to work completing the push-ups, calling out each one completed in a loud voice for everyone to hear. As he approached seventy-five, Sgt. Dixon placed his foot on Sammy's back, pushing toward the ground and letting up just enough for him to straighten his elbows.

"What's the matter Brooks, can't quite make it? Anything you want to complain about?"

"No Drill Sergeant, I can finish this any day of the week," Brooks called out in a clear voice. Finishing his one hundredth push-up, Brooks collapsed to the concrete.

Sgt. Dixon leaned over next to his ear. "Get up and fall in, Brooks. Today is day one, let's see what you got left by the end of eight weeks. Maybe we can make a soldier out of you instead of a smart mouth punk. What I got and what I can do is no affair of yours. Now get up!"

Each day, Tom pushed himself to outdo the other men and never fall behind, regardless of what they were doing. Being an athlete in school, he was a good runner and never had a problem keeping the pace. Most of the time it was Tom, Brooks and another former high school athlete from New Jersey named Emit Surely that led the platoon in speed and endurance. Tom could tell Sgt. Dixon was gunning for the three men. He was just waiting for one of them to mess up so he could make an example of them in front the platoon.

One foggy morning the men assembled in front of the barracks as always, with thirty pound packs and their rifles. At 0700, the company began a march down a dirt road that led to the dense forest west of the cantonment area. The drill instructors continued changing cadence from regular marching to double time for hours without a rest. About 1000 hours, the long column was marched into an open field where they were told to take a break.

Tom sat down on a fallen log next to Eddie Darnel. "How you holding up, Eddie?" Tom asked, as he pulled his canteen free of his web belt.

Shaking his head, Eddie replied. "Man this is tough, Kenrude. My legs are throbbing and my lungs are on fire. I don't know how long I can keep this pace. I don't want to fall out, but I just don't think I can hold on for much longer."

"Don't fall out, Eddie. You've got to hang in there. The last thing you want to do is give Dixon any ammunition he can use to rip you apart. Just keep saying to yourself. "One more step, I can do it. One more step, I can do it. Pretty soon it will be mind over matter. Just don't give the bastard what he's looking for, Eddie."

Before Eddie could respond, Private Frank Batts joined into the conversation. "You got it all wrong, Kenrude. Dixon isn't a bastard, he's just trying to make us into good soldiers. It's all part of the game. If you accept that, everything will go much easier. He wants to see what you're made of and what you can take. Play the game guys, play the game!"

Tom turned toward the smiling soldier. "Yeah maybe, but I don't much agree with some of his tactics, and I don't know that I ever could. Breaking a man is one thing, but constant humiliation is another, Batts. I think you're a damn good soldier, but Dixon hasn't laid his mitts into you yet.

When he does, you might feel differently about all that." Before anyone could respond, the order was given for them to reassemble back on the road. In about half an hour the men were marched onto one of the many rifle ranges on the fort. Throughout the afternoon and early evening, the men practiced shooting on two ranges, one up hill, and the other downhill. Although the training staff was dead serious, allowing no one to break the rules, they were actually very helpful in giving each man the assistance required to become a better marksman.

After eating a hot meal delivered to the field by the mess cooks, the men began the long march back to the cantonment area. It was nearly dark as the men came to a stop in front of the barracks. Sgt. Dixon looked over his tired men.

"Alright, listen up! I want those weapons cleaned and sparkling no later than 2200. Lights out is at 2300, and each of you will be snug as a bug in your racks, no exceptions. Now fall out and get to work!"

Entering the barracks, the men were aghast. Every bunk had been over turned and the contents of every locker spilled out onto the floor. Things had been kicked around, mixing up everyone's property. The tired soldiers stood motionless for several seconds before they slowly began to right their overturned bunks and lockers. Each man sorted through the mess on the floor, attempting to find their property while properly reassembling their lockers. It was nearly 2130 before Tom finally began tearing down his weapon.

At 2155, he walked up to Corporal Edmonds, who was working with the training cadre before attending Drill Instructor School. Tom pulled open the bolt, locking it in the open position as he handed over his weapon.

Cpl. Edmonds pulled the rifle from Tom's hands, holding it up to the light as he looked down the barrel. After turning the rifle around several times, looking it over carefully, he released the bolt allowing it to slam shut.

"I don't know, Kenrude, it doesn't look like you spent very much time cleaning your best friend tonight." With a sly grin on his face, the Corporal continued. "Was there anything that kept you from spending more time on this marvelous piece of equipment, or were you just goofing off trying to entertain your buddies?"

Knowing there was no good way to answer the question, Tom stood at attention keeping his mouth shut as he stared straight ahead. It felt like an eternity before the Corporal threw the weapon back.

"It will pass, Kenrude. If you feel it would serve you well in combat, then you can hit the rack."

Walking up to the weapons rack, Tom placed his rifle in the proper slot. He knew his M-16 was clean and would function well if needed in combat, he would never do anything to infringe upon his own safety. Laying down on his bunk, Tom instantly thought about Mackenzie. He missed her so much, and it felt like forever since he departed Glendale and his caring family.

The week finally came where the men would march out into the hill country and bivouac for eight days. Their packs were heavy as they carried every piece of field equipment they were issued, plus clothing and other personal materials. A hot meal was delivered to the campsite around 1700 by the company cooks. After that, they would survive on C-Rations the balance of the time.

During the long week, the men went through many rigorous training sessions, including more time at the rifle range. On the last night of bivouac, Sgt. Dixon explained how things would go the following morning when they broke camp. When he was finished speaking, Cpl. Edmonds took his place.

After looking over the platoon, he began to laugh. "You all think you are soldiers now that you have bivouacked, and lived on C-Rations. Well, I say none of you are soldiers yet, as you're sloppy and I'll prove it tonight. You see, I'm the duty NCO tonight. So that means I'll be going from tent to tent, trying to see who allows their weapon to be taken away from them while they're sleeping. Believe me, I'll find more than one tonight, and God help the men in the morning that are missing a rifle. I have all night to screw with you, and believe me, I'll make your night a living hell."

Tom had teamed up with Pvt. Marty Spriggs from Wisconsin as tent partners. As the two men buttoned up their tent for the evening, Marty inquired. "Where are you going to put your weapon so Edmonds can't get it?"

Tom smiled. "Between us, right in the middle of the tent, and just under the edge of my sleeping bag. There's no way he can slide his hand under the tent and get it there."

Marty nodded in agreement. "Good idea, Tom. I'll do the same."

Being extremely tired, Tom fell asleep nearly instantly after zipping up his sleeping bag.

However, Marty woke him up with a nudge about 0300. He pointed to an arm that was probing the tent on his side, in search of a weapon to confiscate. Marty quietly pulled his rifle up from under his sleeping bag raising it in the air. When the arm once more reappeared toward the back of the tent, Spriggs slammed the butt of the rifle down on the hand with every ounce of energy he could muster. Outside the tent, a howl went up from the injured man. Seconds later, they could hear footsteps running away from their campsite.

Marty turned to look at Tom. "We need to get up early and tear down our tent, and wake up a couple more guys to do the same. Otherwise, Edmonds may come back to this site and crucify me."

Tom shook his head as he laughed. "Fine with me, Marty. Just so they don't come looking for us before daylight."

At 0430, Marty woke up Tom. "Time to get moving, Kenrude, let's go."

Without hesitation, the men dressed, and began tearing down their tent. Eddie Darnel and Sid Young on their left joined in the early tear down as did Martin and Eugean on their right. By 0500 when Sgt. Dixon began waking the men, the six recruits had their equipment by the road ready to go, along with several other men they had awakened.

From their vantage point, they could see Cpl. Edmonds scurrying about the camp like a lost bloodhound. After the men consumed a fresh hot meal delivered by the cooks, Sgt. Nixon called the platoon together for last minute details of the day's activities. Once again Cpl. Edmonds took center stage when the Sergeant was finished speaking.

Shaking with anger, he held up his bandaged hand. "One of you bastards did this, and I'll find out who you are. I guarantee you will be one miserable son-of-a bitch when I get through with you. You may think it's funny now, but you broke four bones in my hand. That's going to keep me from attending Drill Instructor School for six weeks. Look you low life bastard, it's better you come forward now like a man, than act like a two bit punk and hide like a coward. And I know there's at least one more man that knows what happened, because there were two men in every tent. So, if I find out who you are, you'll also pay the same price. Now that we have an understanding, let's see who has the balls to come forward."

Although no one moved a muscle in the formation, word had spread quickly as to what had taken place. Marty Spriggs quickly became a hero among the men, and they were not about to betray him.

After having the weekend to clean their gear and wax the barracks floor, they returned to training. The next few days were filled with more rifle range, classes in first aid, physical strengthening, and running the obstacle course. Since Tom continued working to his maximum every day and avoiding problems with Sgt. Dixon, things had improved. Problem was, Sgt. Dixon had turned his attention toward Pvt. Johnnie Semz from the hill country of Tennessee. He was a wiry kid with a head full of red hair and a rather crooked smile that made you like him. Although he was strong as an ox, he was very uncoordinated, and didn't do well following or understanding direction. According to Semz, he had only completed seventh grade, as his dad insisted that was all he needed to work in the forest as a logger and earn his keep. When they were in the deep forests of the fort, it was interesting to watch him move about, tracking down animals without being heard. He knew every weed, tree, plant and animal that lived in the forests, and could climb a tree like a squirrel.

However, the only real trait he possessed that the army training required, was his marksmanship. He led the company in scoring every time they left the range. One afternoon as they were making their way back to the cantonment area after another long hard day of training, Semz was sent out to block traffic at a crossroad, while the company passed through the intersection.

Third platoon was just entering the crossing when a deuce-and-a-half came barreling toward them. Sgt. Tillerson, second platoon drill instructor, called for everyone near the intersection to disperse. Everyone made it to safety as the laughing men in the cab sped on.

Once everyone was reassembled, Sgt. Dixon ran over to Semz, grabbed him by his web gear and shook him. "What the hell was that all about? You almost got some very good men killed. Didn't I tell you several times this morning what your job entailed? What the hell were you thinking, Semz?"

Shaking nearly uncontrollably, Semz looked up at Sgt. Dixon. "The man in the passenger seat was giving me the finger, and the driver was waving his hand like he wanted me to get the men out of the way. I kept waving at them, but they just kept coming. I didn't know what else to do."

"Why the hell didn't you warn third platoon at least, why the hell did you just stand there? You are about as worthless a soldier as I have ever seen. Son, I think your days in this man's army are just about through. After you get that weapon cleaned, you come down to the orderly room and see me. We need to talk. Do you understand me, Semz?"

"Yes, Drill Sergeant, I hear you loud and clear," Semz replied, as he continued shaking.

Later that evening after he returned from the orderly office, Tom approached Semz.

"Hey Johnnie, what did Dixon have to say. Is everything alright?"

Johnnie wiped his cheek as a tear began to trickle down. "They gave me one more chance. If I screw up again, I'm through. He said the Army would buy me a bus ticket back home with his blessings. I don't want that, Kenrude, I really want to be a soldier. If I go home as a failure, it will disgrace my entire family. My father will never let me come back to our home and live. You don't know what it's like living in the hill country. Reputation is everything."

Tom was concerned for his friend. "Look Johnnie, quit thinking and just do what needs to be done. You try harder than any man in this platoon, you just overthink everything."

Johnnie nodded his head. "My grandpa use to tell me that when I was just a kid. But I never understood what he was talking about, and I still don't get it. How can you do something without thinking your way through it? It just don't make any sense to me, Kenrude. It just don't."

Tom sat down next to the worried man. "It's like this. When you see what you're supposed to do, let it settle in your gut for a split second and go do it. If you keep it in your head, you just mess it up, as one part of your brain tells you one thing, and the other half tells you something else. Before long you'll screw up as you begin debating which way to go. It's a no win situation, do you understand?"

Shaking his head, Johnnie looked out the window. "Honestly, no I don't get it. If I don't think everything through, I just freeze up. That's always been my problem. I think too much, Pa says."

After checking the time, Tom patted Johnnie on the back. "Look, let's get some sleep. Tomorrow is a new day, and we need to qualify on the range. We need to be rested so we can shoot well. Hit the rack and just forget today. Everything will be better at first light."

Tom walked back to his bunk, knowing full well that everything he just told Johnnie was not going to make one bit of difference. Johnnie was like a runaway freight train heading down hill at full speed. The accident hadn't happened yet, but it was inevitable.

At 1100 the following day, Tom took his position on the uphill range. The coach sitting next to him explained several good points before he was told to take the prone position. Once the firing line was clear, the coach handed him his first magazine. When the order came to commence firing, pop up targets began appearing at random distances on the range. They ranged from 25 meters, to 400 meters. You never knew which target would pop up next. Although the waiting for each target ate at your nerves, time went by quickly as they had to switch firing positions from prone, to sitting, standing, and be ready to fire without notice. Although sweat poured down his forehead, Tom kept his wits about him, scanning the range for the next target, hitting all but one at 400 meters.

When they were told to clear their weapons, Tom gave a sigh of relief, he knew he had passed the morning session.

After consuming a meal of C-Rations, Tom sat under a large tree by himself, waiting to be called back to the firing line. Failing to qualify on the first attempt was a fate worse than death in the Army. He knew he would be harassed and driven ceaselessly by Sgt. Dixon if that happened.

When his group was called to the downhill range, Tom walked slowly with Eddie Darnel. "How did you do this morning, Tom?" Eddie inquired.

"I missed one of those damn 400 meter targets, I don't know if I was wide or too high," Tom explained, shaking his head. "How about you, Eddie?"

Eddie laughed. "Not too bad. I missed a 25 meter target after hitting a

300 meter. I just couldn't adjust fast enough. I saw my round kick up dirt several feet in front of the blasted thing."

Tom smiled as they approached the firing line. He felt better knowing his good friend, who had been a crack shot through all their practice sessions, had also missed one target.

The afternoon session started with the standing position, then sitting and finally the prone. Once again, Tom kicked everything out of his head, continuing to scan the range, squeezing off each round when needed. By the time he reached the prone position, he knew he had hit enough targets to be qualified. Now it was shooting for the record, and he was enjoying every shot as the pressure was gone. After disposing of the last 150 meter target, he was finished.

Standing up, his coach handed him his score sheet.

"Congratulations, Kenrude. You qualified as an expert. You kept a cool head."

After clearing his weapon, Tom walked off the range, handing his sheet to Sgt. Dixon with a smile.

"Hmm, expert. How did you pull that off, Kenrude? I figured you would be back out here for a second try. Good job!" Sgt. Dixon stated with a slight smile.

By the time the platoon prepared to march back to the barracks, Tom was happy. No one in his circle of friends had failed to qualify. Even Johnnie Semz qualified as a sharpshooter. He missed expert by two shots, nothing to be ashamed about, and Johnnie was happy as a lark.

The following Monday morning, A-Company was marched out to the infiltration course. Everyone had heard stories and rumors about the dangers involved. There wasn't one man in the company that wasn't somewhat nervous about the course. Arriving at the training site, the men filed into a set of wooden bleachers. When they were seated, a tall Sergeant with a deep Texas accent stepped up on the podium.

"Good morning, men. This is what we consider to be the most difficult part of your training, and you must complete it. The course which is directly behind me may not look like much to you right now. But tonight, the monster will come alive, and it will eat you sure as hell, if you screw up. I have seen tough men come to tears, refusing to crawl out of the starting pit. So you best listen up. The course is one hundred fifty meters long. You'll pick up a numbered helmet at the range office. You will then enter the starting pit from the far side of the field, and stand against the back timbered wall in single file with your mouths shut. When directed to do so, your drill instructor will tell the first group to jump up on the starting platforms on the front wall. You will kneel down on one knee and wait for the order to go. At this point, we will turn on the .60 caliber machine guns. They will traverse the field on a prearranged course of fire. If you stand up, you are dead. If you get up into the kneeling position, you are dead. If you wave your arm in the air, it may very well be ripped off. If you run into a snake, and this is snake country, lay still until it crawls away. Do not stand up to get away from it. So when you get the order to start, push yourself up and crawl over the top log and begin moving forward. You'll never crawl back into the pit. Once you've started, you are constantly moving forward."

"Moving along, you will come to barb wire and log emplacements. You will need to get under the wire and over the logs without getting tangled up. If you do get tangled up, stop a buddy to help you if necessary, but try and use your own skills to get unhooked. If all fails, just remain where you are until the firing stops.

Out on the course there are pits with high wooden log walls around them. Do not crawl into them, as they have explosive charges inside. We will be setting off the charges as you crawl, to add to the realism you might face in combat. Your last big obstacle is right before the end of the course. It's a double concertina wire wrap you will need to clear. Take your time and don't panic, work together if need be. Once you're through it, keep crawling to the white line painted on the concrete pad you will come to. You may then stand up and report in with your helmet number so we know who has made it through, and who may be stuck out there. You can then take a seat on the bleachers assigned to your platoon. One more important thing. The weather forecast calls for rain tonight. This goes on rain or shine. Rain, lightning and thunder will intensify this event. If you are looking skyward when there is a bright flash of lightning, close your eyes. If you don't, it's going to mess up your night vision for some time, making the exercise all the more difficult.

Now, I want you men to line up on both sides of the field. We're going to have several of our men crawl the course so you can watch. Of course, there will be no gun fire this afternoon. You'll get two opportunities to crawl the course in the daylight, to get ideas of what tonight may be like. In combat, you never know when you'll need to crawl through a wire emplacement, so learn from it."

The men watched intently as four men made their way from the starting platform into the main field. It was clear they had done this many times. Suddenly, one of the men became terribly hooked in the wire and began to panic. Another man slowly crawled over, unhooking him and allowing him to continue.

The training instructor picked up the microphone. "Now, the man who was hooked is my assistant. That scenario was set up for you to learn from. Do what they did, and everyone should clear the field alright. Now go eat your chow and be ready to crawl the field in a couple of hours."

Around 1300, the men filed into the starting trench, lining up against the back wall as they were instructed. Sgt. Dixon walked up to the starting platform.

"Alright men, listen up. You see how you're assembled right now. That's the way you'll line up tonight. So, when I yell out first team, take your positions. The men between the white posts will take their place on the starting bench, and everyone will then move down. When the machine guns open up, it will be loud, very loud, with tracer rounds flying overhead. I'll have a megaphone in my hand to direct you. When I yell go, you'll move out and over the log, and the next group will assemble on the platform without being told, and on it goes, until everyone from the platoon is out on the course. I'll meet you on the other end."

With that, the first team assembled on the platform. As Sgt. Dixon yelled go, they crawled over the log to begin their journey. Several men became hopelessly tangled in the wire as they were more or less hot dogging the course and having fun. Several instructors came to their rescue with a solid ass chewing.

Half way through the course, Tom had just finished moving through a wire when he heard Sammy Brooks call his name. "Over here, Kenrude, I'm stuck and I can't move!"

Tom crawled to his left, finding Sammy tangled rather well. "Hold still, Sammy. It's not as bad as you think. It's hooked to your back pack. I think I would empty some of that before you go through this tonight." Seconds later, Tom had freed his friend, allowing them both to continue the course.

As dusk started to settle over the area, a light rain began to fall, and continued in intensity until it became a full downpour.

Tom's heart beat like a base drum as he entered the pit. They were walking in several inches of water as they approached the white posts. Not a word was being said by any of the men as they awaited orders to climb onto the starting platform. Tom closed his eyes as he attempted to gather his thoughts. Moments later he was jerked back into reality as Sgt. Dixon yelled into the megaphone. "First team, move up on the platform."

Tom was on the platform in seconds, ready to go, and happy he was out of the standing water. Moments later, the air above him was shattered by the most horrendous sound he had ever heard. Looking up, Tom saw thousands of tracer rounds streaking through the dark night sky. He swallowed hard as he drew in a deep breath. He could feel the bench vibrate below him from the thunderous roar. Seconds later, Sgt. Dixon yelled, "Go!"

Tom bolted over the log beside Sammy, heading toward the far end of the field. The two men cleared the first obstacle without a problem, building confidence as they moved along. All around them, explosives were being set off from the pits. Mud and water flew through the air, raining down on the unsuspecting recruits. Tom froze in place for a moment, after a rock slammed down on his helmet. Without thinking he yelled out, "What the hell, knock that shit off!" He could hear Eddie Darnell laugh as he slid up alongside.

"Do you think they're going to listen to you, my brother? Better keep your ass moving, Kenrude. You'll die of pneumonia lying here, and I'll get your share of the hot coffee and cookies they promised us."

"Like hell you will!" Tom yelled back, as he began crawling forward once again.

Somewhere in the distance, Tom could hear a man yelling, "I'm tangled bad help me," but Tom could not be sure in which direction the man was, or how far away he was. After a second of thought, Tom decided there was nothing he could do for the man, so he continued toward the finish line, leaving the helpless soldier to the mercy of someone else close by.

Clearing the white line, Tom stood up. He was covered in mud from head to foot and shivering from the cold. After checking in, he walked over to one of several fifty-five gallon drums that were burning to provide heat to the cold men. He wondered how Johnny Semz had fared tonight, but he wasn't sure which group he was in. This was just the sort of exercise that could catch him off guard, and get him tossed out of the army. As trucks arrived to take them back to the barracks, someone grabbed Tom's pack. Turning, he saw Johnnie Semz standing behind him.

"Hey Johnnie, what did you think of that. Did you ask Sgt. Dixon to do it again?" Tom called out, as he slapped Johnnie's helmet.

"You go twice, and I'll go again, Kenrude. But I'd rather get back to the barracks and get out of these wet clothes and get this filthy rifle cleaned," Johnny replied with a wide grin.

With just two weeks of training left, the men were getting more confident, and were beginning to believe in the new capabilities they had learned since starting basic training. They began looking and acting more like confident soldiers in everything they did. But Tom was quick to learn that anything could go wrong when you least expected it to happen.

On Friday afternoon as the men were hiking back from a training exercise, Sgt. Kendrick led the company into a grassy field at the side of the road. He jumped up on an old tree stump to address the men.

"We'll take a twenty minute break here. Stay in this field. Do not cross the barbed wire fence behind us, unless you want to get your sorry asses killed. It's an impact range for high explosive shells, which means there are unexploded ordnance scattered all over the range."

The men scattered about the field as they smoked, ate snacks or just enjoyed laying in the long cool grass. Tom sat with Johnnie Semz, Eddie Darnel and Jose Martin near a drainage ditch that was empty this time of year. Tom pulled a chocolate bar from his backpack that he had saved from a C-Ration meal earlier in the week. He was about halfway through, when an explosion rocked the area. Nearly everyone stood up, turning to face the impact zone behind them. Eddie turned to look at Tom.

"You wouldn't think they would let us sit in this field if there was a chance a misguided round could go off course and land here. This is crazy."

Before Tom could reply, Pvt. Greg Andover came running up to the fence from inside the impact zone. "Help, someone help! Batts and Eugean are hurt bad. Sgt. Dixon, you need to come quick!"

Without saying a word, Tom raced past Sgt. Dixon to grab the large first aid bag they always took along during training exercises. After scooping it up, he turned toward the barb wire fence.

Sgt. Kendrick screamed at him, "Kenrude, get your ass back here, don't you dare cross that fence, do you hear me, Kenrude!"

Like a typical farm boy, Tom slipped through the strands of wire without getting hooked. Grabbing hold of Martin, he inquired, "Where are they, Martin, you need to show me."

"Naw, that ain't happening, Kenrude. I ain't going back out there and getting killed. You want to go, be my guest, but leave me out of it," Martin exclaimed, pulling away from Tom's grip.

Angrily, Tom pushed Martin up against a small tree directly behind him. "Those men may be dying as we speak. You need to tell me where they are right now."

Shaking his head, Martin exclaimed, "They're both dead, man. I saw them fly through the air with body parts in every direction. It's too damn late, it's too damn late. They're both dead."

Tom pulled Martin from the tree. "Well, you may not want to go, but you sure as hell are going to, now show me where they are!"

Sgt. Dixon was standing by the fence yelling at Tom. "Kenrude, get your ass back here. If you take one more step out there I'll have you court-martialed the minute you return. If you even make it back alive!"

As Tom pulled Martin deeper into the impact zone, he turned to respond to Sgt. Dixon. "If you want to be of some help, send someone back down to that range office we passed about a half mile back and have them get a chopper out here fast."

As the men arrived at the end of the tree line, Martin spoke up. "This is as far as I went. I was scared to go any farther out there. Look just to your left, just by that pile of rocks. That is where Batts stepped on the explosive. He and Eugean are just beyond there, but I ain't going out there."

Tom pushed Martin back toward the tree line before he turned to face the impact zone. He could see fresh boot prints in the soft wet mud in front of him. Carefully, he stepped in each of the boot prints until he arrived at the rock pile. Just to his left lay Batts and Al Eugean. Neither man was moving. Taking a deep breath, Tom followed the last foot prints to the spot Batts had kicked or stepped on the explosive. From here it would become tricky, since Tom had no way of knowing what else was just under the surface of the mucky ground. One step in the wrong place would add his body to the already devastating carnage. Gingerly Tom made his way to Eugean, as he was the closest. As he approached, there was little doubt that the soldier was dead. A large piece of shrapnel had ripped into his chest, tearing away his right shoulder and lower jaw. His internal organs were hanging freely from the cavity. Just to be certain, and using the protocols he had been trained to follow, Tom placed his hand on Eugean's throat to check for a pulse, there was none. As Tom carefully stood up, he heard a moan coming from Batts. That was a good sign, although the man's left leg and part of his left hand were missing. Again stepping very carefully, he made his way over to his friend. Kneeling down, he looked into the man's dark blue eyes, "How you doing, Batts? Can you speak?"

Batts nodded his head, "It hurts bad, Kenrude. I don't want to die. I don't want to die like this."

As Tom quickly placed a tourniquet on the stump of the missing leg, he looked down at the terrified man. "We're going to get you home, Batts. I think you'll make it, just hang in there." Looking into the first aid kit, Tom found two morphine syrettes in a small pocket. Instantly, he broke one open. "This should help, Frankie," he said as it pushed the needle into the man's thigh. "Just give it a couple of minutes."

Tom then carefully ripped open the bloody shirt to find a piece of shrapnel protruding from a wound in his right shoulder. Tearing open a packet of sulfa from the kit, he poured the powder on the wound before wrapping the shoulder with a combat bandage. Finally Tom examined the left hand. The ring finger and small finger had been ripped away with part of the hand itself. However, the heat from the shrapnel had cauterized most of the veins involved, so Tom just gently wrapped the remaining fingers and hand, trying to keep it as clean as possible to avoid infection.

Batts smiled up at Tom. "You wanted to be a combat medic, so I guess I gave you your chance, Doc. Hey, can I get a drink of water? I'm really thirsty."

Removing his canteen, Tom smiled back. "Just a sip, Batts. You're going into surgery when you arrive at the hospital, so I can't give you much."

Batts was fine with that, as he took a small sip from the canteen. Moments later, a Huey helicopter with a large red cross on the side, dove down into the grassy field where the rest of the men were.

As two medics approached the tree line, Tom stood up. "Follow the foot prints and you should be fine. This guy is alive, but badly wounded," Tom called out as the medics followed his instructions for entrance into the impact zone. "I gave him a shot of morphine about five minutes ago, along with a small sip of water. He's doing better now that the morphine kicked in. The other guy is gone, nothing can be done for him." Tom explained as the medics arrived by his side ready to take over.

After looking at Eugean, the medics looked over Tom's work on Batts. "Nice work, Private," one of the medics commented. "Your buddy Darnel said you were in medical school before enlisting, it shows. Glad you want to be one of us, we need qualified men like you."

After arranging the stretcher, the men gently placed Batts on top of it. Tom looked at the two medics. "I'll take the front, retracing our steps. I'll go nice and slow so nobody steps where they shouldn't. Then we can come back for Eugean."

The medic in charge shook his head. "No, we won't be coming back for the other man. Another team will come after him since he's gone. We want to get this man to the hospital right away. You might as well get used to it. You'll run into this all the time once you end up in Vietnam."

Tom just nodded his head in agreement, before turning his attention to the treacherous journey back to the wood line. Reaching the barbed wire fence, the rest of the chopper crew was standing by to help lift the stretcher over the obstacle. As the chopper crew walked off with Batts, Eddie Darnel placed his hand on Tom's shoulder.

"You're going to be one hell of a medic, Kenrude. That took more guts then I have, my friend." Tom smiled at his friend, as several other men came up to shake his hand. However, the friendly compassion was about to end as Sgt. Dixon walked up.

"Kenrude, you best suck up the adulation here and now, because I have three serious charges I am going to write you up for when we get back. Best I can figure, you'll get a dishonorable discharge, or maybe even a little time in the stockade. But you'll pay for not following orders. You think you are Dr. Ben Casey, but you are an E-1 recruit, with no medical training in this man's army. And if you did harm to Batts, you'll pay for that also. Right now we're waiting for the M.P.'s to get here and take you into custody. Then the rest of us will head back for some evening chow."

Before another word could be said by anyone, Pvt. Sid Young stepped forward.

"Sgt. Dixon, you are out of line. I can guarantee nothing will happen to you, Kenrude. Tonight I'll be making a phone call and explain what happened to my father. He'll take care of this in a hurry."

Sgt. Dixon turned toward Pvt. Young. "Looks like I have another man for the M.P's to take with them. None of this concerned you Pvt. Young, you should have kept your damn mouth shut. You think some hot shot attorney you know back home is going to be able to deal with the Military Code of Justice? You got another guess coming, son!"

Sid Young turned to face Sgt. Dixon. "Attorney? Who said anything about an attorney? My father is Major General William F. Young. He's in charge of training programming in the pentagon. I'm sure he'll be interested in everything I have to tell him when we speak on the phone tonight. So I suggest you tell the M.P.'s to leave empty handed when they arrive."

Sgt. Kendrick walked up to the three men. "Enough! Young, is your father really Major General Young?"

"Yes Sergeant, he is. I wouldn't joke about that. After all, I am Jesus Christ," Pvt. Young said with a smirk on his face.

"What kind of crap is that, Young? You just made yourself sound like a fool to every man standing nearby," Sgt. Kendrick replied in an intimidating tone of voice.

"Well Sgt. Kendrick, that's what the drill instructors called me over in the reception station when they shaved off my hair and beard. So, I thought it was high time I performed a miracle. Again, if you want to discuss all of this with my father, go right ahead. The crazy thing is, he wanted me to learn responsibility instead of smoking pot, drinking like a fool, chasing babes and getting arrested all the time. So I either enlisted, or he was kicking me out of the house and stopping my monthly allotment. So, here I am taking responsibility for a change. I have a feeling he just might appreciate that."

Just as the Military Police drove up, Sgt. Kendrick called out for the men to fall into formation. Walking up to the road he put his arm around Sgt. Dixon whispering into his ear. Without hesitation, Sgt. Dixon ran to the road giving them instructions to leave without a prisoner. Arriving back at the barracks, Tom was told to stand fast as the other men were dismissed. Then Sergeant Kendrick instructed Tom to report to the orderly room.

Arriving in the large office, Tom observed Sgt. Dixon, Cpl. Edmonds with his bandaged hand, and Lt. Lopez, their Company Commander, all conferring in the corner. Lt. Lopez walked up to Tom.

"I understand you have a hard time taking orders under pressure. You apparently feel you know more about the code of conduct in our military than my cadre. Why is that Mr. Kenrude?"

Tom stood quiet for a moment before responding. "Sir, I believe in our military. My father fought in World War Two and Korea. I would never disrespect the army, or its leaders in any way, shape, or form. But what happened today was wrong. Batts will survive his injuries, and recover because of what I did out in that field. Had I listened to Sgt. Dixon, Batts would have bled to death long before help arrived. I fail to understand why you're angry over me saving the life of one of your men, sir."

"I don't appreciate your tone of voice or attitude, Mr. Kenrude, and I'm about two minutes away from signing your discharge and sending you on your way home on the Greyhound. We need men who follow the chain of command and perform to the highest level of discipline. That is what makes the United States Army so successful. Your father should have taught you that before you left home," Lt. Lopez screamed as he glared at Tom.

Understanding that he was in a lose-lose situation, Tom looked directly at the angry lieutenant. "Sir, I will not apologize for saving the life of another soldier, even though he made a horrific mistake and failed to follow orders. I cannot excuse his behavior. Nevertheless, I was training to be a doctor before I enlisted. The Hippocratic Oath emphatically states all medical professionals will do their utmost to treat every patient, and that is what I did today. I'm not a doctor yet, but come the day I am, and should you need help, I would perform the same way I did today to get you the treatment you deserve. Now, if you want to toss me out of the army for what I did today, go right ahead. I have a feeling the navy or marines might appreciate the effort I put out today to save a man's life, instead of tossing me to the wolves."

Just as Lt. Lopez was about to speak, he observed several men entering the office. "Attention!" he called out, as Col. Cooper and Major O'Reilly from Battalion Headquarters walked in. Observing the situation, Col. Cooper looked toward Tom. "Are you Kenrude?" he inquired.

"Yes sir, "Tom responded nervously.

"Good, than I don't have to chase you down. I received a call from General Mayer over at the hospital. That was quite the stunt you pulled today. I would never have expected that from a green recruit, but after reading your jacket, I learned quite a bit about your medical training. I'm very proud of you, Kenrude. If I could give you the bronze star for valor I would. But you have to be in combat to receive that particular honor. So instead, I'm authorizing you to receive the Army Commendation Medal. I will award you the medal on graduation day. The army needs more men like you, son." After shaking hands with Tom, he looked at Lt. Lopez.

"I'm sorry Lieutenant, did I interrupt something when I walked in?"

Lt. Lopez shook his head while responding. "No sir! We were just talking to Kenrude, so we could get all the information we needed for the operational report."

The Colonel nodded his head. "Good, get it over to me as quickly as possible so I can use what I need from your report when I write up the commendation. That will work well."

Lt. Lopez smiled as he responded. "It will be on your desk by 0800 tomorrow morning, sir."

Nodding his head in approval, the Colonel turned once more to Tom, shaking hands before exiting the office.

Lt. Lopez turned toward Tom. "You can get the hell out of here and join the men in the barracks. What happened in this office before the Colonel arrived stays right here, do you understand me?"

Tom snapped to attention calling out. "Yes sir, understood sir!"

Quickly Tom spun around heading for the barracks before another word could be said. He couldn't believe what just happened. One minute he was about to be drummed out of the army, and the next he learned he was receiving a medal from the Battalion Commander. This was a story his father would enjoy hearing when he returned home. He also knew Mackenzie would be very proud of him, once she got through yelling at him for entering an impact zone with unexploded ordnance scattered about.

On graduation day, the men were excited to get the ceremony out of the way so they could move on to their advanced training in their assigned military occupations. Some recruits like Tom would stay at Fort Leonard Wood where they would complete their training, while others would go on to different bases. Tom envied the men who were moving on. He had seen enough of Fort Leonard Wood and longed to see another facility, but that was not going to happen.

He thought about the men he had come to know so well. Sid Young was heading to Fort Sill, Oklahoma to attend Artillery School. Sammy Brooks was assigned to Armor School at Fort Irwin, California. Jose Martin was going to Fort Gordon, Georgia, to attend communications school. Johnny

Semz and Eddie Darnel were leaving for Fort Riley, Kansas, assigned to combat infantry school. Marty Spriggs was leaving for Infantry school at Fort Sam Houston, Texas. Emit Surely of all people, had been selected to attend Helicopter Flight Training at Fort Rucker, Alabama. He was a smart guy who already held a single engine pilot license before enlisting.

Had Frank Batts not been injured, he would have stayed at Fort Leonard Wood to train as a heavy equipment mechanic, and Eugean would have been sent to Fort Dix, New Jersey, to become a transportation specialist. It was quite an eclectic group of guys.

All the men had thought about Pvt. Stimson who had gone AWOL back at the reception station from time to time. He had been arrested in his home town and sent to Fort Leavenworth, Kansas to stand trial. However, bad had gone to worse for Stimson, after he pulled a knife and assaulted an M.P. during the arrest. No doubt he was looking at a long sentence in the stockade.

Finally, the men were marched over to the parade grounds for their graduation. Speeches were given by the Base Commander Brigadier General McCormick, Battalion Commander Colonel Cooper, and a Major Haskins from the Pentagon, who happened to be visiting the Fort.

Tom's legs trembled as he was called forward by Col. Cooper to receive his medal. He listened intently as Major Mayer read from the proclamation. After finishing the proclamation, Col. Cooper came forward, pinning the medal to his uniform. Everyone on the parade field applauded and cheered as Tom turned to walk back to his platoon. In all his life, he never anticipated anything like this happening to him. He wished his family could have been there to observe the ceremony.

With graduation activities completed, the men marched back to their barracks as the D.I.'s still had orders to distribute to some of the men. With all the business completed, Sgt. Dixon called the platoon to attention one last time. As the men stood proudly knowing they had completed eight weeks of tough training, Sgt. Nixon smiled. Gathering in a large volume of air he called out, "You are dismissed!"

The men cheered, while slapping each other on the back. Tom shook hands with all his friends before they left for the transportation center. Walking up to Eddie Darnel he smiled.

"Well Eddie, it's been fun, and I'm really glad we were able to have basic together. So you take care of yourself, and who knows, we may just see each other down the road. You never can tell where our paths might cross."

Eddie smiled his big toothy smile as they shook hands. "One thing I know for sure, Kenrude. If I ever need a medic, you damn well better be close. I'll trust you any day!"

Slowly, the crowd in front of the barracks dispersed as the men began their journeys. As Tom picked up his duffel bag to walk the eight blocks to his new training area, Sgt. Dixon stepped in front of him.

"Well Kenrude, you've come a long way since we first met. That was a heck of a way to begin your basic training, but in the long run it probably paid dividends," Sgt. Dixon proclaimed with a smug smile on his face.

Setting his bag down, Tom stared at the grinning Sergeant. "May I speak freely, Drill Sergeant?"

"Why not, Kenrude? You graduated after all," Sgt. Dixon responded with a very cocky look on his face.

Glaring at his former Drill Instructor, Tom began. "I don't think that exercise had anything to do with making me a better soldier. What I accomplished and learned here was important, however, all that first day accomplished was to make me dislike you, and that has never gone away, or will it ever. You may think belittling a new recruit is important so you can break them down and rebuild them, but you never broke me down. I learned long ago how to deal with bullies and individuals who choose to use their power wrongly. I refused to let that first day define me, or allow you to lord it over me. Basically, I used my mind over matter and I didn't allow you to matter."

Sgt. Dixon's smile had by now turned into an angry sneer.

"So Kenrude, what you're saying is, if I was wounded on the battlefield you would step over me and let me bleed to death?"

Angered by the inference that he would allow a soldier to die over personal preferences, Tom stepped closer toward Sgt. Dixon. "As far as I am concerned, you just proved your lack of qualification to be a leader of men. You haven't got a clue what's in my heart. I would treat you no differently than any other soldier on the battlefield, in fact, I would go the extra mile to save your sorry ass. Now, I may not measure up in your mind, but believe me if your ass was on the line, I'm the guy you would want helping you out. That's a whole lot more than you would ever do for many of the men you just had in this platoon. Some of them deserved more than they got, including Batts and Eugean. Thankfully, some of the other platoon Sergeants were willing to step in and help. And your lackey Cpl. Edmonds should never be allowed to become a Drill Instructor. He got what he deserved as far as I'm concerned."

Before an overwhelmed Sgt. Dixon could respond, Tom picked up his bag and walked off toward the north. He felt good about what he had just said to Sgt. Dixon. It allowed him to enter Combat Medic Training with a clear conscience and an open mind. He was glad he would never have to deal with the man again.

CHAPTER 5
MEDI-VAC TRAINING

Arriving at the Medical Training School office, Tom stopped to take a look around. It was a rather new facility with nice brick barracks and surrounding courtyards with flowering shrubs. Tom was ready for a change, and he hoped the constant yelling and intimidation was a thing of the past.

Entering the orderly room, a female First Sergeant looked up from her desk. "Can I help you, Private?" she inquired.

Placing his duffel bag on the floor, he handed her his orders. "Private Thomas Kenrude reporting as ordered."

She eyed him up and down as she slowly took the file. "Oh, so you're the hot shot guy from A-5-2 that treated the injured man in the impact zone. Is that correct, Private?"

Tom did not like being called a hot shot. He just did what was required of him and nothing more. He felt like they were getting off on the wrong foot right away and that angered him, but he knew he had to respond. "Yes Sergeant. That would be me."

Leaning back in her chair she stared up at him.

"'That would be me?' Do you mean you are the man who attempted to save your buddies life, or are you saying you're a hot shot son-of-a-bitch? Because if it's the latter, you can pick up your bag and get the hell out of my office. We don't train hot shots here. We train men and women who want to be medics and nurses, and do the job to the best of their abilities. Now which of the two are you, Kenrude?"

One thing Tom had never appreciated was people who played word games. He appreciated people who came right to the point and asked direct questions. "I apologize for my response, First Sergeant. I am the guy who tried to save Pvt. Batts. I don't look at myself as a hot shot. The medical training I had at the University of Minnesota kicked in and I did what I thought was the right thing to do at the time. I stand by what I did that day. Without immediate help, Batts surely would have bled to death."

Nodding her head, the First Sergeant continued. "I like that response better, Kenrude. My name is First Sgt. Lori Pelzer." Putting down his orders she stood up to look at a large chart on the wall behind her.

"You are in barracks six, second floor, bay five. Everything is well marked, so you should have no problem finding it. Your name is on the bunk along with instructions as to how your locker should be set up. Staff Sergeant Gilitzer is in charge of your floor, and our Company Commander is Capt. Erik O'Shea. He's a fair man and one hell of a pediatrician. He expects the best from each person in this program. You mess up, or fail to complete your training, he will boot your butt out the door faster than you can say Vietnam, here I come. Neither the Captain nor I accept drunkenness, fighting or hostile behavior toward another student. If you have a problem you can speak with me, the Captain or Sgt. Gilitzer. And one more thing, and it's a big one. There will be no fraternization with the females in the nursing program. They are officers and you are enlisted, need I say more?"

"No, First Sergeant!" Tom replied quickly.

"Good. You are dismissed. Go get settled and then find the Staff Sergeant. He will give you the nickel tour and give you your class instructions. Good luck, Kenrude, and remember one thing. Your first impression in the army should be the one you want to live by. Dismissed." And with that, the First Sergeant sat back down at her desk.

Entering building six, Tom found everything just as the First Sergeant had described. While he was setting up his locker, Sgt. O'Shea came walking into the eight man bay with two more new men.

"Well, you must be Kenrude, the First Sergeant called to tell me she sent you over here. This is going to be a busy couple of days as we have an entire new class coming from basic training units all over the country. These guys also live in your bay. Get your areas set up and get acquainted, then meet me down stairs at 1100. I'll have someone there to give you the tour." After shaking hands, Sgt. O'Shea left the bay heading back toward his office.

Tom turned to the new men. "Hi, Tom Kenrude from Minnesota, nice to meet you guys."

"Pat Moran from California," the first soldier stated as he reached forward to shake hands.

The second soldier stepped forward with a big smile on his face. "Tony Sedgwick from

Baltimore, Maryland. Nice to meet you Kenrude. Looks like I sleep right across from you. It might be best we get moving if we want to keep the Sergeant off our butts. I want to start out on a good footing here, not like basic training. Damn, I couldn't do anything right the first week or so. I got tired of hearing my name there for a while."

Tom and Pat laughed as they went to work on their lockers and beds. "Yeah, that was something I do not wish to repeat for another lifetime. You'd think those guys would get tired of yelling all the time. I know it's partially a game, but eight weeks was about enough for me. I hope the instructors around here are more like what we were used to back in school," Pvt. Moran replied.

At 1100, the men joined a group of ten more recruits in front of building six. A Sgt. Woodrow took them all on a tour of their school building and the hospital, where they were able to meet several of their instructors.

In the emergency room they met Capt. Fenwood, the chief instructor of the school. He was a tall balding man with deep lines in his face, and he walked with a slight limp. After shaking hands with the men, he leaned back against the wall.

"Remember one thing while you're here. Each of your instructors has seen at least one tour in 'Nam. Most of them have seen two and some three, such as myself. What you learn here is damn important, and I don't care what other kind of training you already have. Yes, you may want to remember it, but what we teach you here is the way we want things done. Everyone will have the same equipment and everyone will be operating on the same wave length. When you get out to the battlefield, the only thing standing between death and survival for those grunts may be you. They're relying on you, and they hope to God you know what the hell you're doing, and that you're doing it right. You may never get a thanks from most of them, as they're on their way to the hospital as soon as you get them on the chopper. But do they respect you? Hell yes! That's why most of them are going to call you Doc. They look at you as a doctor, knowing that you're there to save their lives. Never let those guys down. Also, you will hear much discussion about carrying weapons. I'll tell you right now that it's in your best interest to be armed at all times, whether it be a side arm or an M-16. The Viet Cong would rather see you dead than most of the grunts. So there it is. You have just received medic training 101. Everything else starts in earnest on Friday. Glad to see you guys here, we need good medics."

By Thursday evening, the barracks was full of new trainees from every Basic Training base in the United States. Tom was stunned when a soldier from Illinois stepped up to talk with him. "I heard your name is Kenrude, and you're from Minnesota. Is that accurate?"

Tom nodded his head, smiling as he looked at the name tag on the man's shirt.

"Don't tell me your dad is Oscar Joblinski?"

The man smiled as they shook hands. "Yeah, he sure is. In fact, Mom named me after him, I'm Oscar Junior. Dad talked about serving in World

War Two with your dad, Harry Jensen and Franny Doogan all the time. It's almost as if I got to know them pretty well myself. I actually met Harry a few years ago when he came to Illinois for some big agricultural show. He was something else, it was almost like meeting a real live legend. I'm glad we're in the same bay. I'm looking forward to getting to know you."

Tom shook his head. "I can't wait to tell Dad that Oscar's son is here with me. He'll get a big bang out of that. I told him that one way or the other, I was going to chase down Franny and have a beer with him before my three years are finished. It would be cool to have you there too. Franny would get a big kick out of that. He's a real neat guy, although he's a bit rough around the edges."

As the lights went off in the barracks, Tom was excited about the next day. He couldn't wait to begin his training. He knew he had a leg up on most of the men, but there was going to be a lot to learn. Everything they would do on the battlefield was a life and death matter. From his experience at the university hospital, he knew better than most of the men what that could be like. But on the battlefield, they wouldn't have nurses to assist, or modern equipment to aid them. All he would have is what he had learned and the meager supplies he carried on his back.

The first classes the men took were standard first aid. They learned how to apply bandages, slings, tourniquets, splints and how to make stretchers out of ponchos, shelter half's, rifles and other materials they might find on a battlefield. Throughout training, small groups of men were taken to the airfield where they trained on loading and unloading patients from choppers, as well as what they were expected to do once they arrived in a combat zone.

Every one of the chopper crews had seen combat, and were more than willing to work with the new medics. Every man was required to fly several training missions into mock combat zones, where they worked on men who were pretending to have various combat injuries and wounds.

Instructors graded the men on their skill levels, and explained procedures if the men failed to follow through with what they were taught. What Tom hated most, was when an instructor required him to explain every step he was taking to handle the injury he was assigned. It was much easier for him to just perform the task, than talk it through with someone that was judging and grading his performance. It actually made him forget what he was attempting to do at the time.

The new medics were also allowed to gown up, and watch doctors at the hospital perform actual surgeries. Tom found it very interesting, asking many questions after the surgery was completed. This was exactly what he wanted to do when he finished medical school.

One Saturday night, Tom, Oscar and Tony went to one of the eating establishments on base to relax. As they sipped a beer waiting for their pizzas to arrive, Oscar looked intently at Tom. "Are you afraid of going to 'Nam? I know we'll all end up there at one time or another, but I'm nervous about it. I know I'll be able to do what we have been taught, but having those assholes trying to kill us first pisses me off, and scares me to death. How the hell do we deal with all of that?"

Tom shook his head as he looked about the room. "Look around you, Oscar. Maybe half of these guys are alive because of a medic. We'll just do what we have to do once we get in combat. There won't be time to think about or analyze the situation, you just have to go to work, because that was what you were trained to do."

After refilling his glass Tony looked at Tom. "Is that what pushed you in basic when those guys were injured in the impact zone?"

Tom leaned back in his chair. "Yeah, I had quite a bit of training at the university. I didn't know what I was going to run into, but I realized I was the only person there that could help them. So I grabbed the first aid kit and ran. But believe me, when it came to walking out in that impact zone, it was the scariest thing I have ever done. There was a moment when I almost backed out. I knew if I got hurt, I was just one more casualty someone would have to deal with, and I wasn't doing anyone any good. But something inside told me how to get out there and help Batts. I guess flying into a combat zone will be about the same. We land, we jump off the chopper, we start attending the wounded, and God willing we get back on the chopper and get the hell out of there."

Oscar and Tony were quiet for a moment before Oscar once again spoke up. "Dad told me about how they had to treat their own men at times since they didn't have a medic with them. Damn, that had to be scary for them. He told me how your dad and Harry took care of him until he could be evacuated. He was lucky, even though he lost his leg. He came back with a good attitude and made something of his life. He never felt sorry for himself, and he and Mom were as normal as any other couple I knew in Cicero. It was because of what happened to Dad that I wanted to become a medic. I want to let the wounded guys know there is hope when they get back. I can tell them Dad's story."

After grabbing a slice of pizza Tony nodded his head. "Wow that's great, Oscar. My dad was in the Pacific on several ships. He never had one sunk, but a lot of guys had serious injuries from Jap plane attacks and shelling. Dad was hit in the leg by shrapnel once. A doctor on board yanked it out, sewed him up, and sent him back to his battle station. He didn't mind though, he wanted to shoot down the Jap that dropped the bomb, nothing personal you know." Oscar and Tom laughed as Tony imitated a man firing an anti-aircraft weapon.

Tom continued laughing as he put a piece of pizza on his plate. "When my dad was wounded he figured he'd had it. There was fire all around and everything was exploding. Somehow Franny pulled him out of the building and saved his life. He had several surgeries in England before he returned to the war. He really praised the medics, doctors and nurses that took care of him. In a way, he's partly responsible for making me decide to get into the medical profession. The other part was my aunt Christine. She was an emergency nurse in the Glendale Hospital. I was always fascinated by her stories of accident victims and how they treated them. It was pretty damn amazing."

After finishing their pizzas, the men strolled back to the barracks. When they arrived, they found First Sergeant Pelzer coming out of the orderly room. She looked over at the three men and smiled. "Blowing off a little steam tonight? They have kept you pretty busy the last few weeks."

Oscar shook his head. "Actually, First Sergeant, a big pepperoni pizza just sounded too good to pass up tonight. Not knocking the food in the mess hall, but the pizza just plain won out."

Laughing, the First Sergeant stopped in her tracks. "Damn, if that don't sound good! I think I may have to shake my friend Joannie from her rack and get her interested in a pizza and beer."

Training became more intense as they began dealing with radical amputations, severe burns, and abdominal and head injuries. The instructors liked calling on Tom since he had dealt with Batts when his leg had been blown off. Tom didn't mind being called upon, but he would have been more comfortable if the instructors explained their histories with these types of injuries.

Although no one ever wanted to leave a man behind if he were killed, the men were taught how best to leave the corpse if they couldn't evacuate it. One of the man's dog tags was to be inserted between his teeth, and they were to pocket the other one. This way the man could be identified when someone was able to retrieve him. Nevertheless, the Viet Cong had a sick way of desecrating the dead if they were left behind, so there never was a sure fire way to mark a corpse for future identification. Tom made up his mind during training that he would never allow the Viet Cong an opportunity to desecrate an American soldier on his watch, he would bring them back no matter the cost.

One of the toughest segments of training was how to teach the men to start inter-venous lines, and give injections to their victims. Every class had new recruits that were squeamish when it came to using needles. Tony had a particularly tough time starting inter-venous needles, often becoming physically sick. In order to cure Tony, they sent him over to the reception station to give injections to all the new recruits. By the end of the second week, he was more than ready to continue his training with the rest of his class, as needles were no longer as issue for him. He estimated he had given over five hundred injections while working in the reception station, while dealing with the many new recruits who passed out before or after getting their shots.

During the last two weeks of training, the men were dispersed among the many dispensaries on base, where they helped doctors and physician's assistants treat the many injuries that take place on an army base. Tom's favorite part was running with ambulance crews on emergency cases. This was giving him good experience dealing with patients immediately after their trauma had taken place. He found that dealing with small children that were the dependents of soldiers was the hardest. Not only was the patient most often unwilling to allow a stranger to help them, but their mothers were frequently a bigger problem. Often, it appeared the parents needed sedation more than their child did.

During the last three days of training, the new medics completed a battery of tests to find out if they were ready to take their place on the battlefield. The written tests were tough, requiring much thought to very complicated questions, often with limited time constraints to see how the men could answer under pressure. Failing the tests meant starting the courses all over again with the next class. If they failed a second time, they would be transferred out for reassignment to another military occupation, which normally meant they would become regular infantry soldiers. After a short stint at an infantry school, their next stop would automatically be Vietnam.

On Thursday evening, the men anxiously waited for the scores to be posted in the barracks. Everyone wanted to begin packing, but they were afraid to assume they'd passed. At 1800, First Sgt. Pelzer entered the barracks. Walking up to the bulletin board in the day room she called out.

"No crowding, pushing or shoving gentlemen, you have all passed with flying colors. Congratulations. You can check your scores if you want. We'll be passing out your orders in half an hour. Get your gear packed up so you'll be ready to vacate the barracks by 1000 in the morning."

First Sgt. Pelzer and Staff Sgt. Gilitzer took over a table in the day room at 1830 to distribute travel orders for the new medics. Although Tom was heading home for a short leave, he knew his future was lying in an envelope on that table, and he was very nervous about what was about to happen. Stepping up to the table, First Sgt. Pelzer handed Tom his orders as she said, "Best of luck, Kenrude."

By the tone of the Sergeant's voice, Tom instantly knew he was bound for Vietnam. His hands shook and he found it very difficult to breathe as he pulled the papers out of the Manila envelope. He closed his eyes in disbelief after seeing the words on line five of the orders.

'Reports to Saigon, Vietnam.'

Pat Moran walked up to Tom, "By the look on your face, I can tell you just received the same orders I have. I wasn't ready for this at all, I wanted to go to Germany so bad."

Tom nodded his head as he forced a slight smile. "That was my hope also, I don't know how I am going to tell Mackenzie or my mom about this, they are not going to take this well."

After shaking hands with everyone Tom slowly walked back to the barracks to pack. Although he was looking forward to going home and getting married to Mackenzie, suddenly part of the gaiety of the event was gone. He had prayed so hard hoping they would go to Germany, where they could spend some quality time together.

The night went by quickly for Tom after he finished packing. Tomorrow he would be back in Glendale, sleeping in his own bed at home, and in just a few days, he would marry Mackenzie. However, he knew from this point forward, the life he and Mackenzie had hoped for would need to be placed on hold, she may even decide to wait with the wedding until he returned. He was angry with himself for automatically assuming he would not go to Vietnam right away, and for attempting to convince Mackenzie he was right. Tonight his entire world had turned upside down, and there was nothing that could be done about it.

The following morning, Tom caught the bus taking him to St. Louis, where he would catch a North West flight for Minneapolis. As he walked through the terminal, Tom began to think back on the past eighteen weeks. It had gone by so quickly, it almost felt like it had been a dream. He arrived there a raw recruit, and was now leaving as a soldier, a combat medic with real responsibilities that had to be taken seriously, because men's lives would depend on his decisions. Although this is exactly why he joined the army in the first place, right now he had misgivings about that decision.

Flight 1148 was just beginning to load as Tom entered the waiting area outside Gate 25. He watched people hugging and kissing, before their loved ones walked into the jetway for a journey to Minneapolis or beyond. Finally Tom took his place in the boarding line, walking down the long aisle to his assigned seat. After fastening his seat belt, Tom removed his hat and closed his eyes. All he wanted to do was get some sleep before he arrived back home where he would have to give Mackenzie the awful news.

CHAPTER 6
RETURN TO GLENDALE

North West Flight 1148 from St. Louis slowly descended through the thick clouds toward Minneapolis International Airport at 1100hrs. Sitting in seat 26C, Tom watched the clouds pass by the wing tip, nervously waiting to get on the ground. He knew that inside the busy terminal, his future wife Mackenzie was waiting for him. Although he couldn't wait to throw his arms around her and give her a kiss, he was sure she would know something was not right. This was to be a grand homecoming as they were going to get married in just four days, and then fly off to Germany where they would begin their lives. Mackenzie had been counting on it since Tom left for basic training and had written about it many times. Now Tom wondered if there was going to be a wedding at all, or if Mackenzie would even want to continue their relationship after being so let down.

Suddenly the clouds broke, giving Tom a clear view of the suburbs that adjoined the massive airport. He watched vehicles race down I-494 as the pilot guided the 727 toward the runway less than a mile away. The tires chirped as they bit down on the warm asphalt, giving Tom a sense of comfort that he was home. It would be wonderful to see his family again, but under these circumstances it was going to be anything but pleasant. In short order the pilot had the aircraft parked at Gate 37, on the B-Concourse. Once the jetway was in place and the door opened, passengers began disembarking. After grabbing his small carry-on bag from the overhead compartment, Tom walked tentatively up the aisle toward the door. Clearing the jetway, he looked around for some sign of Mackenzie among all the well-wishers standing near the gate.

Without warning, she popped up from behind the North West ticketing desk, grabbing him by the arm. "Looking for anyone in particular soldier? How about your future wife?" She smiled as she questioned him before kissing him on the cheek.

Dropping his bag, he grabbed Mackenzie, threw his arms around her and kissed her like he had never done before.

After a long kiss, Mackenzie backed away. "Wow, if being apart from you is what it takes to get kissed like that, we need to separate more often," she exclaimed with a smile. "You have no idea how much I've missed you," she continued as she kissed Tom again.

Tom was happy those first few minutes had gone well, he really needed that. Slowly the couple walked down the concourse hand in hand, heading toward the baggage claim area.

Arriving at Mackenzie's car in the parking ramp, she handed the keys to Tom. "You get to drive home. I just want to cuddle up against you."

Tom laughed slightly as he placed his duffel bag in the trunk. "No complaint with that idea, sounds like a winner to me."

In no time, Tom cleared the heavy traffic near the airport, as he cruised toward Glendale. Mackenzie talked about school and her job for a while then looked over at Tom. After studying his face, she asked.

"Tell me, Mr. Kenrude, what's going on? You can't hide anything from me, you are way too tense and quiet, Tell me!"

Tom turned off the road into a parking lot and stopped the car. "I wasn't sure when to tell you, but I guess the time is now. Sweetheart, there is no way to sugar coat this so I won't attempt to do so, my orders are for Vietnam."

Mackenzie shrieked and began to sob as she leaned over on Tom's shoulder. Tom held her tightly for several minutes before she sat back up. "Do you go as soon as you leave home?"

"Yes. My orders take me to Oakland, California and then on to Vietnam," Tom replied, attempting to figure out what Mackenzie's face was telling him.

After wiping her eyes and taking a deep breath she nodded her head. "To be honest, over the last week I had that feeling, so it did not come as the major blow that it might have, if I was still determined to live in Germany. I don't like it, but I'm ready for it. I spoke to Mom and Dad about it several times, and what I would like to do while you are over there. Honey, I was part way prepared for this, and now I know. So we're still going to get married and you are going to get me pregnant before you leave. And that's an order soldier!"

Tom had to laugh at Mackenzie's last comment. All the fear and anxiety he had been feeling since he opened his orders was gone, although he still had to face his mother. After talking for a few more minutes Tom drove back out on the highway heading west toward Glendale.

Everything looked totally familiar as they passed through Howard Lake and Atwater. Finally, the sign he was waiting for arrived, *'Glendale Two Miles.'* Then there was the big sign for the Eagle Lake Creamery Association his dad belonged to when they had milk cows.

Now, he was just about home. He could nearly smell the fresh chocolate chip cookies his had mother promised him, sitting on the cooling racks in the kitchen. As Tom turned into the driveway, Mackenzie reached over, laying her hand against the horn, giving it a long sharp blast.

"We have to give you a proper entrance Private Kenrude. You are the man of the hour."

His parents exited the house along with his sister Abby, his younger brother Peter, and Christine, his aunt. Bosco their black lab, ran alongside the car yelping as Tom waved at him from an open window.

Exiting the car, Tom gave Bosco a big hug before walking up to his family. Karen grabbed her son holding him securely as tears rolled down her cheeks.

"It's so good to have you home, Thomas. You look great. The army must agree with you."

After kissing his mom on the cheek, he shook hands with his father before exchanging hugs with his siblings and his aunt Christine. With all the handshakes and hugs completed, Tom looked toward the house as he sniffed the air.

"Tell me those are fresh chocolate chip cookies I smell. I've been dreaming of them for the last week. You just can't get anything like that in the army, no matter how hard they try," Tom stated with a laugh. Placing one arm around his mother, and the other around Mackenzie, they strolled happily toward the house.

After changing out of his uniform, and downing several fresh cookies, Tom and his father sat down on the back porch with a cold beer. Steve looked intently at his son. "Any talk about you going to Vietnam? I really do hope you can avoid that damn war. Believe me, it's not anything you need to get involved in."

Tom was quiet for a moment before he responded. "I wasn't sure how or when to bring this up, but that's where I'm headed when I leave home. Mackenzie already knows so you are going to have to help me with Mom."

Steve placed his bottle down on the floor as he stood up. Turning back toward Tom he shook his head. "Do you understand what you are about to get into and how this is going to affect that young lady?"

Tom stood up from his chair. "Yeah Dad, I do, and there is nothing I can do to change any of it. It's not what I wanted right now for damn sure, but it is the hand I was dealt. We discussed the wedding and Mac wants to go through with it no matter what, and so do I."

Steve paced back and forth for a moment before leaning against a post. "I'm not sure that is such a good idea, and your mother will never go for it. Do you understand what this will do to her? Maybe you guys need to reconsider the marriage."

Tom shook his head. "That's not going to happen, Dad. We are getting married as planned, and are going to Duluth for our honeymoon as planned. We want you to be part of it, but if you and Mom want out, that's the way it will have to be."

The two men changed the conversation quickly as Karen, Christine and Mackenzie walked out onto the porch.

The big dinner that was planned in Tom's honor with all the relatives that evening went off without a hitch, although no one noticed some of the uncomfortable glances between Tom and his father.

Tom pulled Mackenzie out onto the back porch after dinner to inform her about the conversation with his father. After Tom finished she turned toward him. "Neither your parents or anyone else is going to keep me from being Mrs. Thomas Kenrude. I love you with all my heart and we are still going to live in the mud hut one way or the other, my dear."

After kissing Mackenzie, he laughed, "It shall be a grand mud hut, and I want you to be my wife more than anything else in the world!" Walking over to the far end of the porch, Mackenzie looked seriously into Tom's eyes.

"When are we going to tell Karen and the others? I told Mom and Dad when they first arrived tonight, and they are sad, but happy we are still going to be married. They told me I can live with them until you come back, if I decide to take a break from school. They are completely understanding."

Tom nodded his head. "I saw you talking to them in the driveway when they first arrived. I figured you were giving them the news. And then your Mom kissed me on the cheek before dinner and said they were a hundred percent behind me. That felt good after the conversation with my dad. I think we should tell Mom in the morning and get it over with. What do you think?"

Mackenzie placed her arms around Tom's neck. "I think that is a bold and sound idea, and I agree one hundred percent."

The rest of the evening Tom enjoyed talking with family members and enjoying their company. Talking with his cousins Greg and Matthew, who were both now totally involved in operating Kenrude Farms was fascinating. It was unbelievable how many different things they had their fingers into, and how much new equipment they had purchased while he'd been away. They both told him if he ever changed his mind they would love to have him come work with them. But the two of them were also very interested in hearing about the army and basic training. Tom was also happy to hear Matt had just become engaged to a girl from Willmar, who was not able to make the dinner tonight.

Early the following morning Mackenzie drove into the Kenrude yard as Tom sat on the front steps drinking a cup of coffee. After the happy couple kissed, Mackenzie turned to her fiancé.

"Well, are you ready for this my love?"

Tom nodded his head as he looked over toward the house. "Yeah I told Mom, Abigail and Peter to wait around, that we wanted to talk to them. We can tell Mike and Glenda and my grandparents later. I know my grandparents may be just as tough as Mom, but it has to be done."

Slowly Tom and Mackenzie made their way into the cozy kitchen where Karen was washing breakfast dishes and Steve was looking over yesterday's mail. As Tom came through the door, Steve stood up giving Tom a dark stare he had never experienced before.

As Karen looked over from the sink she said, "What's wrong?"

Tom placed his arm around Mackenzie as he looked at his mother. "Mom, I told Dad last night, so he knows what I'm about to say. The orders I received when we finished school are for Vietnam."

Karen froze in place as she took in what her son had just told her. She shook her head several times before raising her hand and pointing at Tom.

"NO! I will not allow you to go over there! You get those damn orders changed or I will do it myself. I knew something like this was going to happen the day you told me you had enlisted. Now you get on that damn phone and call whoever you need to call and get those orders changed. Do you understand?"

Tom looked intently at his mother. "Mom, I know you know this. There is no way my orders can be changed, and there is no one we can call. This is the way it is."

Karen threw her dish towel on the cupboard and walked part way into the living room before returning to the kitchen. Looking at Mackenzie she asked, "So I'm sending my baby off to war because you didn't have what it takes to talk him out of the idea of joining the army when he brought it up? Do you understand where we're at now?"

Mackenzie folded her arms across her chest as she glared back at Karen. "Remember, I am sending my husband off to war. My husband, my future! Do I like it, no, not one damn bit. Am I scared, yes. Scared as hell! Do I feel this was my fault? No. Thomas came to me with his feelings, and I believed in him then, as I believe in him now and always will. I wasn't happy with his decision, but I loved Tom and could not handcuff him, and restrict him to do only what I wanted him to do. What kind of a relationship would that be? I am sorry that you've never gotten over it and apparently never will, but our lives will go on and we will live out our dreams. Whether you are happy with everything we do or not."

Karen leaned into her husband as she contemplated everything Mackenzie had just said. "I just can't accept my baby going off to war. I just can't."

Mackenzie nodded her head. "I get that, I really do, Karen. But your son is not a baby anymore. He is a man that believes in himself, believes in his convictions, believes in helping others, and believes in me and the love we share. That is what I love about your son, and that is what makes me want to be his wife forever. Most of all, loving someone means you have to allow them to be themselves, you can't control them or they will just wither and die. And I don't want for Tom to ever wither and die. He is too good of a man for that, Karen."

Karen walked over to Tom, placing her arms around his neck. As tears rolled down her cheeks she looked into his eyes. "Thomas, I will always love you and respect your wishes. I know that you are a grown man and I know we raised you well. I will always say I don't agree with this whole army thing you chose, but I will respect your decision to do what you need to do with it."

Turning to Mackenzie, Karen shook her head. "Honey, I am sorry. I accept you as my daughter- in-law and a part of my family. Can you still accept me?"

Mackenzie looked down at the floor for a moment before responding. "Of course I accept you, and Steve, and everyone else in your family. But if I may be so bold, you have not gotten past that Sunday, when we told you. I always pray that you do, because I really want to be close to you, but I always feel animosity and it hurts."

Both Karen and Steve were taken back by Mackenzie's response. After a moment of silence Karen nodded her head. "You're right, I haven't been able to get past it, and honestly, I don't know how. It will take time, I guess, so please give me time if you can. That is all I can ask for."

Mackenzie nodded her head. "Time we have, and it does heal all, they say."

Placing his arm back around Mackenzie Tom half smiled. "We need to go tell Mike and Glenda, and Grandma and Granddad, so we are going to get moving. We'll talk later. Remember, the Bishop side of the family is having us over for dinner tonight, so it might be late when I get home.

Glenda and Mike were stunned by their announcement, but accepted it calmly. Alex and Nancy did not take the news so well, with Alex explaining everything that was wrong with the role the United States was taking in South East Asia.

Over the next few days, time flew by as everyone prepared for the wedding. Tom spit polished his shoes, and shined the brass on his uniform so it looked impeccable.

Although Steve was excited about Tom's wedding, he was just as excited to see his best friend Harry Jensen who was coming in from Iowa. They served together in World War Two and Korea, becoming as close as brothers.

That night, Harry walked out on the back porch with Tom.

"So, you're getting married and going to Vietnam. I remember when your dad first told me about your birth, he was so proud. And he's never stopped being proud of you, I hope you know that. Every time we talk, he tells me what you're up to, and how you're doing. Thanks for inviting us up here for the wedding."

Smiling, Tom gave Harry a hug. "We couldn't have been married without you and Marilyn here. It would have been like having part of the family missing. We invited Franny, but he couldn't get away from the project he's working on with the army. It sure would have been nice to have the three of you together again, though."

"It's really great to see your folks again. So, how have they been doing?" Harry inquired.

After a moment of silence, Tom continued. "The folks are fine. But be honest, you really want to know how they took the news about me going to Vietnam, right? Dad was really angry, in fact, I'm not sure I have ever seen him that mad. And Mom, well she went off the way I knew she would. She and Mackenzie really had words. Mom admitted she has never really gotten over me enlisting, and still holds a bit of a grudge toward Mac, which is really unfair, since it was my decision. To be honest, Harry, I'm not sure she'll ever let it go."

Harry nodded his head. "Yeah, the four of us have discussed it a bit. I think your mom understands how much the two of you love and support each other, and I think the day will come when she will work through it.

She is a good woman and I believe that time will heal her heart. It was tough for her when the day finally came for you to start making your own decisions, and you made a big one. Just let it go now, Tom. You are proving yourself every day, so keep up the good work and just love your new wife. You chose well. And you're right, having Franny here would have been great. He has a way somehow of turning things into a three-ring circus. Damn, I miss that crazy guy."

On Saturday morning Tom arose at 0600 and walked down to the kitchen. Just as he started making coffee, his mother strolled in. "Big day, soldier!"

Tom laughed at his mother's comment before giving her a big hug. "Yes it is, Mom, and I can't wait to make Mac my wife. We're going to have a great life together. Just like you and Dad."

Karen smiled as she wiped a tear from her eye. "My baby talking like a real man. I'm so happy for you and Mac, honestly I am."

As eleven o'clock arrived, the church in Glendale was packed with the family and friends of the young couple. Tom stood near the vestibule with his three groomsmen, his brother Peter and his cousins Matthew and Greg. Several times, Tom had Peter step outside to get a breath of fresh air since he was so nervous. He was totally afraid Peter would pass out at the last minute. After motioning Tom to take his place in the front of church, Rev. Hamlin signaled Mrs. Crosby to begin the wedding march. Immediately Tom's nervousness disappeared. This is what he had been waiting for.

One by one the groomsmen started down the aisle with their bridal attendants. Peter took a deep breath and started shaking when Anna Marie Morgan took his arm. Attempting to calm his nerves, she whispered softly, "I don't bite, Peter. And someday you'll think this is really cool."

Peter forced a slight smile as several beads of perspiration rolled down his forehead.

Moments later, Mackenzie began her walk toward the front of the church. Her father beamed as he escorted his eldest daughter down the aisle. Tom stood motionless, watching every step his bride took, as she walked closer to him. He wanted to look over at his mother to get a reassuring smile, but he couldn't take his eyes off Mackenzie.

Moments later, Mackenzie and her father stopped at the front of the church about six feet away from Rev. Hamlin. Tom stepped forward to take his place beside Mackenzie to finish the walk. Bill Bishop stepped away from his daughter, extending his hand to his soon to be son-in-law.

"Take care of her Tom, she means the world to me, and she loves you with all her heart."

As the men shook hands, Tom replied, "You need not worry, sir. I love your daughter more than anything else in this world. All I want to do is make her happy."

Taking Mackenzie's arm, Tom smiled at the beautiful woman who would be his wife in a matter of minutes now. She leaned over toward him, whispering.

"Bring on that mud hut, I'm ready soldier."

Tom laughed out loud as he shook his head. Before moving forward toward Rev. Hamlin he whispered back to her. "Be careful what you wish for, sweetheart."

Finally, the couple stood before the minister who was enjoying their antics. He read several short passages from scripture before leading them up to the small altar. After having them take a seat, Rev. Hamlin read several longer passages from the bible that the couple had chosen for the ceremony. After giving a short homily, Rev. Hamlin directed the couple to walk back to the front of the altar. As the couple held hands, they exchanged the vows they had written long before Tom joined the army.

Tom looked deeply into Mackenzie's eyes as he spoke, knowing he had truly found the woman of his dreams. A true partner that he could love and cherish forever.

As the service came to an end, the couple began their slow walk down the aisle toward the rear of the church. Tom felt like he was in a dream, and everything appeared to be moving in slow motion. Cameras flashed and people stuck their hands out to congratulate him, as Mrs. Crosby continued hammering away on the organ and Bosco stood in the entrance of the church barking with excitement as Tom's friend Sam held him back. It was all overwhelming for the young couple.

Exiting the church, Tom was hugged by more women than he had ever experienced in his entire life. Most of them were crying, leaving tears on his uniform. Finally his father pulled him from the well-wishers, directing the couple to the car so they could get over to the reception where dinner was waiting for them.

After eating and dancing with his new bride, Tom felt it was time to get moving. After changing clothes at the Bishop house, they were going to drive to Duluth for a four day honeymoon, before Tom had to leave for Oakland.

The drive took about four hours, but was well worth it. Cresting the hill leading down into the city, the setting sun was reflecting off the smooth placid waters of Lake Superior. Neither of them had ever seen anything like it before, and Mackenzie felt it was a good omen for their marriage.

The young couple had an exciting four days as they visited all the sites they had read about in a travel magazine Mackenzie had purchased in Minneapolis Their last night in Duluth, Tom took his bride to a very nice steak house, where they toasted one another with wine as a man playing the violin roamed from table to table. As a tear slowly rolled down Mackenzie's cheek, she squeezed Tom's hand.

"I shall never forget this evening, as you've made it an absolute dream for me. I will think of this night often while you're away."

Tom smiled at his beautiful bride. "Honey, when I get home, I am going to bring you right back up here and we'll do it all over again, but this time we may have to find a babysitter. We'll sip champagne and sample some of that goat cheese, while we listen to our waiter sing that crazy song again. It will be grand."

Mackenzie laughed as she thought about their singing waiter. "Mr. Kenrude, I'm going to hold you to that promise. I can't wait to hear that guy again, he was so funny. That sounds so fantastic." After a moment of silence she looked seriously at her new husband. "A whole year, how am I going to last all that time without you?"

Taking Mackenzie's hands, Tom smiled at her. "Like you said, it's only a year. I promise you sweetheart, time will go by quicker than you think, and we'll be right back here."

Mackenzie smiled. "Hmm, maybe you're right. But when you get home you better be ready because I am seriously going to jump your bones!"

Tom almost choked on the sip of wine he had just taken. "Jump my bones? What would your mother say if she heard you talking like that, young lady?"

Laughing, Mackenzie took Tom by the hands. "Remember, I am not the proper Miss Bishop anymore. I am now officially certified as Mrs. Thomas Kenrude, and if I choose to jump your bones, my mother has nothing to say about it. In fact, she might just agree with me, although not necessarily in such descriptive terms."

It rained the following day as the couple reversed their course and headed back to Glendale. Mackenzie was a bit depressed as she knew on Saturday her new husband was flying off to Vietnam and a war she was learning to hate already. But a year was not a lifetime, that was true. However, being without Tom now seemed like a death sentence. All she wanted was to be with her new husband for the rest of her life.

Arriving back in Glendale, the couple took time seeing all the family members in the short time they had left together. Tom began dreading leaving his sweet wife behind as he flew half way around the world to a brutal war.

Thursday morning as Tom cleaned out his room, Karen came walking in. She looked in a box marked, *Donate to Church.* Inside she saw a snow globe Christine had given him when she was going to school in Chicago. "So are you getting rid of this?"

Tom nodded his head. "Yes, I asked Christine if she minded and she said she was fine if I donated it to the church sale."

Karen shook her head. "Do you mind if I keep this, Mr. Kenrude?"

Tom stopped working and looked at his mother. "No that's fine, you can keep it. Is there something on your mind you wanted to talk about?"

Leaning back against the door frame, Karen said, "You're giving away your snow globe, you're giving away a life on the farm. Why, why give it all away?"

Tom stood silent for a moment. "Mom, Matt and Greg love farming. I want to be a doctor, I've always wanted to be a doctor. I thought you and dad raised us to be our own person, to do what we needed to do with our lives. I'm not walking away from my family, I just don't want to be a farmer."

Karen walked toward her son. "Do you realize how much of himself your dad has put into this farm? Do you know how much he wanted to leave you and Peter a legacy you could build on? Do you realize how you have let us down?"

Tom threw up his arms. "And marrying Mackenzie fits right into your problems. Well Mom, I am going to be a doctor and we will live wherever my job takes me, and that is our dream. And you better get used to my leaving, because I can tell you for a fact there is a good chance that Peter may not want to farm either. We have talked about the ideas and dreams he has for his life, and I don't see farming being there at all."

As Tom turned to leave Karen took him by the arm. "Honey, everything is so messed up, everything has been turned upside down in our lives. Tell me how to cope?"

Tom looked seriously at his mother. "Mom, I love you and Dad with all my heart. But you need to let me live my own life, even if it isn't what you wanted. When you accept that, you will find some peace, and I pray that you do."

As Tom left the room, Karen sat down on the bed, placing her hands over her face as she wept. She was experiencing the same fear she had when Steve was called back to Korea, and it scared her even more than she remembered.

The plan Tom and Mackenzie had worked out was for Mackenzie to continue with school and live with her parents on the weekends. She was not sure when she would finish her degree, but right now that was not important to either of them. What she hoped for most was to get pregnant during their honeymoon. It would be their child, made out of love for one another. A child they could nurture and raise. She and Tom couldn't think of anything better.

Friday evening as the couple prepared for bed, Mackenzie sat down next to Tom. "Are we going to talk about the five hundred pound gorilla that keeps walking around us, or are we going to ignore that it is here?"

Tom looked over at his beautiful wife, puzzled. "What are you talking about?"

Mackenzie shook her head before getting up and walking toward the window. After looking outside for a moment she turned back toward Tom. "You know darn well, my love. We need to be honest with one another. What happens if you should not come back?"

Tom walked over to Mackenzie as she began to cry. Holding her in his strong arms, he said, "I want you to go on, I want you to have a good life. Don't stop living because of me."

Mackenzie looked into Tom's eyes. "Tell me how to do that. Tell me how to walk away and let go of the love we have for one another. Can you tell me that Mr. Kenrude?"

Tom realized there was nothing he could really say to ease the feelings she was having. Taking her over to the bed they sat down. "Sweetheart, I really don't want to think about it, but I know that possibility exists. I am serious when I say I want you to carry on with your life. Maybe someday you will find another guy that can give you everything you need. Just know you have my blessing to carry on, with whatever you need to do."

Mackenzie shook her head. "I never expected to have this conversation, never. But all I can say is this. "You better come back home to me because you are the love of my life."

As the young couple cuddled together in bed, Tom was not sure if what he had told Mackenzie made any difference, and he knew she would struggle with it if the worst case scenario ever happened.

As Saturday morning finally dawned over Glendale, Tom finished packing his duffel bag and a small carry on, as Mackenzie made sure his uniform was put together properly. At 0800, the young couple began the long drive to the Minneapolis Airport. Abby wanted to drive with them, however, Mackenzie decided to go straight back to her dorm afterwards, instead of driving back to Glendale. She wanted Tom alone at the airport, and then time to herself to think and get used to being alone again without her husband.

Tears welled up in Mackenzie's eyes as they reached departure gate B-32. She smiled at Tom as she placed her arms around his neck, giving him a big kiss.

"So this is where we part, my love, I can't wait to see you again. When you get home we can start the life we planned on. I am so excited."

Tom smiled intently at his wife. "It will be fabulous. I can't wait either!"

After kissing Mackenzie one more time, Tom picked up his carry-on bag and walked toward the jetway. Stopping at the door he blew his wife a kiss, yelling out, "We'll find us a nice mud hut!"

Mackenzie tried to laugh, even though tears were streaming down her face.

Tom dropped down into seat 28A feeling sick, as if someone had knocked him off his feet. This was going to be harder, now that he was married to Mackenzie, after seeing how great it had been being with her every day and night. His heart ached as the plane backed away from the terminal, but he knew it was only going to be a year, and then they would have a lifetime together.

Mackenzie stood by the large glass window near gate B-32 as she watched the plane back away from the jetway. She could feel her heart break as her new husband flew off to war. She hadn't told Tom, but since arriving back from their honeymoon she felt different inside. She placed her hand over her abdomen, hoping she was pregnant.

In what felt like a fast three and a half hours, the pilot announced they were preparing to land in Oakland. Tom peered out the window, marking time until the plane rolled to a stop.

Unbuckling his seat belt, he quietly said, "First leg of the trip is now history." After picking up his duffel bag, Tom walked up to a sergeant that was checking off names of men who were reporting to him.

"Kenrude, Thomas S." He stated loud and clear.

"Kenrude, Thomas S., let me see your orders," the sergeant replied, holding out his right hand. After looking over the orders he handed them back. "Take a seat on one of the three buses outside the door. Don't try and run off, we'll do a head count, and we'll track you down like a dog if you go AWOL on us. Understand!"

"Yes Sergeant, I do," Tom responded before exiting the terminal.

Once the buses were filled, another head count was completed to ensure everyone was accounted for. The buses were driven to an Air Force hanger where Braniff International Airlines Flight 1023 stood on the tarmac. Once loading was completed, the pilot taxied the commercial jet toward the runway.

CHAPTER 7
WELCOME TO VIETNAM

The flight was to be a long one with stops in Anchorage, Alaska and Okinawa before arriving in Cam Ranh Bay, South Vietnam.

The morning sun was just peeking over the horizon as Flight 1023 rolled to a stop on the tarmac. As Tom exited the aircraft, it felt like he was punched in the face with a fist. The humidity, coupled with the stench of rotting jungle, was ten times worse than anything he had ever experienced back home in mid-August. It didn't take long before bags were unloaded, and groups of men were assigned to waiting C-130's for the short flight over to Long Binh where they would be processed.

Processing at Long Binh was very organized and efficient. It didn't take long for the men to complete every step required by the military, so they could be assigned to their respective units.

Tom was excited when he heard he was being attached to the 82nd Medical Evacuation Unit at Binh Thuy. After a long day of flying and processing, he was worn out and hungry. After being assigned to a barracks for the night, Tom joined several other men that were walking over to the mess hall to grab a hot meal. He had barely sat down with his tray when a grizzled looking Master Sergeant walked up to the table. Looking down at Tom he pointed to the seat across from him.

"Is this seat taken, Kenrude, or do I just kick your ass over it?"

Startled, Tom looked up quickly at the Master Sergeant's uniform. Seeing the name on the uniform, Tom bolted from his seat, his best angry look on his face.

"Well, Master Sergeant Francis Martin Doogan the Third, if you feel you need to kick my butt over an empty seat, then let's have at it!"

With that both men laughed, as the veteran sergeant placed his tray on the table. After a long hug, Tom turned toward the men who were sitting nearby, not sure what to make of the entire incident.

"Guys, this was one of my dad's best friends in World War Two and Korea. Although he's a Master Sergeant, I just refer to him as Uncle Franny."

Sitting down, Tom was amazed how fast Franny could devour the food from his tray. Looking over at Tom, Franny inquired. "How's that dad of yours doing back on the farm? I hear he's really expanded the operation."

"Yeah, he and Mike have purchased several other small farms. They now have nearly twelve hundred acres under plow. It's quite the operation," Tom replied with a smile.

Looking serious, Franny continued. "I spoke to your Pa about a week before I left Fort Lewis. I hear Karen's not doing so well with your decision to join the army, or your marriage."

Tom nodded his head. "Yeah, she really lost it when I enlisted, and she partially blames Mac for my decision. Sure, we spoke about it, but this is what I wanted to do. Mom nearly kicked her out of the house that Sunday. I thought she might mellow a bit while I was away at basic training and all, but that wasn't the case. When I came home with orders for Vietnam, she went off the deep end again, especially since Mac and I were getting married. Mom had my entire life mapped out. She figured I would spend my life working on the farm, where I would always be safe and sound. But that's not what I wanted. She doesn't know this but she's got another go round coming in a few years when Peter tells her he wants to be a naval pilot."

Franny shook his head. "I always respected your Mom. She and Steve make a good couple. But she went through hell with your dad in two wars, you need to understand that, Tom. She's just plain scared for you, and there's plenty to be scared about in this damn place. Believe me, this is my second tour, and my last, if Darcy has anything to say about it."

"I know Franny, but I needed to do what was right for me, and Mac understands that and mostly accepts it. I know she has her fears and concerns, but she deals with it, where Mom won't even try," Tom replied, as he stared intently at Franny's face.

Franny looked down at his watch for a moment. "Well Tom, I have to be at a meeting shortly so I need to leave. I found out that you're headed to Binh Thuy, the same place I'm located. If you ever want to talk, get a hold of me. I'm a liaison NCO with the 632 Combat Support Group." As Franny stood up to go, he looked at Tom once again. "Don't give up on your mom, son. She's been through hell and back more than once, and you have reawakened all those fears. Give her some time."

As Franny turned to leave, Tom called out. "Uncle Franny, just one more thing before you go. If I should get killed over here, will you escort my body home? It would mean a lot to Mackenzie, and to my folks."

Spinning around, Franny looked sternly at Tom. "Son, don't you talk that way! I'll not listen to you talking about dying over here, do you understand me! You're going home when your tour is finished, and that's final. I'll not hear another word about it." After backing away from the table, Franny quickly walked off.

As Tom lay in his bunk that evening, he was angry at himself for what he asked of Franny. He knew Franny would get over it, as he understood the fear any new soldier heading into combat was feeling, but it still felt like a bone headed move. Closing his eyes, Tom was ready to get some well-deserved sleep, as it had been a very long day.

However, at midnight, two loud explosions shook the barracks. As the men jumped from their bunks, heavy machine gun and rifle fire echoed across the base. Two sergeants carrying M-16s ran into the building telling everyone to stay where they were and not to leave the barracks. Each man covered an exit until the all clear was signaled around 0200.

A bit shaken, Tom went back to his bunk. He understood now what he had signed up for, and that is was going to be a long year. He drifted in and out of sleep the balance of the night, as every strange sound jolted him awake.

Although Tom was ready to go, he ended up spending two more days at Long Binh with not a whole lot to do. He tried to get a hold of Franny, but was told he had departed for Saigon.

The third morning, after breakfast, Tom was told to be at the airfield by 0900 for his flight to Binh Thuy. Ground crews for a C-130 stood aside their aircraft as pallets of equipment and fresh troops were loaded on board. As soon as loading was complete, the load master closed the rear door and the plane began to taxi.

Binh Thuy was the southern-most military airfield in all of Vietnam. It was located near the Mekong Delta, a hot bed for Viet Cong activity, and a transportation route for the delivery of weapons and munitions to the enemy in Vietnam and Cambodia. The flight there was uneventful, though it was very stuffy inside the secured cargo plane.

Tom was amazed at the base as he exited the aircraft. You could tell the United States built the base with the intention of making a statement to the North Vietnamese government. It was a rather sprawling compound, with many well-constructed buildings and aircraft maintenance hangers. The American forces were here to stay for the long run, no matter what Uncle Ho had in mind in Hanoi.

Tom walked with the rest of the men to a small administration building, near the end of an unloading apron for cargo aircraft.

After handing his file to a sergeant at a large desk, the man yelled out, "Eliot, put down that coffee cup and take your new man over to the Evac Center."

A smallish Spec. 4 jumped from a chair smiling at Tom. "Romey Eliot at your service. Come with me for a short ride to your new home."

Climbing in to a jeep that appeared to have seen better days, Eliot raced down a small service road. "Didn't catch your name back there," he called out.

"Kenrude. Tom Kenrude. Glad to meet you, Romey. What do you do with the unit?"

"Medic, just like you. Really quiet today, so Sgt. Shills told me to grab the jeep and pick you up. You'll like First Sgt. Shills. He's experienced, a second tour man and a cool head. He really cares about his crews. No one screws with us as long as we do our jobs, and we do them damn well. So if you want to fit in around here, be on time, be ready any hour of the day, do your damnedest when you are on a mission, don't think you know better than the pilots, and don't piss of the brass."

Tom laughed, "That's quite a laundry list Romey, but I think I can manage all those requirements just fine."

Arriving at the 82nd Air Ambulance Squadron, Romey led Tom over to Sgt. Shills, who was looking at an operations board that stood against the west wall of the office. Turning to see who had come in, Sgt. Shills put down an eraser.

"You must be Kenrude? Glad to have you on board. We're short two medics right now. Kind of hard to stretch things to the breaking point at times. You'll be with Squadron One, Evac Chopper Three. Your pilot will be Warrant Officer Three Rick Palmero, co-pilot is Warrant Officer Two Chuck Johnson, Crew Chief is Eddie Lemieux. They all know the score and work well together.

Once you have stored your gear, Romey will take you over to the hanger to get acquainted, and go for a quick shakedown flight. You never know when you may have to go out for real. Our Squadron Commander is Captain Samuel Trajillio, X-O is First Lt. Alfred Jurgins. Any questions Kenrude?"

Tom smiled. "No, I think you covered everything I was wondering about."

Finding his bunk, Tom tossed his duffel bag onto the mattress. "I'll settle in later, Romey. Can you take me over to meet my crewmates?"

Sitting outside a maintenance hangar were several Bell UH-1 Iroquois Helicopters, better known as Huey's. As Tom approached the first one, he had to laugh at the name painted on the cowling. It said, 'Palermo's Hot Pepperoni.' No doubt, this was definitely going to be his bird.

Tom shook hands with the crew while listening to their comments, suggestions and directives. Things they felt were most important for the crew to operate efficiently. During their conversation, two of the evac choppers scrambled for rescue missions.

Shaking his head, Rick Palmero stated, "Looks like it's going to be a very busy day. Let's get this shake down flight over in case we're called upon. Just so you know, the bird is loaded with all the equipment you'll need on a rescue mission. If you don't like the way it's organized, feel free to set it up any way you like when we get back."

Tom and Eddie Lemieux settled into the cargo bay of the chopper as Rick and Chuck aimed their bird into the morning sky. As they flew low over the Mekong Delta, Eddie pointed out landmarks, described which vessels on the water belonged to the United States, and where the Viet Cong were known to load contraband for the trip up the river. In the distance, Tom was able to see thick black smoke on a hill top, most likely the result of combat action. As they flew low past two river patrol boats, the crews waved while yelling their approval.

"We've picked up several of their men over the last six months." Eddie explained. "They know we're here for them and they appreciate our help. Keep them happy!"

Turning north, Rick followed the Mekong River for several miles before turning back toward the east. They had flown just a short distance before co-pilot Chuck Johnson came on the intercom.

"Your lucky day Kenrude, we have a mission. Several wounded men from an infantry unit on a small hill just to the northeast. We should be there in fifteen minutes."

Tom leaned forward to look out the windshield. The hill they were headed to was the one he observed with the black smoke. Taking a deep breath, he looked over at Eddie.

"Kick me in the ass if I screw up, I don't want to let these guys down!" Tom called out nervously.

Eddie laughed as he punched Tom in the shoulder. "You'll do fine, Kenrude. Just think of this as your first time in bed with your girlfriend. You weren't a hundred percent sure of what you were supposed to do, but you had the general idea. Just go for it, you'll figure it all out."

Tom shook his head and smiled as Rick prepared to set the chopper down. The odor of diesel fuel filled the cabin. Tom knew from his father's explanations about Korea that napalm had been dropped on the hill.

Eddie leaned toward Tom. "Kenrude, what you're about to see may haunt you forever. Just take a deep breath and go, or you won't be able to help anyone."

Jumping off the chopper, Tom was momentarily taken back. What had been jungle early this morning, was now a charred landscape. Trees that had been torn from their trunks, continued burning on the ground that was now baked hard from the extreme heat of the napalm canisters.

Dismembered, burned bodies of Viet Cong lay everywhere, still smoldering, and fouling the air with a horrid stench. Shaking off the desire to vomit, Tom ran to the first injured man he came upon.

The medic had wrapped a bad shoulder wound with a battle dressing, so the man was in no immediate danger. "Just stay put. I'll be back for you when we load," Tom told the injured soldier.

He again found that the next three men had also been treated by a medic and were in no real need of his attention. Running toward a lieutenant that was waving at him, he observed a young medic, attempting to treat a very bad abdominal wound. Dropping down beside the medic, Tom began pulling equipment he needed from the heavy bag he was carrying.

"Ever started an IV?" Tom asked the medic.

"Yeah once, and I didn't do so well," the nervous medic responded.

Tossing an IV bag toward the man, Tom responded. "Better luck this time, you need to get it right first try!"

As Tom finished bandaging the wounded man, he noticed the IV was in and running. "Let me adjust the drip, go get a stretcher from the chopper."

Moments later as the medic returned with the stretcher, the lieutenant and one of his men picked up the litter, carrying it back to the chopper. As soon as it was loaded, Eddie had the other men climb aboard, with some of them sitting on the edge of the floor with their feet hanging outside.

In seconds, the air ambulance was en-route to the hospital.

Tom looked down at the severely injured man. "Just hang on, the hospital is only twenty minutes away. Try to breathe evenly in short breaths, it will hurt a lot less."

The man smiled at Tom, taking hold of his forearm. "Thanks Doc. I didn't want to die out on that God forsaken hill. I got a daughter back home, she's just a year old. She needs me."

Tom smiled, "She'll have her daddy back good as new, just hang in there."

Tom was happy to see the hospital coming into view as Rick descended to the landing platform. When the chopper had come to a stop, staff from the emergency room rushed out the door rolling gurneys and carrying stretchers.

As they pulled the stretcher from the chopper, Tom told the nurse nearby what his vital signs were. Nodding her head she replied, "Good, we got this, help get the others inside."

Rick was already beginning to run up the engine of the chopper as Tom ran from the hospital with a replacement stretcher. Tossing the stretcher into the outstretched hands of Eddie, Tom jumped aboard as Rick began to lift off.

Eddie looked at Tom. "How you feeling, Doc?"

Tom smiled, "I'm alright," he said. "What's the big rush?"

"We have another mission. Several marines were injured by a land mine. These aren't pretty, Kenrude. Get ready for some real gore," Eddie explained. "By the way, you did good back there, with one little mistake. When you have that many wounded, it's better to have some of the men that aren't injured severely, spread out and wait for the next chopper. They become real targets sitting there grouped up the way they were, but we handled it. Good job!"

Tom smiled at his partner. It was nice to know he had passed the test on his first trip, and he knew full well if he had screwed up, Eddie would have told him about it.

Shortly the chopper began to descend onto a field filled with tall grass. A sergeant stood nearby waving for help. Grabbing the stretcher and his bag, Tom raced through the grass following the sergeant. Laying just at the edge of the jungle were two blood soaked bodies. Stopping at the first it was evident he was dead. Half his head was missing, and there was a large hole in his midsection.

Without saying a word, Tom ran to the next man. His left leg was gone below the knee, and he had a severe wound to his left arm.

Just as Tom pulled a tourniquet from his bag, the jungle became alive with automatic weapons fire. One bullet struck the tree next to Tom's head, another dug into the ground mere inches from his medical bag. Several rounds flew by so close to his ears, he could hear their whine. Gathering every ounce of strength in his body, Tom began treating the wounded man. But bullets kept slicing through the air around him, as the balance of the marine force fought desperately to protect him. With the IV started, Tom yelled at a marine nearby.

"You take the front. I'll take the back and hold the IV bag. Let's go!"

Placing the bag in his teeth, Tom grabbed the back side of the stretcher as they ran for the waiting chopper. Just fifteen feet from the helicopter, the lead marine tumbled forward, causing the stretcher to dig into the ground. Eddie ran full speed out into the field to grab the stretcher. After sliding the stretcher on board, Tom ran back to the marine that was attempting to regain his feet.

Tom looked at the marine, "It's a through and through. Bullet went straight through without hitting anything. You'll be just fine after some minor surgery and recuperation. Congratulations, you just won the purple heart."

The relieved marine nodded his head. "It will be my second, Doc, I stopped a hunk of shrapnel about four months ago in my right thigh. Ten stitches and I was back to work in two weeks."

As Tom attended to the wound, Rick poured fuel to the spinning rotors, raising the chopper back into the sky.

Landing at the hospital, medical staff removed the stretcher and the wounded marine in mere seconds. After spraying off the floor of the chopper, Rick flew the Hot Pepperoni back toward their base, a short distance away.

Several mechanics approached the chopper when the engine stopped. They began counting bullet holes in the fuselage, while examining the machine for any other combat damage. The lead mechanic smiled at Rick.

"Not bad, sir. Just ten holes to patch, but we need to look at your rudder controls a bit closer. You're done for the day."

As the men walked back toward the hanger, Rick took hold of Tom's arm. "You did damn good out there today, Kenrude. But next time, make sure you have your side arm, and get an M-16 to keep in the chopper. You saw today what can happen in the blink of an eye, you never know when you may have to cover yourself, and believe me, the gooks would rather see you dead."

After drawing weapons from the armory, Tom spent the balance of the afternoon resupplying his equipment and reorganizing the chopper to fit his preferences. Eddie helped out so he knew where everything was, so he could assist Tom when needed.

That evening as heavy rain poured down over the Mekong Delta, Tom began making a tape for Mackenzie. He wanted to tell her how much of a difference he had made his first day on the job, but not about being shot at or the horrible hill top experience. He knew from now on, he would have to censor his tapes or letters, so as not to scare his new wife.

After completing the tape, and a letter to his parents, Tom dashed through the rain to the Post Exchange just a short distance from the barracks. Even though he had eaten dinner in the mess hall, he had a tremendous craving for a slice of pizza.

After ordering two slices of pizza and a Coke, he sat down at a table by himself. Seconds later another medic from his squadron strolled over.

"Hi, I'm Gabriel Hartman, friends call me Gabe. You must be Kenrude. Mind if I join you?" The smiling medic inquired.

"Hell yes, have a seat. Nice to meet you Gabe, I'm Tom Kenrude. First day on the job and it was an eye opener," Tom explained.

After sitting down with his hamburger and fries, Gabe began. "Things can get pretty dark around here at times. All we see is death, dying and men torn to bits. You need to find a way to deal with it so it doesn't eat you up. I try to run every day and hit the weights when I can. Relieving stress that way works for me. We also have a Catholic Chaplin that served in Korea that is good to talk with. His name is Father Neederman."

Tom set down his Coke. "John Neederman? A real tall guy with kind of a southern accent, a paratrooper in Korea."

"Yeah, that sounds like him, and he talks about his paratrooper days. Why, do you know him?" Gabe inquired.

"My dad served with a John Neederman in Korea. He told me what a great soldier John was, and that he counted on him all the time. He said the man became a priest after the war. I really need to meet this guy. I wonder if he knows that Master Sergeant Doogan from the 632 Combat Support Group is stationed here also. I ran into him at Long Binh, he served with my dad in World War Two and Korea," Tom explained.

As heavy rains and driving winds kept choppers out of action the next day, Tom was able to meet the rest of the men assigned to Air Ambulance Squadron One. He had already met combat medics Romey Eliot and Gabe Hartman, so it was good to meet the last two, Corey Frantz and Moe Ashton. They all seemed to be nice guys who knew their jobs extremely well.

The crew of Palmero's Pepperoni was sent on calls nearly every day over the next month. By now, Tom had proven himself to everyone in the 82nd Evac Unit, and he was proud of what he had accomplished. Up to this point, every wounded man his crew delivered to the hospital had survived. But there was little doubt in his mind that statistic would change in the future.

What really amazed Tom, was that each man had a short timers calendar they attended to every day, so they could tell you exactly the day they would be going home, back to the world. One evening their able co-pilot Chuck Johnson handed Tom a calendar of his own.

"Kenrude, everyone has one and so should you. I got Lt. Trajillio to give me the stats from your file, so I could set one up for you. Make sure to keep it up to date. They actually are a morale booster. Let me tell you, every night I can cross off another day it feels good. Forty days and a wake up and I'm out of this damn country."

Tom accepted the calendar graciously from his friend, knowing he had gone out of his way to get the information he needed to make it.

Tom was happy that night to sit down with his tape recorder and tell Mac all that happened throughout the day, including the funny ceremony the men had when he was presented with his calendar. He knew things like this kept her mind off the worst possible scenarios. But as the tape spun, Tom was having a tough time talking. There was no way he could ever communicate to Mackenzie what he was seeing over here, and it bothered him immensely. They had always been so close and shared everything, but this was not normal, this was something no one should ever have to experience. Tom was slowly beginning to understand why his father refused to answer his many questions regarding the wars he had fought in.

CHAPTER 8
CAMBODIA

Nobody paid much attention as a single green Ford staff car drove slowly down the busy crowded streets of Saigon. In the back seat sat two very experienced special forces men. The oldest was First Sergeant Ed Mecklenburg and the other was Capt. Walter C. Holloway.

Capt. Holloway was nearly a legend among the special forces in Vietnam. This was his third tour of duty, he had been awarded three Purple Hearts for injuries received in combat, along with three Bronze Stars, the Silver Star and two Army Commendation Medals. There was no longer anything that bothered him with this war. In fact he spoke his mind so often, it was rumored he had lost his promotion to Major by telling the Secretary of Defense face to face that he had his head up his ass. Although many in the army figured that was the end to his military career, officers that were in the know, understood the army needed the Captain and his capabilities, and his promotion was waiting for him at the pentagon when this tour of duty was over.

First Sergeant Mecklenburg had been the Captain's right hand man over the last two years, and would do anything to protect him. The Sergeant had been awarded two Bronze Stars, two Purple Hearts and one Army Commendation Medal. When he spoke during a meeting, officers listened and very seldom attempted to argue the point he was attempting to make.

These two men had trained many of the special forces soldiers currently under their command, and they knew their capabilities extremely well. This team was known so well throughout Vietnam that when they walked into a meeting, everyone automatically knew there was a problem way too big for conventional forces to deal with. These men were the fixers!

Not a word had been exchanged between the two men since they had entered the vehicle at Tan Son Nhut Airbase. When they were about six blocks from Military Headquarters, Sgt. Mecklenburg stated, "What kind of shit has the army gotten into now that they need us, Walt."

Capt. Holloway shook his head. "Tough to say, Ed, we'll just go in there and listen to whatever it is, make a plan and get the job done as we always do. I am getting kind of tired of these pansy ass politicians getting our army into affairs well over our heads, and then calling on special forces to bail them out. That is not want we were set up to do. Our missions are suffering as we have too many men tied up covering the president's ass."

The Sergeant had to laugh as he shook his head. "Well said sir. But I believe that is exactly why we were told to drop what we were doing and get over here right away. Major Howard sounded pretty upset when I spoke with him. I don't think this is going to be a good deal."

Arriving at Major Howard's office, it was a bee hive of activity. Men in uniform and business suits were looking over maps, as a young woman wearing a staff sergeants uniform was passing out packets to everyone.

When the Major observed Captain Holloway enter the room he yelled out. "Alright everyone, we need to move to the conference room right now."

With everyone seated, Major Howard walked to a podium. "Captain we have a serious problem in Cambodia. The CIA set up a special operations team to locate and identify enemy munitions caches. They have been marking them so South Vietnamese Air Force pilots have been able to destroy them. They have been doing an outstanding job up to this point. However twenty-four hours ago their mission was compromised and several of their men were killed. The four that have survived are ready to be evacuated. As their radios still function, they send out coordinates every half hour so we can track them. The information they have gathered regarding troop movements, the Ho Chi Minh trail and operations in Laos is damn important to the war effort. We need to get them out, plain and simple!

Captain Holloway stepped forward to look at the maps. "They knew enough to get in there, why can't their people or SOG go in and get them out?"

Major Howard shook his head. "I don't have an answer for that. Orders from Washington state we are to use special forces to get the job done. And the job falls on your shoulders Captain. How many men do you want to take with you?"

The Captain turned to Sgt. Mecklenburg, "Ed what are you thinking?

After a moment of silence, Sgt. Mecklenburg walked up to the map. After examining all the notes on the map, and looking over the packet he had been given, he sighed. "I am thinking no more than twelve total, more likely two teams of four and a couple of medics in case those guys are in tough shape. We need to be mobile and small to avoid being picked up by the VC. This is their backyard and they know the game very well. I think we should go in during the dead of night with a large sampan. Our naval boats are too loud and attract too much attention. We get them and move for extraction by dawn with a navy landing craft, with two gunboats to back us up."

Major Howard nodded his head. "Your plan makes a lot of sense, Sergeant. We can get you anything you want wherever you want it."

After studying the map once more, Capt. Holloway pointed to a small inlet on the Mekong River about ten miles below their planned insertion point. "This is where we load onto the sampan. We will carry everything we need so the sampan can be empty except for the operator. I prefer a naval patrol boat navigator as our skipper. We want to arrive at 2200hrs and push off shortly thereafter. That should get us to point Zulu no later than 2330. We will want a medi-vac unit standing by in case anything goes south."

Turning to Sgt. Mecklenburg, Capt. Holloway asked, "Is there anything I missed, Ed?"

Shaking his head he replied, "That should do it, sir. I know who we should take from the team already. Before we leave I'll call Ton Son Nhut and have them get ready."

As the meeting broke up, a Mr. Clyborn from the CIA approached Capt. Holloway. "Captain, this mission has to go off perfectly, we need those men back here like yesterday. We can not lose the intel they have or the maps they are carrying. Do you understand?"

The Captain turned toward Clyborn with a look of disgust on his face. "Sir, I never much like these covert missions you people cook up. They are dangerous, costly and most of all, unnecessary. I just don't understand why you don't send some SOG people to get them out, you guys are all cut from the same piece of shit."

Clyborn stared angrily at Capt. Holloway. "First off Captain, SOG is only in the minds of men like you, they don't exist. Secondly—"

Before he could finish, Captain Holloway jammed his index finger into Clyborn's chest, "Listen to me you jackass. I know South Vietnam better than most people back home know their own states. I know what goes on, I know who the bad actors are, and I know when I'm getting lied to. So get out of my way so I can bail out your operatives."

Arriving at their base of operations at Ton Son Nhut, Sgt. Barkins came running out of the hangar to meet them. "Captain we have a very serious issue inside. It's Frampton, he's gone off the deep end refusing to go on the mission, I think you need to speak with him right now!"

Walking into the ready room they found Frampton sitting on a metal folding chair holding his .45 pistol in his hand. As Sergeant Mecklenburg stepped forward, Frampton raised his pistol. "That's close enough, Sarg.! I ain't going on this mission, nor am I going on anymore missions, it's over with, I'm done, Sarg."

Capt. Holloway stepped up aside Sgt. Mecklenburg. "Son what brought this on? Can you tell us what's going on here?"

"That girl, that girl I killed on the last mission. She should not have died, sir. I killed her, and I can't change any of that. I can't eat, I can't sleep, my hands shake all the time. I need to go home, sir. I need to get back to the world."

Capt. Holloway nodded his head. "Frampton, there was nothing anyone could have done to save that girl. She was scared, she didn't realize what she was doing, she simply ran into the line of fire and was cut down. We all feel bad, and we have all seen it happen before. It's not your fault, it's not anybody's fault, it simply happened. So if you can't deal with this anymore no one is going to be upset. We'll get orders cut and send you home, no problem, son."

Frampton jumped up from the chair, knocking it over, as he swung the pistol from side to side. "Well who's going to take her out of my head? Who's going to make me feel whole again, huh? Can you tell me that? You people fucked me up, you people used me up and now you just expect me to go home to Mom and Dad and act like nothing ever happened over here? Well, that's just plain bullshit. I can't do it! I just can't!"

Capt. Holloway took a step forward reaching out his left hand. "Don't worry son, we'll take care of you. We won't let you go through this by yourself. Just hand me the gun. Hand me the gun and we can work this out. No one has to get hurt here today."

"Yup, lock me up in a mental ward, lock me away and fill me with drugs. You think that will cure all that ails me, but it won't, it never will." Before the Captain could say another word, Frampton pointed the gun at him as he backed away toward the collapsed folding chair. "We're all going to hell one way or the other, sir. I'm just going to get there ahead of you."

Swiftly Frampton raised the gun to his mouth and pulled the trigger.

His body flew backward about ten feet before crashing to the ground as blood and debris splattered against the brick wall.

Captain Holloway looked down at the floor and shook his head. "How the hell did we miss this Ed? What the hell are we doing to these kids?"

After talking with the rest of the team, Captain Holloway inquired as to who else wanted to be left out of this mission, or simply wanted to get out of the special forces. Not one man spoke up, instead they all volunteered to take Frampton's spot.

At 2030hrs, a Huey touched down in front of the special forces hangar. Quietly, eight men clad in jungle camouflage and carrying large packs on their backs walked silently toward the chopper. Once everyone was onboard, the pilot lifted off from the tarmac heading south-westerly toward the inlet on the Mekong River.

As planned, the pilot set the chopper down on a small sand bar near a waiting sampan at 2145. Quickly the men jumped from the chopper before wading into nearly knee deep water to climb aboard the small river craft.

With everyone on board, the naval officer that was operating the sampan shook hands with Capt. Holloway. "I'm Lieutenant jg Davis. I know this section of the Mekong very well, we patrol it all the time. We will be there on time as planned if you are ready to get going, sir?"

Patting the young lieutenant on the shoulder, Capt. Holloway smiled. "Make it happen, son, we're on a pretty tight schedule."

Moments later the Sampan was out in the middle of the Mekong River heading north. Sgt. Mecklenburg and Capt. Holloway took up positions on the bow of the boat, scanning the shore on either side of the dirty brown river, looking for any activity.

Thick low hanging clouds shut out any light from the stars, as a light drizzle now made it nearly impossible to identify anything on shore. All that could be heard was the low thump, thump, thump of the single cylinder engine that powered the sampan.

Capt. Holloway stared into the darkness, haunted by what had just happened with Specialist Frampton. He had never lost a man to suicide before, but now he wondered what happened to the other brave men he had led into combat once they returned to the real world. They had all seen too much killing, they had all seen things no person on earth should ever have to see, and many of them like Frampton, had killed women or children in the line of duty. As he had told Frampton, it wasn't anyone's fault, shit just happens in combat that no one can explain.

Halfway to point Zulu, Sgt. Mecklenburg leaned over toward the Captain. "So far so good, sir. I think the heavy mist is keeping everybody off the river, so we should get there in good time."

Keeping his sight on the river the Captain responded. "I think you're right Ed. I just hope those lousy agents can keep it together and don't screw things up. But I got a bad feeling, Ed." After a moment of silence he looked over at his trusted Sergeant. "Turn on the radio, let's see if we can pick up their broadcast. They were told to start listening for our reply about 2300. If we catch their signal give them a rough e.t.a to point Zulu. We can figure it out from there."

At 2250, Lt. Davis turned off the motor allowing the boat to glide up against a three foot bank on the Cambodian side of the river at point Zulu. The men grabbed onto branches to pull the sampan to a stop, as they quickly jumped ashore. With everyone off, Sgt. Mecklenburg gave the sampan a solid push to get it back out into the current. As the current was moving fairly swift, the lieutenant did not fire up the small motor again until he was several miles from the drop off point.

Captain Holloway looked at Sgt. Mecklenburg. "Still no signal from them?"

The Sergeant shook his head. "No sir. I even checked with Thorpe to see if he picked up anything on his radio and he hasn't. What's our plan, sir?"

Captain Holloway shook his head. I don't know Ed. You got tickets for the White Sox game tonight? That sounds like a better plan to me."

"Fraid I'm all out of those, sir. But I heard the Ice Capades are in town tonight though." Sgt. Mecklenburg responded with a broad smile.

Shaking his head, Capt. Holloway responded. "Ice Capades, really!" Looking eye to eye with his best friend the Captain continued. "I'm nervous, Ed. What if their radios have been damaged and they can't call? What if they are all lying dead in the jungle and we have no way to confirm it?"

Seconds later, Sgt. Mecklenburg grabbed the hand set to the radio. "Copy 451. We are at point Zulu. Commencing our run on your coordinates. Keep radio on so we can track you. Over."

After quickly scribbling down the coordinates he was given, the two men looked over the map. After verifying the position, the team moved out into the dark jungle.

About a half hour later, heavy gunfire erupted followed by the thud of mortar rounds exploding off to the north east. Captain Holloway stopped his team. "Ed, call them, see if this battle involves them. We can't move in on the attack unless we know for sure."

After the third call Sgt. Mecklenburg raised one of the CIA agents. After a short conversation the radio went dead. "Sir, 451 says they were discovered and the VC forces are all over them. They are heading out to a secondary position they have in mind. They'll let us know when we can come after them."

Captain Holloway was angry. "They have two radios. Get back on that thing and see if you can reach the other damn radio. We can coordinate their movements so we can get them out of here."

After four attempts Ed shook his head. "No response sir."

By now the firing had subsided, and the jungle was once more dead silent. Not even the nocturnal animals were making any sounds. This was when the jungle was the most terrifying, and caused many a good man to break. Sometimes you were almost afraid to breathe, thinking the enemy was going to hone in on the sound.

Carefully, the team once more began working their way toward the original position they were given. Arriving at the coordinates, you could still smell the cordite from the mortar rounds and see the torn tree trunks, but there was no sign of anyone. Just as the Captain was going to look at the map, gun fire erupted to the north of their position. Several mortar rounds crashed into the jungle, followed by a lot of yelling in Vietnamese. Had they finally caught their prey and were celebrating, or had they once again found nothing?

Moments later, the radio crackled to life. Ed grabbed the handset to listen. After several seconds Ed said, "Negative 451, bad idea. You are moving farther away from us. You need to follow our instructions."

Hanging up the handset there was no doubt in anyone's mind that the Sergeant was way past upset. Pulling out the map and a flashlight with a red lens, he began tracing his finger across the plastic coated paper. "Here. This is where they are headed, sir. It's about two clicks farther north and they are going to end up with this gully at their backs. They don't have a clue of what they are getting themselves into."

Captain Holloway shook his head. "Damn it. Alright. All we can do now is head to that point and hope they stay put. Once dawn comes over this damn jungle we are in big trouble. Let's move out."

Fifteen minutes later, what appeared to be the sound of two grenades exploding was followed by a short volley of fire, once again directly to the north. This time the Captain continued forward, ready to take on any V.C. they might meet.

Once again, the CIA agents had left the rendezvous point and had disappeared into the jungle. Two minutes later the radio crackled with a call. Sgt. Mecklenburg grabbed the hand set and listened while looking at the map. After a moment he replied. "Roger that. We are about one mic away. Stay put and lay low, we are on the way."

Shaking his head, Sgt. Mecklenburg looked grimly at the Captain. Those grenades caused damage. They have several wounded, but they were able to kill the four attacking V.C, so their location should be good."

Wasting no time, Capt. Holloway signaled his men forward, keeping a close eye out for enemy activity.

Arriving at the last location they were given, they found the CIA operatives in rather dire straits. One of the men had a serious abdominal injury, and two others were wounded, but not seriously.

Capt. Holloway looked under the bandages the agents had placed over the abdominal injuries. "He needs an airlift, we can't move him like this." Looking over the other wounded men he shook his head as he continued. This guy has a badly broken arm, he needs to go too. Damn it to hell!"

After a moment of silence he looked over at Specialist Thorpe. "Order up an air evac. This man is going to die if we don't get him out of here ASAP. We need it like two hours ago, put a rush on it!"

Back at Binh Thuy, Tom and Geno had been put on alert in case medics were needed for some sort of special mission. They had played cards and drank coffee all night in the hospital in case a call came in. In seconds, they picked up their weapons and were out the door running toward a solid black Huey, operated by a South Vietnamese army crew.

When they were airborne, Moe leaned over to the flight engineer. "Where are we headed?"

The man laughed as he looked at the two Americans. "I suppose I can tell you now since we're on the way. Our destination is Cambodia."

"Cambodia! What the hell are we going there for?" Tom inquired nervously.

Once more the engineer laughed. "You Americans get all nervous every time Cambodia is mentioned. The war exists there as in Laos, but your leaders wish to not speak about it. Unless you send troops into those countries you cannot win this war."

"So what is going on that they need medics?" Moe questioned.

"I am a flight mechanic paid by your CIA. All I know is there are wounded to be picked up and we have a lift for a basket so we can pull them out of the jungle. Sit back enjoy the ride, and don't get so excited about Cambodia. It does exist!"

Both Tom and Moe were upset by the comments of the engineer, and realized he was not going to tell them anything he did not want them to know. About forty-five minutes later the engineer called out, "We are just about there. We'll lower you down by cable with your equipment. When you are ready we lower the basket for the wounded and take you back to hospital. Simple, simple!"

Tom was the first to be lowered by the cable with one of his bags, followed by Moe and a second bag. Kneeling down by the severely wounded man Tom shook his head. "He is in bad shape, and he's lost a lot of blood. We can patch him up a bit better and start an IV, but that is about all we can do. He needs a hospital. Moe splinted the other man's shoulder as Sgt. Mecklenburg called the chopper to send down the basket.

The basket was about half way down when the helicopter began taking fire from V.C. forces in the area. The pilot poured power to the engines while banking hard to the east and disappearing into the night sky.

"Bastards!" Tom called out as he looked skyward to where the chopper had been.

Not wasting any time, the lead CIA agent stepped forward, firing two shots into the wounded man's head. "We need to leave, we can't deal with him." After folding the man's arms across his chest, the agent placed a white phosphorous grenade under the arms and pulled the pin. Immediately the grenade exploded, covering the body with the hot burning chemical.

"They won't be able to identify him now, they won't be able to connect him with the CIA. Let's get out of here before the V.C. come roaring in," the agent ordered as he looked over at Captain Holloway.

Noticeably angry with what had just happened, the Captain knew the lead agent was right and they had to get moving. Quickly he signaled one of his men to take point, moving the small group farther north towards the prearranged pick up point designated as Apache.

After moving at a rather good speed for nearly a half hour, Capt. Holloway brought the group to a stop. Dawn was just about two hours away and there was no way they would make Apache in time. Looking over at Sgt. Mecklenburg, he said, "Call housekeeping. Tell them the limo left and the tenants will stay longer. We'll let them know when and where we will need the escalator. Tell them one of their butterfly's escaped."

Without saying a word, Sgt. Mecklenburg transmitted the pre-approved code.

A hazy dawn broke over the triple canopy jungle of Cambodia as Capt. Holloway and Sgt. Mecklenburg poured over the map once more. Pointing toward a small line on the map that crossed the gorge that was about a hundred yards in front of them, the confident Sergeant spoke up.

"That could mean there is a small foot bridge over the gorge, sir. That may be our only escape from the V.C. that are out there searching for us. Without that, all we can do is parallel the gorge to the Mekong River with those dinks in hot pursuit."

Looking up from the map Capt. Holloway responded. "Ed, you're right, that could be a bridge. That is if our mighty Air Force hasn't blown the thing to pieces by now." After a moment of silence, he continued. "Alright, it may be our only chance right now. Let's parallel the gorge as you suggested until we get to the bridge and see for ourselves. By now there has to be several hundred V.C. scouring these hills searching for us."

After informing every one of the plan, Specialist Phritz took point and moved out. About twenty minutes later a small explosion resounded throughout the jungle. Sgt. Mecklenburg and two of his men raced forward. They found Phritz lying on the ground with blood covering his right leg.

"Damn, Sarg., I was being so careful, but I never saw the wire. I'm sorry Sarg!"

Sgt. Mecklenburg smiled at his soldier as he waved for Tom and Moe to come forward. After examining the wound and removing several larger splinters of wood and metal, they poured sulfa powder on the wound and wrapped the leg securely.

As Tom was checking the dressing one more time, he looked down at the soldier. "You are damn lucky that was a poorly placed hand grenade trap instead of a land mine. Otherwise, you would most likely have lost most of your leg or been killed. We're going to need to help you as we move out, I don't want you putting your full weight on that leg."

Just as the men prepared to move out, a heavy volley of AK-47 fire descended into their location.

Capt. Holloway grabbed the handset from the radio. "House Keeping this is Grab Bag, we need an immediate air strike on the following coordinates." After reading off their position he awaited a return call, but was angry with what he was told.

"Grab Bag this is House Keeping, sorry to say you are not in our backyard. I will have to check with others to see what can be done."

Keying the mic button Capt. Holloway yelled over the roar of gun fire. "You best divert a Phantom from another mission or we're all dead, you jack ass. We were promised priority, get your head out of your ass before we're all dead!"

Everyone continued firing as the Captain looked at the radio, waiting for some type of response. However, his answer came in the sound of two F-4 Phantoms with South Vietnamese markings on the fuselage, roaring in from the east. They pummeled the hill with rocket and cannon fire from east to west. As the pilots climbed and prepared to make another pass, Capt. Holloway yelled, "Go, go now, we need to move out now!"

It was evident their position could easily be on the receiving end of the next attack if the pilots didn't back off as they were ending their strike. Steve and Moe pulled the wounded soldier to his good foot and supported him as they tore through the underbrush, keeping the man with the shattered arm nearby, hoping there wouldn't be any more trip wires to contend with.

By mid-morning, the men were on a slight rise over-looking a well worn dilapidated wood, vine and rope bridge that had probably been there for decades.

After scanning the span with his binoculars, Sgt. Mecklenburg shook his head. "There are several places where the plank walkway is missing. She's in bad shape, sir."

While looking over the bridge with the Sergeants binoculars, Capt. Holloway shook his head. "Yeah, she ain't much but she's the only ball game in town. Problem is, it may be wired with explosives and the locals know it, and know how to avoid them." Looking over his shoulder the Captain called out, "Lucas, check it out and see what we've got for explosives."

Dropping his pack, Specialist Lucas ran toward the bridge. Getting down on his stomach he began crawling across the rickety structure. About midway across he observed a trip wire attached to one of the ropes. It was attached to a detonator that was inserted into a small block of C-4 plastic explosive. Very carefully Lucas disassembled the bomb, throwing everything down into the gorge but the plastic explosive, which he slid into his pants pocket. After finishing the bridge, he continued checking around the path on the far side, finding two land mines. After checking another ten feet he was satisfied the area was clear. Taking a deep breath, he ran back across the bridge, throwing the land mines into the gorge.

Captain Holloway smiled as his demo man returned with a broad smile on his face. He knew the bridge was clear and ready for them to cross. After discussing his plans with the men, Lucas once more ran toward the bridge. About twenty seconds later, Sgt. Mecklenburg followed.

The three CIA agents went next in rotation, however the man with the broken arm fell, landing on his shattered arm. He howled in pain, without making any attempt to get back up. Without being told, two of the special forces men charged forward onto the bridge. One soldier picked up the screaming man as the other knelt down facing back across the bridge, ready to supply cover fire if needed.

As there was just Capt. Holloway, Tom, Moe, Specialist Phritz and two more special forces men left, the Captain turned toward Tom. "How do you want to do this, Kenrude? It looks like it will be three of you at a time. Do you feel comfortable with that?"

Before Tom or Moe could respond, Corporal Dinzer stepped forward. "Sir, why don't you go now, then we can send the medics with Phritz while Urbanski and I follow up close to aid with fire if necessary."

After a moment of thought the Captain nodded his head, and double timed for the bridge. Twenty seconds later, Tom, Moe and Specialist Phritz started their move.

As the three-some neared the far bank, Sgt. Mecklenburg jumped up and down yelling encouragement. Dinzer and Urbanski were nearly half way across when heavy machine gun fire erupted from the far bank. Dinzer threw himself to the boards and began low crawling as fast as he could, but Urbanski was hit on the way down and wasn't moving.

As Dinzer cleared the span, Moe yelled, "Cover me!" before dashing out onto the bridge. Grabbing Urbanski by the pack straps he pulled him up onto his shoulder and ran back toward the bank. He continued running until he was about five yards into the jungle where he and Tom could look over Urbanski's injuries.

Everyone continued firing back at the enemy while Lucas began setting charges on the ropes and vines that attached the bridge to the bank. Since he didn't want to use all the explosives he was carrying, he cut the block of C-4 he had taken off the bridge into smaller charges, and plugged detonators into them. Pulling the power cords back behind a nearby tree, he waved at the Captain.

"Fall back, fall back!" Capt. Holloway yelled as he took cover beside Lucas. "Wait for it, wait for it, Lucas. On my command."

They watched as about fifteen Viet Cong rushed onto the bridge after the firing stopped. When they were about halfway across Capt. Holloway yelled, "Now!"

All the charges fired at once, allowing the structure to collapse down into the gorge, carrying the enemy soldiers with it.

Captain Holloway joined Sgt. Mecklenburg near the medics as they worked on Specialist Urbanski. Kneeling down next to his wounded man he inquired. "How are you doing, son. You had us scared for a few minutes."

Urbanski attempted to smile as he replied. "Well, sir. I won't be ready to play tackle in today's football game, but I should be ready by next Sunday for sure."

"The Captain patted his man on the shoulder as he looked at him with pride. Good, I'll leave your position open then. I think we play the Ho Chi Minh all stars next week, you best be up to it."

Laughing slightly, Urbanski replied. "Sir, if these guys were the practice squad, we can take the first string with no problem."

Standing up, Capt. Holloway responded, "I'll bet you can, I bet you can, Urbanski."

Walking up to Tom and Moe he inquired, "How bad is he."

Moe shook his head. The round went in on his left side and came out the left front. I'm guessing he may have a broken rib, but we can't be sure if there is any serious internal damage. Good thing is he's not bleeding real bad. We bandaged him good and wrapped him pretty tight. That's the best we can do out here. He can walk with help, but we won't be able to push it, sir"

The Captain nodded his head as he looked intently at Moe. "Son, when we get back, I am writing you up for a Bronze Star. That took guts to run out onto that bridge and carry him back here. Job well done, I'm proud of both of you!"

Walking over to Sgt. Mecklenburg, Captain Holloway asked, "Well Ed, what does the map tell us now? We need to figure something out before long, we have a lot of wounded men."

"Sir, the problem is, I only have an inch of map left. If we go that far to the north we run out of map. I suggest we try and make our way east, but there is not much on this side of the gully marked out for us. No one ever expected us to be in this mess," Sgt. Mecklenburg explained.

"That's why they call us special forces, Ed. Everything we do is special, and every damn mess we get into is special. Every time we make it back we prove we are special, and every time we take on another ridiculous mission like this, we prove we're special besides being just plain stupid." Captain Holloway chuckled at his own joke. "Go east young man, go east. Put Corporal Dinzer in the lead."

By late afternoon, the small and badly beat up team was making rather good time as they were moving downhill toward the Mekong River. They had seen little evidence of the Viet Cong along the way which gave them a chance to breathe.

About 1800 hrs., Captain Holloway ordered the column to halt and take a break. After studying the map, he and Sgt. Mecklenburg found a small cove that would make a great pickup point. After writing down the coordinates, the Captain took the radio hand set.

"House Keeping, this is Grab Bag, do you copy?"

"This is House Keeping, where the hell have you been, Grab Bag, we've been concerned?"

Smiling, the Captain responded, "House Keeping we took the P.M. off to tour our new estate. We found a great place to take a bath. We will need an LCVP with medical service, and suggest two escorts at 2030 hrs. Can you comply?"

"Grab Bag, that's as good as done. Give us your coordinates and we will be there. Good luck until then."

After the Captain read off the coordinates for the pickup, he instructed the men to move out as they still had some tough terrain to navigate.

With Specialist Cohen now taking point, the men were being more cautious as the deepening evening shadows concealed many obstacles and possible booby traps. As Cohen stopped to decide the best way to continue down the steep slope, a shot rang out, sending him rolling down the embankment. Dinzer charged off to his left as he saw a figure running to the north. Lucas followed but stayed a bit closer to the steep embankment. After several minutes of searching, Dinzer pointed toward two downed trees covered in jungle vines. Lucas removed a grenade from his belt and pulled the pin. When Dinzer had taken cover, Lucas pitched the weapon into the twisted pile of debris. When it exploded they heard a scream.

Cautiously, they made their way toward the trees, to find an older woman lying against a tree stump holding an AK-47 on her lap. She was bleeding from a severe wound in her chest and neck. Lucas reached over and removed the weapon from her grasp although she attempted to hold on to it.

Tom came running up to see if his services were needed, while Moe went to attend to Cohen. Looking down at the pitiful shabby woman, Tom shook his head. "This crap just gets to me. We never know who the hell we're fighting over here."

As he was about to kneel down to see if he could do anything for her, she spit blood at him while yelling something in Vietnamese. As her breathing became more labored, it was evident she was going to die. She was going to die a lonely death in the middle of the Cambodian jungle with no family or friends around her, where her body may never be found, and her family would never be sure what happened to her.

Without saying a word, Tom backed away from her and stood up, not quite sure what they should do with her.

After spitting blood one more time she turned her head from side to side looking at the three American soldiers. In broken English but still understandable she said, "Do it!"

Lucas looked over at Tom. "Do what?"

Before Tom could respond, Dinzer fired one shot into her forehead.

"She said do it. She wanted us to finish her off so she wouldn't have to suffer," Dinzer responded, as he watched the old woman slide off to the side of the stump.

Tom looked at Dinzer. "What the fuck, man? We should have left her just die on her own time. This fucking place sucks! Let's go see what's happening with Cohen."

None of the men said another word about it as they went to check on Cohen, although in all reality, Tom did not have a problem with what had taken place.

They found the rest of the team near the bottom of the deep slope, with Cohen leaning up against a tree as Moe was about finished wrapping his right shoulder. Walking up to Moe, Tom inquired. "How is he doing?"

"The bullet shattered his left scapula and ricocheted down inside somewhere. Like these other guys, he needs a hospital and a surgeon. I gave him a double morphine as we are going to need to move him to the pick-up point. He wouldn't be able to handle the pain otherwise. What did you have, did you get the prick that did this?"

Tom nodded his head. "It was an old woman, she had to be seventy plus. The grenade did a number on her, nothing I could do for her. She didn't make it."

Moe nodded his head in understanding. "And the gun shot?"

"No big deal. Dinzer thought he saw something, but it was all good," Tom responded, feeling no one needed to know what had taken place.

Slowly, the battered band of men covered the last mile to the small cove where they would be picked up. Capt. Holloway prayed the Viet Cong would leave them alone until the barge arrived. They no longer had much of a force to resist any type of attack. It would be either fight to the death or surrender and watch their wounded be shot, and the rest of them marched off to an uncertain future.

Just prior to 2030, all the men could hear the low rumble of a naval diesel engine approaching from the south. Sgt. Mecklenburg walked along the shore line, signaling the Boatswains mate where to turn his LCVP.

When the front ramp dropped down, several medics ran forward with stretchers to carry the wounded onboard, and several doctors stood ready to begin giving them advanced treatment before they could get to the hospital for surgery.

Out in the river, two large naval gun boats sailed slowly back and forth, waiting for the LCVP to back out into the river for the trip back south. Tom sat down against side wall of the barge as the Boatswain backed his craft back into the river. Moments later the small convoy sailed back south toward a predetermined destination.

The last forty-eight hours had seemed like a lifetime to Tom. He and Moe had done everything they could do to repair wounds and keep men alive that should have been sent out on medi-vac choppers right away. He was proud of what they had accomplished, but right now he was physically and mentally worn out. He closed his eyes and quickly fell to sleep as the low rumble of the engine blocked out all that was going on around him.

About ninety minutes later, Sgt. Mecklenburg walked over and shook Tom by the shoulder. "We're going to be docking at the river boat base in just a few minutes. You and Moe can get off and spend the night here. Tomorrow, you will be flown back to Binh Thuy."

Tom stood up and walked over to Moe who was also preparing to go ashore. As they stood in silence, Capt. Holloway walked up to them. "Gentlemen, you really proved yourselves well out there. If anything could go wrong it did. Turning to Moe he continued. "Ashton, I will submit the request for the Bronze Star when I arrive back in Saigon tomorrow morning. I'll personally walk it over to Westmoreland's office so it doesn't get lost in the shuffle."

Moe thanked Captain Holloway just as the ramp dropped to the ground. After shaking hands, Captain Holloway, Sgt. Mecklenburg and what remained of their team, walked off to a waiting Chinook Chopper that was running on a landing pad.

A young Ensign walked up to Tom and Moe. "Welcome men, we have a hot shower, hot food and a warm bunk waiting for you. You will be out of here around 1000 in the morning.

Tom and Moe walked slowly toward the helicopter landing zone around 0930, discussing all that had happened over the last few days. Arriving near the landing zone, Mr. Merchant, the lead CIA agent stepped up to them.

Handing them a form, he said, "You need to sign this nondisclosure form. It states you will not disclose anything that happened on the mission, nor can you admit you were in Cambodia, nor can you disclose the names of anyone else involved in the mission under penalty of court martial."

Moe laughed as he handed the form back to Agent Merchant. "You can take my form and cram it up your ass."

Before the angry CIA agent could respond, Tom handed back his form. "I don't have one ounce of belief in what you are doing here. Like Moe said, you can cram it."

Merchant took a step toward them, shoving the forms down inside Moe's shirt. Screaming over the noise of the landing chopper he said. "Do as you are told and don't be stupid!"

As the chopper began to lift off the ground, Moe ripped up the forms and threw them out the door as he waved goodbye to Agent Merchant.

CHAPTER 9
WAR KNOWS NO BOUNDARIES

A heavy mist hung in the air, making the darkness of 0530 appear to be blacker than normal. Tom and his favorite sidekick Romey Eliot walked toward the operations office where they were to be briefed on the first mission of the morning. Entering the briefing room, they walked up to Lt. Jurgins, who was studying a small map. Looking up from the paper he frowned at the medics.

"I was beginning to wonder if the two of you were going to show, I really wanted you to be here for the briefing. Glad you finally made it," the very capable lieutenant commented with a stern look, before returning to study his map.

"That's my fault, sir," Romey responded. "I didn't fill my medical bag last night like I should have so we had to make a quick visit to the supply room.

"Shit happens, Eliot. I'm sure it won't happen again," Lt. Jurgins replied with a wink.

Seconds later, Col. Andre Hernandez, the Battalion Commander, walked up to the small podium. "Good morning, everyone. We have a tough mission this morning. Three days ago, we dropped a platoon of Air Cav. to perform reconnaissance work around Vinh Long. Yesterday morning we received word they had been hit hard by an overwhelming force of Viet Cong and North Vietnamese Regulars that came in by barge overnight. They took heavy casualties but were able to withdraw to a small hillock three clicks to the east," the Colonel explained pointing to a large map.

"We've been supporting them with gunship and fighter aircraft over the last 48 hours. Nevertheless, there is no way for them to break out of there with the number of casualties they have, and we won't leave them behind. Our plan is to have a Chinook drop down and load as many troops and walking wounded as they can and get the hell out of there. We'll have three Huey's circling, ready to drop in with medical staff to retrieve the seriously wounded. All the while, we'll continue hammering the enemy with every bit of air power we can muster. Get in there, do what needs to be done and get the hell out of there. Any questions?"

Captain John Allison from the Air Cav. unit stood up. "Sir, are we going to send any infantry along to protect the perimeter as we evacuate?"

The Colonel nodded his head. "Yes, Captain. We have men standing by the flight line just for that assignment. We're not sending any of your men up there, as we understand the casualties you've taken over the last few weeks. But these men know what to do and will get your men out."

The Captain shook his head. "Sir, with all due respect, I would feel better if my men were going out there to pick up their team mates. It just makes more sense to me."

"Sorry, Captain. This was discussed at the highest level. We want to rebuild your unit when we get them back. We don't want you taking any more casualties, and there's a good possibility of that."

The Colonel spoke for several more minutes regarding the operation as he pointed toward the map behind him. Turning to face the men who sat patiently in the briefing room, he added.

"The operation has been moved back one half hour to give us a little more day light before we fly in there. Take off will be at 0730. That's all, good luck."

Lt. Jurgins turned to the two medics. "You guys will be on that Chinook. When it sets down, get the hell off and get to work. Choppers from

Squadron Four will be there to back you up. Patch them up and get them loaded as quickly as you can. There are a lot of enemy troops down below who are itching to make a mess out of this operation and take down the choppers if they can. Do you understand?"

Both medics nodded in agreement as the lieutenant turned to leave.

Departing the briefing room, the men walked to the hangers where their helicopter was waiting for takeoff. Approaching the Chinook, Moe Ashton came running up behind them.

"Hey Kenrude, wait up," he called out as he neared them. "Why am I in a Huey and not going in with you guys? What's the deal?"

Tom shook his head. "Can't answer that, Moe. My thinking is they don't want all three of us on one chopper in case it gets hit. Why weren't you at the briefing?"

Moe shook his head. "I was scheduled to go with a bunch of Rangers on a quick mission, but it was canceled. I was just told of the change about fifteen minutes ago. I've got everything I need in my bag and more. It sounds like there are a lot of wounded to contend with."

After shaking hands with Moe, the men climbed aboard the Chinook to get out of the drizzle as they waited for their mission to begin. Although Moe was visibly upset, he turned and darted across the tarmac to his Huey. Because of the heavy weather, the flight line was unusually quiet this morning, allowing the Chinook to taxi immediately when the call came for them to depart.

However, off in the distance, the ominous sounds of exploding artillery and mortar rounds appeared to be louder and closer than normal.

At 0715, chopper crews sat ready in their machines, awaiting orders to leave, as a deuce and a half with thirty heavily armed infantry soldiers arrived near the rear of the huge Chinook. As their commanders spoke with the pilot, the soldiers loaded all their heavy weapons on board.

Moments later, the air outside the huge Chinook was alive with the sound of warming jet engines. The huge helicopter shook and vibrated as its massive rotors spun overhead. Tom never really appreciated flying in a Chinook. It was a slow and cumbersome helicopter, which presented a much larger target to the enemy below. Although Huey's were still susceptible to ground fire as they were descending, the pilots were champions in maneuvering their machines, making them harder to hit, or at least it appeared that way to the medics on board.

At 0730, just as planned, the Huey's lifted from the tarmac heading toward Vinh Long. Seconds later, the Chinook pilot began to taxi forward until the giant helicopter lifted into the thick morning air.

With the rear ramp open, Tom peered out the back of the chopper. Everything appeared dark as the thick, moisture laden clouds closed in around the dense jungle below. Closing his eyes, Tom went over bandaging procedures, IV placements and proper methods of loading wounded men on litters.

He now had plenty of experience in such matters, but it always comforted him to go over the routines in his mind on the way to a mission. The last thing he ever wanted to do was make a mistake that would cost the life of a brave soldier. After what seemed like an eternity, the pilot said he was circling the small hillock and was preparing to land. The last thing Tom did in preparation for landing was to remove his sidearm from its holster, slide the safety lever to fire mode, and chamber a round.

Moments later the top of the hill came into view, where wounded men sat awaiting extraction. When the chopper touched down, the medics and infantry raced down the ramp. The medics began grabbing wounded men that could walk, or those not requiring heavy medical assistance, and directing them into the Chinook, while the infantry began re-enforcing the perimeter against an all-out assault by enemy forces.

Tom and Romey were nearly finished with their work, when a sergeant waved at Tom from a short distance away. He was shielding a wounded man from flying debris after a mortar round exploded nearby. Dropping to his knees, Tom shook his head as he removed the quickly placed makeshift bandages covering the man's abdomen.

"He's lost a lot of blood since he was hit yesterday afternoon. I'm surprised he made it this long," the sergeant called out above the roar of the Chinook and the raging battle around them.

Tom nodded as he went to work on the soldier's mangled body. "Hang in there, Corporal, I've seen worse. Give me a minute, and we can load you on the Huey coming in. But I need to start an IV first."

With machine like efficiency, Tom had the IV flowing in mere seconds, despite two close calls with incoming mortar rounds. Moments later, Moe and his flight mechanic raced over from their chopper with a litter. As soon as they loaded the corporal onto it, Tom took off running toward a small dugout, where another soldier was lying out in the open. However, he had to drop twice on the way there, as mortar rounds continued pummeling the hilltop.

Dropping to the ground by the dugout, Tom heard the wounded man called out, "Who's there?" as he reached for his M-16.

"I'm a medic, Tom Kenrude. No need to shoot me," Tom called out as he examined the man's head wound.

"Okay! I thought you were a V.C. coming to finish me off. I can't see a damn thing, Doc, and I keep losing consciousness. What can you do for me?"

Part of the man's skull was missing and several shards of metal were still sticking out from his brain. As Tom began wrapping the horrible wound, he inquired. "Can you move your legs?"

"Yeah a little," the soldier replied, with very slurred speech. "But they don't move the way they should. I can move my right arm but my left just lays there. Will I be alright? I have a little boy at home that needs a papa that can teach him about football and baseball. Do you think I'll be able to do that?"

As Gabe and another soldier arrived with a litter, Tom replied to the worried soldier. "We'll do what we can for you," he said, although he knew the prognosis was not good.

Heavy fire from the north side of the hillock was concerning to Tom, as the small infantry unit that was protecting them had their hands full already. Several more mortar rounds slammed into the hill, sending showers of hot shrapnel slicing through the air. Just as Tom was about to get up from the last explosion, a Cobra helicopter screamed overhead, machine guns blazing away at the approaching Viet Cong nearing their position. Things were beginning to get desperate for the medics and their awaiting choppers.

After Tom finished working on his last soldier he headed toward the Chinook, as the pilot waved at him frantically. Moe was climbing back onto his chopper, as Romey came running from about twenty yards away, with two soldiers carrying a litter with a seriously injured man.

Romey was holding an IV bag in his mouth as he continued applying pressure to the soldier's massive abdominal wound. Tom heard the scream of another incoming mortar round, and he knew it was going to be close. As the hill shook, Romey and the two soldiers disappeared in a cloud of dirt and debris.

As Tom prepared to race back toward Romey, the pilot screamed out, "Kenrude, get your sorry ass on board! I'm getting the hell out of here now, do you hear me? "

Nevertheless, as the Chinook lifted off, Tom and Moe raced toward the men lying in twisted forms on the ground. Arriving aside of Romey, it was clear that nothing could be done for him. His head had nearly been severed by the deadly shrapnel. Turning to his left, Tom observed one of the soldiers withering in pain with his left arm torn off at the elbow. As Tom knelt down to administer aid, he recognized the soldier as Johnny Semz from Basic Training. Shaking his head, Tom began placing a tourniquet just above the elbow joint as he called out, "Johnny what kind of crap did you get yourself into?"

Johnnie looked up at Tom forcing a slight smile. "Hey Kenrude, can you fix me up? I'm no good in the woods this way, my lumber jacking days will come to an end. You gotta do something, like you did for Batts back in basic. Help me out here, Kenrude!"

Tom nodded his head. "I got you Johnnie, you're alive but you got to help me here, or we'll all die. Get up, you need to walk, get off you ass or we'll all be blown to bits, come on Johnnie, damn it, walk with me!"

Approaching one of the Huey's, the flight engineer jumped out grabbing Johnnie allowing Tom to run back to help Moe. They loaded Romey's body onto the litter with the man he had been trying to help, who was also now dead. The second litter bearer was able to hobble back to the closest chopper after Moe had bandaged his leg.

Although the pilot from Moe's chopper was screaming at them to get their asses in gear, they made no attempt to listen until they had everyone on board needing evacuation.

With the evacuations completed, all three Huey's were in the air, as two Cobra's once again raked the hillsides with 20mm cannon fire, keeping the Viet Cong from gaining the summit.

As Moe's chopper turned to leave the area, the co-pilot screamed. Two bullets ripped through the fuselage of the helicopter, striking the young Warrant Officer in the shoulder and left leg. Blood sprayed all around the cockpit as the femoral artery had been damaged. Grabbing a tourniquet from his bag, Moe climbed onto the co-pilot's lap, struggling to get the tourniquet in place to stop the blood flow. With the help of the flight engineer, Tom was able to cut the flight suit off and get a battle dressing on his shoulder. Once more Moe checked the tourniquet to be sure blood flow had all but stopped. Looking into the co-pilot's eyes he inquired, "How you doing sir?"

Trying to force a smile the co-pilot nodded his head. "Not going to make it. There's a photo of my wife in my upper pocket, and a letter I started. See to it she gets it. She deserved better than me to begin with. Tell her I died trying to do what was right."

Moe shook his head. "No, damn it, you're going to be alright. A few more minutes and we'll be on the ground. I promise you I'll get off your lap and let the medics get you in the hospital. How do you think your wife would feel if she heard the last thing you did was have some guy sitting on your lap when you died."

The pilot busted out laughing as Moe placed a big kiss on his co-pilots forehead. "Now you'll have to explain that to your wife for good measure, after I write that letter, since I have witnesses."

Forcing a smile, the co-pilot looked up at Moe. "Alright Doc, let's do it your way. You can hold off on that bullshit letter."

Seconds later the chopper skidded to a stop near the aid station. Doctors and nurses ran toward the three helicopters to triage all the wounded.

After Tom slid open the side door, he jumped out to open the co-pilot's door. "I got a high profile right here. He's bad, lost lots of blood."

Several corpsmen removed the wounded co-pilot from the damaged aircraft, rushing him into the operating area.

After all the wounded men were taken inside, Tom grabbed his blood covered medical bag from the chopper and turned to leave. The pilot walked over to him, extending his hand.

"I apologize for yelling at you back there. You guys do a hell of a job. My co-pilot Dave has his first child on the way. That's all he's talked about since he arrived here three months ago. Thanks to you he'll get to watch her grow up. Thank you for what you did."

Taking a look at Tom's uniform, the pilot continued. "Damn. You are covered in blood from head to toe. Don't know how you do it, Kenrude."

After the pilot walked off, Tom looked down at his uniform. The pilot was accurate. Not one part of his uniform from his neck to his boots was free from blood. Even his chest was sticky with the co-pilot's blood, as it had sprayed on his neck and ran down inside his clothing.

Moe grabbed Tom by the arm. "Come on, let's go get cleaned up. The hospital corpsmen can spray out the choppers."

Tom shook his head. "No, I have to check on Semz and Romey. I just can't leave those guys like this. They deserve better, Moe."

"There's nothing you can do, Tom. The surgeons will take care of Semz, and he'll be sent to a state side hospital. And for Romey, you saw him, he was dead before he hit the ground. They'll clean him up and send him home. That's all anyone can do for him now."

Tom shook his head. "No, I need to see Romey. I need to say goodbye. I just can't walk away like it doesn't matter. You can come with me or go, your choice."

Moe nodded in agreement as he placed his arm on Tom's shoulder.

Entering the hospital, Tom walked up to one of the corpsmen. Do you know where they put Specialist Eliot's body? I'd like to see him."

"Yeah, he's right around the corner, second cart on the left. It's been a busy day here," the corpsman responded as he looked at the blood that covered Tom."

Walking up to the black bag on the gurney, Tom stood motionless for a moment. After taking a deep breath, he slowly unzipped the heavy zipper. Whoever placed Romey in the bag had positioned the head as close as possible to the way it belonged. Moe also observed a large piece of shrapnel sticking out of his chest.

"Poor guy never knew what hit him, and he never had a chance. I'm betting he never even heard the round coming in," Moe explained, as he made the sign of the cross.

Tom shook his head in agreement as he stared down at his close friend. "He was a great guy, Moe. He wanted to be a doctor real bad. He thought coming here would give him some good experience that would help him down the road. He was special and he really knew what mattered."

Looking down at his own uniform, Moe finally realized he was not in much better shape than Tom. "Come on man, let's go shower and get cleaned up."

Tom shook his head. "Go on ahead, Moe. I'll catch up later. I want to stay with Romey a while longer. He shouldn't be left alone out here in this hallway."

"Look Kenrude—" Moe began, before giving his comment a second thought. "Yeah, that sounds good. I-uh, I'll see you later."

After Moe walked away, Tom sat down on the floor across from the gurney. He looked at all the body bags lining the corridor. There were fourteen bags filled with the remains of boys. That was all they were. None of them had a chance at life. Now they would be cleaned up, redressed, placed in a metal military casket and be sent home to grieving families. Some of them like Romey would be labeled, 'REMAINS UNVIEWABLE.' What kind of closure would that give his family? Was it possible to have closure when a son this young was killed in a war? A war that increasingly made no sense to anyone but the politicians.

In mid-thought, a surgical nurse named Roxy walked up to Tom. "Hey, this is not where you belong, Kenrude."

Looking over toward Romey's body, she zipped the bag shut. "He's not here, he's with God now. You need to go get cleaned up and take care of yourself. That's what he would have wanted, soldier."

Slowly standing up, Tom looked almost coldly at Roxy. "No, this isn't what Romey would have wanted. You didn't know him like I did. You never talked about the future with him, his plans, his ideals, his desires. You didn't know him."

Roxy nodded in agreement. "Your right, I didn't know him like you did. But I have gotten to know you two a bit since you've been here. I know that you loved Romey like a brother, and that it's hurt you terribly to see him get killed like that. But you have to let go now and move on. I believe that Romey wouldn't want you sulking over him like this. What did he always say? It was something about not getting—"

Before she could finish, Tom cut her off, "Don't get stuck in the mud, put it in four wheel and get your ass moving."

"Yeah, that's it." Roxy said, smiling now. "So when are you going to get out of the mud, Kenrude?"

Tom walked around Roxy, reaching once more for the zipper to the body bag.

Roxy placed her hand on top of Tom's.

"No Tom! You've seen him. Go now and remember him as he was, not like this. Keep those good memories alive. Now get the hell out of here. I mean it, Kenrude. That's an order!" Lt. Roxanne Proctor demanded.

Tom glared at Roxy for a moment before nodding his head. "Yes, Ma'am," Tom replied feeling somewhat angry with the way she pulled rank on him.

As he turned to leave, Roxy stepped in front of him. "Be mad at me if you will, Tom Kenrude. But look at you! You're covered in blood from head to toe. Other people's blood. You need to trash that uniform, take a shower, and get your head straight before you're called on again. You're no good to anyone if you're in that bag with Romey. He'll be fine. Right now that's more than I can say for you, and you're still alive."

Tom stopped and turned to face Roxy, snapping into an erect posture.

"Understood, Lieutenant. Will there be anything else?"

Throwing up her hands she shook her head. "I'll just chalk this up to a bad day, so go, get out of my hospital."

Angrily, Tom did a perfect about-face and left the hospital at a brisk walk.

After he was out the door, Roxy turned to Romey's bag. Placing her hand on top of the bag she whispered. "Give your partner some strength, soldier. If he stays in that frame of mind, he'll be joining you all too soon."

After turning on the shower, Tom leaned against the partition and wept. He cursed his father for never explaining what it was like to lose a close friend in combat. Why didn't he take time to prepare his son for the worst? Was this the reason his father went for long walks by himself sometimes? Were the memories too tough to bear? Did the pain never go away?

After putting on a clean uniform, Tom walked outside. He looked toward the mountains in the distance where the sun was beginning to set. Suddenly, he realized, there was no way for a father to prepare a son for what happened today. No one could prepare you for this kind of crap. Looking at the golden sunset, Tom said aloud, "I guess war knows no boundaries."

Realizing what kind of a jerk he had been toward Roxy, he walked over to the hospital. Entering the triage area, he ran into nurse, Lt. Kimberly Nesbit.

"Hey Lieutenant, is Roxy still around here. I need to talk with her, and give her an apology." Tom explained.

Shaking her head, she responded. "No, she went back to quarters a while ago. She was pretty wiped out, they had a tough tour today. You'll have to catch her tomorrow."

Tom nodded his head in agreement. "Yeah, we brought them a bunch of patients that were in pretty tough shape. I can understand what they went through."

Slowly, Tom wandered over to the mess hall to grab a bite to eat. It had been a long time since breakfast that morning. Going down the chow line the only thing that looked appetizing was the meat loaf. Adding a couple slices of bread, cheese and a cup of coffee, he was set. He sat by himself near the back of the room, not wanting to talk with anyone tonight. Finishing his meal, he slowly walked back toward the entrance to the hospital where the choppers unloaded. A jeep was parked near the entrance, facing west. Tom took a seat in the jeep as he listened to the far off explosions in the hills to the west. Somewhere out there men were dying, some would die alone in the dark, others would scream for help until a medic arrived, or they simply passed out or died. Everyone knew the Viet Cong rose to the height of brutality in the dark. You were better off dead than being captured after nightfall. From the dark behind him the familiar voice of Roxy spoke out.

"Is it alright if I join you?"

Tom turned quickly in the seat. "Yeah, I would like that."

After sitting down, Roxy turned, half-smiling at Tom.

"Look Tom, I'm sorry about pulling rank on you today, but you were in a bad place and not listening to reason. It seemed like that was all I had left."

Looking over at Roxy Tom nodded. "I'm the one who needs to apologize. I didn't give you much choice. I still can't even believe Romey is gone. It happened so damn fast, he never had a chance. Every day he helped me get through the crap, and drove me to go on. He could talk me out of a funk faster than anyone I have ever known. Damn, I'm going to miss that laugh."

Roxy sat quiet for several moments, allowing Tom to feel his pain. Reaching over she placed her hand on top of his.

"War is hell Tom. I know that's an over worn cliché, but it's just the plain truth. We all lose friends regardless of what we do, or how hard we try to help them. It just can't be helped. But in the end, we need to put it behind us and do our jobs, because these brave men depend on us every single day. We can't wallow in our grief because it will just wear us down."

Tom nodded in agreement. "Yeah Roxy, I know what you're saying. When I enlisted I knew what I wanted to do. I wanted to save lives, and get these guys back home. Maybe I didn't think it through all the way. Maybe I was naïve, or maybe I just wasn't cut out to be a combat medic. But this is way tougher than I ever imagined. I feel so much pain for these guys and it never goes away."

Roxy smiled as she gazed at Tom. "You're good at what you do, and you'll make a fine doctor someday. The problem is, you're a good, caring person, Tom Kenrude. Look, this is my second tour over here. You are one of the best combat medics I've seen, and I've seen quite a few come and go. Keep doing what you're doing, and remember it's alright to feel the pain.

That is what keeps you human. I feel the pain every day. You can't shut off your humanness. It just isn't possible."

Looking over at Roxy, Tom wanted to take her in his arms and give her a big hug. But he knew that was totally out of line. She was an officer, he was an enlisted man, and that sign of affection would destroy their working relationship forever. Instead he changed the subject. "So, is there a guy waiting for you back home?"

Roxy had to laugh. "Well, kind of I guess. There's an orthopedic surgeon back in Akron, Ohio that attempted to give me a ring when I came home from my last tour. I didn't take it because I knew I was coming back here. He was devastated. I felt bad but I didn't want to be engaged and be over here, so instead I broke his precious heart. You can't get much crueler than that, I'm guessing. We didn't talk the rest of the time I was home. About a month after I returned, I received a letter from him. He asked if I would reconsider when I returned." Roxy was quiet for a moment as she stared off into the distance. "You know, Kenrude, if he was more like you, I would jump at the chance to spend the rest of my life with him."

Taken back by Roxy's comment, Tom swallowed hard before responding. "He sounds determined, what are you going to do?"

Taking a deep breath, Roxy turned toward Tom. "I'm still a work in progress. I'm mulling it over. But I need to do something right now I might regret in the future." With that she leaned across the jeep, throwing her arms around Tom's neck, she kissed him. After withdrawing to the far side of the jeep, Roxy jumped out. "This never happened, Kenrude, I mean, well you know what I mean." Before he could speak, she disappeared into the hospital.

Tom climbed out of the jeep, standing motionless for a moment. He had been afraid to give her a hug, and now she had kissed him. Slowly, he walked back toward his quarters. Lying down on his bunk, he found it hard to sleep, as visions of Romey lying in the dirt with his head torn lose from his body kept reappearing over and over.

When he tried to put Romey out of his mind, the kiss from Roxy bothered his soul even more. After all, he was married to Mackenzie, and he loved her with all his heart. Plus he was hoping she was pregnant so they could have a family when he returned. To be sure, this was the most complicated night of his entire life. It was well past midnight before sleep finally overtook his weary body.

In the nurse's quarters, Roxy also found it hard to sleep tonight. She had broken a serious army regulation, no fraternization with enlisted men. Technically, she could be court martialed and sent home for that kiss if anyone reported it. In the real world, being four years older than Tom was not as big of a deal as it had been twenty years ago. But was it love, or just loneliness that she was feeling.

Suddenly, she felt very alone in the middle of a war, surrounded by constant death and hundreds of lonely and desperate soldiers so far from home. She had returned to Vietnam because she wanted to help the wounded soldiers and do something good in her life. But since arriving in Binh Thuy three months ago, fear was her biggest challenge every day. There was no doubt in her mind that she should have never returned. Instead, she should have taken up the position at Akron Children's Hospital that she was offered by her boyfriend, Dr. Scarborough. Maybe he did know what was best for her after all.

Roxy knew she would have to find time tomorrow to speak with Tom, and somehow deescalate the situation between them. It was either that or ask for a transfer to another base in Vietnam, and she didn't want that.

As dawn broke over Binh Thuy, Tom was already preparing his equipment for the day. After placing his sidearm in the holster, he walked nervously toward the hospital to restock his medical bag. Moe attempted to start several conversations regarding two pro baseball games that had taken place the day before back home, but Tom just tried to ignore the small talk.

Moe and Specialist Warren Wymann were first in line at the supply station. Tom watched Roxy make small talk as she filled their bags and sent them on their way. When Tom walked up to the counter, Roxy smiled.

"Good morning, Kenrude. What do you need today?"

After handing her his list, she looked it over carefully before replying, "Why don't you go around the corner and come in here, you need a lot of things."

Once Tom was in the supply room, Roxy walked him to a small office. Taking a deep breath, she looked at him intently.

"Last night, well, that just shouldn't have happened. I mean, we can't allow it to continue. You need to understand that we both could be court martialed over it."

Tom smiled back at Roxy. "Understood. There won't be a problem."

After looking down at the floor for a moment, Roxy looked up at Tom.

"Look Tom, I know you love your wife very much, just as I love Phil, honestly I do. I thought about it a lot last night. Being the wife of a great orthopedic surgeon is not a bad deal. I sent him a quick note this morning telling him so."

Tom smiled as he nodded his head. "I'm happy for you Roxy, or should I say lieutenant."

"No, Roxy will always be fine. Look, I better get back out there. I just wanted us to be on the same page. Thanks for being so understanding," Roxy said, as she turned toward the door.

Before leaving the hospital, Tom walked over to the surgical ward to see Johnnie. He was slightly surprised to see him sitting up in bed after going through all the surgery the night before.

"Hey Kenrude, glad you stopped by this morning. They tell me I'm headed to the Army Hospital in Hawaii later today for some final surgery. Last night I came to realize my life the way I knew it is over now. I don't know what I will do when I get back home. Like I said, not much work for a one arm lumber jack." Johnnie said looking very sad.

Tom was quiet for a moment as he attempted to gather his thoughts.

"Johnnie you are a pretty smart guy, whether or not you want to admit it. Why don't you consider going to school to school to learn a new trade? There has to be something out there you would like to do, give it some thought while you are in the hospital." After looking at his watch Tom placed his hand on Johnnie's shoulder. I have to get going for a mission. Take care and I will look you up when I get home."

After the two men shook hands, Tom left the hospital. He felt somewhat relieved he and Roxie had talked things out. There could be little doubt that he would remember her kiss for a long time to come. But he had someone at home that meant the world to him. Someone who would cross mountains, swim shark infested waters, or live in a mud hut if that's what it took to make a life with him. And besides all of that, she just might be carrying his child, and that was something that made him happiest of all. He felt bad about Johnnie's condition, but some how he knew that kid from Virginia would find a way to pull himself up by his boot straps and make a go of his life. Smiling, Tom took a deep breath as he walked toward the orderly room to find out what missions he would have today.

CHAPTER 10
DISSENSION IN THE RANKS

Tom made his way into the orderly room, although his heart really wasn't set on another mission. Lt. Jurgins was standing behind his desk with Moe, Gabe and several other medics in front of him.

As Tom approached, Lt. Jurgins gave him a disapproving glance for being late. Without saying a word, the visibly upset lieutenant walked over to the staffing board. "Alright, listen up. As some of you know already, we have three new medics in bound this morning. One of them is Specialist Walter Koppelmann, a transfer from Bien Hoa that most of you have no doubt heard about in the news. Yes, he's a conscientious objector that decided to become a medic so he could still serve. We'll treat him like anyone else, and there will be no problems. Do I make myself clear?"

Specialist Frank Ridzik from Flight Four shook his head. "A Jewish conscientious objector that almost got a medic killed down at Bien Hoa, because he refused to carry or pick up a weapon when the shit hit the fan. Yeah, what more could we ask for? Call me what you will, but hell no, I'm not working with him. Court Martial me or transfer me, but I won't be teamed up with no Jew boy, especially one that's a coward to boot."

Moe kept quiet, although you could see he wasn't happy with the new replacement. Medics Boulder, Martinez and Sarducci from Squadrons Four and Two stood quietly near the desk not saying a word.

"Well, we sure as hell have ourselves a problem before the man even steps foot on base. I hate being heavy handed with any man in my command, but this kind of attitude just isn't going to work!" Lt. Jurgins barked in a loud voice as he paced back and forth. "Command sent him here so we could put his services to work. What the hell am I supposed to do with him?"

Moe looked at Lt. Jurgins. "Put him in the hospital. Take Grissom out of the hospital and assign him to us. End of problem, sir."

Lt. Jurgins walked up to Moe standing nearly nose to nose with him. "So each time we have a guy we don't like, we hide him out somewhere regardless of how good he does his job, is that right? What happens if someday the guys don't like you any more, then what do I do?"

Before another word could be said, Tom spoke up. "Put the guy in Romey's place, I'll give him a chance."

Martinez glared at Tom. "What the hell, Kenrude? You got a death wish?"

Before Tom could answer Moe stepped forward. "Look Tom, this guy is bad news. He wouldn't even defend himself or another medic. Yeah, medics aren't supposed to carry weapons, so it fits right in with being a conscientious objector, I know. But remember what you were told when you arrived in country. The V.C. will kill a medic sooner than anyone, so you may have to defend yourself. Hell, we've both carried M-16's, in additional to our sidearm at times. Why put yourself in that kind of predicament?"

Lt. Jurgins looked intently at Tom. "Well Kenrude, what do you say now?"

Tom stood quiet for a moment as he stared down at the floor. "Look this isn't easy for any of us. I heard what happened over at Bien Hoa, same as the rest of you. But I also heard this guy is a great medic, and will jump through hoops to help the wounded. I don't know guys, I think this man deserves a chance. I'll talk with him and see how it goes. I'm sure the chopper crew will take him, they're a pretty laid back crew."

"See how it goes? Damn Tom, if he screws up it might be you we're picking up off an L.Z. next time. Come on, don't put him back out there!" Moe yelled defiantly.

Tom took a minute to look at his friend before repeating his decision. "Look Moe, I appreciate your concern, I appreciate every one of you caring about me, but I made up my mind. I want to give him a chance if the chopper crew will, Lieutenant. Then let's just see how it goes."

Lt. Jurgins shook hands with Tom. "Thanks for working with me on this. If at any time you feel the need to back away from it, and feel that he's dangerous out there, you just let me know."

As the men walked back toward their barracks Ridzik turned to face Tom. "Kenrude you're a damn good medic, fearless as hell. I wish I had your balls sometimes. But this time you've gone over the edge. I'll work with you anytime, but you need to keep that yellow Jew away from me, especially in the field. You got that!"

Moe pushed Ridzik back a few feet before taking up a position between the two men. "Listen up you guys! Tom did what he did for his own reasons, and I give him credit, although I think it was a dumb ass idea. No one here needs to take this out on Kenrude. We all have a job to do and we all need to work together when the shit comes down. I recommend we all give this some thought before we do or say something we'll regret the rest of our lives."

Returning to the barracks, the men picked up the gear they would be carrying with them on today's missions. It was clear that Ridzik was still in a hostile mood and not ready to accept the new man under any conditions. Sarducci walked up to Tom as they left the building.

"Hey Kenrude, Wymann is on hospital detail, so I'm flying with Romey's crew today. Are we good?"

Tom had to laugh. "Geno Sarducci, we are as good as a bottle of Chianti and garlic bread."

Geno laughed as he patted Tom on the back. "You need to come to New York to have some of my mama's homemade lasagna someday. That, and a bottle of Chianti is what this world was made for. Let me tell you, Kenrude. You ain't eaten Italian until you've had Mama Sarducci's cooking."

Tom laughed as the two men approached their waiting choppers.

As the men began stowing their bags, Martin Westhaven, the Warrant Officer Three who flew Romey's chopper, the 'Westward Ho,' approached the door.

"Glad to see you guys are in a good mood. We got a tough one that's going to require two birds, let's ride!"

Moments later their Huey's were airborne flying north toward My Tho. Sarducci's smile and humor disappeared as he stared out the open door. Tom sat quietly looking forward, trying to see what was coming up through the windshield. After several minutes of flying, smoke appeared on the horizon to the west of the town.

"Napalm! A jet just dropped two napalm canisters," Sarducci called out to his crew chief Jack Calle, as he pointed toward an F-4 that was rapidly gaining altitude as it streaked off toward the east. "Damn, I hate that stuff. It just makes everything worse, I hate the smell of burning flesh!" Sarducci added.

Seconds later Westhaven and Palmero set their choppers down on a dirt road leading toward a neighboring village that was fully engulfed in flames. Several Marines came running toward them, carrying a wounded soldier and a civilian.

"We got about four more back by the tree line that are in bad shape. Can you take them all?" a lance corporal called out.

"Yeah, we can," Tom called back as he jumped from his chopper. Looking over his shoulder toward Sarducci, he called out, "Geno, you see to these guys. I'll head over to the tree line and see what we've got over there."

Tom ran full speed behind the corporal, as screaming civilians with most of their clothing burned off ran in the opposite direction, attempting to evade the roaring wall of flame.

Kneeling down by the first soldier, Tom yelled out, "He's had it!" Continuing on to the next soldier, Tom observed the man attempting to stand up, although his left foot was torn nearly completely off.

"Marine, take a seat, you're in no condition to walk. Let's bandage that up," Tom called out over the tremendous volume of noise emanating from the fire and ongoing battle. After securing the foot as best he could, he placed a tourniquet near the ankle to control the bleeding. Moving on to the next Marine it was evident there was nothing that could be done. Once more he called out to the waiting Corporal, "He's had it, there's nothing I can do for him."

The fourth Marine had several injuries needing sulfa, bandages, and immediate treatment for horrible burns. With both men ready to be moved, several Marines helped deliver them to the evac choppers. Tom followed the line of wounded men, until he observed a young pregnant woman lying on the side of the road. She was horribly burned, with her left hand all but gone. Quickly Tom applied a makeshift tourniquet to the woman's wrist and bandaged several of her burns. After giving her a small dose of morphine since she was pregnant, he began picking her up.

A Marine running from the burning village stopped beside Tom. "What the hell man, let the bitch die. She'll just give birth to another fucking V.C. Here let me help you out!" The soldier yelled as he turned his sidearm toward the woman.

Swiftly, Tom pushed the gun away from the woman's head. "Get the hell away from me, Marine. She's my patient. My patient! And she's coming with me. You shoot her, I shoot you," Tom screamed at the top of his lungs.

"Kiss my ass," the Marine called back as he ran toward several arriving Marine choppers.

Moments later Tom arrived at the very cramped choppers. "We can't take her! Both birds are full Kenrude," Sarducci yelled, as he pointed to the injured men on board.

Shaking his head, Tom called back. "I'm not leaving her." Turning toward his flight mechanic he continued. "Eddie, those guys should be good until you get to the hospital, just keep an eye on them. I'll find room on another chopper." Hitting Palmero's door, Tom gave him the signal to leave.

As both choppers began lifting off, Tom raced down the road as quickly as he could. He observed two more rescue choppers touching down about twenty yards away. Moe was helping two badly wounded Marines on board, just as Tom arrived at the door nearly out of breath. Setting the young woman down on the edge of the floor he looked at Moe. "She's bad, real bad, we need to take her on your flight."

Moe nodded in agreement as he lifted the injured woman up toward his flight mechanic. "That fill's us up. Jump on Kenrude, let's get the hell out of here."

Tom took a moment to look around the chopper. The floor was covered in blood. There was blood on the ceiling and walls, everywhere you looked was blood, torn bandages and morphine suretes. Tom quickly realized that Moe and the crew of 'Dragons Tail' had been having a very bad day. He watched Moe work on a man who had lost most of his right arm and was severely burned over half his body. Suddenly the man gasped, before going into convulsions.

"Come on man, hang with me. No, no, don't give up on me. We can do this!" Moe yelled as the Marine jerked once more before closing his eyes for the last time. "Damn it, Damn it to hell!" Moe called out, slamming his fist into a medical bag. Sliding down to the blood covered floor, he ripped off his helmet, throwing it out the open door. Tears streamed down his face as he began to shake with anger.

Tom knew the feeling, and understood there was nothing he could do for Moe right now. He simply would have to let his pain run its course.

Arriving back at the hospital, Roxy and one other nurse began to triage the patients and get them off the choppers as quickly as possible. The dead Marine was placed on a stretcher and carried away, while two more medical aids lowered the pregnant woman onto a gurney. Two hospital assistants cleaned debris from the chopper before hosing it out best they could before the crew prepared to fly back to the village. Tom walked up to Moe who was standing near the hospital door.

"Both choppers are ready to go back there. Can you make it?" Tom inquired of his good friend.

Looking over at Tom he nodded his head. "Yeah, let's go pick up some more of those kids. You know they're nothing more than that, just damn kids." As they walked toward the choppers, Moe ripped a helmet off one of the hospital aids. "You don't need this here, go find yourself a new one would you?" With that, he rushed over to jump back on his bird.

Tom ran forward to his chopper as Eddie extended his arm to help him aboard. After giving a quick thumbs up to Palmero, the chopper roared airborne once again.

Arriving back near the burning village, Tom jumped from the chopper with Sarducci running over from his left. Suddenly a shot rang out close by, ricocheting off the front of Sarducci's helmet, knocking him to the ground. As Tom turned to check on his friend, he observed two V.C. running out from the thick vegetation alongside the road. Dropping to his knees to cover Sarducci, Tom began firing his sidearm, striking the first man. Before he could switch directions, Sarducci fired off two rounds right under Tom's arm, striking the second enemy soldier in the head.

Tom looked down at Geno. "You could have shot me you crazy son-of-a-bitch! If I moved just a fraction of an inch, you would have torn my damn arm off!"

As Sarducci stood up he smiled that wide Italian grin. "Yeah but I didn't. Did I ever tell you the story of how my grandpa taught me to shoot back in New York?"

Before he could answer, Tom smacked his friend on the back of his head before tossing his helmet back toward him. "I would get a new one when we get back if I were you. Send this one back to Mama to show her you really are in a war."

The two men laughed a bit as they raced back toward the burned out area that had been a tribal village for probably hundreds of years. Moe and Martinez arrived moments later to assist in treating the wounded and getting them back to the waiting choppers. Two more times they would fly back to the hospital, unload their patients, grab more medical supplies, and return to the burned out village to search for civilians and wounded Marines. However, they would never be sure how many inhabitants had fled into the jungle to die a slow agonizing death.

As night fell overtaking Binh Thuy, a very tired Tom Kenrude walked toward the barracks. Once again his uniform was torn and covered in blood, vomit and mud. He was tired, hungry and mentally exhausted as he walked through the door.

As he grabbed his shower gear, a voice came from behind him. "You must be Kenrude. I'm Kopplemann. Walter Kopplemann. I hear I'll be flying in tandem with you starting tomorrow."

Tom nodded his head. "Look, it's been a bad day all around. I need a shower, clean clothes and something to eat. Why don't you join us in the mess hall in about a half hour. We can talk then."

As Tom entered the mess hall he observed Moe, Martinez, Ridzik, Sarducci and Boulder already at a large table. After moving through the chow line Tom sat down across of Ridzik. "How's the chicken, Frank?"

"Actually pretty good, so are the green beans," Ridzik replied with a smile. "I see your new partner is here, have you spoken with him yet?"

Tom nodded his head as he shoved a fork full of potatoes into his mouth. After swallowing, he looked at Ridzik. "I asked him to join me here, is that going to be a problem for any of you?"

Ridzik frowned for a moment. "No, not after today. I'll give him his due. But I guess he won't handle shit like we did today, not from what I hear about him. But let's see what the Jew can do."

Before Tom could reply, Kopplemann and another new man, Everett Tomlin, approached the table with their trays. After introducing themselves, Moe and Tom gave them a quick rundown on how the medical staff operated. Both men listened intently, asking several good questions. As Ridzik stood to leave he gazed at the new men.

"Armory is back by the orderly room. Make sure you draw your weapons before your first mission tomorrow. Tom and Sarducci needed theirs today. You just never know when you or your partner might be the next target," he explained, looking straight at Kopplemann.

Not saying a word, Kopplemann finished his coffee and stood up. "Do you have something you want to say to me?"

Before Ridzik could speak, Lt. Jurgins walked into the mess hall.

"Attention!" One of the cooks called out.

As the men began to stand, Jurgins called out, "As you were, men." Walking over toward the medics he glared at the two men who appeared to be squaring off for a fight. "Let me make one thing absolutely clear, gentlemen. I'll not have my medics brawling like a couple of immature punks. If you don't like being here or can't handle each other, I'll transfer your asses up to the gal damn DMZ. Then you might think twice about what kind of a bad ass you really want to be. Do I make myself clear?"

"Yes sir!" The men called out in unison.

"Good, that's absolutely fucking outstanding! Kenrude, Kopplemann, your choppers are scheduled for a mission at 0130 to accompany a special forces mission. Go get some sleep and be on the strip by 0100." After glaring at his men once more he walked from the mess hall.

Tom did not sleep well, his head overflowing with vivid photographs of the days actions. Even worse was Kopplemann's refusal to draw weapons from the armory before turning in for the night. Today, if it had not been for Sarducci's quick action, he would be dead for sure. Now he would have a partner that was totally against killing anyone and with no weapons to boot.

At 0100, Tom and Kopplemann walked up to the waiting choppers on the tarmac. The night air was heavy with moisture as thousands of bugs flew in every direction. It shouldn't have mattered as Tom had been on night missions before, but tonight nothing felt right.

Moments later, several deuce-and-a-half's drove up by the choppers. A young lieutenant walked up to the medics. "Gentlemen, I'm Lt. Stevens. You're to go along with my men up to hill 356. It's quite a ways up north. Our plans are to eliminate a V.C. command post. There'll be friendly's on the ground to guide us in to a narrow valley about five clicks from the base of Hill 356. From there we hoof it up the hill and take out the command post. We leave in 20 minutes." Looking at Kopplemann, the lieutenant asked the obvious question. "Where is your sidearm or rifle, soldier?"

Kopplemann shook his head, "I'm a conscientious objector, sir. I'll not carry a weapon."

The lieutenant shook his head, "Have it your way, son. But let me assure you, if all hell breaks loose, we can't follow you around like a mother hen. You may end up on your own, and that's just plain dangerous." Without saying another word, Lt. Stevens walked off to join his men.

At 0130, the choppers climbed into the night sky. In the past Tom's crew had made several night extractions, but this was the first time they had accompanied a specialized night attack mission, and he was nervous, and to be honest, more than a bit scared. He knew it was luck that saved Sarducci yesterday, as they both used their weapons to take out the V.C. Now his partner was unarmed, and almost arrogant about it. Maybe he had made a bad decision taking the man on as a partner.

Forty-five minutes later the choppers began descending into the valley below. Looking out the door, Tom could see several red marker lights on the jungle floor, set there by the advance force of Green Berets. As the choppers touched down, the special forces operatives exited the machines quietly as they prepared for their assault. Lt. Stevens walked up to the medics.

"You follow us up there and be quiet. Do not, and I repeat, do not stray from us. We will not come back to find you. You get lost you are on your own. Do I make myself clear?"

Both men nodded in the affirmative as they joined up at the end of the short column that was already beginning to move forward.

The ascent was slow and treacherous as the men slipped on the muddy trail and tripped over lose rocks. It made Tom very nervous as they moved slowly forward in the dark moonless night. When the column finally came to a stop, Lt. Stevens whispered to the medics.

"Alright, listen up. You men stay here. We'll move forward to set our charges. If you hear gunfire break out, get your asses up to the crest of the hill and wait for directions."

With that the Special Forces disappeared into the dark night, their silhouettes fading away as the dense jungle growth engulfed them. Sweat poured down Tom's face as he impatiently waited for the return of Lt. Stevens. Every sound, every screeching jungle animal made the hair on the back of his neck stand up.

In the thick underbrush, Tom could hear nocturnal jungle animals flitting about. He prayed that none of them would come forward and bite as they knelt silently on the hill. His heart began pounding and his breathing became labored. He was on the verge of having an anxiety attack and this was neither the time nor the place for that. Tom carefully and quietly pulled his side arm when he heard the sound of bodies coming down the trail directly toward them. Was it the men returning from their mission, or was it V.C. out on patrol? Should he fire and possibly alert the camp, or should he wait until they were right on top of them? Aiming his weapon up the trail he was happily overwhelmed when he heard the lieutenant quietly call out.

"Kenrude, you guys still here?"

Taking a deep breath, Tom replied. "Yeah lieutenant, we're here, and glad as hell to see you."

"Alright. Let my first squad pass and then follow them. The rest of my team will follow you down."

Descending the hill was just as tough as going up, as they constantly tripped over lose rocks and jungle roots covering the trail. Arriving at the landing site, Tom was shocked. Both choppers had departed and were airborne somewhere up in the distant night sky.

Several South Vietnamese guerrillas came forward, shaking hands with the American force. One of them made a call on a handheld radio as he waved a red tipped flashlight in the air. Moments later, the choppers once more dove down into the dark valley, where they hovered several feet above the ground. Tom jumped on board helping the soldiers who were weighed down with their large packs. The third person Tom pulled forward was a V.C. soldier that was shaking like a leaf. Once they were airborne, one of the men looked over at Lt. Stevens.

"Do we still want this piece of crap or can I flush the toilet."

"Flush it," the lieutenant replied.

Instantly, the large soldier pitched the struggling Viet Cong soldier out the door. Tom looked over in horror as the men laughed.

Seeing the incident from his chopper, Kopplemann yelled at the soldiers sitting next to him.

"What the hell is the matter with you people? That man never had a chance, his hands and feet were tied and he was gagged. You just murdered him!"

An angry soldier glared at Kopplemann. "You want to join him, you yellow piece of crap? We all know what you're about. You may be a medic, but in the long run you're a coward. I suppose you would have liked it better if I gave him a parachute and an AK-47. Dead is dead, whether you're shot in battle, or tossed out the door. The only good V.C. are dead V.C., no matter how they die." After spitting on the floor of the chopper the man sat back shaking his head.

Moments later a large explosion rocked Hill 356, sending flames and debris in every direction.

Arriving back at Binh Thuy, Lt. Stevens approached Tom. "You guys did alright out there tonight. I'm happy we didn't require your services."

As the lieutenant turned to join his men, Tom began walking toward their barracks before Kopplemann grabbed him by the arm.

"Will you co-sign a formal complaint against those men? They murdered that man, they need to be held accountable, and I'm guessing the Lieutenant gave his permission to do it. They all need to be court martialed."

Infuriated, Tom stopped dead in his tracks, and dropping his bag he glared at his partner. "Look Kopplemann, I didn't like what they did to that poor S.O.B. any more than you did. I'll see that in my head for a long time to come. It made me sick. But no, I'll not co-sign a complaint against any of them. That would make my life worthless, and there would be hell to pay with the rest of that platoon."

Tom turned away from Kopplemann and was about to grab his bag, but instead he spun around, grabbed Kopplemann by the shirt and pushed him up against the barracks wall.

"You need to think, Walt. Everyone around here knows about what happened over at Bien Hoa. Word travels fast around here. These guys may appreciate you as a medic because you may have to save their sorry asses. But on the other hand, they would just as soon toss you out the chopper the same as that V.C. kid. Now, I volunteered to work with you, and I will. But you best understand what you're up against, or you may get us both killed. Do you understand me?" Tom yelled, as he shook Kopplemann.

Totally caught off guard by Tom's actions, Kopplemann nodded his head. "Yeah, yeah I got you Kenrude. But one thing does not change. I'll not carry a weapon, and I will not take the life of another human being. No one can make me do that, not now, not ever. Do you understand me?"

Leaving go of Kopplemann, Tom stood silent for a moment. "Yeah, alright. Let's leave it there and get some sleep."

Tom's message had definitely sunk into Kopplemann's mind. Over the next six weeks, he kept his mouth shut while doing his job to the best of his ability. He avoided confrontations at any cost, and pretty much kept to himself between missions. In a way, Tom felt bad for the man, but knew full well his attitude that night could have resulted in both of their deaths.

Never once did Tom waver on his support for Kopplemann, or his willingness to serve with him, until another mission where they were to follow Special Forces operatives into battle again.

After being debriefed on the mission, Tom turned to Lt. Jurgins. "Sir, I'm not sure Kopplemann should go with me. He really pissed off these guys on that last mission. I don't think it would take much for one of them to put a bullet in his head. If possible, I would like to choose someone else to take his place. That's just my opinion, sir."

Lt. Jurgins looked squarely at Tom. "Kenrude, you're a first rate medic and a good soldier. I trust your instincts, and believe your opinion is well placed. Nevertheless, Kopplemann in my book is no different than you when it comes to a mission. He'll go with you, and there will be no argument about it. Do I make myself clear?"

Tom nodded his head. "Yes sir, understood."

As Tom prepared his equipment for the mission, Kopplemann walked over to his bunk.

"Taking your sidearm and your rifle? What's up with that? I haven't seen you take both of them with you for a while."

After slamming a magazine into the rifle, Tom took a deep breath. "Just a feeling, that's all. I want to be prepared."

Glaring at Tom, Kopplemann replied. "And you feel that I should be doing the same?"

"No, that's not my feeling or desire for you. You have to do what's right for you, I told you that about six weeks ago. I just have a feeling that this time out, I may need the weapons. I'd rather be safe than sorry," Tom replied, sliding his sidearm into his holster. "Let's go. They're waiting for us."

Tom was totally surprised, but none of the Special Forces men said a word about Kopplemann assisting them on their mission. Although some of them gave him menacing looks, they kept quiet.

After a thirty minute flight to the west, all three choppers descended onto a field covered in grass about two feet high. Immediately, the men jumped from the choppers, allowing them to take off. Lt. Stevens pointed at the big sergeant that had tossed the V.C. out the door. Without saying a word, he began moving toward a tree line about two hundred yards away. It was eerily quiet as the men moved forward at a slow run. Arriving at the edge of the tree line, the sergeant placed his arms straight out from his body. The rest of the men formed a long line before kneeling down. Moments later the sergeant waved his hand in the air and the men moved cautiously forward. Tom hated the jungle, especially the thick triple canopy like this was. It was dark and smelled of rotting vegetation, and whatever else was decaying on the dark steaming jungle floor. The smell gagged Tom, but he refused to let it get the better of him.

Nearly fifty yards into the jungle, Tom understood what made the odor so bad. They came across nearly twenty V.C. bodies in various stages of decomposition. Flies and other assorted bugs crawled in and out of the rotting bodies. It took only seconds before Kopplemann began vomiting and knelt down on the ground.

"Get up, Kopplemann. If they see you like this they're apt to slit your throat and leave you with these bodies," Tom whispered in his ear.

After taking a quick drink from his canteen, Kopplemann rose to his feet nodding his head. The flies were so thick Tom had a hard time breathing without sucking the little bastards into his mouth or nose. He had never seen so many huge flies in his entire life.

Walking another fifty yards they came across a small stream that flowed north to south. The men stopped and knelt down as the sergeant whispered a directive to the two men to his right. Cautiously, they crossed the stream before disappearing into the dense jungle on the far side. Moments later they returned, signaling the platoon forward. A short time later the Sergeant signaled the men to stop and kneel.

The soldier to Tom's left crawled forward a short distance before returning. Lt. Stevens and the sergeant conversed with him for a few moments, before the sergeant once again signaled the platoon forward.

They entered an area in the jungle that had been completely cleared of vegetation. It had seen a lot of foot traffic, most of it coming from the east and north. The special ops team went to work searching the ground carefully with their bayonets. After several minutes of probing, three men signaled to the sergeant they had found what they were looking for. Two men cleared away brush that camouflaged entrances to tunnels. The third man found a large hollowed out area full of weapons, ammunition and explosives.

Lt. Stevens smiled at their find, as he signaled the sergeant and several other men over to him. After a quick conversation, two of the soldiers dropped their packs, took out their pistols and proceeded down into the dark tunnels.

Tom had heard of tunnel rats since arriving in Vietnam, but he had never met one. These guys had more guts than anyone else on earth. They would crawl through tunnels with just a flash light, pistol and bayonet for close in fighting, as they searched for enemy activity.

The first tunnel rat was back in seconds, explaining to Lt. Stevens what he had found. Quickly, the soldier picked up a satchel full of explosives and dropped back down into the tunnel. The second tunnel rat came back, bleeding from his arm. Tom raced forward, setting him down on the ground. After cleaning the wound he quickly bandaged the deep knife cut, as the soldier explained to Lt. Stevens what happened.

"There were three of them, sir. I shot one, but the second man dropped down on me from a type of shelf. He's the one that stabbed me, causing me to drop my flashlight. Luckily I was able to shoot him in the gut. The third son-of-a-bitch nailed me in the face with his fist. He disappeared with my flashlight. I don't know where he went or what's down there. Never found anything but solid tunnel walls."

Lt. Stevens directed two more men with explosives to enter the tunnels as other soldiers prepared charges in the weapons cache. After a very long half hour, all the charges were prepared, and everyone was accounted for. Kneeling down, Lt. Stevens checked his watch before signaling for his sergeant to join him. They spoke for several moments before Lt. Stevens signaled his forces to withdraw back toward the landing zone.

Moments after crossing back over the stream, the jungle was rocked by several massive explosions.

Lieutenant Stevens smiled, knowing they had completed their mission, costing the V.C. a hefty price. But he had no way of knowing what was waiting for them. About halfway out of the jungle, an undetermined number of V.C. ambushed the retreating Special Forces team. Bullets whizzed overhead, slamming into trees all around the Green Berets. Wounded men screamed on both sides as the fire fight was ferocious.

Tom crawled forward toward the first man he saw withering in pain. He had been struck by two rounds, one in the leg and the other in his shoulder. As Tom worked on the soldier he observed a second man down just a few feet away, his head covered in blood. Completing his work on the first soldier, Tom crawled toward his second patient.

The special ops man looked up at Tom. "What the fuck, Doc? What the hell happened?"

Tom could see the bullet had entered the soldier's right cheek, glanced off his jaw bone, exiting out his left eye socket. A second and third bullet tore open his abdomen. Quickly, Tom attempted to stem the bleeding, but the damage was intense. Just as he was preparing another battle dressing for the abdominal wound, the brush in front of him began to move.

Without hesitation, Tom grabbed his M-16 and rolled to the side.

Three Viet Cong rushed forward, the last one taking a moment to bayonet Tom's patient in the throat. But that was as far as he got, as a quick volley of fire from Tom's weapon dropped him to the ground. The lead V.C. hadn't seen Tom as he raced forward. Hearing the sound of gunfire behind him, he instinctively turned to see what was happening.

That became his fateful mistake, as Tom let go two rounds, striking him in the head. The second V.C. disappeared into the jungle to Tom's left. Before he could get up off the ground he heard a shrill scream. Without thinking of his own safety, Tom jumped up, racing in the direction of the sound. He found Kopplemann nearly disemboweled as the V.C. soldier continued stabbing him. Tom fired several rounds into the Viet Cong's back as he rushed forward. Kneeling down by Kopplemann's lifeless body, he shook his head.

"Why the hell didn't you listen to anyone? What the hell, Walt? What were you trying to prove?" Taking his hand, he gently closed Kopplemann's eyes.

As Tom picked up Kopplemann's bag, the battle was breaking off. He found Lt. Stevens standing beside several wounded men needing assistance about thirty feet away.

"Where the hell is Kopplemann?" The lieutenant barked angrily.

"He's dead, sir," Tom replied, as he knelt down to help out the first patient.

Nothing more was said as Tom finished treating the wounded. Lt. Stevens appointed several men to load their four dead men into body bags, as he called in their choppers. As the Huey's set down about fifty feet from the edge of the jungle, Tom helped a man with a serious leg wound move toward the L.Z.

The flight back to Binh Thuy felt different than it ever had before. Tom had now witnessed two good medics being killed on missions. Although this loss really hurt, he knew it could have been avoided if Kopplemann would have carried a weapon, and would have been willing to use it.

As usual, medics with gurneys waited at the hospital for their arrival. They made quick work of getting the wounded inside for further treatment. After all the patients were rolled into the hospital, Tom turned to leave.

"Hey Kenrude," the big sergeant called out as he walked up to him. "You did well out there. You're a good medic. I saw what you tried to do for Belmont before the V.C. arrived. That was good work. But as for your partner, well, it's a good thing he's gone. We didn't need a morale killer like him soiling our ranks."

Before he could say another word, Tom dropped his bag on the ground before landing a solid blow to the sergeant's face.

"I don't give a shit about what you've done here or who you think you are, but that man was a medic. He saved lives every mission we went on. Today he made a bad mistake, he should have had a weapon. But he was still a man that deserved better then what he got, and I don't appreciate your holier than thou judgmental attitude!"

The sergeant looked at Tom for several seconds before responding.

"Yeah, maybe you're right. But I heard what happened at Bien Hoa and—"

Tom cut him off. "It doesn't much matter anymore, does it? He's dead, your free from a yellow bastard, his family will have a funeral to plan and the war goes on. Stick it, sergeant."

Walking up to the operations office, Tom felt like vomiting. He didn't want to face Lt. Jurgins to inform him of the loss of Koppelmann, but he had no choice in the matter. Just as he approached the door, lieutenant Jurgins was exiting. He stopped as he took a long look at Tom.

"What happened, Kenrude? I can tell by your face this isn't good."

Tom shook his head before looking up to make eye contact with his boss. "Kopplemann is dead, sir. We were attacked by three V.C. as we were attending wounded. I killed two almost immediately, but one got away. When I heard Kopplemann scream, I knew where the man had gone.

When I arrived, it was too late to save him. We brought him back, his body went straight to the morgue. If he'd had a weapon—"

Lt. Jurgins cut Tom off in mid-sentence. "Yeah, I know the drill, Kenrude. If he would have had a weapon he most likely would not have been killed. That was his choice, nothing we can do about it. Go get cleaned up and get some rest. You're off the call duty roster the rest of today."

Tom sat quietly on his bunk with his recorder in hand, ready to tape a message to Mackenzie, but nothing came to mind. All he saw in his head was the torn up body of his partner, and the V.C. being tossed from the chopper. He couldn't talk about those things. No one ever needed to know the horrors of this war. It would be impossible for them to ever understand how their sons were being changed forever. Returning his recorder back to his foot locker, Tom sat on the edge of his bed. He vowed to finish medical school when he returned home and to be the best doctor possible so he could somehow make up for all the violence and death he was seeing each day. It was not much to ease the pain that tortured his soul right now, but it seemed like a beginning.

CHAPTER 11
MACKENZIE'S SECOND THOUGHTS

With the first rays of a new dawn peeking through Mackenzie's curtains, she rolled over in bed once more after a long night of fitful sleep. Looking over toward her night stand, she gazed upon a photo of Tom in his dress green uniform, which sat beside a photo of the two of them together down at Eagle Lake. She reached over, picking up the photo of them by the lake. Slowly, she ran her fingers over the photo and smiled.

"Where are you my love? Are you safe today?" She whispered softly.

Placing the photo down over her chest she closed her eyes, trying to remember all that happened that wonderful summer day, just before Tom left for basic training. What was it he had said that made her laugh after she climbed out on the rocks with him? She felt frustrated when the memory of that day fell short of her expectations. She longed to have Tom next to her just for a moment, so she could hold him tight in her arms. There was nothing in the world that made her happier than being married to Tom and she felt blessed knowing she might be pregnant.

Tears began streaming down her soft cheeks as the pain of loss filled her heart. Once more a feeling of guilt gripped her soul, as it had several times since Tom had departed. Did she make the wrong decision agreeing with him to join the Army? Was it going to be her fault if anything happened to him? Would Karen and Steve blame her for the rest of her life if Tom failed to return?

Mackenzie jumped up in bed holding the photo in her hands, pressing it tight against her. This wasn't the way it was supposed to be, or at least she'd thought it would be different somehow. But each day of separation from her husband brought on new fears she found extremely hard to handle.

After getting dressed and having a cup of coffee, she looked around the small dorm room that appeared to be getting smaller each time she looked around. Suddenly she was angry and regretted enrolling in the summer semester. She could have been home in Glendale working in the garden, or volunteering in the hospital. Nothing appeared to be under control in her life, and she longed to be near someone who loved and cared for her. Grabbing her keys, Mackenzie headed down the stairs to the sidewalk in front of her building.

She stood near the curb sucking in copious amounts of fresh air. After a moment, she looked around the usually bustling street. However it was fairly quiet for a Saturday morning. Slowly she made her way across the wide boulevard to a small park that had comfortable benches near several well-groomed flower beds.

For several minutes she watched three squirrels chase each other around a large oak tree. She had to laugh as the first squirrel stopped dead in his tracks, causing the other two to run into each other and flip over. In an instant they scurried up the tree, disappearing into the heavy green foliage.

Arriving at the far end of the park, Mackenzie turned left heading toward a small coffee shop many of her friends frequented. Passing by the huge glass window, her best friend Anna Marie jumped up from her seat to bang on the window.

As Mackenzie entered the coffee shop, Anna Marie Morgan ran up to hug her. "Where have you been the last couple of days? The gang has missed you. Are you alright?"

Mackenzie nodded as she smiled at her friend. "I'm fine, just a little down. I turned in my papers for our biology and pharmaceutical classes on Thursday. Then I went to the lecture at the surgical school Thursday night, instead of yesterday. I just needed some time to think, but I'm not sure it did any good. I keep coming back to the same conclusion over and over."

Anna Marie led her over to a large table where three other girlfriends were seated. "Do you want to tell us what the problem is?" Anna inquired, as she studied Mackenzie's face.

Sitting down, Mackenzie stared at the table for a moment. "I don't know if I should have agreed with Tom so fast about enlisting in the Army. I'm not sure I did the right thing. He is over there getting shot at, and going through some really terrible things. He tries to play it off on his tapes, but I can tell by his words that it's really affecting him. He seems down, and there's not a thing I can do about it now."

Sarah Clausen, who originally roomed with Mackenzie when she started school, spoke up.

"Honey, no matter what you said to Tom, he really had his mind made up already. I don't think you could have talked him out of it, unless maybe you had already been pregnant or really sick at that particular time."

Everyone at the table laughed as the waiter came over to check on any new orders.

Mackenzie smiled at Sarah. "Well, the first issue was out of the question since we weren't even married yet, and thank God I've not been critically sick. But I do know where you're coming from. I just think maybe I should have talked him out of it, or at least tried. He wouldn't have been upset with me, as he always wants me to say what's on my mind. Right now this entire situation feels like it's on my shoulders. I think I should go home next weekend and talk with Mom. Maybe then I'll feel better. She is the wisest woman I have ever met. I can't talk to Karen, because she'll just agree with me that everything is my fault. I can't deal with another screaming match with her right now."

After the waiter brought Mackenzie her coffee, Anna Marie spoke up. "Now let's talk shop or guys or something else. We all need to decompress after this past week."

The following week Mackenzie buried herself in school work and hospital rounds in order to keep busy. When Friday afternoon rolled around, she left St. Paul heading home to Glendale.

Saturday morning, she drove toward the Kenrude home, even though she had told her girlfriends she couldn't speak with Karen. She slowed for a moment on the road before entering the driveway, remembering full well the screaming match that took place the day Tom announced he was joining the Army. And again when he was preparing to leave. She wondered how Karen would respond to the news that she was now having second thoughts. In a way, she was terrified to bring up the subject, but for some reason it felt like something she had to do.

Just as Mackenzie was about to climb the steps to the back door, Karen came walking out with some letters to place in the mailbox.

"Well Mac, what are you doing here? We didn't think we would see you until semester break. Is everything alright?" Surprisingly, Karen stepped forward, giving her a hug. "Give me just a minute to put these letters in the mailbox, then we can talk until the cows come home. I have a fresh pot of coffee on that should be just about ready."

Sitting at the kitchen table, Karen poured out two cups of steaming coffee. "So Mac, what can I do for you, is everything alright?"

After taking a drink of coffee, Mackenzie looked intently at Karen. "I'm not sure how you're going to take this. But I'm seriously having second thoughts about backing Tom's decision to join the army. All his arguments sounded good and proper, and I know he wasn't very happy with school the last few months. His plans caught me totally by surprise, but at the same time, it all made sense to me. I love him with all my heart, and I only wanted to be supportive. So now I question if I made a bad choice, and it scares the hell out of me."

Mackenzie shook inside as she awaited Karen's response, she was not sure what to expect.

Karen sat motionless for several moments as she mulled over everything Mackenzie had just said. After taking a deep breath, she smiled slightly at Mackenzie.

"Sweetheart, I have never been able to come to grips with that God awful decision he made. But, when I read his letters, it always sounds like he's happy doing what he signed up for. I can tell you it scares the hell out of me every blessed day, not knowing what's happening to my boy, and it royally pisses me off. Steve and I have had so many conversations regarding you and Tom. I know I haven't acted like it very much, but I do love you, Mac, and I'm beyond excited that we're possibly going to have a grandchild. It's just that it's been so hard on me to have to worry about another loved one being in combat. Honestly Mac, I don't think there was anything you could have done to change my son's mind. He's like his dad, uncle and grandfather. He is a Kenrude, stubborn from stem to stern." After laughing for a moment, Karen continued.

"There's no doubt that Tom had his mind made up before he spoke with you. No matter what you would have said against his decision, he would have gone. He told me in a letter when he was in basic training that he didn't want to lose you, but he had to make you understand it was the best thing for him. I know it took me a while to accept his decision, but I have, and now I have to trust in God. There was absolutely nothing you could have done to change his mind. Nothing."

Stopping to take a sip of coffee, Karen took a breath and continued, while Mac sat there, stunned at this turn of events.

"Mac, your heart was in the right place, and still is, or you wouldn't be here baring your soul to me of all people. Our family totally accepts you, and always will. You are a Kenrude woman, like it or not, and that comes from the heart."

As Mackenzie wiped at the tears streaming down her cheeks she squeezed Karen's hand.

"I've told my friends about the problems we've had in the past, but I've also always told them what a very special person you are, and how much I'd rather be your friend than your enemy. I know you're a very understanding woman who cares very deeply about your family. I just hope you'll always accept me and the baby we may have, no matter what happens in the future."

Karen smiled. "You always have been accepted into this family, honey. I've just not truly shown you how I felt. Sometimes anger can be a devastating thing and we just don't realize it. Mac, you are a very understanding and caring woman yourself. That is one of the virtues Tom sees in you, and Steven and I see it too. That's what will make you such a great nurse, a fantastic wife and an amazing mother, you'll see. Now, let me go get that letter from basic training so you can take it with you and read it. I know right where it is."

Returning, she handed Mackenzie several letters. "Actually, you should read all of these. They will give you true perspective and ease those fears you have forever."

Taking the letters from Karen, Mac placed them in her purse. "I'll guard them with my life and get them back to you before I head back tomorrow."

"No, I want you to hang on to them a while so you can reread them. Or you can make copies, whatever you decide to do. But they are important for you to read and understand," Karen explained.

After several more minutes of conversation, Mackenzie left the Kenrude home feeling relieved and happy. She really felt accepted by Karen, and now hoped they could be close the rest of their lives, although there was still a nagging doubt in her mind regarding Karen's hidden feelings.

Sunday morning after church services, Mac observed Alex and Nancy

Kenrude, Tom's grandparents, walking toward the coffee shop. Turning toward her mother Edna, she looked at her expectantly.

"Mom, do you think the Kenrude's would mind if we joined them?"

"No honey, I don't think they would mind one bit," Edna replied.

Entering the coffee shop, Mackenzie walked up to Nancy. "Would you mind if Mom and I joined you for your morning coffee.

"Absolutely not, honey. Come on over here and sit down, both of you," Nancy responded, as she pulled another chair over to the table. "I hear you were over to see Karen yesterday. She told me all about your conversation. Believe me Mac, Karen is right, Tom had his mind made up long before he spoke with you. Like father, like son. It's just taken Karen a long time to come to grips with it, and it hasn't been easy for her. We've discussed all of this, during many heart to heart conversations. I can tell the difference in her since she has begun accepting everything. And Mac, she really loves you very much. But enough of that, we're not going to beat a dead horse on such a lovely Sunday morning. It's all well and good, as it should be. So, how is school going?" Nancy asked warmly.

"Things are good, but they keep us busy. I'm learning a lot, although I do wish I hadn't signed up for summer semester. It's been really tough on me the last month or so, but I know it will get me to graduation a bit faster, so that's good. I keep wondering what I will do If I'm pregnant. I'm just not sure about all that yet." Mackenzie replied smiling.

"Yes, I remember when Christine went to nursing school," Alex said, shaking his head. "Sometimes she would come home totally exhausted needing a break from it all. But look at her today. She's a wonderful nurse and it was all worthwhile."

After leaving the coffee shop, Mac and her mother strolled along Main Street for several blocks before Edna spoke. "How long can you keep up your schedule? Eventually, you'll have to drop out of school, you know. All that stress is not good for you, or the baby if you really are pregnant. You need to think about that, and make it a priority."

Mackenzie peered into the plate glass window of Gordon's Flower Shop for a moment. "I know, Mother. Believe me, I know I am going to have to make some serious decisions. Tom would like to see me quit right now. But I just can't do that. I need to finish the semester or all the grades I've been working for won't count. I'm kind of stuck between a rock and a hard place right now."

Edna looked back down the street toward the church as she thought about it. "That makes sense, but honey, I think you should decide that school is over at the end of this semester. Otherwise you'll be in the same boat should you have no choice to quit mid-semester. Then you can move back home as we all talked about. Tom would be very happy about that, too."

Mackenzie smiled at her mother. "You always know what's best for me and how to say it. Most often there's no way I can argue with you, as everything you say is based on logic."

Taking Mackenzie by the hand, Edna continued walking back toward the church. Arriving near their car, she asked a question she'd been wondering about for some time.

"Honey, what have you and Tom thought about doing when he finishes medical school? Is he planning to work in the hospital here, start his own practice, or work down at the university? Any thoughts on the issue?"

Mackenzie leaned against the trunk as she gazed at her mother. "Tom would like to either come here, or maybe go up to St. Cloud, since they have that big hospital up there. He says the St. Cloud area is growing, so the hospital will have to grow with it. I don't really want to live in the Minneapolis area, so I'm hoping for the first two. But then again, he can use the G.I. bill to finish medical school, so there might be a chance he will want to be an army doctor. I kind of like that idea too, and we could live all over the world. I would like to live in Germany and travel around Europe, so I guess I could be happy with that as well. I've always told Tom all I needed was him and a mud hut."

Edna laughed as she unlocked the doors. "Now that's what I call true love."

On Monday morning, since Mackenzie did not have classes, she went to the Glendale Clinic for a checkup. She had felt different over the last two months so she wanted to confirm her suspicions that she was pregnant. After the doctor announced she was in fact pregnant, she screamed with delight. Immediately, she drove around Glendale informing family members of the good news. Mackenzie was proud to announce that if the baby was a boy, he would be called Sean Thomas Kenrude.

CHAPTER 12
THE MOVE NORTH

Sunday morning came much too early for Tom's liking. It had been a long miserable night for him, as Koppelmann's death weighed heavily on his mind. It almost appeared as if it was inevitable, since no one wanted to be around him. No one trusted him. It almost appeared as if Walt was trying to prove a point as well, a point that eventually was going to get him killed. So now there was nothing more to talk about, no one had to argue about serving with him, he was gone, plain and simple, and everyone would be alright with it. A precious but troubled human life swept from this earth forever, and no one here was going to grieve for him. Just send up the next contestant from the audience to play another round of, 'See Who gets Killed Today.'

After breakfast, Tom walked over to the chapel to see if Father Neederman was available. Just as Tom was about to enter, the tall thin priest came walking out wearing his vestments.

"Are you Father Neederman?" Tom inquired.

"Yes, I am, can I help you?" he replied with a smile.

"Yes sir, I'm Tom Kenrude. You served with my dad in Korea, Sgt. Steve Kenrude," Tom explained.

"My goodness, yes. I'm so glad to meet you, Tom. I heard a lot about you from your father and Sgt. Major Doogan. We shared a lot about our families when we were in Korea. It always felt good to leave the war behind for a while, as we talked about home. Your father was a good leader, he really looked out for his men. So Thomas, what can I do for you today?"

Tom hesitated for a moment before telling the priest about Koppelmann, and how the other men seemed to despise him. Then continued with how he died, and what was going through his own head today.

After listening intently to everything Tom had to say, Fr. Neederman nodded his head. "I knew all about Walter, in fact, I spoke with him when he first arrived. He was a very troubled soul, a draftee that should never have been sent here. I do believe his conscientious objector status was real, and not something he made up to avoid combat. Back in World War Two, many people of the Quaker religion held the same status, and served proudly in many non-combat capacities. His problems began long before he arrived here, and unfortunately, his reputation followed him. I was sorry to hear he was killed, but I'm not surprised that it happened. Walter would never lift a hand against another human being for any reason. Truly, that is a marvelous but rare virtue. So Thomas, what do you need of me today?"

"I don't really know. Peace of mind maybe, and I think you already explained that pretty well. I'm still kind of angry about the way the men treated him and bad mouthed him. I liked Walt, he was a good guy."

Fr. Neederman looked skyward as an F-4 flew past. "Men in combat, including medics, look out for each other, and are willing to do whatever it takes to stay safe, and keep their buddies alive. When someone like Walter comes along, it scares them. They can't understand, and in most cases, they don't attempt to understand why anyone who thought the way Walter did, would be in a combat zone in the first place. They actually may feel their safety is threatened by him. It's hard to know what's in a man's soul when he goes face to face with death every day. I have been there, and I can't even explain it for myself."

"Yeah, I think I understand, Father. It still hurts to have seen him get killed like that. He had every opportunity to defend himself, it just hurts me that he didn't try," Tom replied, shaking his head.

"Death always hurts, no matter the situation, but adding the complexities of one's faith to the brutalities of war creates a crisis of conscience within most men," Fr. Neederman explained.

"That makes good sense, Father," Tom responded. "Well I guess I better make my way over to operations to see what's happening today. Thanks for talking this morning, it meant a lot to me. I'll let Dad know I ran into you. He'll be happy to know you're doing well," Tom added with a smile.

"You are most welcome, Thomas. Don't be a stranger, you know God will let you into my services no matter your faith. Also, did you know Master Sergeant Doogan is stationed here? He's also a very good man to talk to when things are bothering you. I can speak from experience, we have spoken several times since he arrived," Fr. Neederman stated as he shook hands with Tom.

Feeling much better now, Tom walked over to the operations office to see if anyone had been assigned to take Kopplemann's position yet. Everyone knew two medics from Westward Ho had been killed in short order. The way things happened in Vietnam, he was sure most medics would begin thinking the Westward Ho crew was jinxed, and would want not part of it.

Tom found Geno Sarducci speaking with First Sgt. Shills when he entered the office. "Just in time, Kenrude," Sgt. Shills called out. "Sarducci would like to leave Squadron Four and take over Koppelmann's spot with Warrant Officer Westhaven. You guys have worked together before, any problems with it?"

Smiling, Tom responded. "No, that would be great, I enjoy working with Geno. Who will you put in his spot?"

"Grissom wants out of the hospital in the worst way. The doctor says he's fit to return back to flight status, so he'll gladly fill that position."

Before the men could walk off, Sgt. Shills called them back. "Don't go too far. The Battalion Commander has an important announcement to make shortly, and it'll affect you guys.

About fifteen minutes later, Col. Hernandez entered the office along with Capt. Trajillio, and the Commanders of the other three squadrons. "We knew this was coming a week ago, we just weren't sure how it would affect us. The 101st airborne is planning a huge operation up near the A Shau Valley. They have requested rescue choppers from several detachments. We're sending all of Squadron One to help out, as well as two surgical teams from the hospital. We have no idea how long you'll be up there, or if in fact you'll be sent back here once the operation is completed. Get up there, do the job and be safe. God willing, you'll all come back here when the operation winds down." After looking over the crews, the Colonel departed without saying another word.

The following morning all four choppers from Squadron One, and a Chinook carrying the medical staff and equipment, flew north toward Quang Tri, to take up their new assignments.

Tom stared out the door toward the large mountains forming the spine of South Vietnam all the way to the DMZ and beyond. The dense triple canopied jungle valleys below were layered in thick rolling fog this morning, making them look terribly menacing. He was amazed at how many variations of green existed in those dangerous jungles, where death waited man at every turn.

Every so often, small hamlets with rice patties were visible in clearings, or along the dirty brown winding rivers that flowed through the dark valleys. This was the sacred home of the Viet Cong. Some were farmers by day, and terrorists by night, people who could never be trusted. They were on the side of whoever was winning, or whoever offered them the most to comply. Of course the constant threat of violence by the V.C. always won out.

The base at Quang Tri was much larger than Binh Thuy, but it was still subject to rocket and mortar attacks on a regular basis. Underground emergency shelters dotted the compound, while huge entanglements of concertina wire and observation towers encircled the very important base.

Here at Quang Tri, the men lived in tent structures that were dug down about three feet into the ground. The sides were built with boards to hold back the earth, while the top was made of thick green army canvas. The canvas sides could be rolled up to allow air to flow through the screen netting.

Capt. Trajillio called his men together once everyone was settled. "Tomorrow, we'll be expected to join the fight. We already know of an operation being put in place with the 101st Airborne. At 0600 Lt. Col. Fargo will explain the mission to us. I can tell you this for fact. The area we're going into is occupied by North Vietnamese Regular Army units, and the Viet Cong. This is not going to be a picnic by any means. Get some sleep tonight and be ready to go."

At 0600 the following morning, all the crews were assembled on the flight line. As the airborne troops began loading, Lt. Col Fargo walked over to the medical staff. "Good morning men, and welcome to Quang Tri. Today we are starting a campaign to wipe out enemy forces located in the A Shau Valley. This is not going to be an easy job. They have been operating out of that area for years, allowing them plenty of time to fortify their positions, set booby traps, dig tunnels and most of all know the terrain better than we can ever hope to. There are hundreds of tunnels that will need to be destroyed, along with gun emplacements and well-fortified bunkers dug into hill sides. Every major hill in the area will need to be taken, so we can use them for fire bases. Do your jobs and get my wounded men out of there as quickly as you can, as you know time equals survival."

When he finished his explanation, he walked among the crew shaking hands with each man. Arriving at Tom he looked at the name on his uniform. "Kenrude? Any relation to a Steven Kenrude from Minnesota?"

Tom nodded his head. "He's my father, sir."

"I'll be dammed. He was a great soldier and an all-around great guy. So how's he doing these days? Wait, first please reassure me that there are no relatives of Harry Jenson with you." Lt. Col Fargo said, with a smile.

"My dad's doing fine, sir. Doing what he loves best, farming. And no sir, there are none of Harry's family close by that I know of." Tom replied with a smile, feeling very comfortable talking with the Lt. Colonel.

After giving Tom a slap on the shoulder, he continued to make the rounds, shaking hands with the rest of the men.

At 0645, the humid morning air became alive with the sound of sixty spinning rotors. Tom could count twenty assault helicopters, six gunships, and their four medical choppers warming up.

Moments later, the swift Cobra gunships roared into the misty dawn followed by the assault choppers, with the air ambulances bringing up the rear. It was an incredible sight watching the armada form up before turning to the northeast.

Thick black smoke rose from the soon-to-be battle ground as Air Force F-4 Phantom fighter bombers, Naval A-6 Intruders and F-8 Crusaders, were already busy dropping heavy ordnance on suspected enemy positions.

At the same time, well placed American artillery continued firing salvos of high explosives on the heavily dug in enemy. However, Tom remembered his father telling him how often heavy bombardments before an attack were not always successful in destroying well entrenched forces.

Quickly five choppers peeled off to the right, heading straight for a mountain top. Five more dropped off to the left, flying toward a mountain plateau where black smoke rolled skyward The gunships had already dropped down to strafe an area around a grassy field where the last ten choppers were now headed.

The four air ambulances began circling to the west as they waited to see where they were going to be needed first, and it did not take long.

Rick Palmero yelled over the intercom. "Tally ho guys, we're going in."

The Huey dove for the valley floor at a tremendous speed as the runners under the chopper dragged against the tree tops. At the last second, Rick pulled the nose of the chopper up, allowing the rear of the chopper to set down first. Smoke rolled up from a burning Huey as mortar rounds slammed into the valley from every direction.

Tom dove from the chopper, running toward a combat medic that was waving at him. "I got three to go here. Two are real bad."

Tom knew full well that one man was not going to make it as his right arm and shoulder were gone and blood flowed from his mouth. The second man had a gaping abdominal wound with his intestines protruding. The third man had several bullet wounds in his legs and arms.

Eddie Lemieux grabbed the man with the bullet wounds, as Tom and the medic stretchered the other two men. In minutes Rick had the chopper airborne, racing back to the hospital, while Tom worked diligently, attempting to control the bleeding on both of his seriously injured patients without much luck.

The soldier with the abdominal injury grabbed Tom's arm. "Call my mom, tell her I need her, I need her bad. Tell her I'm sorry for getting hurt, you tell her that, Doc."

Nodding his head, Tom placed another battle dressing over the horrid wound. "We'll call her when we get to the hospital. You just hang in there, soldier."

With that, the man's hand slipped from Tom's arm as his eyes closed. Shaking his head he turned his attention to the man with the gunshots. He appeared to be doing fine with the bandaging the medic had done. Moments later the Huey slid to a stop near the hospital. Tom and Eddie helped unload the chopper as one of the corpsmen quickly hosed blood and debris from the chopper floor.

As Rick began his ascent back to the battlefield, Tom could see two more ambulances preparing to land at the hospital. It was going to be a rough day for everyone involved. This time as Rick aimed toward a mountain top on his left, two bullets came through the open door, striking a body support beam just inches from Eddie's head.

"Damn!" Eddie called out as he examined the embedded bullet. "Two more inches and I'd be a goner," he called out to Tom.

As Rick brought the chopper within feet of the ground, Tom and Eddie began to jump clear of the fat target with the big red cross on its side. Instantly, something struck the rear rotor, causing it to blow apart. High speed shrapnel from the disintegrating blades flew in all directions. Without the rotor, Rick could not control his massive machine. It gyrated out of control, spinning on its own axis, finally tipping over on it's right side. The huge blades from the main rotor slammed into the ground, sending more deadly shrapnel through the air. Tom and Eddie lay frozen in place, hoping all the flying debris would pass over them. Once the shower of helicopter parts ended, Tom and Eddie jumped back on their feet, racing over to the smoking wreck. Flames were beginning to rise from the engine cowling as fuel from the shattered tank began running on the ground.

Tom grabbed hold of the co-pilots door pulling it open, as Chuck was attempting to climb out of the tipped over wreckage. As soon as Tom handed him down to Eddie, he jumped into the cockpit where Rick was fighting with a jammed seat belt. Quickly Tom pulled out his surgical knife, cutting the belt away from the buckle.

"Come on Rick, give me your hand, this thing's going to blow!" Tom called out over the rage of battle that was taking place just yards away from them.

"My foot! My right foot is jammed. The seat broke lose, I can't get my foot out, Tom," Rick shouted as he once again attempted to pull his foot lose from the twisted metal.

Leaning over, Tom could see one of the floor supports had popped free, jamming Rick's foot. Grabbing hold of the piece of steel, Tom pulled on it with all his strength as he yelled out, "Pull, Rick. You got to pull harder, I can't move it any farther."

As Rick pulled and twisted, his boot finally popped lose. Grabbing Rick under the arms, Tom lifted him up onto the co-pilots seat, so he could shove him out the door. Flames were already licking through the roof of the chopper as Tom dropped down beside Rick. The two men ran toward Eddie and Chuck who had taken refuge behind another downed chopper about twenty yards away.

With a giant whoosh, Palmero's Pepperoni was engulfed in a giant fireball. Rick watched as his beloved Huey was reduced to a charred frame. "She was a good bird. Hope my next one is just as good. Think I'll name her Hot Pepperoni Two."

Eddie laughed as he placed his arm around Rick. "Big thing is Rick, you still got your crew."

Smiling at his flight engineer he nodded his head. "Thank God for that, Eddie, Thank God for that."

Rescue choppers continued picking up wounded from the mountain top, but were unable to take the four men back to the base, as there simply was no room for them, with all the injured soldiers needing evacuation. Tom and Eddie worked with the medics on the ground patching up the wounded men before loading them on to choppers. Rick and Chuck picked up weapons left behind by wounded men, providing cover fire for the medics as they worked.

The rage of battle began to die down on the mountain top around 1700hrs, as additional troops were delivered to the battle. As Eddie monitored several wounded men, Tom ran over toward a Corporal, who was crawling away from an open tunnel entrance on the north side of the embattled plateau. The man held out his hand as Tom slid down beside him.

"Damn Doc, I can't feel my legs. They just won't work. I don't know what the problem is," the Corporal cried out.

Tom did not need to investigate the problem, the answer was very clear to him. A large piece of shrapnel stuck out of the man's lower back, most likely severing the spinal cord. Rick ran over placing a stretcher beside the man, just as shots rang out over their heads. Both men dropped to the ground, hoping to evade the automatic machine gun fire.

Chuck came running forward, firing the M-16 he had picked up toward the open tunnel entrance. Dropping down to one knee behind Tom, Chuck covered his crew members until they were ready to remove the Corporal to safety. Just as the Viet Cong jumped up from his hole again, Chuck let go a long burst of fire. The man slid back down into the hole leaving a trail of blood behind him.

"Grenades. Grenades on my chest." The wounded corporal called out.

Rolling him over slightly, Rick was able to safely dislodge three grenades that were attached to his web gear. Running over to Chuck who was covering the hole, Rick pulled the pin from the first grenade, throwing it down the hole. Both men stood back as the grenade exploded. Running back toward the hole, Rick tossed both remaining grenades into the cave, before diving back out of the way. There were two explosions, followed by a much larger detonation that shook the north end of the plateau. Camouflaged covers blew off two more tunnel entrances nearby, as smoke and dust rolled skyward.

Chuck looked over at Rick. "What the hell did you hit?"

A stunned Rick Palmero looked toward his co-pilot, "How the hell would I know, you want me to crawl down there and check it out? Or maybe I could just ask the next V.C. we come across. Will that work for you Mr. Inquisitive?"

Both men laughed for a moment before jumping up to help Tom and Eddie with the wounded men they were attending to.

As dusk began settling over the plateau, only sporadic gunfire could be heard. The 101st had secured this important prominence, allowing artillery to be brought in the next day. That would be the first chance for Rick and his crew to get airlifted off the mountain. Tonight they would have to hunker down in fox holes, as there was little doubt the still dangerous and active enemy would be dropping mortars on them as they attempted to regain the plateau in the dark. Unfortunately, there was no barb wire, or anything else to build a safety perimeter to protect the scant American forces holding the plateau, that would all be arriving tomorrow.

Tom and Eddie began digging holes near one of the wrecked choppers, using it to protect their backs. Rick and Chuck scurried about picking up weapons, ammunition and C-Rations left behind by the wounded.

As darkness overtook the plateau, every man surviving the battle settled into their holes, hoping they were deep enough, and in the right spots. As expected, mortar rounds began slamming into the hill at intermittent intervals. Men screamed as hot slivers of shrapnel from exploding mortar rounds ripped into their bodies. However Captain Branigan from Baker Company, admonished the chopper crews to stay put in their holes. The enemy loved waiting a few minute between rounds, in hope of catching medics out in the open tending to the wounded. The tired medics assigned to the 101st worked bravely throughout the long night, trying to save the lives of men with the little equipment they had left.

Around midnight, a large group of Viet Cong struck the plateau after crawling up the north side of the mountain. They raced in every direction, throwing grenades and firing at anything that moved.

Rick quickly dropped two V.C. as they ran toward the wrecked chopper. Tom fired on another that approached from the east. Suddenly the men realized, the chopper wreckage was not going to be the safe haven they thought it would be, instead it had become a magnet for the attackers. Sadly, at this stage of the game, it was too late for the chopper crew to move anywhere else.

Out of the dark, a grenade landed about five feet from another stranded pilot dug in near Rick. Incredibly fast, Chuck jumped from his hole, grabbed the grenade, and tossed it back out into the darkness, as bullets slammed into the metal skin of the chopper.

Flame from the exploding grenade allowed the men so see about a dozen V.C. moving up onto the plateau from the mountain side. Everyone dug in near the chopper opened up, spraying the area with automatic weapons fire. Earlier during the evening, Eddie had stored a grenade he picked up in his medical bag, for just such a situation. After pulling the pin, he tossed it as hard as he could, in the direction of the attackers. Screams of pain filled the dark night as bullets and shrapnel from the grenade found targets.

After several more minutes of battle, Rick told them to cease fire. All around the plateau, the battle appeared to be slacking off, but no one was willing to bet the end was near.

As the sound of running feet approached from the east, everyone once again answered with full automatic fire, although they could not be sure they were hitting anyone. Suddenly another grenade bounced off the side of the chopper, landing just inches in front of their position. Once again Chuck jumped from his hole, grabbed the grenade and prepared to toss it back. Just as he let go of the deadly weapon, it exploded. Shrapnel bounced off the chopper as Eddie and Chuck screamed in pain.

"Go, help them," Rick called out as he continued firing.

Tom maneuvered his way over to Chuck first, who was half out of his hole. "How you doing Warrant Officer?"

"Not so damn good, Kenrude. I think my flying days are over," he explained while holding up his right arm minus his hand.

Quickly, Tom placed a tourniquet on the wrist before giving him a shot of morphine. "Where else are you hit?" Tom inquired, as two bullets slammed into the metal behind him.

"My right side, it hurts like hell, doc. What the hell?"

Turning their brave wounded co-pilot over onto his left side, it was clear to see a large piece of shrapnel sticking out of his ribs. Shaking his head, Tom went to work placing a large battle dressing around Chuck's abdomen, securing the shrapnel in place to prevent any major bleeding.

"Lay still, Warrant Officer, the morphine will kick in real soon. That's all I can do for you right now, I have to go check on Eddie," Tom explained, as he began to move toward his injured friend.

"How you doing Eddie, where ya hit?" Tom inquired, as he watched Rick slam another magazine into his weapon.

"My right leg, it burns like hell, Tom." Eddie replied, as he continued firing.

Looking down at Eddie's leg he could see a piece of metal sticking out of his upper thigh, but there was not much bleeding. "Okay Eddie, I see it. You have a hunk of shrapnel in your thigh. It must have been hot when it hit, it appears to have cauterized most of the blood vessels around it. We can't take it out here or you might bleed like a stuck hog. I'll wrap it up and let the doctors deal with it when we get back in the morning."

"You mean *if* we get back, don't you, Kenrude? I don't think we'll survive the night," Eddie yelled back.

Tom grabbed him by the shirt, looking directly into his eyes. "Shut up, Eddie. We'll get out of here in the morning. You'll be just fine, but Chuck doesn't need to hear your negativity. He's in tough shape," Tom screamed back.

After checking on Chuck once more, Tom took his place back in his hole, picking up his weapon. Thankfully, the fighting had almost died off.

Looking down at his watch, Tom was stunned to see it was almost 0500, so dawn would shed it's beautiful light on this plateau of death before long. He couldn't believe how fast the night had actually gone.

As the sun broke over the mountains to the east, Tom, Rick and the four other men that had dug in with them climbed out of their holes and scanned the battlefield. All around them, bodies of black clad Viet Cong lay in grotesque shapes where they had fallen. Some were torn open by grenades, while others had been ripped apart by heavy weapons fire. Within a half hour, rescue choppers began arriving on the plateau. Tom and one other man took hold of Chuck, as Rick pulled Eddie to his feet.

"I'm not going home, Rick. No way in hell am I leaving this crew," Eddie barked as he hobbled toward one of the choppers.

As Rick slid him onto the chopper floor, he smiled. "Let's see how you come out of this. If possible, I'll pull some strings with the old man to keep you here if that's what you want."

Eddie nodded his head, giving his pilot a thumbs up as the chopper began to climb.

Tom helped out where he could until around 1000hrs, when he and Rick finally climbed aboard an army assault chopper for the flight back to Quang Tri.

Upon landing, Tom ran toward the hospital to see how Eddie and Chuck were doing.

Inside the hospital he ran into Roxy, who had come along with the surgical teams. "Eddie and the Warrant Officer, how are they doing?" Tom asked, nearly out of breath.

"Eddie will be fine. We took two pieces of shrapnel out of his leg while putting in fifteen stitches. We'll hold him over night and he can go on light duty tomorrow if that's what he wants. But Warrant Officer Johnson, he'll be going to a rear hospital for more surgery on his arm. We did all we could for him here. You did a good job wrapping his abdomen and securing that hunk of metal. He has a broken rib and ten stitches, but for sure, that will be the least of his future problems. He's in recovery, so you'll have to come back later if you want to see him. He will most likely be on the evac flight at 0700 in the morning."

Walking back to his tent, Tom ran into Moe. "Wow, Kenrude, that must have been one hell of a night out there on that mountain top. Then seeing two of your guys getting busted up right in front of you had to be real tough. We helped evac three loads before we ran into a fuel leak on our bird. I couldn't believe what I saw on that plateau from the air. You were lucky, my friend."

Tom nodded his head. "It was quite a night and I hope I don't have to do that again real soon. All I want to do now is get a shower, a hot meal and a clean uniform before we go back."

Moe looked intently at Tom. "Go back! Are you crazy, don't go looking for trouble if you can help it. Our bird is down until tomorrow, I see that as a good deal, plus you lost your co-pilot and chopper, do you think those things grow on trees?"

Tom forced a slight smile. "No, they don't. But I'm sure Lt. Jurgins is already on it. I'm going to check with him before I get showered. Moe, we need to get out there to help get those guys that are in tough shape, if we don't, who will?"

Walking into the operations office, Tom observed the lieutenant talking with Rick Palmero. After a moment Lt. Jurgins called Tom over to his desk.

"Kenrude, you look beat. I have a chopper that Warrant Officer Palmero can take over, and a co-pilot that's waiting for a crew. He is Warrant Officer Two Gus Brady, and we have a flight engineer by the name of Tim Stewart that can help out until Lemieux is back in action. The chopper isn't ready yet, so why don't you grab some chow, get a shower and be ready in about two hours. I know you're all tired, but we need to get these evacs back on line in a big damn hurry."

Tom nodded his head. "I'll be ready to go by then, sir, not a problem."

Rick Palmero walked up to Tom. "You did real good out there last night, Kenrude. You proved yourself to me in many ways. I'll have the chopper by the hospital, you can meet us there."

After a shower and a hot meal, Tom sat by himself in the mess tent finishing his coffee. Reaching for his cup, Tom felt a slight tremor in his hand. Quickly he pulled his arm back as he stared at his shaking hand. Instantly he realized both his hands were shaking. Closing his eyes, Tom took several deep breaths hoping that would help calm his nerves. Just as he was about to open his eyes, a voice made him jump.

Geno Sarducci was just preparing to sit down across from him with a full tray of food.

"Taking a power nap, Tom? That crap never works for me, I need to be in bed with a pillow and a good amount of quiet in order to sleep, something that is totally lacking around here."

Tom smiled at his friend before taking another look at his hands that were solid as a rock once more.

"So, what's happening with you guys? I heard you almost went down on your last run back here." Tom inquired

Geno nodded his head as he began making a sandwich from the roast beef on his tray.

"Yeah, we had a bullet strike part of the hydraulic system. It was a hard landing to be sure. We should be ready to make at least one more run before it gets dark. How about you, heard your bird is gone and your crew was shot up."

Tom's right hand began shaking slightly as he began to speak.

"Yeah. Warrant Officer Johnson lost a hand, Eddie stopped a bunch of shrapnel, and the chopper is burnt to a crisp. But we have a new bird and new crew members on the way, so I need to get moving."

Geno smiled as he looked up at Tom. "Stay in the groove my friend, and stay out of trouble."

As Tom left the mess tent, he shook his hand several times as if trying to get the blood flowing better, but it didn't appear to be working. Flight mechanic Stewart was loading several stretchers into the chopper when Tom arrived.

"Here, let me show you where I want them placed. And we need to rearrange those three bags by the other door. I want the blue one on top of the big black one and the smaller black bag behind the co-pilot's seat. I kind of have a system in my head that works the best for me," Tom explained.

"Hey, no problem, you just tell me what you like and I'll get it done. I'm Tim Stewart from Anderson, Indiana, just down the road from the home of the Indianapolis 500."

Tom laughed, "Tom Kenrude from Glendale, Minnesota. Just down the road from rows and rows of corn, soy beans and wheat. But at least we never go hungry."

Thankfully, his hands were steady as the two men shook hands. Tom didn't want his new flight mechanic being concerned about his abilities to complete his mission. That was something Tom wanted to deal with on his own terms

Moments later Rick and Gus Brady arrived in a jeep. After exchanging a few pleasantries, the two pilots climbed aboard, preparing to fire up the Huey. Tom took his place beside Tim as they prepared to lift off, just as two more rescue choppers were returning from the A Shau Valley. Rick throttled up the powerful engine, sending the chopper airborne. Looking through the windshield, Tom could see smoke rising from a valley just a few miles ahead, and he knew they were back in the battle mentally ready or not.

Minutes later Rick dropped the chopper down into a rather large field where the twisted wreckage of three burned out Huey's littered the valley floor. Immediately, medics carrying stretchers ran toward the choppers.

As Tom helped slide the first stretcher inside, the medic yelled out. "Radical amputation, lower left leg. He's wiped on morphine, don't give him any more. Your next patient has several gunshot wounds. He's lost a lot of blood, but seems to be holding his own."

Seconds later the Huey was airborne as Tom began checking over the men to see what else he could do for them. The field medics had done a good job, leaving little for Tom to do in this case.

After unloading the injured men, Rick looked at his watch. "They need several more evacs before it gets dark, so saddle up, we're going back one more time."

The sun was beginning to set over the mountains to the west when the chopper once again settled down among the smoking wreckage. A medic was signaling for Tom near the tree line about fifty yards away. Grabbing a stretcher and his blue bag, Tom raced toward him. Laying on the ground was a young lieutenant who was screaming and thrashing about. His right leg was gone at the knee and his left arm was missing near the elbow.

"I gave him as much morphine as I can, but it doesn't seem to be working," the medic explained. "I just don't know what more we can do for him."

"Get him on the stretcher, we got to get him out of here now," Tom called out as several bullets dug into the ground nearby.

As the medic and an infantry private placed the screaming lieutenant on the stretcher, Tom started an IV in his good arm. Before placing the bag between his teeth Tom yelled, "Let's go!"

Another medic had just delivered a soldier with a head injury seconds before Tom arrived. "Put him behind the co-pilot, I need room to work with this guy!" Tom yelled up at his new flight mechanic.

Tom knew he had to get the lieutenant to calm down one way or another to save his life, as his heart was pumping incredibly fast. Just as he reached into his bag for another morphine syrette, the officer grabbed him by the arm with a death grip.

"My wife, she can't see me this way. What the fuck, doc, this wasn't supposed to happen. Sew me back together, Doc. Don't let her see me this way. Oh God, I promised Maria I would come back to her."

"You will, Lieutenant. You will," Tom exclaimed, jabbing the syrette into the officers left leg.

"Tell her, tell her… damn it, tell her I—" Those were his last words, as his tortured body laid quietly on the blood soaked stretcher.

Tears rolled down Tim's cheeks as he placed his hand on Tom's shoulder. "You did all you could, Doc. He was just too far gone. No one could have saved the poor son-of-a-bitch."

Tom stepped over the stretcher to check on his second patient, as the western sky turned a brilliant pink, with several large bands of deep orange running parallel clear across the horizon. The beauty of it was lost on Tom, however, who was now consoling another soldier, a young man who was now blind in one eye.

Touching down at the hospital, Tom directed the medics toward the soldier with the head wound. Several moments later another crew arrived to take the lieutenant to the morgue.

It was just another day in Vietnam for the medical staff at Quang Tri. Repair the injured, console those who were maimed for life, and prepare the dead for transport home.

This day would end for the doctors, nurses and medics, but they all knew it would begin once again when the sun rose in the morning. More young men torn up by bullets and jagged shrapnel, more young men with limbs radically amputated by mines, mortars and artillery, more young men fighting for their lives that would be forever changed. They should all be back home playing baseball, courting their sweethearts, enjoying their youth. But this was Vietnam, a bloody, deadly hell on earth that chose no favorites, and took the best America had to offer.

CHAPTER 13
VIET CONG

Torrential wind driven rain drenched the base at Quang Tri, as Tom awoke early one morning. The howling damp wind blowing in around the flimsy door made him shiver. He was happy to be sleeping in a tent, instead of being out in the middle of the jungle where little or no shelter could ever keep a man dry. He already knew what it was like to put on his driest pair of wet socks, several times a day, in order to prevent foot fungus or many other types of jungle illnesses that could destroy your feet. It was hard to believe he had already gone through several pairs of combat boots, as they appeared to rot right off his feet. Many a soldier in the field who failed to take care of his feet, or heed the warning signs of infections or fungus, had paid a heavy price.

After a good warm breakfast, Tom sat with Moe, Geno and Gabe in the mess tent, discussing the battles of the past few days. It was clear, Tom was not the only medic having a problem dealing with the constant stress they were under. Each man could tell gruesome stories of horribly wounded men, crying for their wives or mothers before passing, or trying to console men who had radical amputations. The sad thing was, none of it appeared to affect them anymore. It was like they went to the car assembly factory and dropped engines in cars all day, until their shift ended. No big deal, stop the bleeding, apply a tourniquet, give a shot of morphine, stuff a man's intestines back into his body before wrapping him in a battle dressing, and maybe pick up an arm or leg that was still hanging on by a tendon. Maybe a lucky doctor could reattach the muddy torn up limb, so his patient could have somewhat of a normal life. Then go back and do it all over again.

However, none of that equaled dealing with a soldier or civilian who had been horrendously burned by napalm or white phosphorous. What skin was left on their bodies, peeled off like the skin of an onion, and that was if they were not burned clear to the bone. No matter what you tried to do for them, nothing took away their horrendous pain, including maximum doses of morphine. Nothing affected Tom more than the screams of little children who were nearly burned beyond recognition.

Over and over he would pray they would slip into unconsciousness, so he would not have to endure their wailing and screams. There were times he would pray for them to just die, as he understood what their lives would be like if they managed to survive the next twenty-four hours. Tom was not sure how he could ever answer to God, as he prayed for the deaths of another human being, but he was sure God had to understand his reasons. After months in combat, it was nearly impossible to get the smell of burned flesh and the screams of the victims out of his mind. Sometimes at night, as he closed his eyes, the grotesquely burned bodies of the victims he had treated marched in a macabre procession through his dreams, shaking him to the core.

If that wasn't enough, the Viet Cong's treatment of the dead or prisoners they captured, was beyond what any normal human being could ever fathom. Bodies were booby-trapped with explosives, they were hung on posts with their limbs cut off, and heads were used to decorate fence posts in nearby villages. Even if bodies were not totally desecrated, their eyes and tongues were usually cut out. It gave little wonder as to why some Americans who spent large amounts of time in the jungle wore necklaces made of ears from the V.C. they killed in combat.

Late in the afternoon, Tom, Geno, Moe and Everett Tomlin were called to the operations office. Inside, they found Lt. Jurgins and Capt. Trajillio standing near a map conferring with a Major and Lt. Colonel from the 101 Airborne.

"Come in gentlemen, and grab a cup of coffee," Lt. Jurgins stated in a somber tone as he continued listening to the officers.

As the conversation came to a close, the three medics were walked into the Captain's office.

"Men this is Major Brandon and Col. Whetner. They have put together a plan to try cut off reinforcements and re-supply to V.C. and North Vietnamese Regulars battling us in the A Shau Valley. They are planning to land 250 airborne soldiers, and 200 men from the 5th Infantry at what appears to be good choke point." Walking up to a map, Capt. Trajillio pointed to an area near the northeast corner of the large valley.

"They will start the battle from here with full air support. They plan to meet up with Marines coming over from the west, and slam the door shut. Anyone left in the valley will be decimated by air power with no way to get out, and no way to be resupplied. The plan is to have the valley secured within 15 days, or 20 at the most."

We expect casualties to be heavy, which brings us to why you men are here. The four of you have seen more combat than any other medics in the squadron, plus you have demonstrated your medical abilities quite well. So you'll be taken out of your choppers, and will accompany the ground troops, assisting their medics during this operation. The operation will jump off at 0600 tomorrow, as our weather people see a 48 hour break from this storm.

Believe me it will be tough going, and you will need to continue on regardless of the weather. Sometimes evac may be hard to pull off, but we are counting on you men to make the difference. Questions?"

Moe stepped forward, "Sir, what happens if we have so many injured men the choppers can't get them all out during the day and we have to contend with them all night long with the little resources we have?"

Major Brandon nodded his head. "You will triage your wounded, get the worst out, and hold the balance for morning. If push comes to shove, you may have to decide who lives and who dies, depending on the severity of their wounds. There are no guarantees for any man once this mission gets underway. We will evacuate the wounded and dead, and bring in replacements to keep up our strength as needed. That's the best I can do for you, Specialist."

Moe looked at the other medics for a moment before nodding his head. "Yes sir, thank you."

As the men arrived at the airfield the following morning, there were rows of Huey's and Chinook choppers loading equipment and men. The four medics were assigned to a Chinook carrying soldiers from the 5th Infantry, including 20 Green Berets Special Forces soldiers, and two intelligence men, most likely from the CIA.

At 0550, five F-4 Phantoms and three Cobra Gunships departed Quang Tri to soften up the landing zones for the armada.

Exactly at 0600, the first choppers lifted skyward, followed by the largest assembly of helicopters Tom had ever witnessed. Light rain fell from the low heavy clouds as the armada raced north over the top of thick triple canopy jungle. Tom figured this would be the last time he would be totally dry for the next month.

He looked across the chopper toward his friends who were seated near the Special Forces men. They all had their eyes closed as they clung to their M-16s. Although they were not making parachute jumps, Tom completely understood how his father had felt before jumping from transport planes into a heated battle. By now the enemy knew something big was happening, as the F-4s and attack helicopters were striking at their positions to clear the landing zone. They would only lay back for so long before attempting to upset the landings, and kill as many Americans as they could before they were able to establish a perimeter.

Tom began preparing himself for the absolute worst, knowing some of the medics he knew so well could also become casualties before this day was over.

As the chopper began its decent, Tom could hear explosions and cannon fire from the air umbrella, attacking anything on the ground that moved.

When the Chinook touched down, everyone dashed down the rear ramp, following orders how to deploy from the officers and noncoms, who had landed on the first choppers. Wave after wave of helicopters descended on the battlefield, disgorging their loads, before taking off again at full speed.

The C-130 Specter Gunships and Cobra helicopters circled the perimeter, firing rockets, machine guns and cannon rounds into the jungle, keeping the enemy at bay.

As the medics arrived at their assembly point, Tom took a moment to look around. There were no burning choppers, and no mortar or machine gun fire was tearing into the hundreds of assaulting soldiers. As the last choppers departed the LZ, everything appeared to be strangely quiet, with the exception of the circling attack aircraft just waiting for the enemy to show themselves.

No doubt there were dead or wounded enemy laying out in the jungle after such a heavy bombardment, but that was not going to be a concern for the medics. Any wounded enemy they ran across, would become the instant property of the Special Forces and CIA, whose job it was to collect intelligence, period!

Several minutes later Major Brandon arrived with four Lieutenants. "Medic Ashton, you go with Lt. Savoy, Sarducci you're with Lt. Brazil, Kenrude follow Lt. Mapes, Tomlin you'll go with Lt. Tripp. Grab all the gear you think you might need over the next day or so, or at least what you think you can carry. We'll be resupplied as needed, but you need to think ahead throughout this battle as to where you might end up, and the number of casualties you may have to contend with."

Lt. Mapes led Tom to Delta Company from the 5th Infantry. "Alright, Kenrude, we start the battle here. You'll need to help our medics whenever and wherever you can. Just give these guys a chance if they get hit. We do not, and I repeat do not, give medical aid to the enemy. Do I make myself totally clear on that point?"

Understanding Lt. Mapes was a fully battle tested soldier, and dead serious regarding his orders, Tom replied, "Understood."

Minutes later the men began moving into the jungle intending to destroy all enemy forces they came across, and seal off the valley with all due speed.

Tom was not the only person surprised when the battle hardened enemy made no attempt to impede their movement. There were clear signs the enemy had been close by, but so far they had chosen to melt back into the thick jungle, waiting for a better chance to attack.

As an early dusk caused by dark low hanging clouds began settling over the valley, the decision was made to halt their movement, just on the east side of a narrow north-south river. A perimeter was established, giving serious attention to the river and it's sandy banks.

Tom placed his shelter half over some downed tree limbs, giving him just enough cover to get out of the falling mist. Troy Goozman, a medic from Delta Company, added his shelter half to Tom's makeshift awning, giving them additional protection and space.

After opening their C-Ration cans, Troy looked at Tom. "Guess this is not what you expected to be doing. I've always kind of envied you guys in the choppers getting the hell off the battlefield for a time as you flew the wounded back to the hospital."

Tom smiled at the battle tested medic. "Yeah, it was a shock to me. I miss that big old Huey already, although we had one destroyed back in the valley on a mountain plateau. We see the same things, and deal with the same issues as you do. It's not much prettier to tell you the truth."

Seconds later, automatic weapons fire broke out down by the river, as mortar rounds began falling all around the jungle. Tom and Troy slid into the large hole Tom had dug, hoping to avoid contact with flying shrapnel from the exploding shells, or sharp wood splinters from air bursts in the trees. Just as quickly as it started, the attack ended. This went on all night long, keeping the men from getting any real sleep. Surprisingly, only six men from Delta Company received medical attention for small cuts the following morning.

At first light, Huey and Cobra gunships struck the west bank of the river with a vengeance, allowing the attackers to cross the river without any hindrance from the enemy.

However it did not take long for the enemy to strike back, with more sadistic and unpredictable attacks that unnerved even the best jungle trained soldiers. The Viet Cong had placed trip wires attached to grenades, mines, artillery shells and bamboo spikes that struck with such ferocity, they would penetrate completely through a body or remove a head.

Every type of Soviet mine was placed in the soft moist ground, including the much feared Bouncing Betty, created in Nazi Germany during World War Two. When this mine was set off, a small charge would send the main container about four feet into the air before it exploded. These mines could be filled with nails or ball bearings, creating horrendous damage to a body for several meters around. They could also be hooked together in groups, so setting off one, meant three or four would explode in unison, preventing soldiers from finding a safe path of escape.

Of course all the booby traps were continually backed up by snipers, who would attack out of well concealed spider holes in the floor of the jungle or from the tree tops. They were experts in camouflage and evasion tactics, being able to live off the jungle for weeks while waiting for their prey to arrive.

It did not take long for the medics to have their hands full as men were struck down with horrific wounds or radical amputations. Although the medics could work diligently to save their lives, getting them out of the jungle to a hospital was now a major task. At times the men had to move the wounded back toward jungle clearings in order for evac choppers to get them out, while constantly dodging well aimed sniper fire. All too often rescuers became victims, creating huge gaps in the amount of medical staff available to treat the wounded.

One week into the operation, Tom felt like he was beginning to run on empty. He no longer had any dry socks, and the ones he had left were beginning to rot away. Lack of sleep, incessant rain, over-whelming humidity, stench of the jungle and a vicious enemy at every step, was beginning to wear on everyone. The worst was to see all the body bags piled in a clearing, waiting to be removed along with the fresh crop of wounded soldiers. Sadly, there never appeared to be a shortage of new faces to send into this meat grinder they found themselves entrenched in.

The stench of the rotting jungle was amplified by the thousands when they ran across rotting corpses of Viet Cong who had been killed days earlier by air attacks. The bloating corpses were covered by thousands if not millions of big black flies and other jungle rodents, feasting on the decaying flesh. Entrails and other body parts hung from low level tree branches, wretched evidence of men blown apart by bombs.

As they prepared to set up camp for the eighth night, the enemy struck from all sides in a well-coordinated and vicious attack. Grenades exploded as heavy automatic weapons fire ripped through the air. As the perimeter had not been totally set, the enemy was able to run through it, killing defenders before they could respond. Attempting to take cover was not an option, as enemy forces were firing from every direction. Tom dropped down behind several fallen trees to tend to three wounded men that were in bad shape. As bullets whizzed over his head and slammed into the trees, Tom began wrapping a serious head wound. A wounded corporal attempted to slide closer to Tom for help, but was struck by a bullet in the forehead. Knowing there was nothing he could do for the corporal now, Tom crawled over the top of him to check on the third patient.

Seeing the man had a large gash in his throat, Tom began to pull a battle dressing from his bag. Before he could retrieve it, a Viet Cong jumped over some logs, stabbing the soldier in the leg, striking the femoral artery. Blood gushed from the wound, as Tom attempted to roll away from the sharp bayonet now being thrust at him. As the determined enemy swung his AK-47 toward Tom's head, he let out a scream. Blood ran from a large exit wound in his chest, as he fell forward missing Tom with his bayonet by mere inches.

Looking up from the ground, there was no way to know who had just saved his life, as there were men still running all around, trying to kill the attacking enemy where ever they could.

With his patient now dead, Tom picked up his bag and M-16, and ran toward a sergeant who was propped up against a tree several yards away, with a huge gash in his side. Although seriously wounded and losing blood quickly, he continued firing at the enemy every chance he got.

Kneeling down beside the staff sergeant, Tom tore open his bloody shirt revealing a nearly ten inch gash that had penetrated to the ribs.

"Fix me up, Doc, I got to get back into the fight. I can't sit here like this while those bastards are still killing my men," the sergeant yelled above the commotion.

"Hold still, damn it." Tom called out as he attempted to push the man back down as he struggled to stand. "You're going to bleed to death if you don't let me to get this wound taken care of. You're in no shape to continue fighting."

Once the bleeding was controlled, Tom looked over at a soldier that was lying about five yards away. "Stay here, I'll be right back. I've got to check on that man," Tom demanded as he crawled over to the wounded soldier.

Just as Tom arrived at the wounded a man, a lone V.C. came running toward them, bleeding from a facial wound, oblivious to their position. Without thinking, Tom raised his M-16 cutting lose three quick rounds, striking the screaming man in the chest. He continued stumbling forward about six more feet before falling to the ground with a solid thud. Knowing he was no longer a threat, Tom bent over the wounded soldier,

"Where are you hit?" Tom inquired, as he could see no blood with his first inspection.

"I don't know, Doc. All of a sudden I couldn't move my legs and I'm having a hard time breathing. I don't know what happened. I'm scared, Doc. You got to help me!"

Tom did a second survey of the man's body, but found no signs of injury anywhere. "I can't find anything, you got to help me out here. What happened?" Tom questioned, as the man began to cry.

"I was standing over there about fifteen yards away, when there was an explosion about three feet behind me. Something hit me in the neck and my legs just collapsed. I haven't been able to move them since. What the hell happened?"

Examining the back of the soldier's neck, Tom could see a large red spot at the base of the hair line, but no cuts were visible. You could have been hit be some piece of debris from the explosion. It must have hit you hard enough to stun your system, I've heard of that before. It may take a few hours or a few days for your body to recover from the shock," Tom explained, hoping the force of the extreme blow had not severed the man's spinal cord. However right now, there was nothing he could do to help the injured soldier, and he certainly didn't wish to add more trauma than was necessary, suggesting he may be paralyzed. It would be a wait and see situation once he was taken to the hospital.

Slowly, the attack began to subside, as the enemy's strength had taken a serious blow. After a tight perimeter was set in place, medics began moving all the wounded into an area near a small clearing just big enough for choppers to land the following morning.

Body bags were already being stacked at the edge of the tree line for evacuation, after all the wounded were removed. Tom knew the battle had been tough, but he was stunned as the pile of bags continued growing.

Attending to the wounded would be an all all-night affair, requiring the vigilance of every medic. Several times Tom walked around the area where the wounded men were collected, looking for Moe to no avail. About midnight, Lt. Savoy walked up to Tom as he was speaking with Geno.

"How's it going guys? Do you have everything under control? I know you went through a lot of supplies today. We'll be resupplied in the morning, as soon as the first chopper can get in here."

Geno shook his head. "We're doing the best we can, sir. It would have been nice if we could have gotten a bunch of these guys out today. There are several that may not make it without surgery soon."

Lt. Savoy nodded his head. "We know, Specialist. But we just couldn't chance bringing in that many choppers this late in the day with the weather front moving in. I hope to God things are better in the morning so we can get these guys out of here.

As Tom turned to walk back toward the wounded men, Lt .Savoy grabbed him by the arm. "Kenrude, I need to talk to you about Pvt. Bright. Is he faking his injuries, or is he actually wounded. I have a bunch of guys that feel he faked his injury to back out of the battle. It's not sitting well with them. What can you tell me for sure, right now?"

Tom shook his head. "I don't know, sir. I've read case studies back at the University of Minnesota, where the central nervous system can undergo a tremendous shock causing partial or complete paralysis for hours or even days. I can tell you, there is some swelling at the base of his neck along with a sizable bruise. Geno has also looked him over, and feels the injury is possible. Only doctors at the hospital will be able to tell us for sure, if their x-ray equipment can see a problem or not."

It was clear Lt. Savoy was not happy with Tom's answer. "Let me tell you right here, right now. If that man's faking his injury, he'll be court martialed to the extent of the UCMJ, and you'll be called as a witness. My men will never tolerate a yellow son-of-a-bitch, and neither will I."

As the lieutenant turned to walk off, Tom stopped him. "Sir, we've been looking for Moe Ashton, one of our medics. Was he one of the men killed?"

Lt. Savoy turned back toward Tom and Geno. "We have taken several head counts since the battle ended. Right now Ashton is one of six men listed as MIA. That's the best answer I have for you. Maybe his body will turn up in the morning when we search the area again. I hope to God he hasn't been taken prisoner. That would be a fate worse than being in one of those body bags!"

During the night two men passed away from their injuries, while three more soldiers arrived wounded by sniper fire, and one man arrived after being bitten by a venomous snake.

Just after first light, the sound of an approaching Chinook raised the spirits of all the medics. As the large chopper set down in the clearing, men began off-loading crates of supplies, as medics began loading the wounded. No sooner had the first chopper lifted off, a second touched down, following the same procedure. In nearly an hour, all the wounded and dead had been evacuated, and the medics were able to resupply their nearly empty bags.

Everyone held their positions in the perimeter as gunships and Naval A-6 Intruders hammered away at suspected enemy positions deeper into the valley. Around 1000hrs, the resupplied force continued its painstakingly slow eastward drive into the thick jungle.

As Delta Company arrived at a stream about six feet wide, the men froze is place. On the far side of the stream were the bodies of three Americans hung from posts. Two appeared to have been crucified, while the third was hanging upside down with both arms and his head removed.

Lt. Mapes carefully scanned the area with his binoculars for several moments before saying a word. "For God's sake, it looks like the man on the right cross is still alive. But we have to be damn careful how we approach this. No doubt there are booby traps or mines we will need to contend with. Charlie would never let us get to these guys without a cost. Son-of-a-bitches!"

Before he could say another word, Everett Tomlin grabbed his medical bag, charging across the stream toward the man on the cross.

Tom jumped up from his position screaming. "Tomlin get the hell back here, Tomlin, stop!"

At that instant, Tomlin's foot snagged a trip wire setting off four Bouncing Bettie's, buried at the far side of the stream. Tomlin flew back several feet as the round steel balls shredded his internal organs and face in a split second. Another mine directly behind the crucifixes exploded toppling them into the stream.

"Damn it, damn it!" Lt. Mapes yelled. "No need to be in a hurry now."

Tom knelt down beside the angry officer. "Maybe he's still alive, sir. We need to go check on him before he drowns. There's always a chance, sir!"

Lt. Mapes looked coldly toward Tom. "I will not risk you or any of my men in a hastily improvised operation to rescue a man I feel is dead. We do this by the book, Kenrude, there may be more trip wires or mines out there."

Turning back toward the Special Forces men, he called out, "Sgt. Dickerals. Take your men and sweep that stream, give us a safe passage lane. Then check around the area for mines or booby traps before we attempt to retrieve those bodies.

The men waited patiently as the Special Forces soldiers worked diligently removing two booby traps and another trip wire. Once they were sure the area was secured, Sgt. Dickeral motioned for Lt. Mapes to bring his men across.

There was no doubt the exploding mine had killed the soldier they hoped to rescue. Most of the shrapnel had ripped his back open. Tom stood motionless as he realized the second man on the cross was Moe Ashton.

Geno knelt down beside the body of their friend. Looking up at Tom he shook his head. "He was dead before they placed his body on the cross, and he's missing some of his organs. The poor bastard was tortured to death before they put their handy work on display. Let's get him down from the cross and get him bagged."

It was not an easy task removing the wooden spikes they had driven through his wrists and arms. As they placed him in a bag, Tom looked down at his friend.

"Rest well, Moe. You would have made one hell of a doctor. You shouldn't have died this way."

After waiting for a chopper to pick up the four bodies, Delta Company continued it's drive against the Viet Cong, who remained a very dangerous enemy, regardless of the losses they had already taken.

The next day they proved that point exceedingly well, when they attacked pursuing American forces from well prepared defensive positions on a small ridge. Although powerful airstrikes pounded the ridge line with explosives and napalm, the enemy continued holding their ground without giving an inch.

Lt. Mapes described the situation with commanders in the rear, inquiring as to what they felt was the best way to take the ridge. He was ordered to pull his forces back about a hundred yards, then dig in and await orders. All night long F-4 Phantoms, A-6 Intruders and F-8 Crusaders bombarded the ridge with a tremendous amount of ordnance. At dawn a C-130 circled the hill several times before dropping a 15,000 pound bomb on a parachute, known as the BLU-82 Daisy Cutter. The bomb contained 12,600 pounds of chemical explosive that would detonate mere feet above the surface of the earth. It creates an over pressure of 1000 pounds per square inch, creating maximum destruction to anything on the ground, and wiping out every form of life within a radius of 900 feet, without forming a crater.

Everyone ducked down in their holes, closing their eyes while covering their ears to help prevent injuries, as they were just at the far end of the weapons lethal abilities.

Seconds later a brilliant fire ball engulfed the ridge line, as a powerful burst of wind raced over the entrenched soldiers. The heat from the explosion was more intense than anyone in the jungle had ever experienced before.

Once the winds dissipated, the men slowly began exiting their holes to see an entirely new landscape. Not a tree or blade of grass remained on the hill. Everything had gone from brilliant green to ashen gray, comparable to photos astronauts sent back from their orbits of the moon. Incredibly, the entire jungle around them was silent. Not a bird or even a chirping insect could be heard in any direction.

Cautiously, the men began moving forward to see if any Viet Cong could have survived the massive fireball. In small cave openings, they found burned corpses aside their melted machine guns. Shattered bones, partial skulls and destroyed weapons littered the ground, but nowhere was there an entire body to be found. The once moist ground was baked rock solid, with the top nearly resembling glass from melted rock.

Tom stood silently with Geno as they took in the unbelievable scene in front of them. "Can you imagine being here when that thing went off?" Geno stated, as he gazed about.

"They never felt a thing. Believe me Sarducci, they were vaporized the moment that thing exploded. Sorry to say, the bastards never suffered," Lt. Mapes suggested as he stopped beside them. "But this will make a beautiful new fire base for an artillery battery. In fact back at HQ, they are already getting everything loaded. They should be here before nightfall and be ready to support our movement tomorrow morning. You got to love it, Sarducci."

Smiling, the lieutenant slapped Geno on the back as he moved up the hill following his men.

Early that afternoon a fleet of helicopters arrived from the south. The first to arrive on the ridge was a Chinook containing combat engineers and a small bulldozer. They were followed by choppers carrying artillery pieces suspended below. Other choppers carried huge pallets loaded with high explosive shells, rolls of concertina wire, sand bags and every other piece of equipment it would take to build a fire base.

The last chopper to set down contained soldiers ready to man the new base, and Lt. Col. Fargo. After watching the engineers and artillery crews begin to build their installation, he walked over to Lt. Mapes.

"Lieutenant, how soon are your men going to be ready to move out. We would like to tie up with the Marines day after tomorrow. They are also tidying up a new fire base in their sector as we speak. I would like to accompany your men on the final leg of this mission."

Lt. Mapes nodded his head. "Sir, we plan to spend the night here to help secure the perimeter, in case Charlie attempts to take the ridge back. The engineers should have everything set by morning, allowing us to move forward."

After once more looking over all the work being done, Lt. Col. Fargo nodded his head. "That sounds like a wise plan to me. I'm going to meet the rest of the officers right now. In the morning when we move out, I would like to follow your company. Is that alright with you?"

"That's fine sir, but it sounds like we'll be taking point as we move out, it could get a little hot out there. We have no idea what we might run up against as the noose gets tighter," Lt. Mapes explained to his commanding officer.

"All the more reason for me to be with you, Lieutenant. I can get a good idea what Charlie is up to and their strengths and weaknesses. Headquarters back at Quang Tri wants me to come back with some idea of what we're still facing out here," Lt. Col Fargo explained before walking off.

At 0730 the following morning, Delta Company began driving east from the new artillery base. Lt. Mapes had his first platoon take point on the south side of the advancing force.

Throughout the morning, only scattered resistance and a few snipers slowed their advance. Special Forces did a good job detecting mines and other booby traps, keeping casualties down to a minimum. About noon, three scouts returned to Lt. Mapes, informing him that a sizable force of Viet Cong were observed coming down from the north, about two hundred yards ahead.

Immediately he brought up reserves, while calling for an airstrike on the coordinates the scouts relayed to him.

Around 1245hrs, once again Naval F-8 Crusaders and A-6 Intruders began hammering the Viet Cong position. Three helicopter gunships circled the area after the fighters departed, firing rockets and 20mm cannons at any movement they could see. A large cloud of smoke drifted over the American Forces as they prepared to attack what was left of the enemy force.

Lt. Mapes signaled his men forward as the smoke drifted off behind them. For several minutes the men moved unscathed through the thick jungle growth, not knowing when, where, or how many enemy forces they would encounter. Suddenly a blast from a Russian machine gun forced the men to take cover. It was followed by a barrage of rifle fire and several grenades. A gunship overhead strafed the area with its 20mm cannons, forcing the Viet Cong to scatter or drop for cover. Quickly Delta Company began moving forward, catching the enemy off guard. The battle was ferocious as both sides refused to give an inch, and men on both sides screamed as they were struck by deadly projectiles, or were killed in hand to hand combat.

Tom had just finished bandaging a soldier when a corporal grabbed him by the arm. "The lieutenant wants you to come back to his position. The colonel's been hit bad."

Picking up his medical bag, Tom followed the corporal as he raced through the underbrush for about fifteen yards. He found Lt. Mapes and his radio man attempting to stop the bleeding on Lt. Col Fargo's chest. Kneeling down beside his dad's former commander, he shook his head. Seconds later Gabe Hartman, who arrived last night to bolster the medical team dropped down beside Tom.

"Damn, Kenrude this is bad. Can you somehow stop that bleeder below his heart or we're going to lose him," Gabe called out.

"I'm trying, damn it, but there's so much damage and there's a large piece of shrapnel stuck inside his spleen that we can't remove. Reaching deeper into the colonel's chest Tom yelled, "Come on Colonel, you got to help us, you got to hang on!"

Seconds later Lt. Col. Fargo closed his eyes as his head rolled to the right. Tom and Gabe sat back looking at the bloody torn body in front of them. Lt. Mapes and Lt. Savoy stood motionless looking down at their dead commander.

"I told him this was not a good idea, I told him we didn't know what we were going to be running into, but he insisted he accompany us on this drive. For Christ's sake, what do I tell headquarters. He was one hell of an airborne soldier from what I heard, I wish he would have stayed with his own men on this mission. Damn it to hell!" Lt. Mapes yelled as he looked down at Tom.

"Nothing you could have done, sir. That mortar round had his name on it, pure and simple. We'll get him wrapped up and bagged best we can. We'll let you know when he's ready for extraction.

Around 1300hrs. the following day, advance units of the 101 Airborne met up with Marines driving from the west. Delta Company met their Marine counterparts around 1345, near a small clearing in the jungle. After securing the area in order to establish a perimeter, several evac choppers arrived to remove wounded, and resupply the combat troops. Everyone involved with the mission was extremely tired and battle weary, after slogging through the jungle for weeks on end, chasing down an elusive and brutal enemy. Over the next forty-eight hours, everyone involved with the battle was withdrawn from the jungles. The Marines set up a front line post at the fire base they secured earlier, in order to continue battling Viet Cong infiltrators in the area.

Arriving back at Quang Tri, Tom went to the hospital seeking out Roxy.

As he approached her, she smiled and put her hands together as if she were praying. "I prayed every day you would not be the next one returning on a chopper. Every time I heard a medic was coming in, it scared the hell out of me." After giving Tom a quick hug she inquired, "So Mr. Kenrude, what can I do for you today?"

Tom smiled at his favorite nurse. "I need some information on a patient I sent you. His name was Pvt. Ernie Bright. He claimed to have been hit in the back of the neck by something after an explosion. He claimed to be paralyzed from the waist on down. I pricked his feet with a needle several times, and he never flinched. What happened to him, can you tell me?"

"He's in Long Binh Jail as we speak, awaiting trial. I was in the triage room when they brought him in. Dr. Culver and I examined him, including the neck area. The doctor couldn't find any swelling near the red mark, which would have shown up after being hit hard enough to damage your spinal column. He never reacted at all when we did the same test you did with a needle on his feet and legs. He was very good at what he was trying to pull off. We barely left the triage room, before he slipped his boots back on and took off like a bat out of hell. We notified the M.P.'s right away. They found him trying to get off the base in a jeep about an hour later. Lieutenant Savoy will be processing the disciplinary charges tomorrow. I have a feeling they are going to throw the book at him, he may grow old in Leavenworth, and that suits me just fine!"

Tom shook his head. "A lot of good men died out there. That chicken shit deserves everything he gets. I just wish I could have caught him before he went on an evac chopper that could have been used by a real injured man."

Roxy smiled. "Don't kick yourself so hard, Kenrude. You had your hands full out there, and didn't have time to deal with him, he was really good at faking it. But, hey, it all worked out in the end, so be happy you made the right call. You just never know what you have out in the field. So look soldier, I have work to do. Go get a shower, some hot chow and some sleep, you guys really earned it."

Leaving the hospital, Tom felt much better regarding the entire situation. He knew for sure Lt. Savoy would pile on every charge possible under the UCMJ, and Bright deserved every one of them. He proved he was a coward leaving others to die, there was nothing more disgusting.

However, the loss of Lt. Col. Fargo weighed heavy on his mind. He knew he would have to write home and tell his father, what had happened to one of the best commanders he ever served under. He also knew Franny and Fr. Neederman would have to be told. Tom was not looking forward to telling those brave combat veterans about the loss of one of their own.

CHAPTER 14
THE MEKONG DELTA

One week later the battered medical unit received its orders to return to their base at Binh Thuy. No one cared about leaving Quang Tri behind. Although they had proven to everyone they were a tough, capable medical evacuation unit, the loss of so many of their men was a hard cross to bear.

The loss of Moe was especially tough on Tom. They had become not only very good friends, but Moe was the type of guy you could open up your soul to, and he never judged or questioned your feelings or motives.

However, Tom understood Moe better than anyone else in their company. He knew the stress of battle was wearing on him, and his breaking point wasn't far away. Twice over the past several weeks, Tom had found his best friend crying when he had been alone. He pleaded with Tom not to tell anyone, as he was just two months short of going home.

The first evening back at Binh Thuy, Tom went to the 632 Combat Support Group in search of Franny. After a short search, he found him in a small office going through a large stack of files.

"Do you have a few minutes to talk, Sergeant?" Tom inquired before entering the office.

"Hell yeah, I got time for you, Tom. I've been thinking about you a lot over the past few weeks. I hoped and prayed you were not one of the medics killed out there. You look a little tired, are you doing alright? Is there anything I can do for you?"

Tom smiled as he sat down across the desk from his father's good friend. "No Franny, I don't think there is much you can do. I lost a real good friend, Moe Ashton was his name. The V.C. captured him and, well you can kind of figure out the rest for yourself. Then Tomlin took off like a maniac trying to help him, and blew himself up. Two good medics gone just like that. Damn, Franny it really hurt, and still does. You've been there, how do you deal with it? I feel just sick!"

After taking a drink of coffee from a well-used mug, Franny sat back in his chair. "When we were in Europe, your Pa and I saw a lot of good men killed. Sometimes a few at a time just like you. I don't know if there's any one thing that gets you through it. You just have to realize that you can't quit or walk away, you just have to dig in a little deeper and work your way through it.

I almost got to my breaking point in Korea. All those paratroopers that were dying around me were from my company, and I was responsible for all of them. Every time I had to send a file back to headquarters for a man killed in action, it felt like a part of me went with it. I prayed every day so God would help me find a way to hang with it and not break. I never told your Pa that, because I know he and Harry were in about the same situation. Look Tom, if you're at that breaking point, no one will call you a coward. You've seen a lot of action. Just go talk to your company commander and request a transfer to a hospital to finish out your tour."

Tom smiled at Franny. "No, I'm not at that point. I want to continue doing what I came here to do, although I understand I could help guys in a hospital just the same. I just needed to talk to someone who has been through this before in a big way. You may not believe it, but just sitting here drinking coffee with you has helped a lot. Plus, I'm worried about Mac being without me when the baby comes. I really wish I could be there for her."

Franny smiled as he nodded his head. "Yeah, I figured you were dealing with all of that, too. It doesn't make things any easier, Tom. Things from home just have a tendency to compound everything when you're at war. Just remember, she is a strong woman, and your folks are there for her. They'll help her through all of it. When you go home, you'll have a beautiful baby to hold and play with the rest of your life. Son, it will all be good, just take your Uncle Franny's word on it."

"There is one more bit of bad news I have for you, Franny. Colonel Fargo was killed during the mission. There was nothing we could do for him. I know you served with him and were good friends. I'm so sorry." Tom explained to Franny.

Nodding his head Franny half smiled. "Yeah, we already knew that. Bad news travels real fast around here. Father Neederman and I took care of the arrangements to send him home. But thanks for telling me, Tom. I appreciate it.

Tom was surprised at how fast two hours passed while he was talking with Franny. But he felt like a huge weight had been lifted from his shoulders. He had survived his first eight months in country, and everything was downhill now.

Since the chopper they had at Quang Tri was in such bad shape, Rick Palmero and Gus Brady flew to Saigon to pick up another unit. No one was surprised to see, 'Hot Pepperoni Two' painted on the front cowling when they arrived.

The next day the men went on their first evac mission, up along the Mekong River. A severely damaged Huey gunship had gone down into the river. A small South Vietnamese patrol boat had rescued part of the crew, but they were in need of emergency medical treatment.

Rick set the chopper down with one runner on the sandy shore, and the other in a few inches of water, about twenty yards from the patrol boat. A Cobra gunship circled overhead, providing cover for the rescue operation.

Tom and Tim ran toward the patrol boat with two stretchers and one medical bag. The pilot was laying on the sand with several battle dressings on his leg and face. The flight engineer was sitting on the edge of the boat with his arm in a sling, and a blood soaked dressing on his right lower leg. Tim helped the flight engineer over to their chopper as Tom knelt down beside the pilot.

"I'm Tom Kenrude, can you hear me?" But he received no answer. Tom continued to speak to the man as he began looking under the battle dressing. The man did not respond, and it was clear why. He had sustained a major head injury, with part of his front skull missing above what was left of his eye. Quickly Tom re-wrapped the wound with a new bandage just as Tim got back. After placing him on a stretcher, the men hustled back to the chopper. Knowing there was nothing he could do for the pilot, Tom went to work attempting to slow the flow of blood from the flight mechanic's leg wound. In order to keep his mind occupied, Tom inquired. "What happened to the rest of your crew?"

"Our co-pilot was dead before we hit the water. A huge hunk of shrapnel from the front cowling all but decapitated him. Our door gunner Mike and I were also hit by debris from the explosion. The chopper turned sideways when we hit the water, I slid out, hitting my arm on the runner when it spun upward, it's broken bad. I don't know what happened to Mike. He must have gone down with the chopper. The poor bastard was only here about a month."

The following day Tom's crew was called into operations along with the crew from the 'Westward Ho.' Geno sat down with Tom as they awaited the morning briefing.

"What do you think is going on? I hope we're not being farmed out up north again. I'm down to six months, so I don't want to go up to the highlands if I can help it. Bad mojo up there if you know what I mean."

Tom nodded his head. "Yeah I know the feeling. The A Shau Valley sucked up a lot of good men, and I don't want to go back up there again either. I'm not really sure we accomplished anything during that damn mission."

A moment later Lt. Jurgins arrived. "Alright, listen up! The brass has decided there's too much enemy activity going on in the lower islands of the delta. They've chosen about a dozen islands and fishing villages they want cleaned out. Tomorrow morning, Marine and Special Forces squads are going to start cleaning house. Your choppers will be added to the operation in order to evac wounded, as there will be several operations going on simultaneously. Wounded will come back here to our hospital. The mission should go on for about a week, maybe longer if the brass feels it necessary. We assigned Frank Ridzik to fill Moe's spot on 'The Dragon's Tail.' They'll be in reserve flying local missions just in case things get out of hand and another chopper is required."

During the first day of the operation, Tom's crew evacuated just one patient from an American gunboat that had been struck in the chest by a bullet. But marine and navy evac choppers had been very busy. On the second day of the operation, Rick received a call requesting an evac near a village on a rather small island. Smoke from burning huts and dried vegetation hung low over the water, obscuring the landing zone when they arrived. Unable to touch down safely, Rick called for an alternate landing site. Seconds later they were instructed to set down on a large pier that ran out about twenty yards from the village.

As Rick swung around to make the landing, Gus called out. "Is that damn thing strong enough to hold us? If not we're going to drop into the water before we can get airborne again, maybe we should hover a foot or so off the deck."

Laying on the floor of the chopper Tim scanned the dock with his binoculars. "Don't set this thing down, everything is tied together with ropes and jungle weeds. Our weight will collapse that thing in seconds. Just hover, I'll call you down."

As Rick approached the dock, Tim began calling out, "Five feet, four feet, three feet, easy now take it slow. One foot, hold us there, Rick!"

Tom jumped off the chopper as four Marines carrying stretchers came running toward them. Tim stepped off on to the shaky pier to assist sliding the stretchers on board. Just as they loaded the last stretcher, a Naval Corpsman came running toward the chopper with a very pregnant young woman.

Tom stopped the corpsman. "Where is she hit?"

"She's not hit, but I think she's going to have the baby pretty soon, we need to get her to a hospital."

Tom shook his head, "Sorry, no can do, there are two more wounded men coming behind you, we can't take her. Get her back to the village."

The corpsman drew his sidearm, aiming it at Tom. "You take her or I'll blow you off this dock, you got that!"

As Tom reached out to help one of the approaching wounded men, the corpsman yelled out. "I ain't playing games here. You best take her or you die. Your decision asshole!"

Before Tom could reply, a Marine sergeant helping the last wounded man toward the chopper stepped in front of the corpsman.

"Get your head out of your ass, son. Take her back to the village as you were told. We don't have time for this crap."

As the sergeant took hold of the woman's arm, the medic aimed his pistol at the chopper as it began lifting off, firing three rounds. Tim screamed as he fell back out the door on to the dock with blood flowing from a wound in his neck.

Frantically, Tom screamed at Rick. "Take it back down, Tim just fell out, he was shot by that son-of-a-bitch!"

"No way Kenrude. That mad man will damage this chopper if he continues shooting, killing us all. We'll have to come back for him. Just help your patients!"

Tom was infuriated as the chopper flew back toward the hospital at

Binh Thuy. He knew he had to take care of the wounded men on board or some of them may die, but he also knew full well that Tim had been severely wounded and needed his help right now.

After unloading all the wounded, Tom jumped back on board. "Come on Palmero, we need to go get Tim, Get this crate in the air!"

Gus turned to look at Tom. "He's coming in with 'The Dragons Tail.' We'll just sit tight a few minutes so you can check on him when he arrives. Plus, we can't take off without having a flight mechanic on board, you know that, Kenrude!"

As 'The Dragon's Tail' began descending, Tom ran forward to check on Tim's status. As he neared the door Ridzik shook his head.

"He was dead before he hit the pier, Tom. The bullet ripped his jugular before slamming into his spinal column. He never knew what hit him."

Tom stood motionless for a moment as he watched medics remove Tim's lifeless body from the chopper. Turning to Ridzik Tom yelled, "He was shot by a corpsman for God's sake! What the hell is going on? We're supposed to save the lives of our men, not take them. I want that man brought up on charges or so help me, I'll hunt the son-of-a-bitch down myself and settle the score!"

Ridzik placed his hand on Tom's shoulder. "Several Marines grabbed that guy before he could shoot again. I have to think they reported the incident, but you can talk to Jurgins about it. I'm damn sure he'll want something done about it."

Tom nodded his head as he stared at Ridzik. "Frank, I'm so tired of this crap, I just want to go home. It just never ends, and the war seems to get crazier all the time. I'm so damn tired of it!"

After reporting the incident to Lt. Jurgins, Tom felt somewhat better. He was also informed that they would have a new flight mechanic in the morning.

Walking into the mess hall, Tom noticed Roxy going through the chow line. After grabbing his meal he strolled up to the table where she sat alone. "Mind if I join you?" he inquired.

"No, please have a seat. It's been a very long day, and I could use some company. I'm sorry to hear about your flight mechanic. Things like that shouldn't happen. I couldn't believe Ridzik when he told me a corpsman shot Tim when you were already in the air. Sure, I can accept the Marine's compassion for a pregnant Vietnamese woman, but to shoot a fellow American trying to make your point is just so horribly wrong. I'm having a real hard time with that entire episode." Roxy explained as she looked across the table at Tom.

Tom was quiet for a moment before responding. "You cannot imagine what that was like. It was kind of like a bad dream out of control in slow motion. You could see him standing there waving his gun as he screamed at us, but it was hard to understand him with the chopper running, and the next thing you know, Tim is screaming as he fell out of the chopper and bullets are still hitting all around me. I kept yelling at Rick to go back, but he had to worry about all of us, so he kept going, which I know was the right thing to do. Every one of us near the door was sprayed with Tim's blood. To be honest, I knew he was dead right away, I just didn't want to accept it. If all that wasn't bad enough, I tried to convince myself I didn't give a crap whether that woman had her baby or not. I never would have thought that way a few months ago, Roxy, I feel like part of me has died."

Roxy forced a slight smile as she looked at Tom. "It's called war, Tom. We not only see the worst, we try and fix it. We hear the screams, we hear their pleas, we hear them beg, and in the end we watch too many die. And yes, with each death, we lose a part of ourselves, a part of our souls. I don't know where it goes, or if we'll ever get it back, but the realities of what we do and see here changes us forever."

Tom nodded his head in agreement, as he was coming to realize that everything Roxy had just told him was painfully accurate. "You know, I expect to hear any day now that I'm a father. My baby will be a new life, and

I'm hoping the birth will be sort of renewal for my soul. I don't ever want that innocent child to have to experience war. Now I understand why Mom got so crazy when I told her I enlisted, though I'm not sure it would have made any difference. I needed to do this, I needed to try and save lives. I needed to make a difference. I think I have. I hope to God I have!"

As Roxy finished eating she reached out for Tom's hand. "You have made a difference, Specialist Kenrude, in more ways than you'll ever know. Just hang in there, we're both getting short, and we're both going to go home and have great lives. You got that Mr. Kenrude, we're both survivors."

Tom laughed as he looked at his special friend, "Loud and clear, Roxy. Loud and clear."

The following day Sgt. Calvin Dozier was assigned to Rick as his flight mechanic. He was already halfway through his second tour in Vietnam, and expected nothing but the best from the men he worked with. His father was a colonel assigned to the War Plans Division of the Pentagon. Dozier made it quite clear he was putting in for Officers Candidate School after this tour of duty.

As fighting continued throughout the islands of the Delta, so did the daily evacuation runs. But each day now, Tom enthusiastically crossed them off his short timer's calendar, as he could see the end was finally in sight.

With a full crew complement, 'Hot Pepperoni Two' took to the skies over the Delta aiding wounded men wherever they were directed. They picked men off beaches, well-built loading docks, rocky shore lines and small jungle clearings. There was nothing Rick wouldn't attempt if it meant saving a life, and he was the best pilot in South Vietnam as far as Tom was concerned.

After dropping off wounded back at the hospital at Binh Thuy, Rick turned his bird back toward the Delta for another rescue run around 1600hrs. There was plenty of daylight available for another run. As they flew over open water Rick began having difficulties controlling the chopper.

Cal crawled up behind Rick's seat. "What's going on, Rick?"

Shaking his head Rick responded. "Hydraulic problems. We must have had a bullet strike a supply line on that last take off, we're losing pressure fast."

Before he could say any more, the chopper went into a spiral as it dove toward the water. "Hold on, we're going to hit hard!" Rick yelled out, seconds before striking the water.

The impact threw Tom up against the roof of the chopper before slamming him back down to the floor. As the severely damaged chopper rolled to the left, the powerful rotors tore from the engine, sending jagged pieces of the blades around the entire area. Immediately, the heavy machine began to sink in the brown waters of the Delta. Tom shook his head, attempting to regain his vision as water began filling the chopper. He saw Cal clutching the back of the co-pilots seat as blood ran from a cut on his forehead.

Grabbing a life preserver from the rack in the back of the chopper, he thrust it into Cal's chest yelling, "Put this on, put it on," as he gave him a push toward the door.

The very groggy flight mechanic slipped his arms through it, as Tom slid around the seat to cut away Gus's safety harness, as he struggled to break free from part of the instrument panel that had bent backward, pinning his right leg. After several seconds, Gus broke free of the wreckage, took the life preserver from Tom, pushed open the damaged door and disappeared outside.

By now the Huey was all but submerged, and any moment now, it would take a quick plunge to the bottom, which could be twenty to thirty feet deep. Taking a deep breath, Tom went under water, attempting to cut Rick's seat belt with his knife to no avail, as the dark murky water began to close in around him. Just as he attempted the dive a second time, the chopper rolled completely over, beginning its final dive. Tom was being pulled down by the suction as he attempted to pull himself back in to the main compartment of the doomed chopper. His ears rang and his lungs burned as he fought to hold his breath just a few moments longer. It began to feel like his eyes were going to pop out of his head at any moment, if he did not find a way out. Reaching out with his left hand, he caught the edge of the rear door frame. Pulling with all his strength, he was able to exit the door and begin swimming toward the surface.

Gus looked over at Cal who was floating about five yards away from him. "You doing alright Dozier, anything I can do for you? That cut looks pretty bad."

Cal shook his head, "No, I'll be alright. But tell me, are there sharks here in the Delta? This blood may attract them, you know."

"No, most of this is fresh water. I think we're too far in for sharks to be around. But to be on the safe side, don't come to close to me," Gus responded with a broad grin.

Smiling Cal looked around, "Looks like we're the only survivors. That damn Kenrude helped push me out the door. Where the hell—" Before he could finish, he gave out a yell, "Sharks! They got my leg, it's pulling me down, I can't get away!"

In an instant, Tom came to the surface directly in front of Cal, grabbing onto him as he gasped for air. After a few moments of heavy breathing, Tom pushed back away from him a few feet.

"Was that you grabbing my legs, Kenrude? Please tell me it was, you scared the hell out of me. I thought I was going to be dinner for some big fat shark!"

"Yeah, that was me. I needed something to lock onto if I was going to make it the last few feet. When I saw your legs I went for them. Sorry, I scared you," Tom explained, as he continued sucking in fresh air that burned his oxygen starved lungs.

Gus was laughing as he made his way over to the two men. "Cal, I wish

I could have taken a picture of your face when Tom grabbed your leg. It would have been worth a million bucks."

Cal shook his head. "Man, I thought I was a goner. You better keep that to yourself, Mr. Brady."

Finally Gus looked at Tom. "Rick didn't make it I presume?"

Tom shook his head. "It was so dark down there, I couldn't see what the hell I was doing, and he wasn't moving. I had to get out or go down to the bottom with the chopper. Rick never got out, he's gone."

The three men were quiet for a moment as they floated in the warm dirty water before Gus spoke up. "Do you need a vest, Tom? I'm a pretty good swimmer even though I think my right leg is broken. When the front of the chopper came back on me, I heard it snap. Without you, I wouldn't have gotten out. So if you want my vest you can have it."

Tom shook his head. "I was a great swimmer in high school, I'll be fine. But we should make a plan where we're going to go before it gets dark. We have a choice of three islands the way it appears. But which ones are controlled by the V.C. is anyone's question."

Gus looked up at the sky for a moment before responding. "That one, the one with the big hill on it. I had just looked down at my chart before things got bad. It said something about a patrol boat base on the north side."

"That sounds like a plan to me," Cal responded, as Tom attempted to place the battle dressing from his equipment belt on his head. "Problem is, I can dog paddle all day, but I can't swim worth a damn. How far do you think it is, Gus?"

"A mile, maybe closer to mile and a half, and to be honest my leg hurts like hell. We need to get it splinted, and the only way we can accomplish that is to get to an island before dark. It will be slow going since two of us won't be of too much help, so we better get moving," Gus grimly replied.

Tom took Cal in tow as Gus was able to swim fairly well, even with one leg out of service.

When they were about halfway there, a small sampan came cruising from the west about a hundred yards away. The three men ceased swimming as they watched the small craft sail along. Gus leaned close to Tom's ear.

"The guy on the bow has an AK-47, so if they see us we're toast. If they come over here we can surrender, or hope our sidearms will still work, and take the bastards on. What will it be, men?"

Without hesitation, Cal and Tom decided they would fight rather than surrender. In unison, they each drew their sidearm from their holsters in preparation for a possible fight. After a very long wait, it became clear the sampan was continuing toward the east, disappearing into the darkening channel. After placing his weapon back into its holster, Gus looked at Tom and Cal.

"So, do we continue on or change course? We don't know where those clowns came from or where they're going," Gus inquired, as he continued listening to the engine now far off in the distance.

"I vote for the island like we planned," Cal suggested. We came this far, I don't want to change directions. I think that's our best option."

With a nod of his head, Tom concurred. "Come on, it's getting too dark to be out here. We need to find protection for the night, and I need to take a look at your leg, Gus."

About forty minutes later the three men hobbled up on the beach. They knelt quietly, listening for any sounds of human activity, but heard nothing. It didn't take long for Tom to determine that Gus definitely had a broken leg. There was plenty of debris laying around the area, for Tom to construct a solid splint. About ten yards in from the shore, Cal found several huge boulders that would offer cover from any prying eyes that might come along the beach during the night.

Tom advised the men to drink sparingly from their canteens, as there was no way to know if there was any fresh water on the island. Gus had two candy bars in a zippered pocket of his flak jacket that had stayed rather dry, so they split one for their evening meal.

Throughout the long night, they took turns keeping watch for enemy activity. Gus saw two more sampans cruising west to east while he was on watch around midnight. Cal saw what he thought was a Navy patrol boat several hundred yards out, closer to the island on their right. It had sailed off to the south at a rather brisk pace. Tom saw two explosions on an island in the distance, followed by a low rumble but nothing more.

At the first crack of dawn, Cal felt it would be a good idea to circumvent the island, to find the Naval Base Gus had seen on his chart. During the long nervous night, Gus and Tom had worked with some thick branches they found to build a rather sturdy set of crutches. After eating the last candy bar, the men began their walk. Several times they waved at helicopters that flew nearby, without attracting their attention. The only vessels they saw all morning were small sampans of different lengths and width, which they did everything to avoid. Around 1300hrs, the men came to the remnants of the small South Vietnamese gunboat base. It was evident that the base had been deserted for some time. Cal and Tom searched through the remaining huts, while Gus kept watch near the pier. Gus was happy to see the two men return with a case of C-Rations that had been left in one of the huts. There would now be enough food for several weeks if they rationed it decently, but they hoped to be rescued long before that.

After having a small snack, Cal looked at Gus. "Do you think they're looking for us?"

"Sure, but where do you start looking when you have nearly 15,500 square miles of islands and water to cover. We told them roughly where we were going, but there were several ways we could have achieved our destination. We just need to keep our eyes open. We have matches now, so we can start a fire if necessary to signal a boat or chopper, and we have huts to keep us dry if it rains. Actually, we're in really good shape for being marooned."

Tom looked out toward the channel for a moment before looking back at Gus. "Any thoughts on how soon someone will be along this route that we can signal? I sure as hell don't want to signal the wrong people. We don't have much for firepower if it comes down to a fight, and we don't even know if our guns will work after being wet for so long."

Gus shook his head. "I'm hoping a chopper comes flying by that we can signal yet today, if those storm clouds don't open up. I got a feeling most of the aircrews have sought shelter by now. Those clouds look like they could drop some big wind and rain on the area in the next half hour or so. Let's pick up some burnable material and put it in one of the huts, that way we'll have something dry to burn if we decide to start a signal fire."

By the time the men gathered a nice stack of debris, the clouds opened up. A powerful wind blew from east to west as rain fell in torrents. The men sought shelter in the smaller of the huts, as it was in the best condition. Cal stood watch in the doorway as the rain began to subside. Just as dusk settled over the Delta, he observed movement on the island, just to the south of their position.

Motioning to Tom and Gus he whispered, "We got company, look just south of the last hut. There are two men standing near that big tree. The closest one appears to have a rifle of some sort."

Just as Gus was about to take a look, both of the dark figures jumped into the open, firing their AK-47s at the hut. The men dove to the floor as bullets ripped through the sides of the hut. As the firing ended, the men could hear several Vietnamese voices discussing the situation. Moments later, several more short bursts of fire came their way, as the sounds of running feet approaching the hut could be heard.

Gus knew their attackers would spray the floor area when they arrived at the door, killing or wounding all of them quickly. In order to draw their attention away from the hut, he threw himself out the door sliding to a stop near a small tree. As he lay in the mud, he hoped Tom and Cal's weapons still worked, or he was a dead man. An instant later Cal and Tom charged out of the hut firing their pistols toward the two men, who had been distracted by Gus, and were looking for him. As they crumbled to the ground, a third person ran toward the south along the coast line.

Tom and Cal grabbed the AK-47's from the dead V.C., giving chase to the third, with Gus a short distance behind them, hobbling on his broken leg. After several minutes of running, the black clad figure disappeared into the interior of the island. Cal and Tom dove behind trees waiting to see what was going to happen.

When Gus dropped down beside Tom he whispered, "There must be more V.C. on the island. The one that got away knows exactly where they are, and went to get help. Lord knows how many there could be. I think we should head back to the hut, gather what we can carry, and find cover somewhere else."

After slowly making their way back to the hut, Cal sat down on the floor. "Where do we go, Gus? Those bastards probably know every inch of this damn island. Maybe we need to swim off to that island on our right."

Gus looked at Tom for a moment before turning his attention back toward the beach. "That's a long swim, and you and I are not in the best condition for that, Cal. Earlier, I saw a very damaged patrol boat pulled up on shore to the north. It's not ideal, but the V.C. won't know where we went for a while. I think that might be a good plan for the rest of the night."

After considering everything Gus had just said, Tom spoke up. "We have no other choice, Cal. Let's head for the boat, at least it will give us cover from the rain for now."

Tom grabbed the case of rations, as Cal took some medical supplies he found on another shelf. Very quietly, the men slipped from the hut, using the jungle for cover.

The boat was in worse shape than they had hoped for, and most likely had been beached for quite some time. However the forward section of the boat was pretty well intact, and would protect them from the elements.

Throughout the night, the men took turns keeping watch from the small control bridge, which offered good concealment.

The rain subsided around 0500hrs, as dawn began to light up the eastern sky. Off in the distance, Tom could see two medium size vessels, which appeared to be American patrol boats. The problem was, now they were separated from their burnable material to use as a signal fire.

Just as Gus crawled up to the bridge, Tom whispered, "Get down. There are four V.C. just at the end of the camp. They're pointing this way, so I think it might be best if we slipped out that hole in the hull and head inland. If we stay here, we're going to be killed or captured."

Quietly the men slipped from the patrol boat, making their way into the dense jungle. They were barely gone five minutes, when a fifth V.C. arrived with an RPG. After taking quick aim, he fired the projectile into the patrol boat. The wooden boat disintegrated, as flames from the remaining fuel in the tanks exploded. Quickly, the enemy soldiers ran toward the flaming wreckage, looking for bodies. It was clear they were angry when they couldn't identify any type of remains.

Tom scanned the delta to the east, hoping the explosion and fire would had caught the attention of the patrol boats, but they had already disappeared behind another island.

As the five V.C. made their way back toward the huts, Gus shook his head.

"I'm open for suggestions. Anyone have any ideas they want to share?"

Cal looked intently at his friends. "We find their base and see how many there are before we decide to leave the island. If it's just the five of them, we take them out and stay put. If there are more, we go swimming no matter the distance once it gets dark tonight."

Tom looked at Gus. "I know this sounds crazy, but I think Cal's right. Let's see what we're up against before we decide to leave. Like Cal said, if it's only a handful, maybe we can take them out. I think it's our best shot."

Gus leaned back against a tree as he watched the fire slowly burn itself out. "Alright, let's see what we can see. No one fires unless I say so, or it's a dire emergency. We can't waste ammo or give away our position."

Cautiously, the three men began trekking through the underbrush heading deeper into the interior of the island. About twenty minutes later Cal held up his hand, pointing to his right. The men knelt down in the tall grass as they observed the five V.C. soldiers walking toward a small hut, where an old woman and another soldier were preparing to cook something in a large pot. A fifteen foot radio antenna was strapped to a tall tree, with the cable leading directly into the hut. A small gas generator which was turned off right now, sat near the hut to provide power to the transmitter as needed.

Gus smiled. "Just like the Australian Coast Watchers in World War Two. They must report to someone on all the boat traffic and aircraft that passes by. We must have caught them off guard last night, and they don't know what to do about it. They're as nervous as a whore in a convent."

Tom leaned close to Gus. "A radio is a radio. If we can jump them, you could dial in our frequencies and call for help. We have two AK-47s and three pistols. With a coordinated move, we should be able to kill all of them, or at least put them down."

Just as Tom quit speaking, three more soldiers walked into the camp from the far side of the island. It was evident they had been out searching and were tired and upset.

"Well Kenrude, that makes eight fighters that we know of, and one old woman. What do you think our chances are now?"

Tom shook his head. "Not as good as it was five minutes ago. The thing is Gus, if we don't do something we can't attract anybody to come pick us up. We have to keep moving to avoid capture, and sure as hell, they'll eventually pick us off one by one."

Cal looked at his partners. "I say we let some of them walk off, then we kill the remainder, and high tail it into the jungle. Then we play cat and mouse with them until we kill them all."

Gus looked at Cal. "Do you realize how long that could take? Plus, they might call for more help, then we're really screwed. No, we need to take them in this camp while they're all together, and hope this is the entire team. Then call for help like Tom suggested."

As the enemy was preparing to have breakfast, Gus pointed out where he wanted Cal and Tom to take up positions. Gus kept an AK-47 with him, while Cal took the second one. Tom took Cal's sidearm and his own, to his assigned spot.

When Gus gave the signal, Cal and Gus began firing their rifles, but Cal's pistol would not fire. Tossing it to the ground, Tom pulled his .45 and pulled the trigger, but it also failed to fire. After chambering another round, the weapon fired, but by now the fight was over, with two V.C. escaping into the jungle.

Slowly the men walked into the small clearing to investigate the outcome of their attack. Five V.C. and the old woman were dead. One wounded man who was hit three times, lay near their cooking fire, but was still hanging on. After looking him over, Tom knew he would be dead shortly.

Gus made his way into the hut to look over the radio. He had barely begun to look at the frequency settings, when two grenades flew through a window on the back of the hut. With no time to spare, Gus yelled, "Grenades!" as he dove out the door. Just as he landed beside the dead woman, one of the grenades exploded. After waiting several more seconds, Gus stood up. "There's one more in there that never went off, stay out of there." Peering in through the doorway Gus yelled, "Damn it, the radio took a direct hit."

Tom called Cal and Gus over to a trail leading toward the far side of the island. "One of them is hurt bad. He left a lot of blood behind, so he's not going to get very far in that condition. The other man must have doubled back to destroy the radio. I say we go after them, we have a good trail to follow. We need to end this if we're ever going to be rescued."

Gus nodded his head. "Alright, I'll lead. You guys keep your eyes open."

After picking up ammo and weapons from the dead the men began their search. Several minutes into their tracking, it was clear the two had left the trail and had turned into the underbrush. Gus felt with all three men now armed with good weapons and extra ammunition, overwhelming the last two defenders should not be a problem.

The trail was still easy to follow, as they found fresh blood on all the vegetation the escaping V.C. touched. It became clear after several more minutes that they were making a turn back toward the old patrol boat base.

Instead of following the blood trail, Gus decided to turn back toward the east, making their way back to the huts cross country, in hope of arriving there first.

Everything at the old base was quiet, and it appeared to be just as they left it the day before. Quickly the men took cover behind trees, giving them good lines of sight into the base. They readied themselves for what should be a final quick fight.

Several minutes later, two V.C. walked into the base supporting the wounded soldier. Gus quickly turned toward Tom. "Where the hell did he come from? How many more are on this miserable island?"

The men watched as the V.C. cautiously walked into the hut where they had piled the burnable material. Moments later, the two healthy men stepped back into the clearing.

"Take them now!" Gus yelled, as he jumped from out behind the tree. Both enemy soldiers instantly dropped to the ground as bullets tore into their bodies. Cal stepped into the hut, firing another round into the wounded man's head.

Tom walked slowly up to the two bodies to make sure they were dead. Just as he was going to roll the bodies over, he heard a slight moan. "It sounds like a woman," Tom called out.

Carefully rolling the body over, it was clear to see it was in fact a young woman, probably no more than fifteen or sixteen years old. Kneeling down beside her it was evident she had been hit twice in the abdomen and was losing blood quickly. Dropping his weapon, Tom placed both hands on the worst wound, attempting to slow the bleeding.

Reaching into his flak jacket, Tom removed a battle dressing, several pieces of gauze, a large surgical bandage, several packets of sulfa powder and a morphine syrette. He was sure there was not much he could do to save her life without a surgeon, but he felt he had to try, after all, she was just a child. Breathing heavily, she gazed up at Tom in fear as he tore her black top open. After pouring the powder on her wounds, he began bandaging her tightly, before administering the morphine. He had just one more syrette left, so he hoped they would be rescued soon.

"Just let the bitch die," Cal said, as he shook his head. "No telling how many Americans she was involved in killing. She's just another fucking Viet Cong."

As Cal lowered his weapon to her head, the girl closed her eyes and shook. Angrily Tom pushed the muzzle of the gun away as he jumped up.

"You already killed one wounded man, I'm not letting you kill this defenseless girl. You pull that trigger, and so help me I'll use it on you!" Tom yelled, as he pushed Cal backwards.

As Cal walked off toward Gus, Tom knelt down by the girl. He brushed her dark hair from her face as he forced a smile, realizing it could easily have been bullets from his own weapon that shot her.

Knowing she could not understand him he said slowly, "We're going to get you back to a hospital and get you help. Just hang on, just hang on."

After looking into Tom's eyes for assurance, she cautiously raised her left hand, removing a medallion from around her neck. Slowly she handed it to Tom, as her breathing became more labored. Tears began flowing from her eyes as Tom took hold of her small blood covered hand. She pushed the medallion into Tom's hand, as she whispered something softly in Vietnamese that he could not understand. Shaking his head, he placed his ear closer to her mouth. Once more she repeated the same sentence, while squeezing his hand shut. Tom wished desperately he could speak Vietnamese, so he could understand and reply to her words. After smiling at Tom, she closed her eyes.

Immediately Tom felt for a pulse on her neck, it was weak and very thready. There was no doubt she had internal bleeding, but there was nothing he could do for her. He was glad the morphine had kicked in, so the pain wouldn't be so intense.

Gus walked over to Tom. "Is she gone?"

"No, the morphine kicked in. I think she's probably bleeding internally, and I have no way of stopping it. She's lost a lot of blood, so I don't know that she'll make it," Tom replied as he once again checked her pulse. "If we could be rescued in the next five or six hours she might have a chance."

Nodding his head Gus knelt down beside the girl. "Damn, she's so young. I know Cal is pissed you are trying to save her, but what you're doing is great. Do what you need to do."

Twice during the next day, they attempted signaling two American patrol boats sailing through the channel without any effect. They watched several F-4s fly overhead, but it was impossible to signal them at their altitude, so another night in the hut was the best they had going for them.

Tom was amazed his young patient was still alive. He shared his water with her, although he knew dehydration was going to become the next issue that could kill her, if they weren't rescued soon.

Just after dawn on the third day, the girl let out a sharp scream as she thrashed about on the bed Tom had made for her from dried palm branches. After placing his hand on her forehead, Tom looked up at Gus. "She's burning up, the compresses I have been using aren't doing the job. Her pulse is very weak, and I'm out of morphine. There's just nothing left I can do for her."

Opening her eyes, the girl reached over to take Tom's hand. She smiled up at him as tears ran down her childlike cheeks. She squeezed his hand tightly with her left hand, as she pointed to his flak jacket with her right. Tom quickly removed the medallion she had given him the day before. She nodded her head, and pushed it back into Tom's vest. Her breathing became very labored as she stared up at Tom. With all her strength, she pulled Tom close to her so she could whisper in his ear.

After finishing what she had to say, she moaned, and closed her eyes for a moment. Reopening her eyes, she placed her left hand on Tom's cheek as she said in broken English, "Good American."

After coughing twice, her lips curved into a very peaceful smile before closing her eyes forever. As her head rolled to the side, Gus wiped a tear from his eyes before inquiring. "Have any idea what she said to you, Tom?"

Tom shook his head. "Sounds stupid I know, but I think she wanted to thank us for not letting her die out here all alone. Enemy or not, I believe it was a comfort for her to have someone with her as she left this world."

Tom was surprised when Cal spoke up. "We can't leave her here like this, we have to bury her. There's no way we can bring her back with us, it could be days before we're rescued."

"Cal is right you know, we'll have to bury her. The sand around here is pretty soft, it shouldn't be too hard to dig a decent grave," Gus explained, as he looked down at the girls peaceful face.

The men were just about finished digging a grave when Cal jumped to his feet. "Choppers, choppers coming from the west. We need to start that damn hut on fire now!"

By now the steady drone of helicopter engines in the distance was apparent to everyone. Quickly Tom set fire to all the dried jungle debris they had stacked in the hut. In mere seconds the hut was a blazing inferno that should easily draw attention from a chopper approaching the island from any direction.

Minutes later three Huey's approached from the southwest, flying about fifty yards off the water. The three desperate men ran out onto the small pier waving and yelling as the thick smoke circled around them. There was no doubt the fire had caught the attention of the lead chopper, as the pilot banked toward the right in order to circle back toward the island.

As the Marine chopper passed overhead, the door gunner waved at the three castaways. After nearly four days of constant fear, they knew their nightmare was about to end. They watched with excited anticipation as the third chopper dropped down near the shore line to pick them up from the beach.

Tom raced up to the door, "We need a stretcher, we have a body that needs to come with us for burial, and I don't want any crap that she was a V.C. She's just a kid!"

Without saying a word, the flight mechanic and door gunner jumped from the chopper with a stretcher.

In a matter of minutes they were airborne, as the pilot circled back out over the channel. As the door gunner talked to Gus about where they came from, Tom looked back toward the island. He felt anguish, knowing he had very likely shot the young woman he had just tried so desperately to save.

Even more depressing, her family would forever wonder what became of this little girl that lay quietly on the stretcher in front of him. Tom reached down and picked up the girls hand, holding it tightly as he closed his eyes for a few minutes of quiet prayer.

The Marines flew the three men, along with the young woman's body, directly to Binh Thuy. Upon landing, Roxy accompanied several medics to the chopper to take care of Gus and Cal. Seeing the young woman on the stretcher, Roxy looked up at Tom. "Is she gone?"

Tom nodded his head. "Yeah, I did all I could, but she had massive internal damage. There was nothing I could do out there to save her life. She deserves a decent burial, she's so damn young"

Roxy nodded her head, instructing one of the medics to take her to the morgue. Tom helped unload the stretcher and place it on a cart. Arriving in the morgue, he walked up to one of the attendants.

"She can't be more than fourteen or fifteen. Clean her up, put her in a body bag, and I'll see about having a small burial service for her."

The attendant smiled at Tom. "No worries, Kenrude. I'll make sure she's handled with dignity, we'll do her up right. I'll let you know when you can see her."

Gus went straight to the hospital to have his leg set properly and placed in a cast, while Cal received stitches in his forehead. Tom was given a clean bill of health after being checked over.

As he walked toward the exit to leave, Roxy yelled at him from a treatment room. Walking back toward the room, he observed Roxy assisting an injured soldier into a wheel chair. Once the man was loaded, she gave a corpsman directions as to where to take him.

Slowly Roxy walked up to Tom as she removed her rubber gloves. "So you're back, had a physical, have gone through hell out there, brought back a young Vietnamese girl to be buried, and you're not going to even check in with me? I thought we had a better relationship than that, Specialist Kenrude!"

Smiling at the obviously unhappy redhead, Tom explained, "I just wanted to get a shower, a change of clothes, and a hot meal. I'm sorry I didn't come looking for you. I figured I would come back later after the morgue technicians have her body ready for burial. Then, I was going to tell you the whole story. I'm just not in the mood to talk right now, Roxy. I really need to sort all this out."

Smiling at Tom she nodded her head. "I understand, Tom. You guys have been through hell. And all the reasons you gave me are pretty damn good ones." After giving Tom a quick hug she continued. "No one knew if you guys were dead, prisoners, or what the hell happened to you. We were all scared as hell, and after nearly three days, a lot of people started giving up hope. I'm so happy to see you safe and sound. You're getting to short to have something bad happen to you. So go get that shower and chow, you can stop back in later or tomorrow, and tell me the story. You'll be grounded for a few days until they can get you another crew and chopper."

"To be honest with you, I was happy to be with Gus and Cal. They never lost focus or lamented our situation. They stayed positive the entire time, which meant a whole lot to me. Too bad Gus is going home. I'll miss him a lot," Tom replied, as he removed the medallion from his pocket.

"Roxy, what do you know about this?" he asked as he handed it to her.

"Wow, this is very ornate. It's Buddhist, I studied the religion when I was in college. The inscription on the front talks about peace and love in your lifetime. On the back in the middle of the wreath is a name, if I'm reading it properly, it would be Minh Pham. Where did you get this, did it come from that young girl you brought in?" Roxy inquired as she continued looking at the medallion.

"Yeah, she gave it to me before she died. She said something to me, but regrettably, I'll never know what it was, even though she repeated it twice. I just don't know enough Vietnamese."

After Tom explained the situation Roxy continued. "What are you going to do with it? Obviously, she gave it to you for a reason, like 'don't forget me,' or 'pray for me,' or 'now you should have this for good karma.' It was sacred to her. Most Buddhists are very fervent in their religion."

Deep in thought Tom shook his head. "I don't know what I'll do with it. I never figured I would know her name, and now I feel even worse that she's gone. You know Roxy, I might have been the one who put the bullets in her to begin with. I guess I'll hang on to it so I never forget her. That's the least I can do."

Roxy could tell how bad Tom felt about possibly shooting the young woman. "Can you remember any part of what she whispered to you, maybe I could translate some of it."

"No, I was kind of shaken seeing how young she was. Every time I worked on her wounds, I would look at her and think that a child like her belonged at home, not in this war. Regrettably, I don't remember any words she spoke, and I'll always wish I did. But I will never forget that sweet smile right before she passed, that I can never forget!" Tom replied as he took back the medallion from Roxy, placing it back in his flak jacket.

Roxy took a deep breath. "I think you have already honored her, Mr. Kenrude, even though she was the enemy, you tried to save her. I believe neither of you will ever forget that. Through those short painful memories, she will always live on in your heart and her spirit will be near. Maybe that's what she was trying to tell you in her own way, although she knew you could not understand her. She knew you were a good person, Tom. Honor her always."

Before going to bed that evening, Tom placed the medallion inside an envelope with a small note which read.

'This belonged to Minh Pham, a soldier with the Viet Cong. She gave it to me before passing away. Her memory must always be honored as she was a young, brave, frightened soldier-child as we all were. God bless her soul.'

The next morning, Tom, Cal and Roxy walked over to the morgue. The attendant unzipped the body bag so they could see her. They had dressed her in a set of Army green coveralls, combed out her long black hair, and placed a light coat of makeup on her young face. Tears rolled down the faces of Tom and Cal as they looked at the young lady. They could not believe how much younger she looked, now that she was cleaned up. Roxy had a hard time controlling her emotions as she placed her arms around both men. After looking at the girl she cried out, "For heaven's sake, she was just a baby."

Around 1500hrs that afternoon, a small burial service was held in a cemetery belonging to the people of Binh Thuy. One of the engineers from the base made a white wooden cross, with her name and date of death, engraved on a metal plate he had fastened to it.

Tom asked his father's good friends Franny and Fr. Neederman to attend the burial. Father Neederman said a few prayers, and read several passages from scripture during the short service.

As Tom and Cal walked back toward their barracks, Cal reached out to take Tom by the elbow.

"Look, I'm so sorry for the way I acted on the island. I had no right.

Maybe I didn't show it, but I'd been scared to death since we went down in that chopper. I didn't think we would ever get rescued and had about reached my wits end. I should never have called her what I did, and I never should have shot that wounded man, although it was clear he was dying. I feel sick about it."

Tom could feel the genuineness of Cal's feelings, and knew he was hurting very badly.

"Look Cal, I understand where you're coming from. I'm not sure what kept me together at times, I was pretty scared, too. Knowing it was probably my bullets that hurt her so badly didn't help. But in the end, trying to help her kept my mind in a good place, and gave me hope. You and I will always be friends, don't ever doubt that for a moment."

Cal smiled as he shook hands with Tom. "So you'll be alright working with me again?"

Tom shook his head, "Absolutely, we have made a pretty good team, and I won't throw that away for anything." Roxy approached the two men before heading back to the hospital.

"Thanks for inviting me, I know this sounds crazy, but being there for that service brought a sort of peace to my heart. I really needed that, I'm tired of war, and what it does to people. We all need to go home and get out of this horrible place."

After leaving the hospital Tom picked up his mail, he could not wait to get back to his bunk to open the envelope from Mac, as he was hoping for another tape. After listening to the tape he yelled, "I'm a father! We had a baby boy. Mac named him Sean Thomas Kenrude. Can you believe it? I'm a father!

Tom had never received so many hugs and handshakes in his entire life. Most of the men asked to send a little message back to Mac, congratulating her as well. He knew it would be a great keepsake, and something he could play back for his son when he was older, allowing him to hear the voices of the men who served with his daddy when he was born. Prior to mailing it, he placed a label on it reading, *'Voices from Vietnam.'*

CHAPTER 15
A NEW CREW

With just under three months left in Vietnam, Tom was assigned to an evac crew being transferred down from Saigon. The pilot was Warrant Officer Three Sy Cumberland, the co-pilot was Warrant Officer One Darnel Franklin. Thankfully Cal was assigned as flight mechanic, which made things a bit more comfortable for Tom. The chopper did not have a name, as Warrant Officer Cumberland felt naming an aircraft was purely bad luck.

On their third mission, they were ordered to fly east along the coast line, joining the search for a pilot from a Naval F-4 Phantom that went down the night before while on a reconnaissance mission. The co-pilot had been picked up about an hour after the crash by a South Vietnamese patrol boat.

Several pieces of wreckage floated near the coast, while an oil slick lingered in the water about two hundred yards off shore. Tom and Cal scanned the water for any signs of life, as Sy flew the chopper merely yards above the rolling waves.

About an hour into their mission, Sy picked up a mayday call from a Naval search and rescue chopper that was experiencing engine problems about five miles from their position. It was clear they were not going to make it back to their carrier, the U.S.S America. Immediately Sy lifted the chopper skyward, turning east out over the Gulf of Tonkin at a high rate of speed. Several minutes later both pilots reported watching the chopper drop into the gulf.

Although Tom was never trained as a rescue swimmer, he prepared himself to dive into the rough wind driven salt water below. Approaching the crash site, he picked out three survivors right away. Since their Huey was not equipped with a hoist, the men would have to be helped onto the runners before being lifted inside the cabin by Cal. As Sy brought the chopper down to wave height, one of the survivors swam toward the chopper unassisted.

"I'm Petty Officer Hernandez, my pilot's hurt bad, he can't swim. My navigator is trying to keep him afloat, but he has a broken arm. I don't know where our co-pilot Commander Walsh is, or flight technician Kraft. I saw Kraft jump from the chopper just before we hit the water, but I don't know where he went. He might have been hit by the blades when we crashed. I'm not sure."

Cal directed Sy to maneuver the chopper toward the injured men as Tom dove from the runner into the warm tropical water. In seconds he had taken the weight of the pilot, allowing the navigator to make his way toward the chopper, where Cal and Petty Officer Hernandez waited to pull him on board. Just as Tom arrived with the injured pilot, Darnel called out there was another man in the water about fifty yards in front of their position, who was attempting to tread water but not swim.

As the pilot certainly had broken ribs and internal injuries, pulling him up into the chopper was not an easy job. With every move he screamed out in pain until they had him on a stretcher on the floor.

As Sy moved the chopper forward slowly, once more Tom jumped back out into the water, swimming toward the injured man. A trail of blood streaked across the water as Tom approached the struggling sailor, who was no longer working very hard to tread water.

Seeing the commander's insignia Tom called out. "Where are you hurt, sir? I don't want to do any more damage if I can help it."

"I have a huge gash on my back and a hunk of metal in my left thigh. But if you help me I can get up on that runner. Just get my ass out of this damn water before I attract sharks. That's the last thing I want to deal with today, Specialist."

Tom motioned for Sy to bring the chopper down a few feet lower, as getting the commander up on to the runner was going to be a tough job. Petty Officer Hernandez dropped down into the water to help Tom, as Cal grabbed hold of the torn life preserver, pulling him up out of the water to safety.

With the commander on board, Cal and the Petty Officer stood on the runner scanning the sea as Sy made another slow search of the area for flight technician Kraft. After several minutes Tom called out. "We're going to need to call this off and get the pilot to a hospital. I'm going to lose him if we don't get help soon. How far are we from the carrier? I'm sure it would be closer than flying back to base, and we don't have much time," Tom yelled out to the flight crew.

About thirty seconds later Darnel called out. "We are about twelve miles from the carrier. I told them we're on the way and they're standing by. They will send another chopper to search the area for the flight tech."

In just a short time Cal called out as he pointed, "There she is, over on the right, what a piece of artwork. Man, she is one beautiful piece of machinery. I can't wait to get on board."

Tom took a quick minute to look at the carrier as they approached, knowing he would never get another chance like this in his lifetime. He had to agree, the America was a very splendid looking warship, as she appeared to skim effortlessly over the surface of the Gulf of Tonkin, despite the howling wind that rocked their chopper. Two minutes later, Sy set the chopper down on a pitching deck that surprised Tom. Looking at the ship from a distance, there was no way he would have guessed it was rolling that much.

Medical staff rushed toward the chopper from the island of the ship, which towered high above the flight deck. As soon as the injured were removed, a small tractor drove forward hooking a cable to one of the runners of the chopper, before pulling it off the main flight deck onto an elevator.

A lieutenant directed the men toward a door near the front of the island. Once they were inside, he removed his goggles and head set. "Welcome aboard and thanks for your help. I'm Lieutenant Mark Sebastian, the landing safety officer. A real bad weather system is coming down from the north, so we can't allow you to head back to your base tonight, so we'll be happy to have you as our guests. Just so you know, our rescue chopper found Kraft nearly a hundred yards from the crash site. How he got that far away that quickly is anyone's guess. You probably would have run out of fuel before you found him. He's a bit banged up but will be just fine. We called off the search for the F-4 pilot, maybe we can look again tomorrow if all goes well." Looking at Tom and Cal the lieutenant shook his head. "Well, we don't have green uniforms for you to wear, but we have complimentary blue navy coveralls after you get a hot shower if that works for you."

Everyone laughed as the men headed down a set of stairs leading to the crew quarters.

After a long hot shower, Tom and Cal joined their pilots in the mess deck for a good hot meal. Although some of the sailors complained about the meal, Tom was totally impressed with the quality and quantity of food on the serving line. However by now the ship was rolling tremendously, as the near gale force winds swept across the gulf. The men found it somewhat difficult eating, as they needed to hold on to their trays, stopping them before they slid off the table.

When they finished eating, Lt. Sebastian had lined up a tour of the ship with one of the ship's yeoman. Reaching the hanger deck, one of the large doors leading to an elevator was partially open. The men stood there for several minutes watching the massive waves. They were glad to be dry and safe on board this huge carrier, as the wicked storm thrashed the Gulf of Tonkin and the Mekong Delta. Off in the distance Tom could see some lights that appeared to be bobbing up and down. The Yeoman explained that it was a destroyer crashing through the heavy swells, thus earning its well-deserved nick name, the tin can.

Upon completion of the tour, the Yeoman delivered Tom and the others to their sleeping quarters.

Like everything else on the ship, the quarters were cramped and tight. Nevertheless, as Tom placed his head on his pillow, he fell asleep quickly. At least tonight he did not have to worry about being awakened by mortar or rocket attacks, or alerts, as enemy sappers attempted to breach the base perimeter.

Darkness came early as the storm raged across the gulf. All combat patrols were suspended for the night as the fleet moved out toward deeper waters.

As dawn crept over the eastern horizon, the storm began to subside. However, wind driven rain continued sweeping across the flight deck of the America, as the sturdy vessel began sailing back toward its assigned combat position.

Although he slept well, and breakfast was warm and tasty, Tom was beginning to feel the bulkheads of the massive ship close in on him. He and Cal walked to the hanger deck so they could get a breath of fresh air and look out across the gulf. As they stood silently watching the angry waves below, an ensign approached them.

"Good morning men, I'm Ensign Cross. According to the radar it looks like the storm is beginning to break up. We're guessing that by about 1200hrs. you should be able to take off. We have fueled up your chopper and given it a once over and everything looks good."

Tom smiled at the news. As the ensign turned to walk off, Tom called him back.

"Sir, do you have any news on how the men we delivered yesterday are doing?"

"Sorry to say the pilot didn't make it. He had some very bad internal injuries, things we just couldn't handle. If we could have ferried him to Cam Ranh Bay, the hospital there might have been able to save him, but he was in bad shape. Everyone else is doing fine. You guys did a good job," the young Ensign responded.

Cal shook his head. "I knew he was bad when I pulled him into the chopper. He had that scared look in his eyes that dying men seem to have so often. And there was just no real easy way to get him on board without a basket and lift."

The ensign smiled. "Don't blame yourselves. Like I said, he was in worse shape than anyone of you could have guessed, you did all you could have done for him."

By 1100hrs the rain had stopped and the wind was manageable for a helicopter flight. A small tractor pulled the Army chopper out toward the middle of the flight deck as the crew exited the island. Tom and Cal carried bags jammed with cookies from the ship's bakery, a gift from the America's skipper.

After running down the pre-takeoff check list, Warrant Officer Cumberland fired up the engine. Moments later both rotors began spinning, blowing water from the deck into a wild frenzy. After receiving permission to take off, Warrant Officer Cumberland lifted his chopper from the America's flight deck, turning due west back to the coast of Vietnam and Binh Thuy.

Peering down from the chopper everything appeared to be normal as they approached their landing spot on the airfield. Tom could see two evac choppers parked near the hospital, meaning wounded men were arriving from combat in the Delta mission.

As Sy set the chopper down, two mechanics came walking from one of the maintenance hangers.

"Hey Cumberland, any problems you need to have looked at?" One of the mechanics inquired.

"Problems no, but I do have a request. I have never liked naming a chopper in the past. But I was thinking on the way back here that I would like to have 'U.S.S. America' painted on the cowling. Do you think you guys could handle that for us overnight?"

"Okay, that sounds good to us, Cumberland. We were always wondering when you would get around to naming your bird. You're the only one that's never baptized your chopper. Consider it done. We'll do it the way the navy does numbers on hulls, white with black trim. It should look pretty cool when we're finished with it." The mechanic called out as he and Warrant Officer Cumberland shared a high five.

Tom picked up medical supplies from the hospital to resupply the chopper, as Cal cleaned the cabin and cockpit. As the men finished their work, dark storm clouds began rolling in from the gulf. It was evident that the storm had not finished giving Vietnam it's final blast. As large rain drops began falling, Tom slid the side doors closed to the cabin, as Cal and one of the mechanics finished securing the props so they couldn't be damaged by the harsh winds before being towed into the hangar.

As the howling winds drove the torrential rains sideways, everything at Binh Thuy came to a standstill. Tom sat on his bunk making a tape for Mackenzie, telling her all about their rescues at sea, and his time on board the aircraft carrier. He knew she would really enjoy the story, as it was something totally different than he usually reported. It was nearly 2200hrs when he finished writing letters home to the rest of his family. He could see Peter going crazy over the fact his big brother had beat him to living on an aircraft carrier, even though it was just for one night. In the envelope he enclosed two U.S.S. America patches that he was given by the yeoman that gave them the grand tour of the ship, knowing that Peter would cherish them forever.

Around 0100hrs Tom was awakened by several large explosions, followed by a tremendous amount of rifle and machine gun fire. Within minutes, Tom was running toward the operations building with his medical bag, as enemy mortar and rockets continued pounding the base.

As Tom, Gabe and Geno entered the building, Lt. Jurgins and First Sergeant Shills were looking over a map of the base. The men stood quiet waiting for orders, as Ridzik, Mark Grissom and Orlando Martinez came running in the side door.

Lt. Jurgins turned toward his medics. "Can't believe those bastards attacked in weather like this. We've been hit bad on the north and northwest side of the base. The enemy has broken through the wire in several places, over running gun emplacements. Kenrude, Sarducci, Ridzik, grab a jeep and head to the northern perimeter. Grissom, Martinez and Hartman grab a jeep and move to the northwest perimeter. Help where you can, and keep your weapons ready. You may do more fighting than anything else tonight, until we can get this mess under control. And for God's sake, watch out for one another out there."

Ridzik jumped into the nearest jeep with Geno jumping into the passenger seat, as Tom jumped up behind the fifty caliber machine gun. As Ridzik let the clutch fly and took off, Tom cocked the heavy machine gun and held on. All along the northern perimeter, American and South Vietnamese forces battled to hold back the surge of Viet Cong and North Vietnamese Regular Forces that had infiltrated down from the north. Just as Ridzik approached a burning deuce and a half, an RPG struck the jeep's right front wheel. Tom was tossed airborne as the explosion flipped the jeep over onto its side. Gabe Hartman, who was driving the second jeep, slammed on the brakes turning hard toward the right to avoid the spinning wreck. As he attempted to back up, another RPG struck the side of his jeep right below the machine gun where Martinez stood. Hot jagged steel and shrapnel from the RPG tore into Martinez as he flew off the back of the burning vehicle.

Still dazed from hitting the ground, Tom struggled to stand up as he looked over at the burning jeeps. Ridzik screamed in pain as Geno worked feverishly on his nearly severed right leg, attempting to stem the flow of blood from the ruptured femoral artery.

Pain shot up Tom's back as he hobbled toward the wreck to assist Geno, who was bleeding from a gash in his left shoulder.

The second jeep had landed upside down, pinning Gabe under the wreckage. Grissom had been thrown clear when the doomed vehicle tipped over. Flames licked at the rear of the jeep as Grissom attempted to pull Gabe free without any luck.

"Get out of here!" Gabe screamed at Mark. "When that gas tank goes we're both dead, so get the hell out of here, just leave me!"

"Kiss off Hartman!" Mark yelled back as he picked up the drive shaft from the road. "I'm going to put this under the front fender and lift, you wiggle your sorry ass out, and don't quit on me."

"My legs, I can't feel them, I don't think I can do much to help you. Just get the hell out of here, go see what you can do for the other guys," Gabe called out in anger.

Disregarding Gabe's pleading, Mark prepared to pry the jeep up. Three soldiers that were running toward the fighting stopped to help. Two of them helped pry the jeep up, as the third was able to pull Gabe free of the wreckage. Grissom slapped the back of one of the soldiers who helped lift the jeep, just as a bullet struck him square between the eyes.

The three soldiers picked up Gabe carrying him safely away from the burning jeep, before grabbing their equipment and disappearing into the night. Gabe sat up against a power pole looking at the bodies of Martinez and Grissom, as the gas tank exploded sending a sheet of flame skyward.

Slowly feeling began returning to Gabe's legs, and he figured the weight of the jeep had temporarily cut off circulation to his lower extremities, causing loss of feeling. Once his legs felt close to normal, he stood up using the power pole for assistance. After taking several deep breaths, he picked up an M-16 that was laying close by, along with his medical bag. Knowing there was nothing he could do for his partners, he knew he had to check on his fellow medics.

Gabe arrived to find Tom attempting to pull Ridzik's feet free from the twisted floor panels, as Geno kept pressure on a tourniquet. A slow trickle of gas was running down the floor of the buckled jeep, directly under Ridzik's seat. Pulling out his bayonet, Gabe began prying on a piece of sheet metal near the gear shift, as Tom attempted to pull the damaged brake pedal off to the left, away from Ridzik's leg.

"That's it, I have his foot!" Gabe called out, grabbing hold of Ridzik so he wouldn't slide out of the jeep too quickly, causing more damage to his leg. Just as the men laid him on the ground, several bullets struck the jeep.

Tom spun around quickly pulling his pistol from its holster, just as Gabe retrieved his M-16 from the back floor of the wreckage. Both men stood close to the jeep using it for cover as they scanned the darkness in front of them. Tom was just about to re-holster his weapon so they could get Ridzik away from the wreckage when several dark figures emerged from the blackness about ten yards away firing their AK-47s.

Gabe dropped to his knee firing at the figures rushing towards them as Tom let loose with his pistol. With only seven bullets in the magazine, Tom was out of ammunition quickly. Before he could reload, one of the Viet Cong threw a grenade over the jeep hitting Gabe's helmet before dropping to the ground. Without hesitation Gabe kicked the grenade out in front of the jeep as he dropped for cover. As the deadly device exploded, sand, mud and debris rained down on the medics. With a new magazine in his pistol, Tom peered around the front of the jeep, as Gabe made his way around the rear of the upturned wreck. Just as Tom cleared the front of the vehicle, Gabe let loose with several shots.

Tom cautiously made his way toward the rear of the wreckage, to find Gabe standing over the body of a dead Viet Cong.

"You alright?" Tom called out.

"Yeah, how about you," Gabe responded as he continued looking down at the dead man.

"I'm good. The grenade took out the other guy it appears. Are you sure you're alright?" Tom inquired as he gazed at Gabe who hadn't moved a muscle and continued looking down.

"I never killed a man close up before. I never had the experiences you, Moe and some of the other guys had. I looked right into his eyes when I pulled the trigger. I saw that sudden fear in his eyes, knowing he was about to die and there was nothing he could do to stop it. It was painful, and I think I saw his spirit slide away when he fell. What the hell did I just do?" Gabe yelled above the din of combat as he walked toward Tom.

"You did what you had to do, what we all have had to do at some point. It's over Gabe, he's gone, we're alive and now we need to get Ridzik and Geno to the hospital. You need to focus because I need your help, Gabe," Tom explained as he watched Gabe look back at the dead man one more time.

"Yeah, I'm good. Let's find a way to get some help for these guys," Gabe responded as he slapped Tom on the shoulder.

Moments later a five-quarter ton truck came inching down the road. Tom signaled to the driver to stop as he explained their situation. Without hesitation the two men in the cab loaded Ridzik and Geno into the back of their truck before turning around.

Arriving back at the hospital, Tom grabbed a corpsman with a stretcher to assist in getting Ridzik and Geno to the triage area. Both men were very weak from loss of blood, although Geno refused to be placed on a stretcher.

Within minutes Roxy and several other nurses attended to the wounded men, taking them into treatment areas where doctors awaited them. Tom sat down on the tailgate of the truck as Gabe paced back and forth. Tom knew what Gabe was going through because he had already been there. They were medics, they were supposed to save lives, but in this war, all the traditional lines had been crossed, leaving each man responsible to do what he felt was right. Gabe was a strong man and a good medic. Tom knew it may take a few days, but he would work through it, especially when he came to realize Martinez and Grissom were dead, Ridzik may never walk normally again, if they could even save his leg, and Geno might end up going home because of his injuries.

As Tom jumped off the tailgate, he stopped to listen for the sounds of combat. Only a sporadic shot could be heard now and then coming from the north end of the base. The attack had been repulsed by the valiant soldiers manning the perimeter, and those who answered the call for help. Indeed it had been a bloody night that no one would care to repeat for some time, although in reality, that might well depend on the number of losses suffered by the enemy.

Tom and Gabe quickly returned to the north perimeter to assist medics with all the wounded. As the sun began to illuminate the battlefield, it was clear to see the enemy had taken a severe beating. Combat engineers with bucket loaders began digging deep, huge pits several hundred yards from the outer wire. They then began scraping the ground with their buckets, rolling bodies of the dead into the pits. Inside the perimeter, bodies of the dead enemy invaders were loaded onto trucks before being delivered to the massive graves. It was a sickening operation, but there was no other way to safely dispose of so many corpses, before they began to putrefy and spread disease. As the pits were closed, Father Neederman walked among them saying prayers for the dead. Later in the day wooden signs were erected near the pits in Vietnamese, informing the public of the existence of the mass graves.

As Tom and Gabe prepared to leave the area of the north perimeter, Sgt. Doogan came rolling up in a Jeep.

"Well, Mr. Kenrude, I see you made it through the night intact. I was told several medics from your evac unit were killed, I had to find out if you were one of them. Glad to see you're alright."

Removing his helmet Tom leaned against the jeep. "Franny, I never thought I would lose so many good friends in short order like that. I know you and Dad did several times over in France, but this is tough to deal with."

Franny stepped from his jeep as he wiped sweat from his forehead. "It's war son, pure and simple. No one can ever be ready for it, you never know when it will happen. Just take a moment to grieve for them and move on. That sounds like crap I know. But if you wallow in it, you're no good to anyone. Get back to work, and do your job, that is the best remedy I've found." After shaking hands with Tom and Gabe, Franny jumped back in his jeep and drove off.

That evening Tom walked over to the hospital to check on Ridzik and Geno. He found Roxy sitting at a desk writing in a hospital journal.

"How are you doing Roxy? It must have been hell in here over the last twenty-four hours."

"You don't know the half of it soldier, and I'm all too sure you don't know your friend Frank Ridzik didn't make it either. He lost so much blood before he got here, he went into shock as we took him into the operating area. The doctors did all they could for him, Tom. He just had nothing left to give us back. I'm so sorry, however Geno on the other hand will be fine. We stitched him up after pulling several more pieces of metal from his arm. He argued that he didn't want to be transferred out, so he'll be on light duty for ten days before he can get back into a chopper. I have plenty of work for him to do in the hospital, so he'll be just fine. He's like you, damn the torpedoes full speed ahead. If you want to see him go right ahead, he's bored and a little restless. He asked about you several hours ago."

Tom was silent for a moment. "I really thought Ridzik would make it. I knew his leg might be questionable, but I never thought he would die. That makes me just sick. Who would have ever thought we could lose three great medics in one night, and none of us were even in the air."

Slowly Roxy stood up from the desk and walked over to Tom. "You did all you could do out there. Everything was against you from the beginning.

Listen to me, Tom. You have just a little over two months to go so you need to be careful. Don't dwell on what happened tonight, because it will keep you from doing what you need to do out there. You have a wife and baby that need you back home. Don't make any foolish mistakes, or try to be a hero, it will get you killed."

Tom looked intently at Roxy. "I know what you're saying, and I appreciate your concern. But tonight everything happened so fast, no one had time to think or react the way we normally would have. I'm glad Geno and Gabe survived, although Gabe had a pretty tough time when he killed the last guy face to face. Man, he took that hard, I never saw him like that before."

Roxy smiled slightly as she stepped back away from Tom. "Mr. Kenrude, you are a good man, a great medic, and a good friend, now go visit Geno, he's waiting for you."

Tom smiled at the pretty redhead, "Thanks Roxy, you're the best. I'm so glad we met. You always know what to say to help me get through the rough times. I'll miss you very much when I leave but always consider you one of the special people I met over here. Maybe when you get back to the states we can get together. I would like you to meet Mac and the baby."

"That's a date, Mr. Kenrude. I'll give you my address before you leave. It would be really fun to meet Mac and your new child. I'm going to hold you to that, Tom," Roxy replied with a loving smile.

"Well, I brought Geno a couple of his favorite candy bars, so I should go see him before it gets much later. Thanks again for the talk, Roxy," Tom replied as he prepared to leave.

Laughing Roxy shook her head. "Yeah, that's all I need, Sarducci on a sugar high bouncing off the walls all night. Get out of here, Kenrude, and go see your buddy."

Geno observed Tom walking into the ward. "Hey Kenrude, I thought you forgot all about me. I was hoping you might stop by. I really wanted to talk to you tonight."

Tom laughed as he tossed the bag with the candy bars at Geno. "No way would I forget you good buddy. I had a few other things I needed to do before I came over here. Like getting your groceries from the PX. I knew you would never survive here without them."

"All is forgiven Mr. Kenrude, you came through in a pinch. I guess I'll be on light duty for about ten to twelve days before I can fly again. I kind of have a feeling Roxy is going to make me pay for arguing about staying here. She wanted me to go home in the worst way. Glad the doctor had the wisdom to intercede. I want to finish my tour just like you," Geno explained as he unwrapped a candy bar.

It was nearly 2300hrs when Tom walked out of the hospital. Roxy had told her replacement to allow Tom to stay as long as he wanted, as it was good therapy for both men.

The following morning Lt. Jurgins requested Tom come to the operations office. As Tom walked through the door, the lieutenant looked him over. "Well Kenrude, you look pretty good considering all that happened last night. How are you feeling?"

Tom nodded his head. "Pretty good sir. I had a long talk with Geno last night, and Gabe this morning. It was one of those things that couldn't have been avoided, we were caught between the rock and the hard place simple as that. No one could have prevented it."

"I'm glad you see it that way, Tom. As you know by now, this damn war is a bitch and totally unpredictable. Had I thought for a minute you were going to be attacked like that I never would have sent you guys out there. But we do what we have to do. So now I have three letters to write that I'm dreading. There is nothing I hate more about this job." After a moment of silence he continued. "You won't be flying today. I'm giving you guys the day off to do what you need to do after last night. But tomorrow we continue the mission. I have two medics coming from the replacement center, and Bill Boulder will come out of the hospital to take one of the spots."

The following day all evac choppers were once again in the air, delivering wounded soldiers to the hospital. Tom felt relieved to be back in the thick of things. It took his mind off the bloody night that had claimed three of his good friends.

CHAPTER 16
BABIES AND BROTHERS

After a long restless night, Mackenzie woke up early, not feeling very well. She walked into the kitchen where her mother and father were having coffee. She sat down at the kitchen table and was about to pick up an empty cup when she suddenly felt an intense pain.

"Oh God, I think Sean Thomas might be coming. He isn't supposed to be here for another two weeks. Oh damn it hurts, get me to the hospital. What if somethings wrong?" Mackenzie cried.

In a matter of minutes, the Bishops were flying down Highway 12 into Willmar. Arriving at the hospital, Mackenzie was taken straight into the maternity ward where her doctor had been all night.

"What's happening, Doctor? He's not supposed to be here yet. Not for two more weeks. What's happening? I don't want to lose our son," Mackenzie cried out as tears rolled down her cheeks.

The doctor smiled, "Mac, sometimes babies just don't understand our calendars, and have a tendency to be on their own schedules. You know we just predict as best we can, but that's all it is, just a prediction. From what I can tell nothing appears to be wrong, you're just going to be a mother a couple weeks earlier than you expected. I'm sure Thomas will approve of being a daddy no matter what the date."

While the Bishops waited, they called Steve and Karen. In no time, the Kenrude's joined them in the waiting room, along with Mike and Glenda.

Although time appeared to drag on, in just a few hours a nurse walked into the room to announce that six pound, twenty-two inch Sean Thomas Kenrude had arrived, and mother and child were doing just fine.

After kissing Karen, Steve gave his brother and sister-in-law big hugs, before congratulating the Bishops who were excited and crying.

A short time later the family was able to see Mackenzie and the baby. Karen looked down at her grandchild and cried. As Steve placed his arm around her she smiled up at him.

"He looks so much like Tom did when he was born. It's almost like looking back at his birth all over again. He'll be so happy when he sees his son."

Mackenzie held out her hand toward Karen. "Tom showed me those photos you took of him after he was born. I thought the same thing, Sean really does look like his daddy, and I wouldn't want it any other way. He'll be a tall, blue eyed Kenrude. We may have to wait a while to figure out the hair color though, since Sean here is completely bald."

Everyone in the room laughed as Mackenzie kissed her baby. "I have waited to do that for so long. Sean is a dream come true for us, and the start of our family. I can't wait for Tom to come home and complete the circle. He'll be such a proud daddy."

On the drive home Karen looked over at her husband. "So, how does it feel to be a grandpa? You always said you wanted a dozen grandkids, so now you have a start."

Taking hold of Karen's hand he smiled. "Yeah, this is so great. It's really hard to believe my little boy is now a father. That kid who could never stay clean, could nurse sick animals back to health, and could throw a football better than me, and I was the damn quarterback. I'm so proud of him for all he's accomplished. He and Mac will be great parents, there is no doubt in my mind. How are you feeling, Grandma?"

Karen laughed as she shook her head. "I've always loved Mac, even though we've butted heads over many things. I know she loves our son very much, and will never do him wrong. I like the idea of being a Grandma. I can't wait for the rest of our children to have babies, all kinds of babies!"

The first thing Mackenzie did when she arrived home, was to make a tape for Tom so he could hear his son making all kinds of baby sounds, and especially some crying, she knew that would get to him in a big way. The drug store became very accustomed to Mac bringing in many rolls of film at a time, as she attempted to capture everything their baby did, so Tom would not miss out. But most of all, she prayed every day for Tom's safe return so their family would be complete. At the end of each day, Karen and Mackenzie would cross it off their calendars, as they had been counting down each day since Tom had left. They didn't need to turn over as many pages on their calendars anymore, as his return date was coming closer, and that made everyone very happy.

Tom's younger brother Peter was excited about Sean's birth, but was not really sure how to deal with a baby in the family, or how to hold it when Mackenzie gave him the opportunity. After all he had just turned 16, and was at that awkward age where babies and masculinity were still a jumbled mess. At school the girls liked him, but he was unsure how to deal with it. But he was able to compensate for all of that with sports and academics where he knew exactly what to do. Peter was a star athlete in every sport he attempted, breaking several of Tom's individual records. Academically, he was a straight 'A' student, and often tutored kids who were falling behind. His favorite classes were math, science and chemistry.

However, he was also at the age where he began to wonder what he was going to do with himself when he graduated from high school. Of course his parents hoped he would settle down in Glendale, get married, and spend his life working with Kenrude Farms, Inc. Both of his cousins, Matt and John, were excited and looking forward to operating the huge agricultural enterprise their family had built.

But Peter never shared his growing ambitions to become a pilot with his parents or other family members besides Tom. He read Tom's letters over and over when he wrote about choppers and the fighter aircraft that backed up their missions. Peter never missed the evening news on TV, where they ran combat footage of aircraft attacking enemy positions, or being catapulted from aircraft carriers. Those film clips excited him far more than the big International combine his dad and uncle had just purchased.

One evening after school, Peter watched Erik Preston spraying pesticides on a field south of their home. He watched the bright blue plane make a sharp turn before heading toward the small grass runway on the Preston farm. Starting Tom's beloved dirt bike, he rode quickly down to the small airstrip where Erik was just idling up to his hangar. As Peter rode into the yard, Erik waved from the cockpit of his crop sprayer.

"Well Mr. Kenrude, what can I do for you today?" Erik asked as he jumped down from his plane.

Peter didn't answer at first as his eyes were glued to the blue Stearman bi-plane parked in the hangar.

"She's a great little airplane," Erik stated, as he walked up to Peter. "Want to look in the cockpit?" Erik asked, knowing Peter was chomping at the bit to do so.

"Can I? Would you mind if I sat in it? I've always dreamed of doing that, every time you fly over our house. Today your duster really got to me, so I had to drive over," Peter exclaimed as he ran his hand gently over the bottom wing. "She's a real beauty!"

Smiling, Erik walked up to the plane, explaining how he should get up into the front seat. Once Peter was seated, Erik placed the headset over his ears. "Now you look like a real pilot, Pete."

Gently, Pete took the stick in his hand moving it from side to side as he smiled. "Wow, this is so neat. Where did you learn to fly?"

"My grandfather was a pilot in World War One, and my Dad was a pilot in World War Two. This was my grandfather's plane. He taught me how to fly it when I was about your age, when we lived south of Minneapolis. My Dad inherited it when my grandmother passed away. He did a lot of work on it to bring it back to its present condition. I was already crop dusting when he passed away, so Mom told me to take it, love it, and keep it in good shape." Erik explained watching Peter smile.

"So are you going to take him for a ride?" Anne Preston inquired, as she stood in the doorway. "Anyone that smiles that much at an airplane really should get a test flight, honey. The kids are still napping, so I can wait with dinner. Go ahead, take Pete for a quick ride."

Peter thought his heart was going to pop out of his chest it was pounding so hard, as he and Erik pushed the Stearman clear of the hangar. Once they were buckled in, Erik rolled over the radial engine. After several puffs of black smoke the engine came to life. The plane shuddered as if the engine were going to knock everything loose.

Moments later Erik turned the plane toward the grass runway, as he opened the throttle. In no time the light plane was airborne, heading straight up into the crystal clear blue sky. Peter sat completely still as the cool air rushed over his goggles. After several minutes Erik asked, "How's it feel, Pete? We're heading straight for Eagle Lake right now, then we'll buzz your folk's place."

"This is awesome, Mr. Preston. I never expected this to happen today," Peter exclaimed as he watched the sun sparkling on Eagle Lake. Seconds later Erik sent the plane into a dive over the Kenrude house making a wide circle. Peter waved at Abigail as she sat on the swing set looking up at the plane. He laughed as he watched her run toward the house.

As Erik brought the plane back up to level flight about five hundred feet above the ground he called out. "Alright Pete, take the stick. You're going to fly her."

Slowly Peter grasped the stick, feeling the vibration in his hand. Over the next few minutes Erik explained how to make turns, increase altitude, and descend. After ten more minutes Erik took control of the plane, bringing it back to earth on the grass runway.

After pushing the plane back into the hangar, Erik smiled. "You're a natural, Pete. You never panicked when that gust of wind caught us. You corrected like a pro. I was completely amazed!"

Peter smiled as he shook his head. "That was the most awesome thing I have ever done. I can't thank you enough for the ride."

"Ride hell, I think that was your first lesson. Keep in touch, and when I'm not busy I'll take you up and teach you how to really fly, land and take off. I think you have the makings of a pilot," Erik said, as they shook hands.

Pete's smile disappeared. "I don't have money to pay you for the lessons, and I know my folks won't pay for them either."

Erik smiled. "Well, this old hangar gets pretty dirty with the planes going in and out. Sometimes the fertilizer and pesticide bags mount up, and sometimes Anne could use a hand with the lawn. If you can help me out with those things, I would be more than happy to give you lessons. Last year I had to hire someone to get all that work done. Free lessons would actually be a big financial help to Anne and me. What do you say, Pete?"

"It's a deal, you got yourself a deal, Mr. Preston," Peter exclaimed, as tears ran down his face.

That little hangar was never so clean, and the lawn around the Preston home was manicured as if it were a golf course. Anne enjoyed having Peter around to watch the kids from time to time when she was busy with paperwork, and Peter loved teaching the boys how to catch and hit a baseball.

Although Peter was having the time of his life, and Steve approved of the plan, Karen was very apprehensive of Peter flying around in an open aircraft. More than once she talked to Steve about her fears with Tom flying in choppers in Vietnam, and Peter cruising around Minnesota in an open Stearman. On more than one occasion, she attempted to convince Peter that she would be much happier if he were spending more time learning to operate the combine.

One afternoon after a dental appointment, Peter waited for Karen to pick him up in town. He strolled over to the drug store to look at magazines on flying. He found one that had several articles on the newest naval fighter school in California, called Top Gun. After purchasing the magazine, he hid it inside a folder filled with school papers. He knew his mother would get very upset if she found that magazine. One son in the service was enough for her, and she intended for Peter to help run the farm, not to fly Navy fighters off the deck of an aircraft carrier.

During his study period the next day, Peter went to the office of his guidance counselor. He found Mr. Workham sitting alone in his office grading papers.

Peter knocked on the door frame before entering the office. "Sir, do you have time to answer a couple of questions I have about college?"

Smiling, Mr. Workham pointed to a chair. "I always have time to speak to students about their future, Mr. Kenrude. What can I help you with?"

Peter began explaining about his flying lessons and his love of aircraft. After several minutes he asked. "I would like to be a Navy pilot, so what do I need to do to get into Annapolis?"

Mr. Workman walked over to a rack filled with brochures on colleges. Returning to his desk, he handed Peter a brochure on the Naval Academy.

"This pamphlet really explains the process very well. Your grades are excellent, and you have been taking courses the Navy would be happy with. Continue getting top grades, take more math and science courses, and maybe get your pilot's license before you graduate. All of that will have bearing when you fill out your application and go through the screening process. In fact, I know Senator Henry quite well. If you continue working as you have been, and still want to shoot for Annapolis when you graduate, I'll contact the Senator regarding a placement for you. It would be nice to have a Glendale man go to one of the military academies. I've always dreamed of having one of our students become a military officer. You could be the first, Peter, and I believe you have what it takes."

Smiling Peter stood up. "That would be fantastic Mr. Workman. You can count on me to do my best in the balance of my high school years. I want to go to the Naval Academy more than anything. I just have to convince my folks that it's the best thing for me. Tom kind of got the ball rolling when he joined the army, so he took some of the heat for me."

Mr. Workman laughed. "Yes, I always liked Thomas. I had thought maybe he was the guy that would go to one of the military academies. But he had a dream and followed it, so you can't knock that. I hope he gets back from Vietnam alright and finishes medical school. He will make a terrific doctor, plus he has a great wife. Mackenzie and my daughter are pretty good friends."

Leaving the guidance office, Peter was more excited than he had been in a long time. Finally, it appeared that everything in his life was starting to make sense. He had no qualms about his plans, and there was not going to be anyone, including his mother, that would be able to change his mind. He couldn't wait to write Tom and tell him about his plans. He knew Tom would endorse them instantly, after all he was the first one in the Kenrude family to make it clear that farming was not for him.

Peter understood that it was best to speak with his parents regarding his plans sooner rather than later. After church services Sunday morning, Peter sat down with his parents to have breakfast.

Steve looked at his son for a moment. "What's going on with you, Pete? The last few days you've been acting a bit strange. Have you met a young lady we should know about?"

Abigail laughed, "Yeah Peter, is she cute? Is it Wendy Wilkes? I saw you talking to her the other day on the school bus. I know she likes you a lot."

Peter had to laugh. "No. Sorry Abby, it's not a girl, although Wendy is cute."

Karen sighed, "Wendy is precious and her family is great. You could do much worse than her Peter. But if it isn't a girl, what is it? I've noticed you acting a bit differently the last few days as well. Tell us, what is going on in the life of Peter Kenrude?"

Peter choked down a swallow of coffee as he looked at his parents.

"Mom, I already know how you are going to react, but I've made up my mind. I have a major goal I'm working towards. I spoke with Mr. Workman about colleges this week. After a long conversation, I told him I wanted to attend Annapolis. I want to be a Naval Officer and a pilot."

Karen placed her coffee cup on the table. "That will not make it! I have one son in the army right now serving in a war. I'll not have another son in the service. The answer is no! Forget about it!"

Steve shook his head. "Son, I was hoping you would stay here on the farm and work with Matt and Greg. The three of you could make a great team and take Kenrude Farms to a new level. You guys have the brains and the skill to do great things."

Peter looked down for a moment. "Mom, Dad, I know what your plans are for me. But they are your plans, not mine. Farming is not what I want to do. I love flying, and Erik says I could get my license in about a year. Every time I go up, it gets in my blood more and more. I'm sorry, but I'm going to join the navy and become a pilot one way or the other, with or without your blessings."

Steve and Karen sat quietly looking at each other. After several moments of thought, Steve spoke. "I guess we can't live our children's lives, or demand that they live the way we want them to. Honey, although you hate the idea, we have to consider Pete's happiness and what he wants for his future. I have my own reservations, but he would get a great education at Annapolis."

Karen wiped a tear from her cheek. "Is war the only thing the Kenrude family is good for? Why does this family have to single handedly defend this country when others run to Canada to evade the draft? Can anyone explain that to me?"

Taking a deep breath, Peter reached over, taking his mother's hand. "Mom, I have wanted to serve since Tom joined. I wasn't sure how or where, but I've been interested in flying for a while. Once I got some flying in, I knew without a doubt what I wanted to do. I know I have two years before I graduate, but I know what I want, I know what will make me happy, and I know how I want to live my life. I need you and Dad to give me your blessing, just like you did when I wanted to start flying. Please Mom, give me your blessing."

Karen looked at the ceiling for a moment before looking at her husband. "God knows I fought hard to keep Tom out of the army. I fought so hard I almost turned him away from me. I know Mac still has bad feelings about that entire incident, no matter what she says. I pray someday she'll finally be able to put it behind her and fully forgive me. There is no way I can go through that again, and hurt the ones I love. So Peter, if that's what you want for your life, I'll give you my blessing. I may not like it, nor totally approve, but like your father says, we can't live your life."

Peter stood up from the table walking over to his mother. Bending down he took her in his arms. "Thank you, Mom. I needed your blessing more than you know. I love you guys very much, but I just need to do this. I need to so badly that nothing else matters, including Wendy Wilkes. Although I do have to admit she is really something. Before I graduate, I just might get up the nerve to ask her out."

Karen smiled at her youngest son. "Honey, just take all of this one day at a time. As you said, you have two years of high school left to go. Please keep an open mind, and make sure you make the right decisions."

Later that evening Karen and Steve went for a walk down toward Eagle Lake. As they sat on the rocks Karen looked over at her husband. "You have sure been quiet since we left the house. What's going on in that head of yours?"

After skipping a stone across the water, Steve took in a deep breath. "I don't really know what to say, honey. When we started building Kenrude Farms, I could see Tom, Peter, Matthew and Greg all taking over parts of the operation, making it bigger and better than I ever thought possible. Now it appears it will be up to Mike's boys to continue the dream. In a way that really hurts. When I'm gone, there will be no one from my side of the family involved. Where the hell did I go wrong? Why can't my boys have the desire to build on my dream? I love them both so much, but I know I can't control them."

Skipping another rock, he continued. Karen was quiet, knowing her husband needed to get this out.

"Hell, when Tom graduates from medical school, who knows where he may end up. He could end up being a doctor in Seattle or Miami. If Pete stays in the navy, hell, the skies the limit as to where he may live. If he were to marry Wendy Wilkes, she would have no problem going where ever the navy sends him. It's not like she'll be here raising a family while he's in Hawaii or San Diego."

A few more minutes ticked by in silence.

Steve finally continued. "Maybe Abigail will marry someone from Glendale that will want to be involved. At least that would keep our side of the family in the mix. But that's a long shot at best."

Karen looked at the wild flower she had picked before sitting down. For several moments she studied her husband's face before she spoke. "God knows all I wanted was for our boys to be involved in the farm, it was my dream too. It was kind of my way of keeping my two sons safe and happy with their wives and children, right here near Glendale. What a great thing that would have been. But for some reason, God has chosen to reject my dreams and prayers, and I don't understand why. I do know that I fight for peace of mind and understanding every day. I pray now that little Sean might be the one to jump into the farm someday. Tom and Mac will make sure he knows what the family is all about, and what the farming operation means to all of us. So I guess, there's still some hope down the road."

Steve shook his head. "I know for Sean it will be like that World War One song, *'How do you keep them down of the farm after they've seen Paris.'* Tom and Mac will be traveling all around the country, and maybe the world. Sean will never come back to Glendale to be a farmer, not after being exposed to all that culture and life style. I guess we have to admit right now that Abigail might just be our best chance at having a family member involved with the business. There are some young boys her age around Glendale and Willmar that live on farms. Maybe one of them will marry her and see our operation as a good thing to get involved in. But I'm not going to hold my breath anymore."

Karen smiled at her husband. "Honey we have three beautiful, intelligent children. We have raised them well. We've taught them to think for themselves, and take pride in whatever they do. And I'm very proud of all of them. I guess we need to just enjoy the kids as they are, and give them the tools they need to keep going forward, wherever that might take them."

The following morning Steve stopped by his parent's house for coffee. As they sat at the table he explained about Peter's plan to attend Annapolis and not work on the farm.

When he was finished talking, Alex leaned forward. "Son, I ran into Art Young at the hospital in Willmar the other day when I went in for a check-up. He owns about eight hundred acres west of Willmar. He told me his oldest son is attending Veterinarian school in Ames, Iowa, and his youngest boy just joined the Fire Department up in St. Cloud. He talked about how bad he felt that there was no one left in the family to take over when he retired. But we are lucky in a way, because Mike's boys still want to farm, so the family legacy will be solid for twenty to thirty years. And you never know what may happen with grandkids or Abby, you never know who she may marry. So look on the bright side, son. Kenrude Farms is alive and well, and still has a great future."

Steve smiled at his father. "You always have had a way to find the silver lining. When you explain it like that, it all seems better. I guess I'll just have to see what comes down the road before I get excited. Besides, Mike and I still have a lot of years to work."

Nancy smiled as she set her coffee cup down. "And remember one big thing, Steven. All we really want is for our children to be happy and productive. If they are happy, healthy, and doing what they enjoy, we have done a good job."

As Steve went to work with Mike, he understood everything his parents had told him. He realized his work and investment would be safe for generations to come and that was worthwhile.

CHAPTER 17
UNREST BACK HOME

Unhappiness regarding the Vietnam War continued building across the United States, as more young men were dying for a war no one really understood. It had already destroyed the Presidency of Lyndon Johnson, and was now causing problems for President Richard Nixon, who had vowed to end the war if he were elected. All across the nation, anti-war protests broke out on college campuses. ROTC buildings were burned, sit-ins occupied University Administration Buildings, and National Guard troops were called in to restore order, while politicians, clergy and other prominent Americans, spoke out against our involvement in South-East Asia, on television on a daily basis. America had become a nation of Hawks, who supported the war, or Doves, who sought peace. It was nearly impossible to find any middle ground on the issue.

Many Minnesotans were hoping a peace deal could be achieved, if Vice President Hubert H. Humphrey could defeat Nixon in the 1968 Presidential election, since he had been their U.S. Senator for many years. However, his reputation had been severely tarnished by being Johnson's Vice President. Now they had to place their hopes on a President they disliked and unapologetic-ally called, 'Tricky Dick.'

Glendale had always been a rather conservative community, but voted democratic in most elections, except when Eisenhower ran for president. He was seen as the hero of the war in Europe that everybody loved and admired. Nearly every car in Glendale wore an 'I LIKE IKE' sticker on their rear bumper.

Although Eisenhower was the first president to send advisers to Vietnam, they mostly blamed Kennedy for the war itself. He believed in the Domino Theory, that if Vietnam fell, so would all of South East Asia. And now Nixon was promising the same as he asked congress to allow bombing of North Vietnamese sanctuaries, and supply lines in Laos and Cambodia, just as Kennedy had predicted would happen.

Glendale was no different than any other community in Minnesota, where daily discussions and arguments regarding the war took place. However they were usually peaceful, with both sides willing to argue their points over a hot cup of coffee at the local cafe, and in the end, they usually agreed to disagree, as they knew there was nothing anyone in Glendale could do to end the war.Obviously, there wasn't a home in the Glendale area, where the war news was more closely watched and studied than the Kenrude and Bishop homes. Although Steve, Peter and Abigail watched the five o'clock evening news regularly, Karen had a tendency to avoid it, unless she heard a headline that drew her into the living room. She would never watch the network's one hour expose's, where their anchor men went to the war zone to gather human interest stories, or to explain why America was losing the war. It was always too painful to watch, and she was always afraid she would see Tom's crew rescuing a bloody soldier during a combat mission.

It was just the opposite with Mackenzie, who hoped she would see her husband on the news. At least she would know he was safe, for that period of time. Around town most residents knew by now not to discuss the war when Mackenzie was around. If there was any negative discussion going on, Mackenzie would be on top of it like frosting on a cake, and she never backed down. After all, she was defending her husband, so no one's opinion mattered when she spoke her mind.

Although St. Cloud was about sixty-five miles from Glendale, it had the closest Federal Office Building with a social security office. As Steve needed to purchase repair parts from an implement dealer near the city, he brought Peter along, so he could apply for his social security card.

As they walked down the Germain Mall toward the Federal Building, they observed about two hundred people pointing toward the building as they chanted, "Hey, hey, it's not okay, how many kids did you kill today!"

Taking Peter by the arm, Steve walked across the mall toward a bank where they could watch what was happening. Two women broke from the crowd, running straight toward the Federal Building's main entrance, before being turned back by police. Both of them carried quart jars filled with a red substance appearing to be blood. After the officers blocked their entrance, they began throwing the liquid toward the building as the onlookers cheered their approval. Swiftly several officers detained and hand cuffed the women, as they attempted to run. Four young men standing near Steve cheered when the women were taken away.

Turning toward the tallest of the group, Steve inquired, "I take it you don't agree with the protest?"

"Hell no!" The man replied, "I have a brother stationed at Da Nang, and this crap pisses me off. I would love nothing more than to jump into that crowd and start busting heads. Our guys are dying for their freedom, and this is how they get payed back? How about you, what are your feelings?"

Steve shook his head. "My son is an air evacuation combat medic stationed at Quang Tri right now. I served in World War Two and Korea, so this shit just boils my blood."

One of the men wearing a leather vest stepped forward. "My name is Dan, I served a year over there with the Navy. Do you know what this bunch of heroes is planning? They're going to kill a small dog with homemade napalm, right here on the mall before they leave today. We're here to grab that poor animal before they can do anything to it. Do you want to help us, or are you willing to let this sick bunch of losers destroy an innocent animal for their fun?"

Peter looked up at his father, "Dad, we have to help these guys. Do you know how mad Tom would be, if he found out we allowed them to kill that poor dog? It isn't right, Dad!"

Steve looked grim as he nodded his head. Turning toward the four men he inquired. "What do you want us to do? I don't want my son to get arrested, he's only sixteen."

"No problem," Dan said with a smile. "Just stand by the street corner. If you see someone coming from the north or south with an animal cage, just wave at us, we'll take it from there. No need for you to get more involved than that. We just can't have eyes on everything with this crowd."

"Sounds like a plan," Steve replied, as he guided Peter around the crowd toward the corner of Eighth Avenue and St. Germain Street.

Several minutes later Peter observed two older men approaching from the south, carrying a metal live trap, containing a small dog, and a third man carrying a metal vessel that could have held the napalm.

"Dad there they are, right by that yellow Buick." Peter called out.

Steve waved his arm toward Dan, who had stationed himself midway between his friends who were scanning the mall to the east. In a split second, the four men were busting through the crowd heading toward the men with the dog.

Dan gave a quick shove to the man carrying the live trap. Losing his balance, he reached out for the Buick, allowing one of Dan's partners to grab the cage and run south. Dan and his two buddies acted as blockers, slowing anyone attempting to chase their friend. When the police arrived, they took possession of the metal container and cuffed the three men. It was evident the police were well aware of their intentions.

Knowing the Federal Building would not be open for the balance of the day, Steve and Peter walked back toward the Loop Parking lot. As they approached the intersection on Seventh Avenue, Peter pointed to the man with the cage standing outside of the drug store across the street. When the traffic light turned green, Steve and Peter crossed the street quickly, approaching him.

"Hey guys, thanks for your help back there. It worked out better than we thought it would. We might not have seen them had it not been for your help. So now my girlfriend has a new dog to house break." The young man said with a smile.

Steve laughed. "You better get the hell out of here before any of those protesters come this way and catch you. I'm sure they are not in a great mood."

"Yeah, I agree. Here comes Carla, she just ran into the drug store real quick, so now we'll be on our way. I hope your son stays safe over there, and thanks again for your help." He replied.

Peter was very proud of what they had accomplished today. He felt like a hero saving that dog, even though all he did was alert the four men so they could take action. He couldn't wait to get home and tell Abigail about all that had happened. No doubt she would be upset as she declined the invitation to ride along.

CHAPTER 18
THE WAR WITHIN

Poverty, disease and crime were the hallmarks of Vietnam in the 1960's. Governments in Saigon collapsed on a regular basis, either through military coups, or assassinations funded by the United States, Russia or by the North Vietnamese government itself. Political prominence in South Vietnam depended on money, who was willing to fund you, and who you could trust on any given day. The stability of every government in Saigon depended heavily on American dollars from Washington to keep it afloat. However all too often, corrupt politicians funneled millions of those dollars into foreign bank accounts for their own use.

It was obvious for years that most high ranking politicians in Saigon realized the South would never win the war, and they would have to leave the country quickly to survive. So millions of dollars in cash and gold wound up in safe deposit boxes in the Philippines, Singapore, Hong Kong, France and the United States.

As the war against the North appeared to have no end, the South Vietnamese dong ran an annual inflation rate of two to three hundred percent, making the American dollar the most demanded and collected currency on the streets.

Next to illicit drugs and the opium trade, perhaps the most lucrative industry in the South was prostitution. Street walkers and whore houses could be found on any given street in Saigon. They always turned a good profit, as they had an eager clientele from many South East Asian business men, and soldiers, ready to part with their money for a few minutes of excitement. However all the clients realized they were gambling they would not contract some form of venereal disease, which ran rampant among the young women.

Although authorities claimed to be cracking down on these operations, it was well known by citizens and the American military alike, that many of the brothels were owned and operated by the Canh Sat, South Vietnam's infamous state police who were known as the 'White Mice' for the brilliant white uniforms they wore, and the sneaky underhanded operations they were involved in.

Attempting to cheat or injure one of the women was a serious crime which was always quickly and brutally punished by the Canh Sat.

The war South Vietnam fought against North Vietnam took center stage throughout the world from 1965 through 1975. But the most brutal war of all, was the one perpetrated against average South Vietnamese citizens by the Canh Sat, and their powerful friends in the CIA. Both the CIA and the White Mice had one major goal—eliminate all North Vietnamese sympathizers in the South, and they would go to any lengths to find, torture and eradicate them by any means, whether they were actually guilty or just generally suspected.

For the average farmer in South Vietnam, they knew little about what happened in Saigon or even who their latest leadership was. They were caught up in a war that left them no way out. The South Vietnamese, and the United States military, told them they were their friends, and that they would do everything they could to help them, as long as they distanced themselves from the Viet Cong or the North Vietnamese military.

Consequently, the Viet Cong told village leaders they could either cooperate with them, or they would be killed, their women raped, and their villages burned to the ground. So, America's plan to win the hearts and minds of South Vietnamese peasants was all but lost before it began. Sadly, though understandable, many parents gave up their sons and daughters to fight for the Viet Cong, regardless of what promises were made to them by the Saigon Government. Entire villages handed over animals and their meager crops to feed the guerrilla force that showed no mercy for noncompliance or expectations of complicity with their enemies.

Regrettably, the CIA had the same feelings regarding complicity as did the Viet Cong. If CIA Operatives felt a village was aiding the enemy, reprisals were swift and brutal. There need not be any real probable cause, any overwhelming burden of proof, or factual evidence for a CIA squad to descend into a village, extracting retribution for alleged transgressions against the war effort.

But that was not the worst. In 1962, Military Assistance Command Vietnam (MACV), was established at Ton San Nhut Airbase just outside of Saigon, to be responsible for all American war efforts in country. They reported directly to the Commander in Chief of all Pacific Forces.

However, since the war effort was not moving in the direction desired by the Pentagon and political forces in Washington, an even darker more sinister organization was created in 1964, to attempt to gain control of the south.

It became known as MACV-SOG, which stood for 'Military Assistance Command Vietnam, Studies and Observation Group.' The American public never knew anything about it, and the United States Government denied its existence until 1997. It's members consisted of handpicked operatives from the CIA, along with highly skilled intelligence military soldiers, Army Special Forces, Navy Seals, Air Force and Marine Recon units, along with some specialized South Vietnamese units.

Although their main objectives were listed as Psychological Operations, known as Psyops, and Black Ops, which covered everything from propaganda radio broadcasts into the North, to unconventional warfare including assassinations of military and political opponents, their operations were far from conventional warfare. SOG was given a wide latitude allowing them to operate highly classified military missions into North Vietnam, Laos and Cambodia, that were contrary to the stated objectives of the United States in South Vietnam. As most of their missions were in Cambodia, they divided the country up into three separate commands.

The North, which was the largest, operated out of Quang Tri, the Central operated out of Kontum, and the South which was the smallest, operated out of Ban Me Thout. Many operatives used coded names, carried foreign weapons, and were not allowed to have anything on their person that could tie them to the United States Government.

With the many waterways, marshes and islands in the Delta, the Viet Cong had strong contacts among the local inhabitants that helped ship supplies up the Mekong River, and created safe havens for Viet Cong and North Vietnamese operatives to rest and resupply. Small heavily armed naval boats patrolled the Delta on a daily basis, searching sampans and fishing boats for contraband or Viet Cong.

Around the base at Binh Thuy, the local residents had been quiet, and went about their daily business without causing the base much to worry about, although suspicions always remained regarding their true allegiance.

Several days after the Viet Cong attack on Binh Thuy, Tom was excited to hear that Oscar Joblinski, Jr. and Andre Flinn were assigned to fill the vacancies left by the deaths of Ridzik, Martinez and Grissom. Bill Boulder was happy to finally be assigned to an evac crew, after spending four long months working in the hospital.

Tom made a special effort to be at the airfield when Oscar arrived. The men smiled and hugged each other for several moments. "Damn Oscar, I didn't think we would get together. It's great to see you. Where have you been since we left medic training?"

Picking up his bag from the chopper, Oscar replied. "I went right to Korea after training for a year, believe me, you don't need to go there. Then I went to Fort Riley, Kansas, until I was called up for Vietnam. I've been operating out of Tan Son Nhut until they decided to send me here. I heard you guys have had a string of bad luck."

Tom nodded his head. "Yeah, we lost some really good medics in a hurry. It hasn't been easy for any of us. But I'm sure glad you're here and can't wait to tell Dad we're serving together. He always enjoyed being with your dad in Europe. Hey, and did you know that Franny is here at Binh Thuy?"

"No shit? Damn, I would love to meet him again. I haven't seen him since I was about five or six," Oscar replied, as the men entered the barracks.

As Geno was out of the hospital, he and Tom set up a training session with the three new men. It was clear to see the men were sharp, well mannered, and knew what was expected of them. They asked good questions and took advice from the veterans as if it were gospel.

About midday, several unmarked black choppers sat down near the edge of the airstrip close to the repair shops. Tom was not sure what to make of the men exiting the unmarked choppers as they wore heavily camouflaged uniforms with no military insignia's, and were armed to the teeth with non-American weapons.

One man who appeared to be in charge, directed his men toward the mess hall as he walked straight for their Battalion Commander's office. He wore simple black jungle dungarees, jungle combat boots, and carried a Russian made AK-47.

Andre Flinn shook his head as he jumped down from his chopper. "Those guys are SOG. The man in black was in a village we were helping several wounded soldiers out of before I was wounded. I watched him place his .45 right up against the side of a young Vietnamese girl not much older than fourteen, and pull the trigger. Her parents screamed with horror and rage as other family members held them back. Then he walked over and shot two of their biggest pigs and laughed. When he was finished, he yelled something in Vietnamese for everyone in the village to hear. Then he and the four men that were with him, got into one of those choppers and left. On the way back to the hospital at Danang, one of the wounded men we were helping told me the guy in black and his men were SOG, and to never cross them in any way. I told him I was going to report the murder when we landed. He told me there was no place I could go to ever get away from them and that I was as good as dead if I spoke up. I never said a word, but I still have nightmares watching that pretty young girl die. They are bad news, my friends, really bad news. Stay away from them."

Oscar looked over at Flinn, "SOG? I heard about them all the time up at Tan Son Nhut, since MACV is located up there. But everyone downplayed their existence, saying they were nothing more than a myth. My captain said it was all made up to scare the villagers and take the heat off the CIA. Funny thing was, no one ever said much about the CIA. We were all told to keep our mouths shut around them, no one trusted those guys at all."

Flinn shook his head. "No, believe me, it exists no matter what Saigon or Washington wants the world to believe. Just keep your mouth shut, and your wits about you if you're around them. They'll cut your throat no different than a damn hog."

Tom and the rest of the medics were stunned by Flinn's story. After a moment Geno spoke up, "Sure, I've heard rumors about things like that. Hell, we've all heard rumors about CIA bullshit, and rumors about SOG, but to hear a real eyewitness report is chilling. Why the hell is crap like that allowed? Someone somewhere must know what's happening. That was just to blatant!"

Tom shook his head. "What the hell do you think those bastards are doing here? They sure as hell have something on their minds other than eating chow. They give me a bad feeling, and I don't like it one bit. I wonder what he wants with Col. Hernandez? This ain't good boys!"

As the SOG operative entered the Headquarters building, Colonel

Hernandez was standing in the middle of the outer office with his arms folded across his chest.

"What in God's name are you doing here, Rampart, or whatever your real name is?"

Sneering at the Colonel, he replied. "Come on Colonel, just call me Jack. We've chewed some of the same turf before here in Nam, so you know my name well enough."

Without flinching a muscle, Col. Hernandez glared at the man. "Rampart, I don't like you or your bullshit SOG operations one bit. I would prefer that you finish feeding your men, fuel up if you need to, and get the hell out of here. We want no part of anything you're involved in. Do I make myself perfectly clear?"

Rampart walked over to a desk chair and sat down, placing his feet up on the desk as he glared back at the Colonel. "Well, I sure as hell am upset by your hospitality, sir. I'm shocked by your attitude, Colonel. I should think you would be more grateful to me after pulling your medics out of the crap two years ago. I was sure you would be happy as hell to see me again.

Colonel Hernandez walked forward, brushing Rampart's feet off the desk. "Rampart, you never bailed me out of anything. That village was not a problem until you made it one. Those people did not deserve what happened. My medics went there to help deliver a baby for the Chief's daughter. Everything was going just fine and the people appreciated our help until you and your murdering thugs arrived. My men were in no jeopardy and there were no V.C. In that village."

Jumping out of the chair Rampart laughed. "Tsk, Tsk, Tsk. I feel so reprimanded by your high and mighty morals. But let me remind you Colonel, I determine who the enemy is in this part of the Delta now, and you're going to need to cooperate with me. Need I remind you who I work for, and who gives you your orders? Besides, you got your medics back alive, unscathed, and not one of your aircrews was injured. Why be so petty about such worthless things."

Colonel Hernandez stepped nose to nose with his adversary. "And you slaughtered twenty innocent people for no reason, then you have the balls to question why those people turn against us. Well this time, you're not going to kill anyone if I can help it, not in my area!"

Rampart rolled his eyes as he tossed a packet of papers toward the Colonel. "Sir, you will find in those documents, orders from Saigon to work with me and my men. You'll provide me with two of your best medics, and provide us one dust off chopper to be kept ready at all times. I already have the names of the two men I want written on the forms, Kenrude and Sarducci. They'll be ready by 0600hrs tomorrow. We'll keep them with us as long as we need them. Any questions, Colonel?"

After looking over the documents, Col. Hernandez glared at Jack Rampart. "Fine, I'll follow the orders, but you best bring those men back to me in one piece, or I'll personally hunt you down like a dog."

While glaring at the Colonel Rampart reached into his shirt pocket, pulling out a neatly folded document he handed to the Colonel. "It's signed by Billy Westmoreland himself. I thought you might like to know who authorized this mission in case you want to challenge anything. Get the men assigned and I'll be out of your hair."

As Col. Hernandez opened the document, Rampart strolled from the building calling back, "Times a'wasting, Colonel, Billy might not appreciate that!"

The colonel shuddered as he read the order instructing him to assign whatever resources Rampart felt were necessary in order to complete the mission, and for an unspecified amount of time. He sighed deeply when he realized the order was in fact signed by General William Westmoreland. After several moments of thought, he called for Captain Trajillio.

When the captain arrived, Col. Hernandez handed him the order. "Tell me what you think we should do. For God's sake, Captain Rampart will kill our men just as fast as he would kill an innocent villager. I'm torn as to what I should do!"

After a moment of thought, Capt. Trajillio looked at his colonel. "Sir, if you don't follow through with these orders, you'll be court martialed. You can argue the point with Saigon, but you know who controls that operation, and once more you will lose. Sir, I don't know this Rampart, but I've heard bad things about him and his men. I've heard about the villages they destroyed in the central highlands. I think our best bet is to fulfill the order and hope for the best. Sarducci is a solid medic and soldier, he picked up some good experience before he was wounded. He and Kenrude will work well with any air crew you pick."

"Alright. Get a hold of Kenrude and Sarducci. Give them their orders and send Warrant Officer Cumberland's crew. They have worked together for quite a while," Col. Hernandez directed as he walked over toward the window behind his desk.

Around 1600hrs, Captain Trajillio called the men together in his office. "Gentlemen, I have some new orders for you. As of 0600hrs tomorrow, you're being assigned to work with a specialized combat group operating here in the Delta, or where ever Captain Rampart, or whatever real rank he has, decides to take you. You'll be with him until his mission, whatever it might be, is completed. I can't tell you anymore, as we don't know anything else. All I can tell you is to be careful, and don't trust or cross Rampart and his men."

At 0530hrs, all the SOG operatives stood near the black choppers, as the medi-vac crew assembled by the door of Cumberland's chopper, awaiting Rampart to arrive and give them their orders.

As Tom paced back and forth, Oscar came running up to him. "Tom, be careful out there, and watch your back. I have a really bad feeling about these guys."

Tom slapped Oscar on the shoulder. "No worries, my friend. Geno and

I will cover each other, and you better take care of yourself while I'm away. We need to catch up when I come back."

Before talking to the aircrew, Rampart made one more trip to the Colonel's office. Entering the outer office, he observed Col. Hernandez reading the morning report. After slamming his AK-47 down on a desk, he looked coldly at the Colonel. "My team is here to perform some undercover operations in and around Binh Thuy, or wherever it might take us. We're looking for a large band of pro-communist subversives that are attempting to undermine our Hearts and Minds campaign. As you are aware, even President Nixon believes in our mission, so we can turn this war over to the South Vietnamese Army to fight, and we can all go home. Any complaints, Colonel?"

Col. Hernandez threw the morning report down on Capt. Trajillio's desk, as he turned to face Rampart. "First off, Rampart, and as I have said, I know that's not your true name. Second, you're working for SOG, and could care less about Hearts and Minds. That operation is a joke which allows the CIA or SOG, which ever name you're using today, to commit murder on a wholesale basis wherever you go. So you can get the hell out of my office and clear this base. But you best bring my crew back alive, if you know what's good for you."

Rampart laughed loudly as he picked up his weapon. "Colonel, better men than you have tried to take me on and lost. My work is open ended and I do as I see fit!"

As Rampart approached the flight crew, Tom walked up to the arrogant leader, asking, "Tell me, what is our mission?"

Rampart looked at the two medics with a sneer on his face. "Simple, you will do what we tell you to do, do it well, and never ask any more stupid questions. Now get on board and be quiet."

Angered by Rampart's smart ass response, Tom felt like slamming his fist into the side of his scarred left cheek. However, he knew this man was not only a hired killer, he was a butcher that simply didn't care who he killed, friend or foe. It was best to allow this sleeping dog to be left alone, although Tom was sure they would clash somewhere down the road, and he was not looking forward to the thought of it, or the possible outcome.

Turning toward Warrant Officer Cumberland, Rampart continued. "You and your flight crew will stand down, remain ready, and respond when you're called, it's as simple as that, got it?"

Warrant Officer Cumberland glared at Rampart for a moment before responding. "Loud and clear!"

Tom and Geno sat quietly in one of the unmarked choppers as it took to the sky, heading deeper into the Delta. Tom thought back to the day when their chopper had gone down and he fought to escape the sinking machine. He thought about Warrant Officer Palmero's body down at the bottom of the murky water. His remains would never be recovered, and his family would never really have any closure, and they would always wonder where their son was, although they would know the details of the crash.

Tom was surprised when he realized the three choppers were leaving the Delta and heading up the Mekong River. Below, Tom could see three river patrol boats, skimming along the brackish water as they watched for any type of enemy activity. He could see a fourth boat pulled alongside a larger fishing boat. The crew was searching the boat for contraband, as the owners knelt on the stern with their hands behind their heads.

Minutes later the choppers turned inland, setting down beside a well-built rice paddy that drained its excess water right back into the river. Several farmers worked diligently, appearing not to pay any attention to the black choppers or the men getting off. Once everyone cleared the choppers, the pilots took back to the skies heading south. Tom and Geno were instructed to walk into the middle of the cluster of killers, unaware as to their destination.

A small woman carrying two baskets on a long pole walked up to one of the men, yelling and waving her arms. No one paid any attention to her as they continued to the Northwest. Tom was sure one of the men would shoot her, but no one raised an eyebrow at her rantings.

After nearly an hour of walking, they entered a rather large village where about twenty South Vietnamese soldiers were standing in a group near a hut. As Rampart approached, a small Vietnamese man in his thirties wearing a white suit coat and tan pants exited the hut.

"Ah Rampartsan, you arrived a bit earlier than I thought you would. I told you last week when I wanted you to be here. Do you not trust me, a Captain in the Canh Sat?"

Rampart spit a healthy amount of chew on the ground. After wiping his chin with his sleeve he responded, "That's exactly why I don't trust you, Captain Wong. You would slit your own mother's throat if you thought you could make money off it. Believe me, Captain, I always know who I'm dealing with, and what they're about. You my friend, are a butcher and a fraud."

There was little doubt that the captain was angered by that last statement. Breathing heavily, he looked sternly at Rampart. "If it had not been for me, you would either still be rotting away in that Cambodian prison camp, or be dead. You do not wish to show me a slight bit of respect?"

Rampart took another step closer to the agitated captain. "And I believe if it wasn't for you, I would never have ended up in that mess. I'm only here because my superiors insisted I meet you. So, let's cut the crap and tell me what we're here to do?"

"Your superiors! You say that like they are well-respected men, when in fact your CIA has the bloodiest hands in this entire war. They now hide under the name of SOG, as if no one in Vietnam knows who they really are. I have no respect for them, but I know they will kill me just as simply as they will a dog if I do not cooperate. And you must know they would do the same to you, if you cross or embarrass them. Your day may come Mr. Rampart, or whatever your real name is."

Without warning, Rampart slapped Captain Wong across the face. Instantly, the South Vietnamese soldiers began raising their weapons, but quickly stopped as the Captain raised his hand.

"One day your luck will run out, Mr. Rampart, and you will meet your end. I guarantee that I will never shed a tear for you. You say we are both alike, but I beg to differ with you. Maybe one day I will even have you in my gun sights, and pull the trigger myself. You play a dangerous game, your country and you," the captain yelled angrily.

"Yeah, yeah, you scare me real bad, Captain. Just give me the paper work I need so we can be on our way. I'm tired of this little chit-chat we're having," Rampart replied in a very calm voice.

Visibly angry, the captain reached into a leather satchel that hung from a long strap on his left shoulder. "Here are the documents from Saigon. I have read them, and am not so sure they are accurate. Just take them and be on your way. I'm finished with you and your henchmen."

Rampart scanned the documents for a minute as the captain and his two aides walked toward an older International Scout. Just before they were ready to enter, Rampart yelled out, "Wong, if you ever get me in your sights, you best finish the job right then and there. If you don't, there's no place short of hell you can go to hide, I promise you that!"

After the Scout departed down the muddy trail, Rampart looked at the village chief, who was obviously and rightfully scared of the SOG team that stood in his small village.

"Get the hell out of my face," Rampart yelled as he pushed the scared old man to the ground. "Come on, let's get moving, Sgt. Tran, you and your men take the lead."

They walked for several hours, wading through rice paddies and over man-made dikes that were probably centuries old. As dusk began to spread over the land, they came upon several small hillocks. As they approached the first one, Rampart yelled out.

"We'll camp for the night on top of the largest hill to our right. It'll give us the best view of the area, and it has trees for cover."

After finishing a meal of C-rations, Rampart walked over to Tom and Geno. "Tomorrow will be different. We'll be dealing with tough Viet Cong sympathizers that need to be eradicated if we're going to win the hearts and minds of these village people. Be on the lookout because things can happen quickly out here. I don't want either one of you getting your ass blown away, we may need you."

Geno shook his head. "How the hell do you plan to win the hearts and minds of these people the way you treat them. The way I see it, you're just driving these poor people against us. This whole hearts and minds game is nothing short of a crock of shit."

Rampart knelt down beside Geno. "Listen here, punk. You're here for one year, and then you will take your sorry ass back to the states and tell people, 'I'm a veteran, I served in Vietnam.' Well, I've been here for three and a half years, and I've seen crap and done things you could never imagine. I've watched good men die because of these Viet Cong bastards, and I'll not rest until we have killed every last one of them. If you got a problem with that, I don't give a shit! Just do as you're told, and like I said, earlier, keep your mouth shut!"

Geno looked at Rampart without flinching. "Tom and I were assigned to keep you and your men bandaged up, and save your lives if need be. We'll do our jobs as best we can, what you do is your business, whether I like it or not."

Rampart laughed as he stood up. "Now you're getting smarter, Sarducci. We're on the move by 0500, you best get some sleep, as it will be a damn long day. And just a quick reminder, Sarducci, stay the hell out of my way. Your miserable life means nothing to me!"

At 0500 the following morning, Sgt. Tran led the group off the hillock heading due north. As they approached a small village, two men carrying AK-47's dashed out toward a large mound of straw near the trail and began firing. Sgt. Tran dispersed his men around the village, as Rampart and his four men returned fire. In just a few minutes the firing had ended, as the South Vietnamese soldiers killed both attackers.

Residents of the village were running in every direction as they yelled and screamed, trying to hide their meager possessions from the dreaded security force. The chief and his family stood silently in the middle of the village, attempting to quiet everyone. As Rampart and Sgt. Tran approached, they all bowed in unison.

Rampart stared at the chief for a moment before slapping him across the face, and pushing him to the ground. The chief's wife cried as she knelt down to help her husband back to his feet. When he was standing again, Rampart pulled out his side arm and shot a small pig that was nursing on its mother. As he aimed his weapon at the mother sow, an old woman ran in front of it, pleading with her hands folded in front of her. Tom held his breath, waiting to see what was going to happen, as Rampart was still pointing his weapon in her direction. Suddenly he changed directions, and shot a goat that was tied up to a fence. A young couple ran toward the dead animal, as they screamed what Tom figured were insults and threats

Near one of the huts, Tom observed a woman crying as she held the head of a young boy in her lap. Tom could see blood on the boy's shirt. Picking up his aide bag, he and Geno rushed over to the woman. The boy had been hit during the gun fight, most likely by a South Vietnamese soldier.

Tom pulled up the boy's shirt to take a look. The bullet had hit the boy in the shoulder and deflected off the bone, before passing on through without causing any serious damage. Geno began pouring sulfa on the wound as Tom prepared to stitch the entry wound. Before he could place one stitch, a gunshot rang out. The boy's body jumped, as a bullet smashed into his forehead.

Tom spun around to see one of Rampart's men standing behind him, his sidearm still pointing in the boy's direction. Angrily, Tom jumped up, and swung his fist into the man's nose. As he staggered backwards, Tom continued toward him, landing two more solid punches into the man's face. Blood streamed from his nose and mouth as he fell to the ground. Tom picked up the .45 pistol from the ground, aiming it toward the injured man. "Get up, you son-of-a-bitch! Get your ass up, or I'll shoot you where you lay, you sick bastard!"

Rampart rushed forward yelling, "Kenrude, you drop that gun. Put it down. Don't you shoot him!"

Shaking with rage, Tom pitched the weapon off to his left as he glared at the shaking SOG operative. "You ever pull anything like that again, I'll kill you without a second thought. If you think I'm kidding, just try it!"

Although Geno was angered at what had just happened, he was taken back by Tom's sudden burst of anger with these hired assassins. They could kill Tom in a heartbeat without ever thinking about it. He watched Rampart walk up to Tom with his gun still in his hand.

"Kenrude, you're getting to be more trouble than you're worth. I served with your Daddy in Korea, he was a hell of a soldier and did his job every damn day. You're nothing but a sniveling, peace protester in uniform that should be back raising hell at some college!"

Tom glared at Rampart. "You're right about one thing. My dad was a hell of a soldier, and he had ethics. No way in hell would he ever have killed a little boy that was wounded and needed help. I'm not sure what your end game is, but you sure as hell aren't winning hearts and minds."

Rampart glared at Tom for a moment before yelling, "Burn the damn place, burn it all!"

After Sgt. Tran translated the order to his men, they all began setting fire to every hut, every stack of hay or straw. In minutes, the quiet village became a massive inferno consuming anything that would burn. The screaming villagers ran about attempting to grab their animals and pull them

toward safety, before the laughing South Vietnamese soldiers could kill them.

As thick clouds of smoke spread across the rice paddies, Sgt. Tran led the pack of dangerous marauders toward several hills to the north. Although Tom and Geno were angry, they took comfort in knowing the man Tom struck had a broken nose, and maybe a cracked cheek bone, and was going to be in some serious pain for a while. There was no way he was going to get any medical attention, or pain killers from them, no matter how much Rampart threatened them.

The following day around noon, they entered a quiet village where several men greeted Rampart and his thugs. Taking out the paper work Capt. Wong had given him, the men quickly read the information. As the taller of the two handed the papers back to Rampart, he laughed.

"Hell yeah, we got that bastard and two of his men. We've got them back over there behind the huts. Come take a look for yourself. You'll enjoy their accommodations."

Rampart slapped the man on the back, "Good job, Steinman. Let's have a look see, and we'll grade your work for efficiency."

Rampart's four men along with Sgt. Tran followed by Tom and Geno walked back by the wood line. Tom and Geno were aghast at what they were seeing. The man the SOG operatives were referring to as Ming Hoang, a Viet Cong leader, was crucified upside down on a crudely built cross. He had been savagely whipped over most of his body as he hung there. Next to him, staked out on the ground was a young man with a spear shoved completely through him, with both hands cut off.

The third man, the only one still alive, was tied to a tree. He was bleeding from several massive cuts on his chest and thighs. Rampart and Sgt. Tran walked over to the man. As Tran began asking questions, the dying man slowly answered them. After nearly fifteen minutes of questions, the man's head dropped to his chest.

Rampart turned toward Tom and Geno. "See if he's dead. We're not through with him yet."

Amazingly Geno found a very weak pulse. "If you want him alive, we need to cut him down, stop some of this bleeding and get liquids back into him, or he'll be dead shortly."

Under the supervision of Rampart's men, they began bandaging wounds, while starting an IV and giving him pain killers. About an hour later he regained consciousness, but was running a high fever. Several women from the village continued bringing cool water and compresses.

About 2100, Rampart and Sgt. Tran walked up to Tom asking. "Can the prick talk? We need to get more information from him, and this is no joke, Kenrude."

Tom nodded his head. "He's awake, but very weak. Go slow, and you might get what you're after. He's very scared of you people, and mistrusts us even though we're helping him."

Surprisingly, Rampart and Sgt. Tran went very slowly, without attempting to inflict any more pain on the man as they knelt beside him. After nearly an hour, Rampart stood up. "We got what we wanted and needed from him. Kenrude and Sarducci, go take a hike." As Tom and Geno walked into the center of the village, a single gunshot rang out.

At 0400 the following morning, Rampart awakened everyone. "We have a busy day in front of us, we need to get moving. You got forty-five minutes to be ready."

There was little doubt in the minds of Tom and Geno, that today was going to be much different from what they had experienced so far. Rampart and his men were pumped and ready for action, and Sgt. Tran had whipped his men into a frenzy. As a helicopter landed in a clearing nearby, the three men who had greeted them in the village, along with the man Tom assaulted, piled on. Tom felt a bit better when the man he had injured departed, as he was certain the demented asshole was going to try and kill him one night while he slept.

This morning Sgt. Tran led them to the northwest. Around 1300hrs, they arrived near another village. Sgt. Tran and several of his men went forward to scout the village and its environs. Rampart continually paced back and forth in the wooded area where they waited, until Sgt. Tran returned.

After a lengthy conversation, Rampart and Tran shook hands. Several minutes later, Tran took all but two of his men and departed toward the northeast. Rampart pulled together his four men and the two Vietnamese soldiers to give them orders as to what they were going to do. Walking over to Tom and Geno, he glared at them. "This is what we came for. Today we clean out a hornets nest, and people are going to die, maybe a lot. Just take care of my men and don't worry about the enemy."

Quickly, the seven men approached the village, shooting the first two people they came across. The chief came running from his hut with his hands up, yelling stop in rather good English. His wife and daughter nervously bowed as the men approached them. Rampart grabbed hold of the chief's wife, putting his sidearm to her head. The chief fell to his knees, begging him not to shoot. Ramparts eyes were glazed over like a mad man. Turning toward the chief he yelled, "Huan Loc!"

The chief shook his head while pointing toward the west yelling, "Cambodia! Cambodia!"

Rampart shook his head in anger. "Huan Loc, Huan Loc. Or she dies."

Once more the chief pointed west pleading, "Cambodia! Gone two days, Cambodia!"

Rampart threw the woman to the ground before shooting her three times. Just as quickly he grabbed hold of the chief's daughter. "Huan Loc! Now!"

The chief sobbed as he shook his head mumbling, "Cambodia, gone to Cambodia, gone!"

It was clear to Rampart they had missed the man they were looking for, and he was angry beyond words.

"Burn it, burn it. Send it all to hell! Leave these sorry bastards nothing. Kill all the livestock." As his men started their work, he looked at Tom. "Interfere and she gets a bullet to the brain, your call!"

Tom and Geno stood motionless as one of the South Vietnamese soldiers covered them. Tears ran down Tom's face as he watched precious farm animals being slaughtered, and every hut burned to the ground. One old woman picked up a pitch fork and walked toward Rampart as she yelled. Seconds later she laid dead next to her prized hogs.

Turning to one of his men, he yelled, "This little bitch comes with us, tie her and gag her."

Minutes later, Rampart led his men to the west at a rapid pace. Near night fall they approached the Mekong River. Rampart scanned the Cambodian side of the river for any movement. Seeing none, he sent one of the Vietnamese soldiers across to scout the area. While they waited for him, a small sampan came slowly down the river. Rampart walked quietly along the shoreline to see where it was going.

Returning he was smiling, "There's a large village about three hundred yards up the river.

They just finished loading bags on to a small sampan that headed north, most likely to some Viet Cong hide out. It's too dangerous to attack it in the dark. We'll jump those sons a bitches in the morning. They'll never know what hit them."

Pulling a radio from the pack of one of his men, he dialed up a frequency and made a call. After giving the coordinates, he said, "Be ready to attack on my call, and don't let those army do gooders know what direction you're headed. We'll check for our man first, then when you come, blow it all to hell. Over."

Moments later the Vietnamese soldier returned from across the river, explaining he had seen nothing going on close by, and no sentries patrolling the shore.

There was little going on in the village in the early morning hours, when Rampart led his killers onto the bamboo docks that were built along the shoreline. Several beat up sampans containing fishing equipment were tied to the sturdy pier. Terrified villagers bowed as they approached the

SOG butchers, offering them fruit and vegetables, hoping to appease them. Before anything could be said, Rampart fired two shots into an old man that had knelt down before him. Kicking the body off to the side he mumbled, "You weak simple son-of-a-bitch."

Several villagers ran toward the chief's hut, knowing there were going to be problems. As the chief and his wife approached, Rampart threw the young girl they had taken from the last village on the ground in front of them. As one of the Vietnamese soldiers yelled at them to take care of her, the chief's wife knelt down to comfort the frightened child.

Rampart pulled his sidearm, aiming it at the girl and the chief's wife.

"Huan Loc, Huan Loc!" he yelled.

The chief raised his hands as he pointed across the river. Slowly he knelt down, taking his wife in his arms. Angered, Rampart fired a shot into the ground, missing the chief's wife by inches. As his eyes nearly bulged out of his head, he yelled, "Huan Loc! Now, you piece of crap!"

As the chief began to cry, Rampart yelled, "I'll give you something to cry about." Forcefully he pulled the chief's wife from the ground, nearly ripping her clothing off. Shoving her towards one of his men he yelled,

"Rape her! Let the chief know what kind of fun she can really be!"

As the SOG operative began leading the screaming woman toward the closest hut, Tom ran forward, with his sidearm in his hand, striking the man alongside the head as he tackled him. He jammed his pistol up against the dazed man's head, as he watched the woman run for safety.

Kneeling down on the back of the SOG agent, Tom glared at Rampart, knowing he was going up against the devil himself.

"This ends now Rampart, you son-of-a-bitch! There'll be no more killing, there will be no more intimidation by your evil style of justice. It's over! Throw down your weapon or this man dies. You may get me, but Sarducci will finish you and the rest of your men with his M-16 in one quick blast." Sweat streamed down Rampart's dirty face, as juice from his chewing tobacco rolled down over his unshaven chin. His eyes glazed over, as his chest rose and fell as his breathing became heavier. His arm remained steady as a rock as he continued pointing his pistol at the head of the shaking old man. After rotating his head from side to side a few times, he gave out a tremendous yell that sounded like a wounded animal in the throes of death. Rampart squinted as sweat poured into his eyes. Slowly he turned to look over his shoulder to see where Geno was standing. It was clear Geno had the drop on all of them. He had positioned himself on the pier directly behind Rampart and his men, giving him a clear shot at anyone that made an attempt to move. Tom never flinched, as Rampart turned to look back over at him with pure hatred in his eyes.

For several moments you could have cut the tension in the air with a knife. Not a word was spoken, as first Rampart looked at Tom, who was glaring back with determination on his face.

"It's your choice, Rampart. Think real hard before you act!" Tom yelled angrily.

Sarducci stood like a rock on the pier, as he aimed his weapon toward Rampart. "We're done, this is no bluff, Rampart, there will be no more killing of innocent people. Drop your weapons, or every one of you bastards are going to hell right here and now!"

CHAPTER 19
CHICAGO BURNS

Peter Kenrude was totally excited as he rushed inside through the back porch of the farm house, holding an envelope in his right hand. "Mom, I did it, I won the science fair! I get to go to Chicago for the National Science Contest. You have to read this. I can go, can't I?"

Karen walked over, kissing her son on the forehead as she took the envelope from him. After reading the information, she smiled as she hugged her son.

"Of course you can go, honey. You have worked so hard on this project you deserve it. Your father and I are so proud of you."

Peter smiled as he took the envelope back from his mother. "I can't wait to see a big city like that. I know Minneapolis is big, but Chicago is huge, and has all kinds of famous landmarks. We get to go touring after the contest is over. I need to get a better camera, or maybe I can use yours?"

Laughing, Karen shook her head. "Yes, you can take mine, just be careful with it."

Steve helped his son do some last minute work on the science project, before packing it up for the trip to Chicago. Peter wanted everything perfect, so the judges would have no choice but to hand him the blue ribbon for his work on Nuclear Propulsion.

Peter was happy that Mr. Carrington, Glendale's science instructor, had been picked as one of the chaperon's for the trip, as he had given Peter the idea for his project. The days up to the trip to Chicago were busy, as Peter promised his father he would help get the final fields of corn planted before he left.

On Wednesday morning, Karen drove Peter to the school where John Carrington would pick up his three other students and take them to the bus station in Willmar. Stopping the car near the bus, Karen looked over at Peter.

"Son, you need to behave yourself, and don't cause Mr. Carrington any problems. He has been very good to you, and expects great things from you down the road. But, have a fun time and we hope you take first place. Just do your best, and know we'll be proud, whatever the result."

Peter smiled at his mother. "You know I'll behave myself. I would never do anything to embarrass Mr. Carrington or you and Dad. Believe me, this trip will be a marvelous experience, one I'll never forget, even if I don't get first place."

Karen leaned over, giving her son a kiss on the cheek. "Stay safe in that big city, sweetheart."

Peter had to laugh as he shook his head. "Don't worry, Mom, I got the Kenrude smarts. I know how to take care of myself."

After loading Peter's science exhibit and luggage on the bus, Karen spoke with Mr. Carrington as to what time the bus would return on Sunday. After waving at Peter as the bus drove off, she thought about what Peter had just told her just moments ago, *"Don't worry mom, I got the Kenrude smarts and know how to take care of myself."* If nothing else, that bothered her more, because Peter was just like his father, uncle and big brother—way too self-assured and never willing to back down.

Although the rest of the students slept on the bus, Peter could not. He took in every sight, every sound, and logged his thoughts and ideas in a journal. He understood how his father and Tom must have felt when they left home to join the army.

The city of Chicago was huge compared to Minneapolis. Peter was thrilled as they drove by many of the buildings he had read about in magazines or seen in news stories. Chicago was the big leagues, and now he was part of it, if only for a few days.

After arriving at the Chicago bus terminal, Mr. Carrington led the students to a smaller bus that took them to Columbia College. Immediately, the students went to work setting up their science exhibits so they would be ready for judging the following morning. After Peter had his exhibit set up, he looked over some of the exhibits from his competition. He knew his exhibit was as good as the others, so he went to bed that evening feeling ready to compete in the morning.

The judges asked tough questions of each student, and hung on every word they answered, making sure they knew what they were talking about while attempting to trip them up. Mr. Carrington had played the devil's advocate during the past week, asking them tough questions over and over, preparing them for any and all questions the judges might ask.

No matter what the judges asked Peter, he had a solid answer, and they were not able to trip him up in any way. When it was over Peter felt he had done his best and felt he might be a contender for the blue ribbon. As the ribbons were finally awarded, the judges called Peter and a boy from Oklahoma to the stage. They were hopelessly deadlocked on this competition, so both boys were issued blue ribbons.

Peter was ecstatic. After shaking hands with the boy from Oklahoma and the judges, he raced down the stairs to thank Mr. Carrington for all he had done to help him win. Peter was also proud of his fellow students from Glendale. Two of them were awarded blue ribbons in their categories and one student received a second place ribbon. It was an all-around great showing for Glendale High.

On the following day, the science fair was open to visitors from all over the country. Many of the visitors were scientists who enjoyed discussing every facet of their varied projects, and could speak well on any subject, including nuclear propulsion.

Although Peter was thrilled with the competition, he was equally thrilled about Saturday, when they would get the royal tour of the city. Peter had more rolls of film than a professional photographer, and he hoped to shoot them all.

About midway through the tour on Saturday, the van driver attempted to turn onto the street in front of the Federal Building. However, there were hundreds of people in the street, carrying signs and banners demanding America get out of Vietnam. Groups of people would chant, "What do we want? Peace! When do we want it? Now!"

The driver looked scared, as several men began burning a stuffed figure resembling Richard Nixon. No matter which way he attempted to go, people were pounding on the windows of the van with sticks and signs. Several people moved out of the way for a minute, as the driver blew his horn and began rolling forward into another lane, but that only lasted for a moment until his way was blocked again by angry protesters.

John Carrington was angry. He called to the driver.

"Stop and let me out so I can reason with these people. They don't even realize there are just kids in this van."

The driver glared at Mr. Carrington, "You open that door and they'll pull you out like a rag doll, and there won't be a thing any of us can do to help you.

John Carrington shook his head. "All they need is a calm voice to help them understand we mean them no harm and just need to move on down the road."

Before the driver could respond, Mr. Carrington opened his door and began to step out. Immediately he was pulled from the van, and disappeared into the angry mob. Several of the girls screamed and huddled together, as the driver made one more attempt to back out of the crowd, but the angry protesters would not move.

Seconds later, the angry mob began rocking the van from side to side, as they screamed anti-war slogans. Several people smashed windows as the rocking became more intense.

Peter yelled out, "Were going over on the next one, hold on!"

Seconds later the van lay on its side, as the protesters cheered while dancing back and forth screaming, death to baby killers.

The driver climbed over the seats, and opened the rear door while yelling, "Run kids, this is your chance. Get out now!"

In seconds, the driver was knocked to the ground by a man wheeling a baseball bat. Eight of the students near the rear of the van attempted to run as the driver instructed. Peter saw several of them, including one boy from Glendale, disappear into the crowd, as a boy from Iowa met the same fate as the driver.

Seeing flames and smoke emanate from the engine compartment, Peter looked at the two girls from Glendale that stayed in the van with him. "Listen to me, we need to get out of here before this thing explodes. I'll make a hole for us, you guys hold hands, and listen to what I tell you to do, and we'll get out of this alright. Can you do that?"

Marie Downing replied that she could, but Cynthia Upton began to cry, saying she wanted to stay in the van where they were safe. Peter grabbed her by the arms.

"Listen to me Cynthia, if this van blows up, your dead. Right now I look at our situation like this. If we stay we die. If we leave, we have a chance, and I am not leaving you behind. Now, take Marie's hand and run to the left when I tell you to go!"

Whimpering, Cynthia took hold of Marie's hand as Peter pulled the fire extinguisher from its bracket. After pulling the pin, he jumped over the last seat, and gave anyone nearby a shot of dry chemical powder directly in the face as he yelled.

"Go Marie, go!"

He kept giving shots of powder to people no matter what they were doing, until the three of them were clearing the crowd. As the extinguisher emptied, he slammed the empty vessel into the side of one man's head that attempted to grab Cynthia. Moments later, the three students were free from the mob, running east, as the van became fully engulfed in flames.

Marie hugged Peter when they came to a stop near the steps of a government office building. Breathing heavily, she looked back down the street.

"Where do we go now, Peter? I'm scared. How do we get back to the college, and what do we do about Mr. Carrington and the others?"

The three of them watched as police cars and vans full of riot police, along with several fire trucks, flew past them toward the Federal Building.

Peter thought for a moment before responding. "Alright, we know there will be lots of cops down there in a few minutes to break up that demonstration. We'll wait here until the noise settles down, and then we'll find an officer who can help us."

Cynthia began to cough, "What is that, my eyes are burning, I can't breathe!"

"Tear gas! The cops have shot off a bunch of tear gas, and it's drifting this way. Come on, we need to find cover."

Running toward the south a couple of blocks, Peter realized they were out of the path of the stinging gas. Better yet, they came across a boy named Charlie from Iowa that had also jumped from the van. His left eye was partially swelled shut from being punched by a protester, but he was not going to let that stop him from getting back to find the rest of the students.

After waiting about a half hour, the four scared kids began walking back toward the Federal Building, in the hopes of finding their friends and Mr. Carrington. However, they were unnerved by the number of ambulances taking injured people to hospitals.

Arriving at a police barricade, Peter explained to the angry officers what had happened to them, and inquired about Mr. Carrington and the other students.

One of the officers sneered as he looked at Peter. "And I suppose you're not one of those hippie un-American bastards we had to gas."

Angered by the officer's demeanor, Peter glared right back. "My brother is over in Vietnam right now, so don't you dare put me in with the likes of them. They just tried to kill us. That was our van they tipped over and burned. Did you listen to anything I told you?"

Peter's comment riled the officer even more. "So you're a patriot, good for you. But I think you're one of them punks trying to get away. That's what I think." Before Peter could say another word, the officer sprayed him with mace, and threw him into the back of a patrol car, along with Charlie. After slamming the door he yelled, "Get their asses out of here!"

Marie and Cynthia screamed and pulled at the officer, attempting to convince him they were not part of the demonstration, but to no avail.

Arriving at a booking center, Peter observed Mr. Carrington sitting on a bench along the wall. Pulling free from an officer he called out, "Mr. Carrington, over here, over here!"

Fast as lightening, John Carrington jumped to his feet, running over to Peter and Charlie, hugging them tightly. "Do you know where any of the other kids are? And what happened to your face? Peter, were you maced?"

Peter looked angrily at the transporting officer. "Yeah, I was maced by another officer. Look, Marie and Cynthia were with me, but this son-of-a-bitch wouldn't listen. I don't know where they're at now, and Cynthia is really shaken bad. I could barely get her out of the van."

The officer looked at Peter. "You mean you were telling the truth?" Charlie was about a second away from slugging the officer when Peter took him by the arm.

"Yes, we were telling the truth. I don't know what's wrong with you people in Chicago," Peter screamed, as his eyes continued to water, still burning from the mace.

John Carrington glared at the officer. "First off, I want some medical attention for this boy, and I want it right now! Secondly, radio the officer back at that barricade, and see what the hell he did with those two girls. Believe me, if anything bad has happened to them, I'll hold you personally responsible! There are also other students and the van driver out there somewhere."

Immediately, the officer told one of the dispatchers behind the desk to have a nurse report down to booking right away. He then called on the radio to confirm the whereabouts of the two girls. Within seconds, he was told they had been placed in the back seat of another patrol car that was still parked near the barricade. He informed the officer to bring them to the booking station right away.

Knowing the girls were safe and that Peter was getting his eyes washed out with saline solution, Mr. Carrington pressed the sergeant that had arrived with the nurse, regarding the other students from the van.

It was apparent the sergeant was very concerned, as he began making numerous phone and radio calls. Minutes later he informed Mr. Carrington that two of them were with fire fighters, one was with an officer near the Federal building, and they were still looking for the last three.

When Marie and Cynthia arrived at the booking station, Peter let out a sigh of relief. He was even more relieved when the police brought over a van to return them to the college. He had enough of Chicago, and could have cared less about taking any more photos.

By four o'clock Saturday afternoon, all the students were safely back on campus and ready to head home in the morning. The driver was in the hospital with several broken bones, but would be fine. Chicago no longer held any type of appeal for Peter. He had learned firsthand how dangerous the rioters could be, and that the reported brutality of the Chicago Police was no longer just a questionable nightly news story. In his experience at least, it was an accurate portrayal.

Around five o'clock, a reporter from a local Chicago Television Station arrived to investigate the story he had heard about from firefighters. He interviewed Peter and several other students regarding the incident. After his station aired the story, it was picked up by several of the networks.

So, as it worked out, everyone in Glendale was well aware of what happened to their children and friends, long before they arrived home Sunday evening.

As the bus pulled into the parking lot of Glendale High School, a crowd of about two hundred screamed and clapped as the students quietly exited the bus. Although everyone was treating them as hero's, Peter did not feel like one. The experience had left him empty and cold inside. Even after watching the news reports over and over before going to bed Saturday night, he could not believe that Americans were treating each other the way they did. He still felt shock that the rioters had little or no concern for lives of the young people inside the van, and that he himself had to resort to violence to get away from the angry mob. Most of all, he resented the fact that his brother was risking his life for their freedoms, while the angry protesters in Chicago and around the country showed no concern for the rights, welfare, or safety of their fellow Americans. It made him sick, and he vowed never to return to Chicago for the rest of his life.

Karen and Steve rushed forward, grabbing their son and holding him tight. Karen kissed him on the head as Steve smiled at his brave boy.

"We are both so proud of you, Peter," Steven exclaimed, as he hugged his son for a second time. "You were beyond brave for your years, and you did what you had to in order to protect those girls. Maria and Cynthia along with their families, and the rest of Glendale will never forget what you did yesterday."

After Steve let go, Abigail walked up to her younger brother. "I'm so proud of you, Peter. I've never thought of you as a man, but you've just proved you are one. I must have the best brothers in the entire world."

As they turned to walk to their car, Maria came running over. She grabbed hold of Peter and gave him a huge hug and a kiss on the cheek.

"Peter Kenrude, you are my hero today and always. Thank you for keeping us safe. I really liked what you did with that fire extinguisher. I can still see the faces of the people you shot with that powder. Although it was scary then, now it gives me something to laugh about, and I really need that."

Peter patted Maria on the shoulder. "You were brave, too. You kept of hold of Cynthia the whole time. Without you, who knows what might have happened to her."

Maria looked over at Cynthia, who was sobbing as her mother and father held her. "Yeah, I think it will be a long time before she gets over this, if ever. I'm kind of scared for her." Turning back to Peter she smiled. "Thanks again, I'm back safe in Glendale because of you, Peter."

Although all the admiration and pats on the back were nice, Peter could not bring himself to smile. He still couldn't understand what had happened in Chicago, nor could he understand what they thought they were accomplishing by their actions. America was not supposed to be like this, not when men were dying and being maimed for life. He longed for the patriotism he had heard so much about during the wars his dad had fought in. He just couldn't understand it at all. His heart was broken, and fear for his country haunted his soul.

CHAPTER 20
SHOW DOWN

Forcefully Rampart pulled the chief's wife from the ground, nearly ripping her clothing off. Pushing her towards one of his men he yelled, "Rape her! Let the chief know what kind of fun she can really be!

As the SOG operative began leading the screaming woman toward the closest hut, Tom ran forward with his sidearm in his hand, striking the man alongside the head as he tackled him. He jammed his pistol up against the dazed man's head, as he watched the woman run for safety. Kneeling down on the back of the SOG agent, Tom glared at Rampart, knowing he was going up against the devil himself, "This ends now Rampart, you son-of-a-bitch! There will be no more killing, there will be no more intimidation by your evil style of justice, it's over! Throw down your weapon or this man dies. You may get me, but I think Sarducci will finish you and the rest of your men with his M-16 in one quick blast."

Sarducci stood like a rock on the pier as he aimed his weapon toward Rampart. "This is no bluff, Rampart, there will be no more killing of innocent people. Drop your weapons, or every one of you bastards are going to die right here, right now, it's your choice!"

For several moments you could have cut the tension in the air with a knife. Not a word was spoken as Rampart first looked at Tom, who was glaring back with determination on his face. Slowly he turned to look over his shoulder to see where Geno was standing. It was clear Geno had the drop on all of them. He had positioned himself on the pier directly behind Rampart and his men, giving him a clear shot at anyone that made an attempt to move. Tom never flinched as Rampart turned to look back over at him with pure hatred in his eyes.

Heavy sweat poured down Rampart's dirty face, as juice from his chewing tobacco rolled down over his dirty unshaven chin. His eyes glazed over, as his chest rose and fell as his breathing became heavier. His arm remained steady as a rock as he continued pointing his pistol at the head of the shaking old man. After rotating his head from side to side a few times, he gave out a tremendous yell that sounded like a wounded animal in the throes of death.

Turning his head back toward Tom he yelled out, "Meet you in hell, Kenrude." In a split second, he fired two shots in Tom's direction, as he dove down into the huddled villagers.

The frightened, screaming villagers scattered in every direction, blocking Tom from having a clear shot. As Rampart raced toward the north end of the village, Geno dropped down behind a barrel, engaging Rampart's men with full automatic fire. Before they were able to fire at anyone, Geno cut them down, including the two South Vietnamese soldiers.

As Tom began to pursue Rampart, the operative he was holding to the ground rolled over, pulled his sidearm from its holster, and prepared to fire. However, he was not aware of where Geno was now standing. As he began to take aim, Geno fired the last three rounds from his magazine into the man's body.

Dropping the magazine from his M-16, Geno slammed a fresh one into place as he ran after Tom. About a hundred yards from the village, Rampart turned to fire at his pursuers, but was instead struck down by automatic weapons fire coming from the jungle. As he collapsed to the ground, Tom and Geno took rapid cover behind several trees along the well-worn trail. As the two men attempted to understand what was happening, several Huey choppers flew past the village, very low above the water. Seeing the men taking cover, the pilot of the lead chopper accelerated his machine as he flew off to the northeast.

Moments later, Capt. Wong from the Canh Sat, along with his two body guards, emerged from the underbrush. Tom and Geno looked at each other in amazement as the captain of the secret police and his body guards were dressed exactly as the Viet Cong that stood behind them.

Slowly Captain Wong walked forward kicking Rampart's corpse solidly in the face. "I told you Rampartsan, one day I would get the upper hand, and now I have." Turning toward the village, he observed Tom and Geno coming out from behind the trees.

"So you see, your Rampartsan is no more, he will never bother me or anyone again. Do you care? He was just CIA scum, or SOG, or whatever you Americans wish to call butchers like him." Looking at Geno, he continued. "So, I just watched you shoot all of Rampart's men, and two of mine. Are you also SOG, or are you part of another American operation."

Geno stood motionless for a moment, as he eyed the Viet Cong soldiers standing at the edge of the jungle. It was clear they were not ready to walk away from this situation, as they were firmly in control. Cautiously, Geno lowered his M-16 as he glared at the Captain.

"Tom and I are medics, we were ordered to go along with Rampart on this mission. We are not part of anything that man was attempting to do or did in the past."

After looking skyward to see where the choppers had gone, Capt. Wong looked back toward Tom and Geno. "So all that is left is to deal with the likes of you."

As Captain Wong turned to give orders to his body guards, the two choppers returned, dropping in low over the jungle. Immediately, his body guards raised their weapons to fire, as the Viet Cong fighters retreated back into the jungle. Capt. Wong screamed at them in anger, attempting to get their attention. With all the confusion, Tom and Geno dropped to their knees, opening fire. As Geno sprayed the trail with full automatic fire, Capt. Wong and his bodyguards tumbled to the ground. From the jungle behind the village, a roar of AK-47 fire went skyward, aimed at the choppers, followed by a poorly aimed RPG that had no chance of striking its target.

Door gunners on both choppers began hammering away with their heavy machine guns, as their pilots flew just feet above the tree tops. Three more choppers landed to the south of the village, disgorging a large group of AirCav soldiers.

Slowly and methodically they began sweeping the jungle behind the village, attempting to wipe out any Viet Cong the helicopter gunners had missed. Tom and Geno backtracked into the village for safety, to find a naval river patrol boat tying up to the pier, while another one sat about halfway out in the river with their weapons pointed toward the village.

An army colonel wearing an AirCav patch on his shoulder along with three infantrymen stepped off the patrol boat, walking swiftly over to Tom and Geno. The colonel called out, "My name is Col. Charles Gagne, United States Army, AirCav. Who the hell are you, and what the hell is going on here?"

Tom explained the situation as quickly as he could, to the somewhat angry and impatient colonel. After listening to everything he was told, the officer pushed his helmet back.

"Are you telling me both Captain Wong and Rampart are lying dead on that trail?"

Geno nodded as he replied, "Yes sir, and they are definitely both quite dead."

Turning to one of his soldiers he said, "Get me two body bags out of the boat, I want to personally take those assholes back for ID." Turning back toward Tom and Geno he continued, "Take me to them!"

Arriving at the bodies, colonel Gagne knelt down to search them, as his men kept watch for enemy activity in the jungle. He removed documents from both men that he tucked inside his shirt. After the body bags had been sealed, a Lieutenant from the AirCav team approached.

"Colonel Gagne, we've secured the area, there are about forty bodies in the jungle. I have one slightly wounded. My men are collecting weapons and ammunition." Looking at the body bags, the lieutenant continued. "Whose men are those, sir?"

Smiling, the colonel responded, "Lieutenant, meet SOG agent Rampart, and Capt. Wong of the Canh Sat. We no longer have to search for these two sons-a-bitches."

"Outstanding, sir. I'll get my men to take the bags to the boat when they're finished cleaning up the weapons," the lieutenant replied with a salute before heading back toward his men.

Before the colonel could turn to leave, Tom spoke up, "Sir, I heard Rampart on the radio, telling his men to attack the village with their choppers and wipe it out. He also told them not to let the army know where they were going, or what they were up to."

Col. Gagne nodded his head. "Affirmative, Specialist Kenrude. We are well aware of that call, we were scanning their frequencies. We sent one of our teams in to make sure their choppers never got off the ground. Although this mission didn't go quite as we planned, the results are as good as gold." After thinking for a moment, the colonel continued. "Did either of you ever hear Rampart or the captain talk about a man named Huan Loc?"

"Yes, it was like Rampart was obsessed with him. Several villagers told him Huan Loc had gone back to Cambodia, but Rampart didn't want to hear it. He was ready to kill anyone that didn't give him the answer he wanted," Geno replied.

"Back to Cambodia, you say. It would have been nice to grab him too. Then we could have tied a pretty bow on it and called it a damn good day. Well, Loc will screw up and we'll get the sons a bitch eventually," the colonel responded as he made a notation in a note book.

After returning to the village, Tom and Geno attended to the wounded

AirCav soldiers before helping to load them on a chopper. When they were finished, Tom stopped the colonel. "Sir, if I may ask, what the hell happened here today? And what's been going on with Rampart? We were right in the middle of all this, our lives at risk from all sides from the moment we got the orders. I feel like we've earned some sort of explanation!"

Nodding his head and placing his hands on his hips, Col. Gagne replied. "I was given orders from MACV to find Rampart and Wong and end their operation, no matter what. We've been tracking your movements best we could since you started out. Of course we've also been tracking Wong with great success, as his ego kept him from keeping his mouth shut. His uncensored radio calls allowed us to take out several of his high ranking men along the way. We knew Rampart was playing both sides of the field. He was SOG all the way, and was a ruthless killer that took MACV'S operations to the extreme, and was originally well-liked for it back in Saigon. However, there were other people that were tired of his crap, and wanted it ended now. The problem was, Rampart and Captain Wong had looked out for one another for quite some time. They'd had a lucrative drug smuggling operation for several years and Rampart was skimming profits while attempting to break into the prostitution industry in Saigon, which was Wong's operation pure and simple. Wong's men soon discovered what we already knew, that Rampart was sending hefty amounts of money to a numbered bank account in Australia every month. The more those two battled, the more we were able to close in on them. Yesterday, we learned Wong had slipped out of Saigon and was poised to meet Rampart here to kill him with the aid of Huang Loc and his men, making it look like a Viet Cong attack. However, it appears things went south, and you guys wound up in the middle. I'm truly sorry for that, but I'm happy you guys were able to respond the way you did. My bosses back in Saigon will be very happy you ended the life of that murdering piece of crap Capt. Wong, although SOG or the CIA may not see it that way. We are also on the lookout for another CIA man that went rogue by the name of Sprage. He's just as dangerous."

Tom looked intently at the Colonel. "Rampart questioned everyone we met for the last several days regarding Huan Loc. Who is Huan Loc?"

Shaking his head, Col. Gagne responded. "We know Loc is a major leader of the Viet Cong, but he's also huge in the drug trade, playing one side against the other, allowing him to rake in huge amounts of cash to fund his operations. We would like to see him dead, but he's a slippery S.O.B. with connections all over South East Asia."

Just as the men were ready to load onto the boat, the village chief's wife came running over with the little girl. She began speaking rapidly to the Colonel, who stopped her. He called over a Petty Officer from the boat. "You need to translate for us."

After the woman repeated her message, the petty officer explained. "She and her husband want to know which village she came from. They will take her back and see if they can find her relatives."

Tom and Geno shook their heads. "We walked back and forth all over that damn jungle. I couldn't tell you where we were, or how to find that village again. Rampart had his men burn it, so there is no telling where the villagers may have gone. Just tell her to take care of the girl," Tom replied, as he smiled at the child who was now cleaned up and dressed somewhat neatly.

The petty officer explained the situation to the woman. After hearing what he had to say, she looked down for a moment with a sad look on her face, then nodded her head.

Just as Tom turned to get on the boat, the girl ran up to him pulling on his shirt. Kneeling down, Tom looked into her beautiful brown eyes and smiled.

"You will be fine here. The chief and his wife will take good care of you."

The girl placed her small hand on Tom's cheek and spoke softly. When she finished, Tom asked the petty officer what she had said.

He shook his head saying, "Nothing much, just gibberish. Leave it be, specialist."

Tom shook his head, "No, I want to hear what she had to say. It's important to me."

The petty officer asked the girl to repeat what she had said. She stepped forward, pointing her finger at Tom, and repeated her message even more slowly as she stared intently into Tom's eyes.

"It doesn't make sense, she said, 'Pray that the trial may pass by you, but know it's the master's will it must be done,' you see, gibberish."

As he finished translating, the girl began nodding her head as if she understood every word the petty officer had explained. As Tom reached out for her hand, she backed away toward the chief's wife, hiding her face in the woman's long skirt for a moment.

As Tom stood up, the woman took the girl by the hand, and began walking back toward their hut. Halfway there, the girl turned back to look at Tom. Once more she pointed her finger at him, before placing her small hand over her heart. As their eyes were locked on to one another, Tom could see tears rolling down her soft cheeks.

Nothing the girl had said made any sense to him, but her last gestures gave him an uneasy feeling. Shaking his head, he turned and boarded the boat, as the woman and child entered their hut.

Moments later, the two boats headed south down the Mekong River, as the choppers containing the AirCav team disappeared into the distance.

Arriving at the river boat base, Tom and Geno were given hot showers, clean coveralls and a good meal. Before they could return to Binh Thuy, Col. Gagne, had them each write a complete report on the incident.

It was a big relief for both men when the chopper touched down at Binh Thuy the next day. They were happy to see Capt. Trajillio drive up in a jeep to meet them.

The men shook hands with their captain, who was also very glad to have them back alive. "So, can one of you tell me, why we have a General

Satre in our orderly room spitting tacks? He's about as hostile as Rampart was before you men left. He wants to talk to both of you, now!"

Entering the orderly room, the general stepped forward, staring at the medics for a moment.

"Alright, I don't care if this takes all day and all night, I want every detail on your mission, and I want to know where Rampart and Wong are right now! Gentlemen, you better get this right the first time around, because I'm not in the mood to play games."

Tom looked the angry General in the eye. "You'll find Rampart and Captain Wong burning in hell where they belong. If you feel either of them were assets to this war, than you belong with them. They're both dead, and Col. Gagne took custody of their bodies yesterday. He said he wanted to have an investigation done to confirm their identities."

Before the General could speak, Geno added. "Eventually Manfred and Jungles will be caught up with also. Our men are not going to put up with their crap much longer!"

The general paced back and forth for a moment. "Well, you men got it all wrong. I'm not here hoping that Rampart and Wong are still alive, in fact I hope they're dead, and I hope the rest of those animals like Manfred and Jungles get what's coming to them real damn soon. They think SOG and the CIA are going to win this war for the United States, but all they're doing is making it totally impossible for us to win. You can't judge what they do, as it's all sanctioned at the highest level of our government, and no one is going to change what they're doing, and I mean no one! It won't take them long to have a replacement for Rampart, and the Canh Sat will replace Captain Wong. So the prostitution, assassinations and drug running will continue. How else do you think the CIA funds their operations?"

After a moment of silence, the general nodded his head. "Alright, I have my aide set up in the conference room with a tape recorder. We're going to ask questions, and you can fill in the blanks and give us insight as to what happened and who was all killed. You men are not in trouble, but what you know just might help me when I get back to the United States."

The following day, Tom and Geno were called back to the office. When they arrived, a young Vietnamese man in a heavily starched white linen suit awaited them. He smiled broadly, as they walked up to him.

"Gentlemen, I am Major Ti of the Canh Sat. I am replacing Capt. Wong, who has mysteriously disappeared. I have been led to believe you can shed some light on this matter. After all, it would be best for both our governments if we could handle this matter discretely. I would hate to have to bring you men to Saigon to speak with our interrogators."

Capt. Trujillo stepped forward. "Let's get one thing straight, Major. My men aren't going anywhere with you, so anything you need to ask them, do it here, do it fast, and get the hell out of my office, so we can get on with fighting this war."

The major glared at the captain for a moment, before turning back toward Tom and Geno with the large fake smile.

"So, tell me, when was the last time you saw our captain? Where were you, and what were you doing?"

Tom shook his head, "We couldn't tell you where we were, some village along the Mekong."

"And what were you doing there? Smuggling drugs, sending supplies to the Viet Cong perhaps?"

Geno walked up face to face with the grinning Major. "I don't think so, but the last I heard, Capt. Wong was making a reservation in hell, and we'll be more than willing to make one for you too, just to save you the time and effort!"

Capt. Trujillo busted out laughing as the smile disappeared from the Major's face as he turned and exited the office.

CHAPTER 21
WASHINGTON D.C.

General Edmond Satre and his aide Lt. Jim Ruckles, had just finished their workout in the basement of the Pentagon. As they sat on a bench in the locker room the general shook his head.

"Jim, this damn work out gets harder every week, and you get better and better under that basketball hoop. Did you ever think of playing in the NBA?"

Lt. Ruckles laughed. "No sir, they would eat me alive. I'm not in their league by any stretch of the imagination.

The general laughed as he wiped sweat from his forehead. "So you're saying you're only good enough to take on an old man that is past his prime?"

Smiling over at his mentor and good friend, the lieutenant replied, "So how's that leg coming along, sir. Any problems?"

"Naw, no problems. It's just not as strong as it was before. The doctors in Saigon did the best they could putting humpty-dumpty back together again. And by the way lieutenant, that was a very good segue you used to avoid answering my question. I'll still make a good officer out of you one of these days."

The general laughed as he slammed his hand down on the shoulder of his trusted aide as he stood up. "Now let's get cleaned up. I promised Alice we would be in the office by 0730."

The general passed through the reception room straight into his office without saying a word. Alice Sanborn, his longtime secretary looked at the clock on her desk.

"You're late, General."

"Yeah, yeah, I know, the traffic coming up from the basement was the worst. I had to traverse around two spilled cups of coffee, one dumped file, and had to give directions to a crying intern that was lost. God, I hate it when women cry in front of me. What is wrong with you people?"

The late fifty-something woman, wearing a red dress that fit her slender figure very well, with her mostly silver hair neatly rolled up on the back of her head, smiled. "I'll ignore that last question, as we have been there several times before, sir, and you have lost each time. So, tell me, how is that leg of yours doing today, General?"

Turning to look at his very outspoken secretary, who was now standing in front of his desk with her arms folded, he replied, "You can wipe that snarky smile off your face, Alice. Do you want to know what I weighed this morning, too? Good grief, what's going on around here?"

"Oh, I can find out your weight from your lieutenant, sir. You know, I actually think he may be afraid of me at times. But you failed to answer me, General. How is your leg doing today?"

As the general poured a cup of coffee, he looked at his persistent secretary as she stood like a statue in the middle of his office giving him a menacing glare.

"You know Alice, I can understand why Lt. Ruckles might be afraid of you. There are times, like right now, when you even scare the hell out of me!"

"Well that's fine, General, but you still didn't answer me. That tells me an appointment for therapy at Walter Reed is going to be needed again, Or, I can just call that lovely wife of yours and schedule a nice long chat with her over coffee in the morning. Which is it, sir?" Alice asked, with an intimidating expression on her face as she looked over the top of her reading glasses.

Sitting down behind his large oak desk, General Satre motioned for her to sit down.

"No, Sally knows about my leg. She noticed the last few days I've been limping more, and it is somewhat painful when I go to stand up. Alice, there are times I wish I would have lost the damn leg instead of having it rebuilt like a transmission. I don't think an artificial leg would have caused me such grief. I know the doctors in Saigon told me I was better off keeping my leg, but sometimes I wonder. Yeah, go ahead and make a couple of appointments for therapy, it sure can't hurt."

Alice studied the General's face for a moment. "You do know General, the men that died that day, it wasn't your fault. You could never have known that rocket attack was going to hit in Saigon when it did. I can still see that pain in your eyes, sir."

The general smiled at his good friend, secretary, and favorite confidant. "Alice, I appreciate your concern and dedication. So answer me this, how is your husband doing after his heart attack? Damn. Fifty-nine is way too young to have a jolt like that."

As Alice rose from the chair, she nodded as tears filled her eyes. "He's doing much better, thank you. The doctors say he should get back to something close to normal in about six months. He can do some of his work from home, so that has kept his spirits up, and I'm happy for that. He told me the other day he wants to get back to golf next year, because he wants to kick your butt at least one more time. I pray to God he can keep that golf date."

The general laughed as he put his coffee cup on his desk. "He's a good golfer, Alice, and a better friend. I can't wait to get back on the course with him. Tell him I'll stop by next weekend for a game of chess. At least I can beat him at that."

After looking at her watch, Alice began heading back to her desk in the reception room "Your 0800 appointment should be here shortly."

Before Alice could announce that Agent Carl Sprage from the CIA was there to see him, the door flew open to the general's office. He began yelling, "Who the hell do you think you are, General?"

Alice ran into the office behind him saying, "I'm sorry sir, he just walked right past me, I couldn't get him to stop."

The General raised his hand, "It's alright Alice, just close the door on your way out."

After taking a sip of coffee he looked at Agent Sprage. "Now tell me, what has you all wound up this beautiful morning, or do I need to get used to spooks running off the rails on a regular basis?"

Agent Sprage looked sternly at General Satre. "You have no damn business getting involved in CIA activities in Vietnam. We have a job to do over there, and we don't need a two bit Major General attempting to gum up the works!"

After that comment, the general sprang from his chair like a leopard attacking its prey.

"Listen to me, Sprage. I spent three tours over on that God forsaken piece of real estate, cleaning up messes your people created. You've got butchers like Jungles, Manfred and Laramore, or whatever their real names are, leading execution squads around the south and in Cambodia under the direction of SOG, causing nothing but pain and grief. I've seen the results of their so called, 'win the hearts and minds of the people' campaign, and it stinks to high heaven. Those men just like Rampart are nothing but butchers and should be brought up on charges. I'm surprised that men like you and the director of the CIA could ever endorse such a sick operation as SOG!"

Sprage glared at the general. "SOG? What the hell are you talking about? SOG doesn't even exist, except in the minds of officers like you that are attempting to discredit the CIA for what we're trying to accomplish."

Gen. Satre looked indignantly at Sprage. "So what's going on in Cambodia and Laos is a figment of my imagination, and my men who were killed along the Mekong River with American weapons by South Vietnamese soldiers in Cambodia never happened, right!"

Agent Sprage pointed his finger at General Satre. "You know that attack has never been substantiated. Your men were caught up in the middle of a cross fire, no one was proved to be firing from Cambodia, and you know it."

General Satre shook his head. "Sprage, we found the body of one of your men tangled in the brush on the Cambodian side of the river. We saw Americans heading west when the fighting started, don't stand here and tell me I'm full of shit."

Sprage laughed as he walked over toward the window. "General, did you ever identify the man with the South Vietnamese Army, did you ever recognize any of the so called Americans you say witnessed the attack? Hell no, because those men could have been French, Italian, German's or whatever. You just assume they were Americans because they were white."

General Satre angrily slammed his fist onto his desk. "You are one arrogant bastard. You know damn well members of SOG are scrubbed clean of anything tying them to the United States Military or Government, and none of their files, no matter who they fight for, ever reflect their presence in Vietnam. There is no way to back trace any of them."

Sprage walked back toward the general. "Go ahead, prove any of that, prove just one case."

General Satre laughed, "Look, I'm a Major General, not some two bit reporter you can pay and turn into a puppet to run with every story you lay on them. I know how the system works, I've been over there, and I know SOG exists, and I'll do whatever I can to take it down."

Sprage crossed his arms over his chest, "Well General, sometimes you have to break a few eggs to make an omelet, and I sure as hell am willing to do just that to bring about a final victory. So, you can take your self-righteous attitude and stick it up your ass!"

General Satre charged around his desk, getting face to face with Sprage. "Look you sick son-of-a-bitch, that crap you pull over there isn't going to win this war or any other war. All it does is inflame the people against us, and that's why the Viet Cong have been so successful. You aren't keeping the people from joining their ranks, you're shoving them right into the arms of the V.C. and they damn well know it. I'm surprised Ho Chi Minh doesn't send you a gall damn personalized Christmas card!"

Sprage's eyes narrowed as he glared at the general. "Just because what we do over there upsets your tender stomach, don't think for a minute anyone cares about your simple fucking feelings. I've heard you have an appointment to see the president and his advisors. I suggest you cancel it and leave all of this alone if you know what's good—"

Gen. Satre cut him off before he could finish his thoughts and he slammed his finger into Sprage's chest. "Are you threatening me, Sprage? You have the balls to think you can waltz into my office, and threaten me, a two star general, and get away with that? Well, you better think again. Now, this conversation is over, and I want you out of the Pentagon right now."

Reaching down on the desk he pushed a button next to the phone. In seconds, a military police officer and Lt. Ruckles entered the office from the situation room next door at a brisk walk.

"Lieutenant, escort this piece of crap from the Pentagon. If he resists, shoot the bastard, and pull his ID card. I want him banned from these premises today!" Gen. Satre yelled, so angry he shook.

As Lt. Ruckles placed a hand on Sprage's arm, he pulled away. Before a word could be said, the police officer pulled his weapon from its holster, pointing directly at the angry CIA agent.

Sprage put his hands up in the air, yelling, "Okay, okay, put that damn thing away, I'll go. We wouldn't want to soil the General's new carpet now, would we?"

General Satre laughed, "Hell Sprage, I got plenty of money in the budget for new carpet and your worthless funeral. You can have it any way you want."

Just as Lt. Ruckles was going to take Sprage by the arm one more time, the hostile man turned toward the door. Before exiting, he turned to face the General again. "This ain't over General, not by a long shot. I recommend you watch your six."

The police officer pushed Sprage up against the wall, as he removed his cuffs from the case. After placing them on Sprage's wrists, he read the man his rights.

"What the hell do you think you're doing, officer? Take these damn cuffs off, you have no right to arrest me, I'm a federal agent!"

"You threatened the general in my presence, sir. You'll be turned over to Metro Police and booked downtown," the police officer explained as he pushed him out the door.

After they left, Alice came running into the office. "Are you alright, sir? I called for the police officer the minute that jackass arrived. I knew he was up to no good."

Gen. Satre smiled at his angry secretary as he sat back down behind his desk. "Remember, you need to keep that blood pressure down, Alice. If you can't, maybe I will need to see about getting you an early retirement, and getting a cute young blonde to take your place."

Alice folded her arms across her body as she glared at the general. "Early retirement? Cute blonde? Who the hell do you think you're speaking to? If it weren't for me—"

Shaking his head the general cut her off. "I know Alice, if it weren't for you, I would have to pick up my own pastries every Friday, and make my own golf dates. Yes, you do serve a purpose."

Alice half-laughed as she walked up to his desk. "Oh pooh, on all of that. However, remember you do have an appointment at the White House at 1300hrs. The car is ordered and Lt. Ruckles has all the files you requested. Will there be anything else, General?"

Trying to look angry he replied, "In fact there is one thing. Will you tell the baker to put a little more butter in the danish this coming Friday? They weren't quite as fluffy as normal last week."

Alice smiled, as she walked back toward the door. Do you want me to tell you where the baker can place that butter, sir?"

General Satre laughed heartily as he shook his head. "Thanks for calling the police officer, Alice. I never expected it to get that far out of hand, I really did not."

Nodding her head, she replied. "Any time, General. Besides, I don't retire until you do, so you may have to put up with me for a while, and maybe Friday I won't even pick up the danish, so there."

As she closed the door, Gen. Satre laughed as he said to himself, "I wonder where the Pentagon ever found her?"

At 1220hrs., the General and Lt. Ruckles slid into the back seat of a dark green Chevrolet Impala, with army markings on the doors. In seconds, the driver departed the Pentagon for the short trip to the White House, depending on traffic.

Looking out the window, Gen. Satre inquired, "So, how long did it take the CIA to break Sprage free from Metro Police?"

Lt. Ruckles had to laugh. "They weren't through booking him by the time those clowns arrived at the front door demanding his release, according to the MP. I guess his superiors were hot as hell."

General Satre was quiet for a moment. "I don't think his superiors know exactly what that man is all about." After a moment of silence the General continued. "So, how do you think this meeting will go? Sometimes, I think I should just keep my mouth shut, but Sprage and his kind really upset me. Our boys that are fighting over there, they don't deserve to have SOG and the CIA making things more dangerous for them. How many of our boys are being killed because of the shit they're getting away with. Someone has to take the bull by the damn horns and stop it."

Nodding in agreement, Lt. Ruckles turned to look at the General. "Sir, you are doing the right thing. I saw too much of their so called pacification program when I was over there. I still have nightmares about that little girl I saw mutilated and burned by that monster Manfred. Every time I have those nightmares, I go into my daughter's room and pick her up from the crib and hold her. It's the only thing that soothes my soul."

Arriving at the White House, the two men walked slowly down the hall toward the office of the President's secretary. Just before reaching the door, Gen. Satre took hold of the lieutenant's arm.

"Son, what you are about to witness, is a general committing political suicide. It may not be hostile, it may in fact be a very cordial meeting, but in all reality, I'll never get another promotion, and down the road a year or so, they'll ask for my resignation. So, I want you to keep your mouth shut, hand me any documents I ask for, and leave the room when I tell you to do so. I want you to make this a learning mission as to how not to conduct your career. Do I make myself clear?"

Lt. Ruckles looked down at the floor for a moment before responding. "Crystal clear sir. Permission to speak freely, sir?"

Nodding his head, Gen. Satre replied, "Of course Jim. Your input has always been important to me. Say what you feel is necessary."

After clearing his throat, he looked into the general's eyes. "Then don't do it, sir. Cancel the meeting, give them any excuse you can come up with. But please, don't put your career on the line like this. You have way too much to offer the army and our country, sir."

General Satre looked compassionately toward his aide.

"Thank you for that, Jim. But if I keep my mouth shut, butchers like Rampart, Manfred, Jungles and Sprage keep on killing poor innocent people for nothing, and they win. If I go into that office and attempt to make a difference in the conduct of this war and get canned, they still win. It's a lose-lose situation all the way around. So, then I have to ask myself, will I sleep better tonight if I have the meeting and at least try, or will I sleep better tonight if I turn my back on those poor villagers and our boys dying over there. I think the answer is clear as mud."

Lt. Ruckles half smiled as he nodded his head. "Well then, give them hell, sir!"

The president had just finished a meeting when the two men walked into the outer office. The president's secretary pointed toward some chairs as she went into the Oval Office. Moments later, she returned.

"The president will see you now, gentlemen."

President Nixon was standing in front of his desk with his arms folded across his chest as he listened to a comment from Secretary of State William Rogers. Secretary of Defense Melvin Laird, Attorney General John Mitchell, and William (Red) Evans, a former Vice Admiral, now Assistant Director of the CIA, were sitting on the sofa listening to the conversation.

The president turned and smiled as he walked over to shake hands with Gen. Satre and Lt. Ruckles, "It's nice to finally meet you, General. I have heard a lot about you over the last few months. I was sorry to hear about the injuries you sustained during your last tour of duty and I'm glad you've managed to come back so well. We need good men like you working with us on the war."

"Thank you, Mr. President. I appreciate your concern for my welfare, and I'm glad to have the position in the Pentagon I'm currently serving in," the general replied as they shook hands.

Smiling, the president directed the two men to a set of chairs opposite the sofa. "So, tell me General, what kind of information do you have regarding problems in the operation of the war?"

"Well sir, when I arrived in Vietnam, I was given a policy manual regarding CIA operations in the field." As he spoke, Lt. Ruckles handed the document to the president.

President Nixon flipped through it for a moment before handing it to the Attorney General.

"John, is this the manual we looked over when I took office," the president inquired.

After checking it over, the attorney general replied, "Yes, Mr. President. It has been thoroughly vetted and agreed upon to assure we are not breaking any laws, or stepping on toes at the United Nations. It's the handbook all commanders in the field should be operating with."

General Satre felt a knot in his stomach as the president looked at him. "Mr. President, this next document was compiled during my last tour of duty." Handing it to the president, he continued. "It's a report containing the amount of civilian casualties, villages destroyed, and other crimes committed by SOG hit teams throughout 1968 and the first half of 1969."

President Nixon starred intensely at General Satre. "Look General, we all have heard the vicious rumors concerning SOG, but the organization simply does not exist. We spend time every week assuring the press and our allies that we have no such agency operating in South East Asia." Turning toward William Evans, he continued, "Red, what can you add on this? Personally, I'm tired of telling everyone over and over that this SOG operation just does not exist."

The CIA Assistant Director stood up and walked over to a map of South East Asia that stood on an easel near the president's desk. Pointing at the map he began, "We have our hands full, right here in South Vietnam. We know there are Viet Cong operating in Cambodia and Laos. We do our best to have the local governments deal with those incursions, and they do a good job. Yes, we have many pacification operations going on throughout the south, especially in the central highlands and the delta. So far it appears those programs are working out quite nicely, mothers and fathers are no longer turning their boys over to the V.C., and they are no longer allowing the V.C. to intimidate their villages. In fact, we have heard many stories about how villagers are using captured weapons to fight off the V.C. when they approach their villages. If this continues, Mr. President, Vietnamization of the war will proceed on schedule, allowing us to begin pulling troop out of South Vietnam within the next year."

Director Evans walked over to Gen. Satre. "You stated there have been crimes committed in the South by this SOG group. I haven't been made aware of any crimes committed in Vietnam by my people or any other agencies."

Once again the president slowly looked through the file General Satre had given him, frowning from time to time. Before handing it to Director Evans, he looked over at the general. "General, can you emphatically state these allegations are one hundred percent accurate, that there are no false claims made by field commanders, where they might have assumed there was a bad situation without personally checking into the facts of the case. If there is even one, we'll have to consider this file as inadmissible. Additionally, the term SOG is used again and again, and we all know that organization just does not exist. What do you want me to do, General?"

By now, General Satre had begun to realize he had made a huge blunder by coming to the White House with this information. It was obvious the president was upset this file had been created without the knowledge of anyone in general headquarters in Saigon or the Pentagon.

Standing up, the general faced the president. "I can assure you sir, everything in this document has been checked and rechecked, and every officer reporting the incidents is of the highest caliber, and beyond reproach."

Reaching down to Lt. Ruckles, Gen. Satre took hold of the last document. "Mr. President, this file contains information regarding unauthorized SOG operations in Cambodia, Laos and North Vietnam, during that same period, under the auspices of the CIA. It explains who the ground commanders were, where the operations were launched from, and how many American troops were involved."

William Evans stomped his foot as he faced the president. "Mr. President, I don't know where this man received all this so called information, but I can categorically deny all of these so called operations, and any organization known as SOG. We do not operate in Laos, Cambodia or for God's sake, North Vietnam. I would like to meet these field commanders and question each of them!"

Before another word was said, General Satre ordered Lt. Ruckles to leave the Oval Office. Once the door was closed, General Satre looked at the president. Sir, I'll stake my career on everything I just handed to you. I can assure you, every bit of information I have presented here, is truthful and accurate!"

President Nixon raised his hand. "Calm down, General, no one here is calling you a liar. No one is saying your file is inaccurate. Yes, Bill is a bit upset, but we'll need time to go through all of this and see where it leads. Bill's people will get right on this, interview the field commanders and report back to us as soon as possible."

Shocked, Gen. Satre protested. "Mr. President, giving that file to Director Evans to investigate, is like handing the keys to the barnyard to a wolf. That file needs to go to an independent investigative team, someone who will be unbiased."

President Nixon scowled as he glared at Gen. Satre. "General, are you telling me, that you believe the top people in my government, people that I personally hand-picked, would fail the American people by destroying or lying about the content of a file?"

After taking a deep breath, Gen. Satre replied. "Mr. President, I have the utmost confidence in you and your cabinet members. But sir, I'm all too sure that Mr. Evans knows exactly what's going on in Vietnam, and that he'll do anything to make sure nothing happens to his men or their operations."

President Nixon paced back and forth for a moment before looking over at Melvin Laird, who was now standing next to the general. "I'm amazed at what you brought to this office today, General. However, it's only fair that the CIA get a chance to study the documents, investigate the complaints leveled against their agents, and debunk this SOG situation that has everyone so wound up, before reporting back to me or taking any actions. I'm not sure what you thought would or would not happen here today, but we have your file, we have your concerns, and this matter is now closed. Mr. Secretary, you can escort the General out."

Secretary Laird led Gen. Satre and Lt. Ruckles down the corridor away from the Oval Office. "General, you pissed off some powerful people today. I can't even guess what ramifications will come from this. But I'll give you one strong piece of advice. For the foreseeable future, I would make sure you have your six covered at all times! Sleeping dogs don't like being awakened by an intruder, especially when they feel everything is under control. If I were you, I'd get a hold of our old friend Sid Dittmore. He may just save your butt in the long run."

Before the general could respond, the Secretary of Defense walked briskly back toward the Oval Office without saying another word.

Lt. Ruckles looked at his general. "Where do we go from here, sir? This place and everyone in it is giving me a bad feeling. Should we head back to the Pentagon, or do you want to head home?"

Shaking his head, the general half smiled. "No Jim, I have work to do, let's head back to the Pentagon."

Several days later, Lt. Ruckles drove General Satre to a meeting at Andrews Air Force Base. When the meeting concluded several hours later, the General had agreed to give Navy Lt. Commander Baker a ride back to the Pentagon. As they approached the car, Admiral Wilcox called the General Satre back to the door of the office building to hand him a file. Lt. Ruckles and the commander proceeded to enter the car. Lieutenant Ruckles turned the key to start the engine, so he could get the air conditioner running to cool down the interior. A tremendous explosion rocked the area, as the Green Chevy Impala erupted into a ball of flame. Admiral Wilcox and General Satre watched in horror as the flames consumed the two dedicated officers.

Saturday morning, Lt. Ruckles was laid to rest in Arlington National Cemetery. Although it was a small funeral, the grief displayed by the mourners was very intense.

"How could this happen, General? Who would do such a thing? We need answers, and soon," Alice demanded, as she and her husband walked toward their cars along with Sally Satre.

As the general watched another funeral party start their graveside service, he looked at Alice. "I can't say for sure, but I have a pretty good idea." Taking his wife by the hand he looked into her eyes. "When we get home, I want you to pack a bag and go to your sister's place. I'll have an armed escort pick up Mary at Georgetown, and bring her there also. Brian will be fine at West Point, but I'll make sure the Commandant keeps him that way."

Sally Satre looked sternly at her husband. "No General, I'll not frighten our children, or go running into the night. I have weathered worse and I'll stay where you stay. End of discussion!"

Tuesday evening as the general walked into his house, Sally was busy preparing the evening meal. "Your favorite tonight, Ed. Lasagna, with red wine and garlic bread. Oh and by the way, a box arrived for you from your book club, it's on the sofa."

General Satre looked down at the box for a moment. Several things caught his attention. The label was not in the normal spot on the box, and the tape was wrinkled in two places, which he had never seen before.

Walking into the kitchen, he took Sally by the hand. "Turn off the stove, and come with me out the back door and don't argue." After leaving the house, he led Sally over to their favorite neighbor's place, where he called the police and bomb squad.

About an hour later, a sergeant from the bomb squad walked up to the general. "Good thing you didn't try to open that box. There was enough Semtex in that box to take out several homes. We gave the box to the police to check for finger prints or any other evidence. As you may or may not know, Semtex is a real favorite of the East German Stasi, and many unofficial Russian thugs."

Gen. Satre shook his head. "They won't find a damn thing. That was set up by a pro, my guess is a CIA bomb-maker."

The police sergeant looked strangely at Gen. Satre. "CIA? What the hell are you talking about?"

Walking back to the neighbor's house he knelt down beside his wife. "Will you go to your sister's house now? I can't protect you here."

After a moment of silence, Sally looked intently at her husband. "Arrange for Mary to be picked up, I'll have my bags packed in an hour. Sweetheart, who is trying to kill us?"

With his wife and children safely tucked away, Gen. Satre left the Pentagon the following day around noon, driving to a small hobby farm just west of Alexandria, Virginia, to meet his old friend Sid Dittmore. Sid had been one of the most daring and successful operatives in the Army's Covert Operation section for over twenty years. It was rumored he had actually infiltrated the Russian KGB, where he set up a plan to assassinate Nikita Khrushchev. He still had contacts around the world that rivaled most intelligence gathering agencies.

As he drove into the yard, two men walked over to greet him. "General, this is Guy Ortega. His record speaks for itself. I trust him with my life, and actually, I have a few times," Sid Dittmore explained, as the two men shook hands.

After the General and Guy Ortega shook hands, Sid led them into the small barn.

"Ed, contrary to what you may want to believe, this contract on your life has not been sanctioned by the CIA. My sources tell me it comes from a nasty old KGB agent named Nicoli Kharkov, and a dangerous CIA agent named Sprage, who has gone semi-rogue. He is a first rate rat, and has made big bucks off the war. You have rattled some big shoes, and Kharkov's feet are a perfect size ten. He has two men on his payroll in the United

States to protect his interests. Sprage is one of them, the other is a German assassin named Rudolph Krance, who was a member of the East German Stasi, and more recently up until a year ago, was a freelance hit man for our State Department in Europe. When Sec. Rogers found out about the operation he pulled the plug." Leaning against a stockade gate, he let the general absorb that information before he continued.

"Krance has made big money taking out industrialists, politicians or anyone else the State Department wanted gone cleanly and efficiently. He was a World War Two orphan with a chip on his shoulder from Magdeburg, East Germany. He originally took the job when the Berlin wall went up, all too happy to kill anyone he thought could be responsible for the deaths of his family. No one knows how many people he has killed, probably hundreds. He's like a slot machine. Put in the money and out come the bodies. Ortega's men have a line on Krance right now, but Sprage and Kharkov are in the wind, probably in Vietnam, where they have people that will protect them. However Kharkov has two big weaknesses. He demands power and doesn't care how he achieves it, and secondly, he will do anything for money. He has worked with the mafia here and abroad, and has completed contract hit operations for the CIA.

Ortega stepped forward, handing Gen. Satre a photo of Kharkov. "Like Sid told you, Sprage and Kharkov both disappeared right after you found his bomb. But they won't give up, because Sprage had a brother in Vietnam. He went by Rampart, but his real name was Willy Sprage. He sent millions of dollars in cash and gold bullion to the United States each month to be laundered, stolen from the South Vietnamese government. Kharkov handles the trade and laundering, and your Carl Sprage handles the transport, netting him quite a large bank account in Switzerland."

The general took in all the information he had just been told. "So, where do we start? I'm on a month's leave and ready to finish this thing, so my family can be safe."

Ortega shook his head as Sid looked down at the floor. "Hiding your family is fine. We got them covered, nothing will happen to them. But you need to continue your regular work schedule, or they'll know something is up, and they'll burrow so deep underground we'll never find them. You need to work with us, General. We'll get those creeps, but you need to cooperate."

Nodding in agreement, the general replied. "Is it possible I can get in on the take down?"

Nodding his head, Sid explained. "If they come close to you, yes. But they know what you look like, and if they see you where you don't belong, everything goes to hell. So, stay clear of everything. We've got your back in more ways than one, just don't ask questions, you know who we are."

Shaking hands with Sid, the general replied. "Oh yeah, I know better than to ask questions."

The following morning, a representative from the Pentagon H.R. Department arrived, with a Lt. Nathan Scarsdale in tow. He had been assigned to become General Satre's new aide.

Over the course of the following weeks, the lieutenant had done little to earn the confidence of either Alice or the general. It appeared he was constantly preoccupied with things that had nothing to do with his job.

Since General Satre had taken his car in for service one afternoon, he asked the lieutenant to give him a ride home. The general missed Lieutenant Ruckles very much, as there was never a dull moment when they were in the car. He could banter back and forth on nearly any subject, and his dry wit made the conversations all the more fun. That was not the case with Lt. Scarsdale. He very seldom started a conversation, and was not good at continuing one when it began.

Arriving at Fort Belvoir, where the general had taken up an apartment on officer's row, Lt. Scarsdale turned to look back at General Satre.

"Should I be here at 0500 sir?"

Nodding his head in approval, General Satre replied. "Yes, that would be fine, Lieutenant. My car should be done sometime tomorrow afternoon, just in time for the weekend."

Arriving at his apartment door, General Satre felt an odd feeling come over him. He looked up and down the corridor, but everything appeared normal. After unlocking the door, the general stood to the side as he pushed it open. After waiting several seconds, he walked inside, scanning the room from left to right. Nothing was out of place, and his mail from the previous day was still laying on the coffee table where he had tossed it. Closing the door, he slowly walked into the bedroom. Once again, everything looked just the way he had left it that morning, but still that nagging feeling that something was amiss bothered him. After getting changed, he tucked his .45 pistol into the back of his waistband, before heading toward the kitchen. Stopping in the doorway, he shook his head as he mumbled, "I think this crap is getting to me."

After taking a quick glance out the kitchen window, he turned toward the refrigerator. His hand was just inches from the door, when something told him not to open it. He stared at the door for several moments, not knowing exactly what to do. Walking over to one of the drawers, he carefully pulled out four dish towels. After tying them together, he tied one end to the refrigerator door handle, and took the other end to the door way of the living room. With a quick tug, he pulled the door open, as he threw himself down on the living room floor.

A quick blast blew the refrigerator door off the hinges, scattering deadly shrapnel all around the small kitchen, while blowing out the window. Instantly, the door to his apartment burst open, as a man dressed in black, carrying a sawed off 12 gauge shotgun, charged into the room. Gen. Satre pulled his pistol from his waist band as he cautiously crawled around the large recliner that was in front of him. He watched as the gunman walked to the kitchen door and looked over the destruction. Jumping to his feet, Gen Satre called out, "Looking for me?"

As the man began to spin around, the general placed three well aimed shots into his chest and head. Nervously, the general walked toward the body lying on top of the rubble. Just as he was about to kneel down to remove the gunman's black stocking cap, someone fired two shots into the apartment, barely missing his head, before running down the corridor. As if back in Vietnam, the General reacted swiftly, giving chase to his assailant, determined he not get away.

Both men ran head long down the stairwell toward the front door of the building. Not wanting the assassin to get away, the general leaned close up against the wall, firing two shots down into the open stairwell. The sound of a body falling down the stairs was music to his ears. Carefully, he worked his way down from the second floor to see the gunman struggling to push the door open, as blood poured from a wound in his lower back and upper thigh.

"Drop your weapon, and I can help you out. No reason to die now. Drop the pistol!" The general called out as he took one step at a time down the last flight of stairs.

Taking a deep breath, the gunman began turning his pistol in the general's direction. Well before the wounded man could fire, Gen. Satre fired two more rounds into his body. The general stood motionless as he looked at the lifeless body in front of him. After studying the corpse for a moment he was awestruck. He noticed the collar of a naval uniform, with lieutenant's bars attached to it, protruding out from under the black coveralls. Kneeling down, he pulled the black stocking cap from the man's head. It was the body of his new aide, Lt. Scarsdale.

As General Satre stood up, a black SUV skidded to a stop outside the building. Sid Dittmore, Guy Ortega and two more men poured out of the vehicle. Running up to the general, Sid called out, "Are you alright, General? We've been back tracking Krance's movements all week, but somehow we lost him in the past twenty-four hours. Just an hour ago, we put it all together. We knew he was here and was coming after you. Is this Lt. Scarsdale?"

General Satre nodded his head as Guy Ortega and the other men raced past him into the apartment building. "Yeah, I'm fine. I think you'll find Krance dead in my kitchen. He put a bomb in my refrigerator. After it exploded, he must have come in quick to make sure I was dead, but I got the drop on him when he hesitated. Then the lieutenant fired several rounds at me from the corridor before turning jack rabbit."

Moments later, Ortega and his men returned from the wrecked apartment. "It's Krance alright," Ortega explained. "I found this in his pocket and that answers the other question we wondered about."

As police cars and fire trucks filled the parking lot, Sid took the general by the arm. "Get in the back seat and be quiet. Let me handle these guys."

Ten minutes later, Sid and his crew climbed into the SUV. "We're all good, sir. Looks like it might have been a small gas explosion that killed the occupant of the apartment. The body of the unidentified man found by the door will be taken to the medical examiner at Fort Mead for an autopsy, to determine the cause of death and attempt to determine who he was."

General Satre had to smile. "How the hell did you get that worked out so fast?" After a moment of thought, he continued. "I got it, don't tell me, those were special ops guys and you made the call before the damn bomb went off, or something like that."

Sid looked into the rear view mirror for a second. "Yeah, something like that. Like I said, General, it's best you don't ask questions. Plausible deniability and all."

As the SUV rolled out of Fort Belvoir, General Satre leaned forward. "What the hell did Scarsdale have to do with all of this? He was just appointed to my staff?"

Guy Ortega looked back at the general. "We've been watching him for about a month. He's been working for the CIA and Sprage for quite a while, there's good money in that kind of shit. He was instrumental in hiring Krance to take you out. The problem was, he worked through intermediaries and was hard to pin down. It was a phone call he made early this afternoon that put all the pieces together for us. Part of the call was a ruse, he made it appear he was taking you to the White House for another meeting, which caught us off guard completely. When you failed to arrive for your meeting, we knew we had been taken, and the next obvious place you would be was your apartment. Sorry we were a bit late, we made some calls to round up help as quickly as we could, we really did want Krance alive."

General Satre leaned back into the seat. "I'm not going to apologize for killing that son-of-a-bitch or the lieutenant. Right about now, I'm willing to kill anyone I need to so we can put an end to all this."

Everyone in the SUV laughed, as Sid drove at top speed out of the Washington D.C. area. Arriving at Sid's compound, General Satre thanked the band of men that had saved him.

Turning to Sid he inquired. "So you said this contract came from Sprage and Kharkov, how the hell do we get to them, and what happened to Carl Sprage?"

"Questions General, you've got way too many questions. I told you to leave well enough alone, that we had your back. Alright, so we almost blew it today, I'll be honest. The problem was things were moving too fast. Krance and Sprage both disappeared in a matter of hours. Scarsdale's phone call regarding that meeting was credible, as the CIA Director himself, and the Secretary of State were both called to the White House for a late afternoon session. We were caught flatfooted, I'll admit to that, and I'm damn sorry it happened," Sid explained, as he looked intently at the General's face.

General Satre walked toward the barn for a moment, deep in thought. "No apologies needed, Sid. I've always trusted you and still do. But from here on out, either I'm totally in the loop, or I'll opt out and figure this out for myself."

Sid walked beside his longtime friend as he nodded his head. "Although I don't like putting you out in the line of fire, you proved today you can handle it. Just so you know, about an hour ago, you put in for extended leave to be with your family. Everything is signed and looking kosher. Alice doesn't know what's going on, so she'll not be able to mess things up with her inquisitive crap. Everything is set to look like you and your family are enjoying an extended vacation to Portugal."

General Satre laughed. "You got your hooks into just about everything in Washington, don't you? What was the reason for my leave?

Sid turned to look the General eye to eye. "Things are heating up, it was best you were gone and undercover. We're really close to busting this, so we need you where we want you. The reason for your vacation was family problems, not far from the truth!"

Before the general could respond, Guy Ortega walked up to Sid with several sheets of paper. After reading them he smiled.

"General, how do you feel about an unannounced trip to sunny South Vietnam? I hear the special operations season has just gotten underway.

After a moment of thought, General Satre looked at Sid. "What was in that black book Ortega pulled from Krance's pocket?"

Sid smiled, "Like I said, these guys are creatures of habit and they make mistakes. The book had dates of upcoming operations in Vietnam, unit movements, major supply missions that could be used to smuggle drugs to their desired locations and CIA operatives operating in those zones. Now we have a good idea where we can find Sprage and Kharkov. Ortega is already making some calls to Saigon.

The following morning at 0500, Gen. Satre, Sid Dittmore, Guy Ortega and two other men flew out of Dulles International Airport on a private cargo plane, bound for Tan Son Nhut air base near Saigon.

Heavy humidity and bright sunny skies greeted the men as they exited the cargo aircraft near a military storage warehouse. Walking inside, Gen. Satre was surprised to see his old friend Capt. Walter Holloway sitting on a pallet of C-Rations beside his trusted friend, Sgt. Ed. Mecklenburg.

"Well, well. Never thought I would run into you over here again, Walt. What brings you here to this operation?"

Jumping down from the pallet Capt. Holloway began "This mission is high profile and urgent. The last thing Westmoreland wants is a Russian operative running around South Vietnam. Kharkov and Sprage have been contracted out by the CIA for elimination, but their bodies must be authenticated. Actually my boss was stunned when we were called upon to complete the mission. But we were told to wait for you, as you know how their operation works."

Approximately 0500hrs the following morning, Capt. Holloway led a column of eleven men onto two Huey helicopters parked near the Special Forces compound. The flight took them deep into a dense jungle about one hundred miles west of Saigon.

After departing the choppers, the small team made their way toward a small muddy river that ran down from the mountains to their north. Arriving at a small village, Sgt. Mecklenburg walked up to the village chief who had seen them coming from some distance.

Bowing down, the chief smiled. "Mecklenburgsan, good to see you again. Long time."

After shaking hands with the chief and handing him several cartons of Camel Cigarettes, Sgt. Mecklenburg and Capt. Holloway sat down on a bench beside the chief, showing him photos of Kharkov and Sprage.

"Chief, have you seen these men?" The Captain inquired"

Nodding his head, he smiled, "Three, maybe four days ago. They came through here with about fifteen men. They say they are lost, looking for American forces. I tell them of supply base up river several miles. They leave quickly."

Sergeant Mecklenburg patted the old chief on the back as he thanked him.

Captain Holloway instructed specialist Lucas to take point as they began their trek up hill. Halfway to the supply base Lucas observed six Viet Cong off to their right walking in the direction of the village they had just left. Immediately, he turned back to the team to inform Capt. Holloway.

After hearing the news, Sid said, "Sprage! He paid V.C. to wipe out the village to cover their tracks. We need to go back or they will kill every last villager and burn the place."

Sergeant Mecklenburg concurred with Sid's explanation. Looking at the Captain he said. "Let me take three men back with me. You should have enough men to take out Sprage and his operation if you play it right."

Captain Holloway nodded his head. "Two birds with one stone. Take who you want, we'll continue on."

After grabbing three men from their team, Sgt. Mecklenburg headed back toward the village at a rapid pace. Everything appeared quiet in the village when the team arrived on the far side of the river. After several minutes, Corporal Nelson pointed toward three V.C. that had circled around the village and were taking up positions to the south. Sergeant Mecklenburg looked at Corporal Nelson. "Take Roland and get behind them and neutralize them quickly" Taking Specialist Turner, Sgt. Mecklenburg walked north about twenty-five feet before crossing the small river. Kneeling down on the river bank, they observed the last three V.C. about ten yards from the village holding onto an old woman.

Looking at Turner, he whispered. "You get the guy on the right, I'll get the guy on the left. Than we both take the third."

Turner nodded his head as he brought his rifle up to his shoulder waiting for orders to fire.

Taking careful aim Sgt. Mecklenburg said, "Now Turner, now!"

The two V.C. holding the woman collapsed to the ground, and the third man was killed quickly as he wasted time attempting to see where the fire was coming from. Turner and Sgt. Mecklenburg charged forward as gunfire erupted on the south side of the village.

The old woman looked up at Turner as he held his hand out to help her up. As a tear ran down her cheek, she gave him a hug. Quickly Sgt. Mecklenburg ran into the village as people were screaming and running about. The chief approached him shaking like a leaf. Before he could speak, Turner and Sgt. Mecklenburg ran to see how his men had come out. As Nelson came out of the tree line he smiled.

"I have a gift for you, Sarg. All of the enemy dressed like Viet Cong were actually American, and one was Sprage. I was dumbfounded when I rolled him over."

After confirming the dead man was in fact Sprage, Sgt. Mecklenburg looked up to see a black CIA chopper headed for the supply base. Without talking to the chief, the four men began a quick run to back up their team.

Arriving at the supply base, Capt. Holloway had made contact with the base commander, asking if he had seen the men in the photos. The Captain was upset when he was told Sprage had left the base about a half hour ago with two of his workers and several Vietnamese soldiers. The commander told him he knew the other man as a Col. Underwood, who regularly picked up supplies for CIA activities, and that his men were stacking supplies at the LZ right now as the chopper would be there about 1030hrs.

Capt. Holloway spread the men out as they worked their way toward the LZ. Sid, Gen. Satre and Ortega worked their way around the LZ toward the western perimeter.

As Capt. Holloway watched Sprage's men piling up the crates, he could hear the chopper off in the distance. He knew they could not make a move until the helicopter had landed or they would fly off and Kharkov would remain at large and still be a serious problem.

As the chopper circled the base, Kharkov was looking out the side door, smiling as he took a wave from one of his men.

Captain Holloway was nearly holding his breath as the pilot was now about ten feet from the ground. Suddenly another man they had not seen came running up toward the chopper yelling for them to leave, "Go it's a trap, go!"

Sid opened fire dropping the man, as the pilot began sending power to the massive blades to get back into the air.

Everyone on the team rushed forward, killing all the workers in the LZ before they could attempt to jump on board or escape from the base. Specialist Lucas fired nearly a full magazine toward the cockpit window as he ran forward. Seconds later the huge chopper began to stall out as it swung over to the east and plunged to the ground.

Sid and Gen. Satre climbed up into the chopper to make sure Kharkov didn't get away. But there was no reason for speed. They found the Russian mobster lying in the middle of the chopper holding onto an AK-47 with one bullet wound in his head and two in his chest. As there would be officials demanding the body be authenticated, Sid and Ortega pulled the corpse from the chopper which was beginning to burn.

After placing Kharkov's body a good distance from the flaming wreck, Sid walked up to one of the wounded workers. Kneeling down he asked who else was involved with this operation but the man refused to answer.

Sid looked down at the man and said, "If you want medical care, tell me who else we're looking for."

The man shook his head. "I'm not talking. Go ahead and shoot me!"

Nodding his head, Sid replied. "Alright, we'll do it your way," as he pushed the palm of his hand down hard against the bullet wound in the man's shoulder.

The man screamed as he glared at Sid. "Okay, okay, stop it." After taking a breath he continued. "I only met him once, they call him Rampart, that's all I know."

Breaking open one of the crates, Capt, Holloway smiled. "Yeah, I bet Kharkov and Rampart could afford to operate a chopper like this. There has to be tens of thousands of dollars of cocaine and opium in just one of these crates.

The camp commander was stunned when he saw what was in the crates marked *Medical Supplies*. "Damn. They have been in and out of here for months, we just worked off the paper work we received. Those sons a bitches!"

Sgt. Mecklenburg and his men arrived to find the action already over.

As he looked over what was in the crates he was stunned. "There is no doubt they would have done anything to protect their investment, they were making millions, and by the way Captain, we took out Sprage."

The next morning after agents from the army Criminal Investigation Division arrived to take over the investigation, Captain Holloway walked up to Gen. Satre.

"Well General, it appears we have finished the job we started out to do. Sorry to say I know for a fact someone else will pick up the operation one way or the other. We just stopped if for the time being."

Nodding his head, Gen. Satre replied. "I know you're right. But at least we took out some real bad actors, so we made a difference."

A half hour later the eleven men flew back to Saigon along with the bodies of Sprage and Kharkov. Arriving at Tan Son Nhut, the bodies were transferred to a van that was to take them to a morgue to be held during the investigation.

As Gen. Satre climbed aboard the cargo plane for the trip back to Washington, he felt tired but excited that he could bring his family back home and continue leading a normal life. He now totally understood there was far more going on in Vietnam than most Americans could ever imagine, and there was no doubt the whole truth would never come out.

CHAPTER 22
THE DIRTY STREETS OF SAIGON

No one at Tan Son Nhut Air Base near Saigon paid much attention as a Huey helicopter arrived from Binh Thuy, nor did anyone really care who was inside.

But for Tom and Geno, this was a trip they had not expected to take or really wanted to. Ever since the battle down along the Mekong River, someone was poking around, trying to find out information regarding the disappearance of Rampart and Capt. Wong. However, this time it was different.

They had been called to Saigon to speak to high ranking military authorities, CIA operatives and State Department officials from Washington.

As the men jumped down from the chopper, a young lieutenant came walking up to them. "Gentlemen, my name is Lt. Earnest Bolig. I'm a JAG attorney, assigned to assist you as you go through these investigations. Understand, you have not been charged with any crimes, you are not suspected of committing any crimes, nor are you going to be allowed to incriminate yourselves if in fact you did something against the Uniform Code of Military Justice that we are not aware of at this time. Just follow my lead, and we'll get you back to your base as quickly as possible."

After shaking hands, Tom inquired. "I don't get any of this. I realize a SOG operative disappeared as well as a South Vietnamese Police Captain.

Why the hell is that a big deal? We have soldiers disappear every day in combat, and no one really seems to even care."

Lt. Bolig looked at both men. "You might want to hold back a little on this SOG thing. Every time that word comes up, another star falls from the sky. Believe me, no one will want to hear about SOG, although you and I know that just like hell, it does exist. So, let me take you men to your quarters and get you a good dinner. We'll have our first meeting in the morning with two men from the State Department. They seem pretty level headed, so maybe they can end this."

In the morning, both Tom and Geno were ready to move forward, anxious to get this over with. At 0900, they were ushered into a room with Lt. Bolig, where two men in suits, along with several aides, awaited them.

Once everyone was settled, the younger of the men spoke up.

"Good morning men. We want to get through this as soon as we can so we can all move on with this war, so we'll try to be as brief as possible." After looking over a few pieces of paper, the man inquired. "After the battle was over, you were removed from the village by a naval patrol boat, with a Col. Gagne and several of his men. Where exactly did they take you?"

Geno leaned forward toward a microphone. "We sailed south out into the gulf. We then turned to the southeast for a short time, where we tied up to a dock near a beached naval landing ship. It was a busy place, with about fifteen or more patrol boats coming and going."

"What happened when you arrived, Mr. Kenrude?" the man inquired as he took notes.

"Well, we were taken aboard the ship, given a shower, clean clothes, a meal, and then told to write down everything we could recall from the time we left Binh Thuy until we arrived at the ship. When we finished, the Colonel read what we wrote, asked a few questions, made some notations and told us we could go back to Binh Thuy the following morning."

"We understand there were two body bags on the patrol boat with you when you arrived at the ship. Please tell us about them, Mr. Sarducci," a man from the state department asked.

"Actually, there were four body bags on the boat with us. Two of them were already there when we loaded up. All of them were still on the boat when we were taken to the ship, there is no way I can tell you what happened to them," Geno replied.

After conferring for several minutes, one of the state department officials inquired, "Do you think you would recognize them again if you saw them."

Tom scowled as he leaned close to the microphone, "It has been several weeks since their deaths. With the intense heat and humidity, it's possible they may have decomposed beyond the possibility of facial recognition."

"But would you be willing to try? That is the question, Mr. Kenrude," the angry man asked.

Tom looked up at the ceiling for a moment before replying. "Sure. If you have the bodies, we would be willing to look at them and do our best."

Both men agreed before the same official replied. "Good, we'll accompany you, as we have a South Vietnamese soldier ready to drive us to the central morgue a few miles away. If you can identify them, we should be finished with you, and you may return to your base.

About ten minutes later, the men climbed into an older Ford van for the short ride to the morgue. After leaving the van, they walked toward the front door of the building which faced the busy street. A Vietnamese police officer stood guard at the door. As they prepared to enter, he stepped in front of Geno.

"Are you the Americans who killed our Capt. Wong?"

The South Vietnamese Soldier that drove them, pushed the officer aside. "We are here for legal purposes, you need to stand aside. This does not concern you."

The angry officer stepped back, although he continued to keep his right hand on his pistol.

Inside the morgue, a doctor took them back to a cold storage room. Lying on two stainless steel tables were two body bags. Stopping by the first bag, the doctor spoke up. "This man appears to be American. But we have nothing that let's us know who he is."

After unzipping the bag he took a step back. Tom and Geno peered down at the corpse. The man's face had already turned nearly purple from decay, and the right side of his head was slightly caved in, nearly where the Captain had kicked him after he was dead. Tom looked up at the two State Department men.

"Looking at the size of the man, and the damage to his head, this certainly could have been Rampart."

"How about you?" Lt. Bolig inquired of Geno.

Nodding his head in agreement Geno responded. "It would appear to be Rampart. I agree with Tom."

After zipping the bag shut, the doctor walked them over to the second bag. "This man is no doubt oriental, with a mustache." After opening the bag he walked over to a desk to pick up a file.

Again, the man's face was nearly purple, and it was clear a bullet had hit the left side of his head, damaging the skull, and a second bullet tore open his throat. Tom looked over at Geno.

"I can't be sure. After you fired, we never went forward to look over the bodies, and I never took a close look when we walked Col. Gagne back up there. I'm just not sure, what do you think?"

Geno stood quiet for a moment. "I dropped to my knees when I fired, so I was aiming slightly upward. I saw Wong reach for his throat after I fired the first shot, and he turned slightly to his left before falling. I'm guessing my second shot hit his head spinning him around. I know my third shot went into his side as he fell."

The doctor came over, unzipping the bag farther and rolling the corpse over onto its right side so they could examine the lower left part of the body.

Geno pointed, "Yup, that entry wound is where I hit him. That would have to be Wong."

Both State Department men smiled as Lt. Bolig patted Geno on the back. "Alright, enough of this, let's get the hell out of here and back to the office building so we can wrap this up." Lt Bolig stated firmly as he walked into the outer office.

Just as the South Vietnamese soldier entered the outer office he was met by a volley of gun fire. He flew back into the file room, as automatic machine gun fire riddled his body. Tom slammed the heavy door shut, as Geno pulled the dead man's pistol from its holster. Seconds later more gun fire shattered the windows of the file room, killing one of the state department officials.

Lt. Bolig yelled at the doctor, "Is there another way out of here?"

The doctor pointed back toward the morgue, "Yes, through the delivery garage."

Quickly, Lt. Bolig led the way back into the morgue as bullets tore the front rooms to shreds. After pushing the steel door closed, Tom looked at the doctor. "Do you have any weapons around here? We might need some fire power if we're going to get out of here alive."

The doctor opened a closet door, exposing two AK-47 rifles and a shelf containing six loaded magazines.

Tom and Geno took the rifles, as Lt. Bolig took the pistol from Geno. Come on, let's get out of here before they come looking for us. On the far end of the delivery garage, the men observed a steel door. Lt. Bolig slowly opened the door, peering left and right. Seeing an older American army three-quarter ton truck parked about twenty feet away, he called out. "That's our escape, can you drive that, Kenrude?"

Smiling, Tom exchanged weapons with the lieutenant. "What's the matter, sir? Never learned to drive a manual transmission?"

As they prepared to run for the truck, Lt. Bolig responded. "I grew up in money, Kenrude, everything had automatic transmissions. Why work when you drive?"

The lieutenant jumped in the passenger seat as Geno kept watch by the back of the truck as the state department man and the doctor jumped on board. Just as they were ready to depart, several White Mice came around the side of the building firing pistols.

Lt. Bolig cut them down as he fired out the window of the cab, allowing Geno to jump into the back of the truck. Tom crashed the truck through a fence, over-turning a motorized three wheel taxi, and sideswiping a parked delivery truck, as he headed toward the busy street and safety.

Arriving back at the State Department office, the remaining shaken investigator told Tom and Geno the State Department no longer had need of them. The following day, they received nearly identical questioning from several CIA agents, who repeated the company line insisting that SOG did not exist, they'd never heard of a man named Rampart, and they had nothing going on in Cambodia.

Around 5:00pm, Lt. Bolig informed Tom and Geno that they could return to Binh Thuy the next day, as everyone was now satisfied, and the army did not wish to hear another word about any of it.

Overjoyed that they could return to their base, Geno told Lt. Bolig that they should go out for a drink and a restaurant meal. The lieutenant smiled, "Damn, I was hoping someone would suggest the idea. I know just the place for an excellent meal, and they have great cold beer."

About half an hour later the three men were walking down a busy dirty sidewalk, where street vendors were still working hard to sell their wares. Everywhere they looked, American Military Police and South Vietnamese soldiers patrolled the bustling streets, keeping a cautious eye on everything that moved. They were about a half block from the restaurant when the sounds of beating drums and chanting filled the air. Everyone on the sidewalks appeared to panic as they looked in every direction. Traffic on the streets stopped and angry cab drivers blew their horns and screamed out of their open windows.

Lt. Bolig pushed Tom and Geno up against the front of a barber shop. "Something's going to happen, the drums and chanting are always a sign that Buddhist monks are in the area, and are going to pull of some type of anti-government protest."

It was then that Lieutenant Bolig observed eight yellow clad men with shaven heads blocking the intersection, as several South Vietnamese soldiers attempted to push them from the street.

Screams echoed off the buildings, as stunned people ran from the area in disbelief. Two of the monks had set their gas soaked clothing on fire. The first one fell to his knees as the flames engulfed his body. The second monk made several steps toward the panicked crowd, as he waved his arms in the air, as if asking for their help. As the remnants of the crowd ran away, the monk fell face first onto the asphalt street.

Flames continued roaring over their gas soaked bodies as soldiers slowly made their way into the intersection, to extinguish the flames with fire extinguishers from their jeeps.

What surprised Tom and Geno the most, was how quickly traffic began flowing through the intersection again, as the charred and smoking bodies remained in place. On the far street corner, the remaining monks continued beating their drums and chanting an eerie song. They remained in place until a South Vietnamese ambulance arrived to pick up the bodies.

Tom turned to Lt. Bolig, "Can you explain what that was all about, it was horrifying. I could go the rest of my life without ever seeing anything like that again!"

Lt. Bolig watched as the ambulance crew scraped the remains of the monks off the road.

"The Buddhist monks have been protesting the war since the French were here. Every so often they will do something dramatic to draw worldwide attention to the brutality and illegal actions of the Saigon government toward the peasants living in the countryside. We have not had one like this for some time. As you can see, camera men from all over the world are here to film the demonstration and its aftermath. They are always forewarned when the monks are going to do something like this, and of course, they never tell anyone, because it makes good news for the five o'clock report back home."

Geno looked angrily at Lt. Bolig. "If these guys know what the CIA and SOG—or whatever they want to call it—are doing to the peasants and their villages across the south, they have a right to be pissed off. This is one sad state of affairs, yet these people on the street don't seem to give a damn."

Lt. Bolig shook his head. "You guys come to Saigon for a day or two and see some crap and are outraged. These people see things like this all the time. Monks on fire, Monks slashing their throats in front of restaurants, police shooting suspects in the streets at all hours of the day, and Viet Cong blowing up night spots killing innocent people without warning. They see it all, so the shock factor is gone. They just hope to stay safe until the next government can take over and restore peace, maybe even the communists, but it never happens. Believe me, many of these successful looking merchants and business people you see in the street are making big money because of the war and the Americans. But a good portion of them would just as easily welcome the North Vietnamese to take over, knowing the crime, the burning monks and the Americans would be gone. They just want to live in peace, and few of them believe the South can ever win. Many of them will certainly flee into Cambodia or Thailand when and if that time comes. Who knows, some of them may even be able to buy their way into America."

As the men walked toward their restaurant, Lt. Bolig continued, "You see gentlemen, the streets of Saigon are paved in blood, dollars, and crime of all sorts. Nothing that you or the U.S. Government can do will ever change any of that. We will never know how many people have died in one way or the other here in the capitol city, but be assured, if those streets could talk, no one would believe it."

CHAPTER 23
GOLGOTHA

Dark clouds blanketed the skies above Vietnam, as gusty winds blew everything that was not nailed down across the open runway at Binh Thuy. Several fighter jets had taken off already for attack missions farther to the north, but all the choppers were grounded. Wind driven rain splashed hard against Tom's face, as he walked with the rest of the men from Air Evac Squadron One toward their command building. They were told to meet there at 0900 for a briefing regarding an upcoming mission they were going to be involved with.

Entering the office, Tom looked over at Geno. "You've been pretty quiet this morning. What's going on in that head of yours?"

Geno shook his head, and said, "I don't know Tom. Something just doesn't seem right, but I can't put my finger on it. It's like the stars and the moon are out of alignment. I just have a bad feeling, and I really don't like it. It's time we both got the hell out of here."

Having Geno being so seriously distressed really bothered Tom. Whenever things appeared to be out of control in the past, Geno was always the guy that could bring levity, or help dispel everyone's fears. Not sure what to say, Tom thought it best to just leave it alone for now.

A few minutes later, Capt. Trajillio and Lt. Jurgins walked into the room. After looking over the squadron the captain began.

"Good morning, men. As things have been fairly quiet down here in the delta, headquarters has ordered us to send a medi-vac squadron back up north to Quang Tri. I fully understand that none of you really wants to go, but you were selected by the colonel as the most qualified squadron. The only thing I know right now, is that there are several hills in the area the brass want taken, and they are pulling in units from all over the country to handle the job. I have no idea how long it will take or how long you'll be up there. I truly hate the thought of you men leaving us again, but it just can't be avoided. So get packed, you will be leaving at 1300hrs., weather permitting, or first thing in the morning. Lt. Jurgins will be accompanying you and will be your commanding officer while you're operating up there. That's all I have, any questions."

Warrant Officer Willy Sardozzi spoke up. "Sir, will we be attached to Army or Marines?"

Capt. Trajillio smiled as he looked over at the Warrant Officer. "No Sardozzi, don't worry, you'll be attached to army forces, and I'd bet they'll be AirCav units. I heard last night there are several new AirCav units being deployed to Quang Tri."

As no one else had any questions, the men headed back to their barracks to pack their gear. When Tom had finished packing, he placed a tape in the recorder.

"Hi gorgeous. Wanted to let you know we're being sent north, back to Quang Tri to take some hills. No one in our squadron is looking forward to this at all. Geno is really upset about it. In fact, I've never seen him this way before. But we'll get through it. My tour of duty is getting really short now. I can't wait to come home and see you, and meet Sean for the first time. I love the pictures you send. I keep the one of you and Sean at the park by the rose garden inside my helmet all the time. It's my good luck charm." Wanting to lighten the mood, he changed the subject and continued.

"If you get a chance, see if you can get a brochure on the classes at the university for next semester. I want to get back into med school as quickly as I can. Just think about it, you, me and Sean in a small apartment near the university. It should be a great time. Well, I know this is short, but we need to pick up some medical equipment before we leave, so I better get going. Give Sean a big hug and a kiss for me. Tell the folks it might be a while before I get a chance to send my new address, but I will as soon as I can. Mac, I love the hell out of you. When I graduate from medical school, we should move to Hawaii like you suggested in your last tape. Would that be fun or what? Well, better get moving. I love you Mackenzie Kenrude! Bye for now."

After dropping the tape in the mail box, Tom walked over to the hospital to pick up medical supplies. As he entered the pharmacy, he noticed Roxy writing notes on a clipboard.

"Hey Roxy, what's going on? I have quite a list here of things I want to take with us, can you help me out?"

Putting down the clipboard, Roxy turned and smiled. "For you Mr. Kenrude, I'll make time."

Tom laughed as he handed Roxy his shopping list. "I'm going to miss you while we're up at Quang Tri. I hope all goes well for you while we're gone."

Roxy smiled, "Well Master Kenrude, you better get back before the end of the month for my goodbye party. I'm so short, I can dangle my feet from the edge of my cereal bowl into the milk. I can't wait to get the hell out of here. Plus, I want to exchange addresses so we can keep in touch. I'll be very happy and relieved to hear when you are back home with Mac. And Sean."

Tom smiled, "Yeah, I'll be leaving just about three weeks after you. I can't wait to get home. It seems like it's been a really long year. I need to have some peace back in my life. But I've learned a lot and done a lot of things over here that I can use down the road. It should help me in medical school, too.

"Well then, I better get your supplies before I hold up your departure time. Give me fifteen minutes and I'll have everything ready, or you can just sit there and drink coffee. There's a fresh pot on the hot plate."

Tom looked through several magazines that were lying on the desk as Roxy raced through the supply room filling his order. When she returned, she handed him the box.

"Now, you take care of yourself up there. I don't want to hear about you getting hurt, or being swallowed up by some huge snake in that thick jungle. Get your butt back here for my going away party, and you can consider that an order, Mr. Kenrude."

After giving Roxy a hug and a wink, Tom headed out to the chopper to store everything she had boxed up for him.

Since the weather had broken enough to allow the choppers to take off, Tom hurried to get everything stowed on board, knowing they would likely be off the ground in about fifteen minutes.

As Tom finished storing everything, a very familiar voice spoke up, "So, I hear you're headed up north into the highlands."

Spinning around quickly, Tom held out his hand, "Hey Sergeant Major Doogan. It's great to see you. How did you find out about the mission already? I just learned about it myself within the last hour."

After shaking hands, Franny looked intensely at Tom. "Knock off the Sergeant Major crap, young man. You best refer to me as you have all your life or I'll give that young butt of yours a good whooping, and don't think I'm not still young enough to do it."

Tom laughed as he shook his head. "You never change, Uncle Franny, I love it! I'm really glad you stopped by before we left. I wanted to see you, but didn't figure I had time to get all the way over to your unit and back. To be honest, I'm a bit nervous about going on this mission. I don't know what it is, I can't put my finger on it. Even Sarducci has been off his normal good humor, and when he gets upset, I get upset too, to tell you the truth. Kind of like you, Uncle Harry and Dad."

Franny had to smile. "Yeah, we all fed off each other in more ways than one. Look, don't let your buddy's nerves get to you. I saw that way too much in Europe and Korea. If you let his problems bother you, I damn well guarantee you'll make some bad mistakes. Deal with only your feelings, Tom. That way you won't second guess anything. Be your own man, it works every time."

As the rest of the crew walked up to the chopper, Franny shook hands once more with his best friend's son, and the rest of the crew. Grabbing Cal by the arm, Franny looked him straight in the eye." You guys look out for one another up there, and be a solid team. I expect to see all of you back here when the mission is over."

Cal smiled at the grizzled combat veteran. "Don't worry Sergeant Major, we'll be just fine."

Turning back toward Tom one more time, Franny smiled, "Stay safe out there, Tom. Think of Sean and Mackenzie before you do anything stupid, or feel like being a hero. You're getting short, and that matters big time, you got that?"

As Tom climbed aboard the chopper he looked down at Franny. "I got that Sergeant Major. I'll keep my head down, my nose to the wind, and my feet moving. I'll talk to you when I return. Keep the light on for me, we'll have a cold one together and tell lies."

Franny laughed as he gave Tom a quick salute for luck. As the props began to turn, Franny backed away and covered his face. When the U.S.S. America was airborne, Franny watched the rest of the squadron get in formation before turning north.

After several moments, Capt. Trajillio walked over to Franny. "Is there something I can do for you, Sergeant Major? I know you have family ties to Kenrude, and he's damn proud of you."

Franny saluted the Captain. "Well sir, I just hope that kid keeps his head together up there in the central highlands. He's getting too damn short, and he has a child at home he's never seen. I just pray that he stays out of harm's way best he can."

"I agree with you one hundred percent, Sergeant Major. One hundred percent," After patting Franny on the shoulder, Captain Trajillio walked off toward a jeep that was waiting for him.

Tom sat quietly for some time as he listened to the bantering going on between the crew on their headsets. Warrant Officer Cumberland was a natural comedian who could twist around anything you said to make a joke of it. No one was immune, and absolutely nothing was sacred when it came to his blistering sense of humor. Tom had learned quickly to stay out of conversations when Cumberland was at his best. Although Cal was a pretty smart guy, he fell into Cumberland's traps way too often and there was never any way out, short of surrender. Tom just leaned back against the back wall of the chopper, closed his eyes and listened to the comedy show on his headset.

Arriving at Quang Tri, the men were met by a Lt. Raleigh. He spoke at length with Lt. Jurgins regarding their mission, where they would bunk, and whatever else he felt was important. As a large storm was building off toward the west, the men moved quickly to secure their choppers to prevent wind damage. According to Lt. Raleigh, the weather was going to keep them grounded for the next couple of days. That gave Tom ample time to make another tape for Mac, and write letters home to his folks. Geno had settled down somewhat since arriving at Quang Tri, and was heavily involved in a card game with Oscar, Cal Dozier and Andre Flinn. Andre was a real good card player, who had a tendency to clean house on whoever challenged him to a game of poker. Many men back at Binh Thuy had learned to avoid games with him.

On the second day at Quang Tri, Tom awakened to the sound of F-4 Phantoms and A-6 Intruders streaking skyward as dawn crept over the base. Looking out the window in the barracks, it was evident that the storm had moved out over the Gulf of Tonkin. A brisk wind was already beginning to dry the tarmac around the flight line. There was no doubt in Tom's mind, they would be going out on a mission later today or tomorrow morning.

About 1600hrs, Lt. Raleigh called the medi-vac crews together. After laying out a map on one of the bunks he looked over the men.

"As you noticed, the storm moved out to the gulf. First mission is set to jump off at 0600, so I want one chopper with the teams when they leave, and two more choppers will go about fifteen minutes later. Everyone else will wait until calls come in from the LZ's." Running his finger along a large plateau on the map, Lt. Raleigh continued. "From the intel we have gathered, we believe there to be a large contingent of North Vietnamese Regulars, backed up by VC in the jungle to the north and west of this plateau. Estimates range from about two to three hundred. Exactly what their plans are, we don't have a clue, so we're going to disrupt their plans and kill as many of them as we can, before they can make a mass attack. We'll be using the plateau for the LZ and medi-vac point. Don't take anything for granted, this could get ugly, depending on how well they're dug in. We're going to begin hitting the area with artillery and aircraft strikes about 0400. Anyone have questions?"

After looking over the map one more time, Tom spoke up, "Lieutenant, how long is the grass on the plateau, and is it rocky or fairly smooth?"

Lt. Raleigh folded his arms across his chest. "I'm guessing the grass will be near knee high, and if it's like most plateaus around here, it's most likely rather smooth and free of a lot of obstacles." As there were no more questions, Lt. Raleigh rolled up the map and left.

Returning to his bunk, Tom tore down his sidearm and oiled it one more time, to ensure it was in proper working order. As he reassembled it, Geno walked over.

"Do you intend to use that in the morning, Tom? Or is it your good luck charm?"

Tom turned to face his good friend. "I don't have a clue, Geno. I just want to make sure it won't let me down at a critical time. I think we all better be totally prepared, don't you?"

Geno sat down on Tom's bunk, "I got the jitters real bad, and I just can't shake it, Tom. Seems like the whole world has been turned upside down. I know we have been through this before, but I just can't shake it this time. Something feels like it's out of place somewhere."

Cal looked down at Geno. "Hey I've been there before, just as bad as you. But in the morning when we go to work, everything will fall into place. We'll react as we should, we'll do our jobs, and we'll all be heading home in no time flat."

Tom smiled at Cal. "Yeah, we'll all be going home as we should. I for one am not going to let those bastards mess with me. I'm going to treat and load the wounded, and get off that plateau as quickly as we can. I'm not waiting around for Charlie to dictate anything to me."

By 2300 the building was quiet. Out in the central highlands, nearly eight hundred enemy soldiers slept in tunnels that had been constructed deep underground over the last several months. They were deep enough, and fortified heavily, so that bombs and artillery would not cause them much grief. Those keeping watch above ground kept close to the tunnel entrances, so they could dive in quick if American bombs and shells began descending upon them. No one in the South was aware that this was a well-stocked supply base, allowing fully equipped North Vietnamese Regulars to bring the fight to American Forces all across the south. The base was planned to house nearly a thousand men, complete with hospitals, kitchens and armories.

At 0400, bombs and artillery shells began dropping on the jungles around the plateau. Down in the tunnels, the earth shook and light dirt trickled down from the ceilings, notifying everyone that an assault would be upon them at dawn. To the west of the plateau, not one bomb or shell landed in the secondary encampment where over five hundred enemy slept. Officers began preparing their men for the onslaught that was going to arrive when the barrage lifted. The plan was set, the men in the north and east encampments would surge forward from their tunnels confronting the air assault, while the men in the west would stay in place, until

America forces were fully engaged, before ascending from their tunnels into the battle.

It was 0605 when the first armada of choppers lifted off from the airfield at Quang Tri. Tom and Geno's choppers were to be held in reserve. They stood beside their birds as they watched the sky fill with Huey's, the huge Chinooks and nimble gunships. Four F-4 Phantoms rose into the morning sky, ready to lay down covering fire for the soldiers involved in the massive air assault.

At 0620, the first choppers touched down on the plateau as the F-4s circled overhead, waiting for orders of where to strike, but everything appeared to be relatively quiet. Empty choppers swiftly lifted off, as full ones continued touching down, then quickly returned to Quang Tri to pick up more troops for the battle. As nearly a hundred men now occupied the plateau, they began cautiously spreading out, creating a skirmish line in the tall grass. The never ending flight of choppers continued, disgorging more men and equipment, with still no sign of an enemy force.

Very quietly, at 0650, enemy troops began crawling from well-concealed tunnel entrances to the north and east, setting up small mortar tubes and rocket launchers. Soldiers carrying AK-47s, captured American M-16s and deadly RPG's, spread out near the edge of the jungle, wearing heavy camouflage uniforms that blended in with the tall grass.

Exactly at 0700, an RPG arose from the jungle to the east, slamming into a Huey that was just about to land. It was followed by three more in rapid succession, all of which struck landing or exiting choppers. Burning wreckage and fuel sent clouds of thick black smoke rolling to the east, as every enemy machine gun and rifle opened fire on the attacking forces. Cobra gunships dove into the fight, firing rockets, as their powerful miniguns fired thousands of rounds of 20mm ammunition toward the edge of the jungle. A Cobra gunship diving down from the north, was hit by heavy machine gun fire. No matter what the pilot attempted to do, the stricken chopper had a mind of it's own. It slammed down and exploded, just short of the American skirmish line. Men screamed as flaming jet fuel, unfired rockets, and thousands of rounds of 20mm ammunition exploded all at once, sending a wall of high speed deadly shrapnel upon them.

This is exactly what the North Vietnamese commanders were hoping for. Pilots flying F-4's, couldn't bomb enemy forces racing out from the jungle from the east, for fear of hitting Americans. All they could do was attempt to use their machine guns, although the thick black smoke obscured their targets and the lines of battle.

Calls came in immediately for every available medi-vac crew to respond to the battle. As Cumberland neared the battlefield, Tom looked out the door. He could see burning wreckage all over the middle of the plateau. Toward the east, he could see American and Vietnamese forces involved in hand to hand combat, as more choppers continued delivering additional soldiers. Off to his left he watched a Huey have its rear rotor torn of when it was about twenty feet off the ground. The machine spun on its own axis several times before nosing into the ground and exploding.

As Warrant Officer Cumberland set down, about twenty badly wounded men that had been patched up by medics, scrambled for the open door. Cal and Tom did their best to load as many as they could, before yelling at the flight crew to take off, leaving many frustrated and angry wounded men behind.

The medical staff was waiting at the hospital with stretchers and satchels full of medications and bandages. Once all the men were removed, a hospital attendant sprayed down the floor of the chopper, washing the slippery blood out the opposite door. Seconds later, Cumberland was back in the air flying full speed back to the battle. They arrived to see a pilot of an F-4 let go a canister of napalm into the northern encampment. The thick black, burning gel spread out across the grass and jungle killing everyone in its path. The pilot returned quickly, firing rockets and cannon fire, deeper into the jungle hideout.

Once more, Cumberland slid his chopper across the grass, stopping short of a burning Huey. Tom jumped off the helicopter, grabbing ahold of a very badly burned Warrant Officer that was being held up by a medic. After Cal pulled him on board, Tom helped two medics load four more men that were in horrible condition. Several bullets passed through the cabin walls of the chopper, as Cumberland raced skyward, attempting to avoid another rescue chopper that was on its way down.

Tom grabbed an IV bag full of ringers lactate from his medical bag, in hopes of getting fluids into the horribly wounded pilot, but the man kept pushing Tom's hands away. As Tom attempted one more try, the man spoke, "Save it for the living." With that the man closed his eyes and was gone.

Once more Cumberland placed his chopper perfectly on the pad where nurses and medics awaited him. Jumping off the chopper, Tom looked over at the head nurse. "This guy is gone, take care of the others." Cal and Tom placed the burned man on a gurney before jumping back on board. They didn't even wait for the floor to be washed off, knowing that time meant lives.

It was impossible to know how the battle was going from the air, as smoke covered much of the battlefield, however it was clear to see by the casualties, that the AirCav unit was taking a severe beating.

Once more Cumberland landed his helicopter where it was most needed. Again Tom raced from the chopper as a medic waved for his help.

"You've got to take this corporal, I can't get the tourniquet to stop the bleeding, his lower leg is shattered and beyond repair."

Grabbing the handles of the stretcher, Tom ran toward the chopper as Cal was helping another medic load a man with a missing arm. Just as Tom reached the chopper, he spun around and fell down. Picking himself up, he realized a bullet had struck his left arm, tearing open the outer layers of his flesh. After jumping on board Tom yelled out, "Go, go, get off the ground."

As the chopper flew toward the south, Tom was able to readjust the tourniquet and get the bleeding nearly stopped on the badly wounded corporal. Looking over at Cal, he yelled out. "Come here, you need to bandage my arm. We can't wait at the hospital for them to take care of it." Following Tom's directions, Cal did a solid job of applying the combat dressing.

Medical staff members were once again waiting as the chopper settled onto the landing pad. Tom jumped from the chopper to help unload the wounded, while yelling out instructions as to what he had done for each man he had treated. As they unloaded the last patient, one of the nurses looked at Tom's arm. "Kenrude, come inside so we can take a better look at that arm."

As he watched a hospital attendant spray out the chopper, Tom shook his head. "It'll have to wait for now, we don't have the time. We're heading straight back."

After Tom and Cal grabbed three stretchers and a medical bag with supplies from one of the nurses, Sy lifted the chopper off for another return trip.

Approaching the plateau, it was evident that the situation had indeed changed, and not for the good. North Vietnamese soldiers were streaming onto the battle field from the east, as they swarmed out of tunnel entrances. Several Cobras were strafing the area while firing rockets into the jungle. Overhead two F-4's were circling, waiting for the Cobra pilots to clear the area so they could drop napalm canisters on the attacking hordes.

Just as Sy began his decent onto the plateau, Tom watched an evac chopper from another squadron burst into flames as it was taking off. Debris drifted to the ground as a large ball of red and yellow flames rolled skyward. It made Tom sick to know the entire crew and all the patients they'd attempted to rescue were gone.

When the chopper was still about three feet off the ground, Tom bailed off as he watched two medics struggling with three wounded men approaching the LZ. Quickly, he grabbed a man that had his midsection completely bandaged, but was still bleeding severely. Sy was about to lift off when Tom called for him to wait. Neither Tom nor Cal could believe what they were seeing as a soldier stumbled toward the chopper. He was carrying what was left of his right arm in his left hand, and most of his right cheek was hanging by a thread.

Tom pulled him on board as he called out for Sy to lift off once more. Immediately, Tom shoved a morphine syrette into the soldiers leg, before placing the shredded cheek back onto the soldier's face. Tom placed several bandages onto the cheek, as Cal rolled a large roll of gauze around the man's head.

Cal held up the arm as he looked at Tom. "What do we do with this?"

Grabbing another roll of gauze, Tom wrapped the torn end securely then tied the gauze around the man's chest. Leaning over to Cal, Tom whispered. "It can't be reattached, but we'll let the doctor's deal with him on that. He's calm now, so let's try to keep him that way."

Tom tended to the other three men as necessary as the chopper flew back to the hospital one more time.

Just as the last soldier was removed from the chopper, Lt. Raleigh came running up to Sy's door. Pulling it open, he yelled, "They're pulling out, they can't hold the hill. You've got to get back and take as many men as you can, we can't leave them behind."

Sy nodded his head as he began sending power back to the engine. Thick black smoke rolled over the plateau from burning wreckage and napalm. It was tough for Sy to get a clear view of where he wanted to set down, as medics and soldiers helping wounded men were streaming toward the extremely hot LZ. This time Cal and Tom both jumped from the chopper before it touched down. Both men were instantly thrown through the air as a mortar round slammed into the U.S.S. America. Landing on his knees, Tom stared back at what had been his chopper just moments before. The machine was totally engulfed in flames, and it made him sick to see the corpses of Sy Cumberland and Darnel Franklin slumped forward in their seats, as flames engulfed their lifeless bodies.

As Tom went to stand up, he felt a sharp pain in his left side. Looking down, he could see a piece of shrapnel from the chopper sticking out of his rib cage, as his flak jacket had been shredded in the explosion. Taking a deep breath, he struggled to his feet and continued on.

He grabbed hold of a man that was covered in blood from a head wound. After wrapping the wound best he could, he helped him toward another evac chopper that had just landed. As he turned to help the next wounded man, a bullet ripped into his left shoulder, rending his arm all but useless. Falling to the ground Tom called out, 'Mackenzie! Mackenzie!' as he saw visions of Sean standing on the porch of his parent's house waving at him.

With all his might, Tom raised himself back to his feet while yelling, "No! No damn way!"

His mouth felt parched as if he were in an arid desert, but he had no water available, as a bullet had punctured his canteen. After firing two shots from his sidearm at an approaching Vietnamese soldier, he stumbled forward toward a wounded man that had fallen to his knees. Taking hold of the soldier, he called out, "You need to help me, I've only got one good arm left."

As he said that, a bullet grazed his forehead, throwing him backwards to the ground. He could hear his heartbeat as if it was coming out of his chest, and he could see Mackenzie calling for him as she stood by Eagle Lake, holding Sean. After wiping blood from his face, he picked up an M-16 that was lying near his feet, and fired at several more North Vietnamese soldiers running toward the area. Throwing the rifle to the ground, he pushed himself back up off his knees, so he could return to the wounded man. As he grabbed onto the man's flak jacket to pull him up, an evacuating lieutenant called out as he ran by, "Let him go corpsman, he's a goner, just save yourself!"

The wounded man concurred. "I'm done for, doc. Thanks, but you need to go."

Tom shook his head, "No way, get up. Come on, help me soldier, and we can get you out of here together!"

A blinding flash sent Tom flying backward, as a hot piece of shrapnel tore into his neck and a larger piece smashed his upper left arm, breaking every bone in the shoulder. Tom rolled across the ground for several seconds as pain rushed through his body and mind, jumbling his thoughts.

"I can't quit, I can't quit," Tom mumbled, as he struggled to reach his feet.

The soldier he had attempted to help was severely injured by the blast. Tom knelt down by the dying man, thrusting a morphine syrette into his arm. Gasping for his last breath the man looked up at Tom.

"Doc, I believe you and I will be together in heaven before this day is done."

"No come on, we can get you out of here, you got to try," Tom screamed over the ever increasing roar of battle, as everything inside his head was spinning like a carousel out of control. Realizing the man had died, Tom began to wonder where Cal was. Could he even be alive yet, did he need help? With all those thoughts rushing through his head, Tom pushed himself up yelling, "Cal!"

As he began reaching out to help another wounded man, a second mortar round crashed into the ground about ten yards in front of him. The blast picked him up, throwing him back into one of the destroyed choppers. Before he could react, Tom observed three Viet Cong coming around the front of the burning wreckage from the west. Pulling his pistol, he shot the lead man in the head, as the second V.C. fired a shot into his abdomen. Blood gushed from the wound as Tom slipped down to his knees, just as Cal came running through the smoke and bedlam with an M-16 he had picked up along the way. He fired a short burst from the weapon, killing the second V.C. instantly. However, now the rifle was out of ammunition, and Cal's wounded legs were beginning to fail him. The third V.C. fired two nearly point blank shots into Tom's chest, as he rushed on by him heading towards Cal, who had also now dropped to the ground.

A bright light lit up the universe around Tom, as he found himself inside a broad corridor filled with people walking silently toward a structure emanating soft calming music. Tom attempted to speak with several of the people, but they just kept moving forward, and would not respond, as they all appeared to be either praying or in deep thought. After making about twenty paces, he felt a hand on his shoulder. Turning, he saw a large young man in a white robe, with a gold cord around his waist.

The man looked intently at Tom and said. "Are you sure you are finished, Mr. Kenrude?"

Tom nodded his head. "I lost so much blood, I have massive internal damage, my right lung is nearly shredded, all the bones in my left arm and shoulder are shattered, and I'm bleeding from my brachial artery and have no way to stop it. There is nothing more I can do, I couldn't breathe anymore."

Once again the man looked intently at Tom, "So, you say it is finished then, everything you need to do has been completed?"

As tears rolled down Tom's face he replied, "No, no, it can't end this way, Cal needs help!"

Tom gasped for air with all the strength left in his body, as pain ripped through his abdomen and chest, but he could never allow the last Viet Cong to kill Cal. The pain was intense when he moved, as every part of his broken body had paid a terrible price this day. As sweat and blood poured down over his face, tears welled in his eyes, but he knew he had to shake it off. Struggling to his knees one more time, he picked up an M-16 from the ground. About ten yards away, he observed Cal fighting to pull his pistol from its holster with his severely damaged right hand, as the enemy soldier began lowering his weapon. Bracing the rifle against his left leg, Tom fired the last four rounds from the magazine, striking the attacking Viet Cong in the back, just as he prepared to fire at Cal.

Although completely unable to move, a slight smile broke out across Tom's parched lips, when he realized Cal had not been hit by the Viet Cong's fire. Knowing his final mission was now completed, the small smile slowly evaporated from his face as he felt life slipping from his body. Tom understood completely that he was never going to see Mackenzie again, or ever meet his son. He had run the race and given all he had, now it was time to turn his life back over to his creator. As he lay in the mud and blood gasping for air, the mental anguish was intense. He thought about home, Glendale, Mackenzie, Sean and all his family as he called out for them. The pain of his loss was intense, as visions of happier times streamed through his mind as if on an endless reel of film. As the images of home faded away, the face of the young Vietnamese girl they rescued came into focus. He heard her dire words, *"Pray that the trial may pass by you, but know it's the Master's will it must be done."*

For the first time since that day, Tom realized she had been predicting his death. A tear rolled down his cheek as his eye lids closed forever, blocking out the world around him he had loved so much.

As Cal struggled back upon his torn and injured legs, he attempted to hobble forward as he yelled, "Tom! Tom! Tom!" Although even as he shouted, he knew it was too late. As if in slow motion, he watched the M-16 slide from Tom's hand as he slumped forward. The last thing Cal remembered before a sergeant began pulling him toward a chopper was Tom yelling out, 'Mackenzie!' In an instant, Tom's lifeless, bloody, and mangled body lay among the dead soldiers littering the plateau around the LZ on Hill 843.

Cal stared out the door at the body of his good friend as the chopper rose into the sky. He couldn't believe what had just happened, nor could he believe he had just left the body of Thomas Steven Kenrude behind on that battle scarred plateau.

Colonel Hernandez had just finished speaking on the phone with his counterpart at Danang, when Corporal Rightman informed him he had a call from Colonel Lopez at Quang Tri.

The two men attended West Point together, and remained good friends throughout their careers. Col. Hernandez sat back in his chair, smiling as he picked up the receiver, ready with a smart quip for his long time friend.

"Not a good day for golf, Don. It's been drizzling here all day."

Col. Lopez could neither smile nor laugh at his friends comment. "Andre, this is the worst phone call I hope to ever have to make to you. I have some very bad news regarding your medi-vac squadron."

Slowly, Col. Hernandez leaned forward as he felt the blood drain from his face. Leaning against his desk, he replied, "Give it to me straight, Don. What the hell happened, and how many did I lose?"

"Yesterday, your men were busy pulling out wounded men from a battle on Hill 843. Late in the afternoon, the decision was made to pull the plug on the battle and get the hell out of there. Our intel regarding the enemies strength in the area was totally wrong." "We were told there were several companies in the area, but in all reality, we now estimate there was a regiment of North Vietnamese Regulars, backed up by an untold number of Viet Cong. It was bloody, Andre. Choppers arrived in waves attempting to withdraw all our forces, but many were shot down. There were so many wounded men on that hill, we had no choice but to send in more medi-vac units to retrieve them and get them loaded. Warrant Officer Eddie Jackman's bird went in first. An RPG hit the tail rotor sending the chopper into a spin. According to commanders on the ground, Jackman did all he could do to avoid crashing into the waiting men on the hill. He ended up slamming into another disabled chopper. Jackman, his copilot Stan Levin and flight mechanic Kevin Studer were all killed. Your medic Geno Sarducci was thrown clear of the chopper. He's in serious condition, but he is expected to recover from his injuries. Warrant Officer Cumberland's bird landed safely, but was hit by mortar fire within seconds. Cumberland, and his co-pilot Darnel Franklin were killed instantly. The flight mechanic Cal Dozier was away from the chopper attempting to help your medic Specialist Kenrude with the injured men. Dozier was hit by shrapnel and a few bullets. He's back in surgery right now, and we aren't sure he's going to make it.

Kenrude was hit numerous times as he attempted to pull wounded men to safety and treat them. According to a report filed by a Lt. Lee from the Air Cav. Team, Kenrude was firing at the enemy while dragging men to safety. He would do what he could to stabilize them, then run back out to rescue more wounded. Lee figures Kenrude was hit at least eight times before he died. After a discussion with Lt. Lee, I'm going to recommend Jackman and Kenrude for Bronze Stars."

Col. Hernandez sat motionless as he listened to the details of the battle. Although he had seen tough combat in Korea, he couldn't hold back the tears that ran down his face.

"Six dead and two in the hospital. My God Don, they were all great soldiers and all around good men. Franklin had six weeks left, he was planning to get married when he returned home. Kenrude was also down to about six weeks, he had a young wife and a son he hadn't met waiting for him."

The line was quiet for a moment before Lt. Lopez spoke. "That hill is littered with wreckage and the bodies of men we couldn't get out before the LZ was over run. We plan to go back today to pick them up. Each one of those men had a story as tragic as those you mentioned. They were all heroes in one way or another Andre, and all their families will feel the loss and pain."

After taking a deep breath, Col. Hernandez inquired. "When will the bodies be returned to us?"

"You should have them by 1500hrs tomorrow afternoon, I hope. We have a C-130 set aside for the trip. Just so you know, the bodies of Cumberland, Franklin, Jackman and Levin will all be marked 'REMAINS UNVIEWABLE' as they were burned very badly. Sorry to have to tell you that, Andre."

Nodding his head, Col. Hernandez replied, "I was pretty much expecting that after what you'd already told me. Alright, I'll get the word out here, and prepare to write letters to the families. Make sure you follow up on those Bronze Stars, that's the least we can do for those brave men. Well, I better get moving, Don, thanks for the information, I know it wasn't an easy thing to do. Give your wife all my best. We'll talk again in the next few days."

As he hung up the phone, he finally realized Capt. Trajillio was standing in the doorway of his office. "Come in. Sit down Captain, we need to have a long talk."

After the Captain was seated, he looked up at his commander. "Sir, I didn't mean to eavesdrop on your conversation. But Rightman told me you had a call from Col. Lopez, and your door was open, and I saw—"

Col. Hernandez cut him off mid-sentence. "It's alright Captain. We both lost the same men, we both need to inform our people and prepare for the return of their remains." After explaining all that Col. Lopez had told him, the Colonel handed Captain Trajillio a list of things he wanted him to take care of.

Since the rain around the delta had brought flight operations to a stop, the men from the squadron were all nearby. After assembling the crews, Capt. Trajillio stepped up onto a couple of pallets to inform them what had happened. It was as if a huge vacuum cleaner had sucked all the oxygen from the hangar.Men grabbed their chests and gasped, some looked for anything to sit on, while others stood in place crying while hugging their buddies. After several moments, the captain stepped down and walked among his grief stricken men, attempting to console them as best he could. Leaving the hanger, he dreaded his next stop. He knew going to the hospital would be tough.

Arriving at the hospital, the first person he ran into was Dr. Phillips. He pulled the doctor aside, informing him of what had taken place. When they were finished talking, Dr. Phillips assembled his staff outside the operating area. Once again Capt. Trajillio explained what had taken place on Hill 843, and what had happened to their flight crews. When he came to Tom's name, a scream came out from the assembled staff as Roxy collapsed on the ground. Several nurses came to her aid, helping her back up. With her right hand over her face she sobbed uncontrollably.

As nurse Sylvia Jones attempted to take her to a treatment room to sit down, Roxy called out, "Where is Thomas, I want to see him, he can't be dead. Oh God, he just can't be dead. Please tell me this isn't true." Once more the normally steady, tough, and efficient nurse slipped away from Nurse Jones, collapsing to the ground.

Quickly a medic rolled out a wheelchair, so the staff could get Roxy out of the area. After placing her on a gurney near the pharmacy, Sylvia Jones, who had become best friends with Roxy, held her hand while attempting to console her stricken friend and colleague.

About a half hour later Roxy sat up on the gurney, attempting to force a smile to reassure her friend. She looked down at her trembling hands.

"First off, it's against regs for an officer to be involved with enlisted personnel. But you know Syl, I really came to love Thomas. I never told him my feelings, as I knew he was married and loved Mac with all his heart. I tried real hard to keep my feelings at a distance, and never allowed anything to happen between us. But now my heart aches so much. What do I do with all that love I had for him that I never ever told him or anyone else about?"

Syl stepped forward holding Roxy's head against her chest. "You can still tell him, honey. When they bring him in tomorrow, take a moment to be alone with him and talk to him. He'll hear you. Just let him know your feelings, tell him everything that's in your heart. I wasn't unaware of your feelings for Tom and was always amazed at how you handled yourself around him. You're a stronger woman than I am. I could never have held back my feelings as you did, right or wrong. Why don't you go back to the barracks and lie down for a while. I can cover for you, and everyone will understand. We've all had a terrible shock."

Roxy smiled at her best friend. "Thanks Syl. What would I do without you?"

Capt. Trajillio returned to his office feeling drained and tired, and it was not even 1100hrs yet. After getting a cup of coffee, he picked up the phone to call the 632 Combat Support Group. He hesitated for a moment when the person answering the phone said, "Good Morning, 632 Combat Support Group, this is Sergeant Major Doogan, can I help you?"

"Sergeant Major this is Capt. Trajillio calling from the 82nd Medical Evac Unit. I'm afraid I have some very bad news for you. Thomas Kenrude was killed in action north of Quang Tri, along with five other men from our unit. Their remains will be returned here tomorrow afternoon around 1500. I know you have been close to his family for many years, so I thought you should know."

Franny sat back in his chair for a moment as he attempted to comprehend what he had just been told. Leaning forward again he cleared his throat.

"Captain, what the hell happened up there?"

Capt. Trajillio explained what he had been told regarding the battle, and that Tom and Eddie Jackman were being nominated for Bronze Stars for their bravery and performance.

After hearing everything, Franny shook his head in disbelief. "Captain, when Tom was in the replacement unit when he first arrived, I was up there conducting some business. We ran into each other in the chow hall. I got angry with him over this, but he said if anything happened to him while he was over here, he wanted me to escort his body back to Glendale, Minnesota. I'll be contacting my commanding officer when we're finished here, so arrangements can be made."

"That would be great, Sergeant Major. I'll pass that along to Col. Hernandez and the army burial people. Pack your bags, I'm guessing the men will leave the following morning. Is there anything else I can do for you Sergeant Major?" Capt. Trajillio inquired.

"No, sir. I thank you for the call. I'll see you around 1500 tomorrow." After hanging up, Franny knew he had one more call to make. Father John Neederman, one of the chaplains at Binh Thuy, had served with distinction during the Korean War in Steve Kenrude's platoon.

After Franny related all the information to Fr. Neederman, the priest was quiet for a moment. "I will call my superior officer in the morning to make arrangements for my trip to Glendale, if that's alright with you Franny."

"Padre, it would be a great comfort for me, Steve, and his family to have you there. I was hoping you would want to fly back with me."

Skies were heavy overcast with a slight wind blowing out of the northwest as the huge green C-130 circled Binh Thuy before making an approach to land.

Franny found it hard to breathe as he watched the plane taxi toward the parking area a short distance from the hospital. Father Neederman tried to hide his tears as the ramp at the rear of the cargo aircraft was lowered. Eighteen men from the 82nd Evac unit stood near the aircraft. When they were given permission to board, six men at a time went up the ramp to pick up a black body bag and deliver it to a waiting truck. After they had unloaded the bags, the truck slowly drove over to the hospital.

At the hospital, Capt. Trajillio stood by the truck, announcing the name of each man as they were taken down from the platform and placed on gurneys. Roxy shook and gasped for air as she held on tightly to Syl and nurse Diane Parker. As the captain read, 'Kenrude, Thomas S.' Roxy began to weep.

As two corpsmen rolled the cart passed the mourners, Roxy broke free from her friends and ran toward the cart. Leaning over the black bag, she clamped her hands tightly on to the heavy rubber as she wept. Syl walked over to her friend taking her by the elbow.

"Come with me, Roxy, let them take Thomas inside. These men need to finish their work."

Roxy looked up at her friend, "This wasn't supposed to happen, he had so much to live for. I don't want to leave him this way." With the help of Dr. Phillips, Syl was able to help Roxy back toward the hospital.

Around 1800, Roxy quietly walked back to the morgue, knowing the attendants had departed for the mess hall. She walked over to the bag marked with Tom's name. After standing silently for several seconds, she placed her hand on the bag above Tom's head. Reaching down, she took hold of the large zipper.

After taking a deep breath, she slowly began to unzip the heavy black bag until she could see Tom's face and shoulders. She held her hands over her face as she peered down at the silent figure. His face was covered in blood and dirt that had been streaked from sweat. There was a good size cut on his forehead, and a rather large gash on the right side of his neck. A bullet had torn through his left shoulder, and it appeared his left upper arm had been shattered by a large piece of shrapnel.

Gently Roxy ran her hand across the top of Tom's head as tears rolled down her cheeks. Leaning over near Tom's ear, she whispered.

"Thomas Kenrude, why didn't you make it back?" As she stood straight, she began crying even harder. After composing herself somewhat, she once more leaned over. "You never knew it, and I couldn't tell you, as much as it was killing me. But I loved you with all my heart. Dear Lord, why did this have to happen to you, Tom?" Straightening up again, Roxy walked across the room to lean against the wall. She shook her head as she stared at all the bags lined up, waiting to be taken care of by the morgue attendants. Slowly she made her way back to Tom. Leaning over once more she continued. "I know you had Mac and your new son waiting for you back home, and I knew you would never have done anything to destroy that relationship, but Tom, no matter how hard I tried to ignore my feelings, I just kept falling deeper and deeper in love with you. So what do I do? How do I ever fill the horrible loss I'm feeling right now? Thomas, tell me what to do? I loved you so much." She kissed Tom on the cheek and slightly smiled. "Rest well my love. Have a safe journey."

She was beginning to close the bag when her curiosity overcame her better judgment. Just as she was about to unzip the bag further, a voice behind her spoke up.

"Lt. Proctor, I suggest you leave well enough alone. You have seen enough of your friend, and in all honesty, I should be reporting you for opening that bag, but I promise I won't if you cooperate with me. You don't need to see anymore, it won't make any difference one way or the other. Remember him as he was, not the way he is today. He's gone, Lieutenant, say a prayer for him. He gave the best that he had, and all we can do for him now, is get him ready to go home to his family. We have lots of work to do with Kenrude and the rest, so I'm asking you to leave now. Please don't make me call Dr. Phillips."

Turning around slowly she looked at Sgt. Crestly. "I know you're right, I just had to say goodbye. He really was a great guy and a great medic. He deserved better."

Sgt. Crestly nodded his head as he zipped Tom's bag shut. "They all deserve better, Lieutenant, none of them deserve to pass through this sad little morgue, but its war, which means good men will die, and I hate my job. Nevertheless, families deserve to have their sons, fathers and brothers handled with dignity."

After looking at Tom's bag one more time, Roxy slowly made her way out of the morgue as the other attendants were returning. Stepping outside into the gathering dusk, Roxy walked down toward the airstrip as she watched two F4 Phantom's streak down the runway. As she watched them turn toward the north, she said, "Please come back. God, please let those men come back in one piece."

The following morning, unceremoniously, the C-130 was loaded with eight military caskets, two of them containing remains of men that had been killed a day earlier. Once they were loaded, Franny, Fr. Neederman and three other men designated as escorts walked up into the cargo bay.

Fifteen minutes later, the lumbering C-130 lifted from the runway a Binh Thuy, headed for the official military morgue at Tripler Army Hospital in Honolulu, where the bodies would be completely prepared for burial back home.

When Geno awoke in the hospital at Quang Tri, several nurses began checking his vitals and looking over his bandages. "How are the other guys from my chopper?" He asked one of the nurses.

"I don't know, Specialist. I was off yesterday, and I just came on duty about a half hour ago, so I'm still playing catch up. But right now, worry about getting better yourself," the forty-something year old nurse replied before leaving the room. After a doctor looked him over, he told the nurses to transfer Geno to a surgical ward.

After Geno was in the ward about an hour, he asked the man next to him if he knew if there was a Kenrude, Dozier, Cumberland, Franklin or Studer in the ward. He knew full well that Jackman and Levin had died on impact after the explosion. After a moment of thought, the soldier replied that he had heard the name Dozier a couple of times, but didn't remember the others.

Knowing full well he didn't have much time because the nurses were going to object, Geno yelled out, "Dozier, Cal Dozier, Are you here?"

From just a couple beds away, Cal called out, "Yeah, I'm here Geno. How the hell are you doing?" Cal paused, sickly aware of the impact his next words would have. "I'm truly sorry to tell you, Geno, but we're the only ones who made it."

Geno gasped as tears filled his eyes. "Kenrude and your crew are all dead? No way Kenrude is dead? That's got to be bullshit!"

After a moment of silence, Cal said in a broken voice, "Yeah, we would have landed perfect, but a mortar round landed right on top of the chopper. Cumberland and Franklin never had a chance. I was out of the chopper, preparing to load guys when a second mortar round hit. I fell to the ground, both my legs were pretty torn up, especially my left. As I attempted to cover Tom, I got hit in the shoulder by a bullet that traveled downward, doing some internal damage. Geno, I could barely move, I didn't have much strength left, but I kept firing best I could to help Tom. He battled like a mad man, firing in every direction, pulling men to safety to protect them. I don't know how many times he was hit, but he just kept working, finding a way to save the next man. I saw the mortar round hit about ten feet away from him. Tom was tossed back against a wrecked chopper like a fricking rag doll. I couldn't figure it out, I don't know how he did it. That son-of-a-bitch kept firing, even though his left arm was beyond use. I saw three V.C. come around the front of the chopper. Tom got one of them right away, the second one shot Tom twice before running toward me. I shot him with an M-16 I picked up, but ran out of ammo. The third bastard pumped two or three more shots into Tom, then headed toward me. It became an all-out race as he came toward me firing, and I struggled to get my .45 out of the holster. Before I even realized what was going on, Tom pulled himself up to one knee and fired four rounds into that asshole. After the V.C. went down, I looked over at Tom, just as he slumped forward, dropping the rifle. I yelled for him, but I knew he couldn't hear me. I just kept calling, but he was gone, Geno. He was gone. Then he saved my miserable life after he was dead. I swear he came back and used the last ounce of life he had left to save me, and then finally left go forever. What the hell did I ever do to deserve that kind of dedication from such a loyal friend?"

Tears ran down Geno's face as he wept. "Dear God, he never got to see his son. Please grant him eternal peace, he was the best man I ever knew."

Two days later, several officers came to speak with Cal regarding what had happened before Tom was killed. They were working off the After Action Report, and the request for a Bronze Star that Lt. Lee had filed. The last thing the investigator asked Cal was whether or not he thought Tom didn't deserve a higher degree of medal for what he had done.

Cal looked at the two men, "In my mind he deserves the Medal of Honor, because he just wouldn't quit. He saved a lot of lives, getting them back toward the medi-vac choppers that were arriving. I just couldn't save him, and even after I totally believe he was already dead, he came back and saved my miserable life. In my book he's a real hero. I've never seen anything like that in all my life. He truly came back from the dead to save me, he honestly did.

CHAPTER 24
GRIEF IN GLENDALE

Large bolts of lightning crisscrossed the dark skies above Glendale as cold, heavy, wind driven rain washed over the windows of the Glendale Hospital. Inside the busy hospital, nurses were once again working another round of ten hour shifts.

A very tired Mackenzie dropped down into a chair behind the nurse's station on the fourth floor of the hospital. Her good friend Gloria Bentner looked up from her paperwork and smiled.

"These ten hour shifts are getting to you, I know. Good thing tomorrow is your day off. The weather is supposed to be kind of nice, so maybe you can go out and do something fun."

"You have no idea how good that sounds. I think my feet are about to fall off," Mackenzie responded, as she leaned back in the comfortable desk chair. After looking up at the clock she continued. "I just can't wait for Tom to come home. It seems like an eternity since he shipped out. And you can bet, I'm going to take a few days off regardless of what's going on around here, no matter what Ellen Chandler has to say about it. It's not my fault that old battle ax has never had a relationship in her life!"

Gloria laughed as she threw a pen at Mackenzie. "Wow, you got a case of who gives a damn really bad girl. I wouldn't let Chandler intimidate you, no one on the floor would blame you at all. In fact, I'm willing to take a shift for you if need be, and so would Carla. We already discussed it the other day."

Mackenzie stood up as she looked at the light panel to see who was calling for a nurse. "Oh, that's Mrs. Sandhoff. I'm guessing she needs pain meds. I tried to get her to take it a little over an hour ago, but she insisted she was going without any tonight." As she opened the medication cabinet she looked over at Gloria. "I don't know what I would do without you. You've been such a good friend since I started here. I can't wait for you to meet Tom and it would be really fun to go out sometime with you and Eddie once Tom has his legs firmly back on solid ground again."

Gloria smiled as she picked up the round sheet from the desk. "Oh yeah, we'll go out and kick up our heels and have a ball. Like a double date. That sounds like a really good idea, Mac."

The rain had begun to subside as Gloria and Mackenzie walked across the parking lot toward their cars. "Well Gloria, don't work too hard tomorrow, and get some sleep tonight. In fact, go home and unplug the phone. Eddie can do without talking to you for one night."

Gloria laughed at Mac's suggestion. "Sleep does sound really good right now. I think it might be a bit cool tonight, so I'm going to toss an extra blanket on the bed, snuggle into my extra pillows, and get all toasty warm."

The women waved at each other one more time as they left the parking lot. The streets of Glendale were nearly deserted as Mackenzie drove the short distance home. She was happy to be pulling into the driveway as the temperatures were beginning to fall and the streets were getting a little slippery.

Quietly, Mackenzie walked into Sean's room to check on her precious child. Finding him awake, she reached down into the crib to pick him up. Sitting down in the old wooden rocking chair she had found at an auction, she kissed her smiling son.

"What are you doing awake, Sean? You should be sound asleep. But I'm kind of glad you're not, because I really missed you tonight."

After rocking Sean for several minutes, his tired eyes slowly closed. However Mackenzie was not ready to lay her son back down. She continued rocking him a while as she sang him a lullaby. With her son now sound asleep, she laid him back in his crib, and covered him with a small blanket Karen had made for him. Standing aside the crib she whispered, "Your Daddy is going to be so proud of you, and he's going to love you so much. You two are going to have so much fun together. I can't wait to watch the two of you play. We'll be such a great family. And you know what Sean, we may even have a playmate for you in the future."

As Mac walked toward her room, her mother met her in the hallway. "Was that little rascal awake again? Your father and I had a terrible time getting him down tonight. It was like something was scaring him, but I couldn't figure out what it could have been."

Mackenzie nodded her head. "Yes, he was awake when I went in there. So I rocked him for a few minutes, and he went right back to sleep. I hope he stays that way, because I'm really beat."

Sitting down on her bed, Mackenzie picked up the photo of her and Tom from the nightstand. She brushed her hand over Tom's face and smiled. "I can't wait to kiss you Thomas, damn I miss you so much. And you better remember, I'll still live in that mud hut with you, no matter where it takes us." Placing the photo back on the night stand, Mac pulled the covers up to her chin. Before turning out the light she whispered, "I love you, Tom."

Mackenzie awoke to a misty, heavily overcast Saturday morning in the warm comfortable bed in her parent's home. It had been a long, tough week at the hospital, so she was ready for a relaxing day off. She really didn't want to work on Sunday, but it wasn't possible to get her schedule changed. Nevertheless, she was excited that Alex and Nancy wanted to spend today with Sean, so she could drive to St. Cloud with Glenda, Christine and Abigail, to spend the day at Crossroads Shopping Center. They always had such a great time at the mall, with so many stores and restaurants to visit. She had prepared a shopping list over the last week, which included a spiffy new sport coat for Tom. It was something she had always wanted him to own.

Mac and her mother were having a cup of coffee in the kitchen, just as the small cuckoo clock in the living room chimed 8:00am. She stiffened slightly, as she observed a blue sedan pull up in front of the house. As two Army officers and Rev. Hamlin exited the vehicle, the coffee cup in her right hand crashed to the floor. She and her mother stood silently for several moments as the three men walked up the sidewalk to their front door. Mac took one step forward as the doorbell rang, before falling to her knees. She began sobbing uncontrollably, knowing she would never see her husband again, and that Sean would never get to meet his father.

Edna Bishop nervously opened the door, looking straight into the eyes of Rev. Hamlin. "Tell me it isn't so. Oh Lord, please tell me it isn't so."

Reverend Hamlin took her by the hands as he quietly said. "I'm so sorry, Edna."

Glenda, Christine and Abigail rushed up the walkway, nearly pushing the army officers out of the way. Entering the living room, they dropped to the floor beside Mac, attempting to console her. Glenda looked over at Christine, as tears rolled down her cheeks, "Go call Steve and Karen."

As Glenda held Mac tight, she sobbed and screamed, "Oh God, he's dead. Oh God, he's dead!"

Mac grabbed onto Glenda with all her strength as she looked up into her eyes. "I killed the love of my life, my husband, the father of our son. I should never have let him enlist. Oh God, he's dead, he's dead. What do I do now, Glenda?"

Reverend Hamlin knelt down beside the grief stricken women he had come to know so well.

"It's not your fault, child. God never let's us know what he has in store for us or our loved ones, or when it will be our time. You gave much to Tom, and he loved you with all his heart, and now you have his child to raise in his honor. That is an incredible act of love."

Mac turned her head away from him, grabbing her mother's arm as she sobbed.

"I want my son to have his father, I want to have Tom help me raise our child, he deserved that! Oh God, what do I do now? Why? Why did you take him from me? Where is the mercy and love you have promised us? Tell me God. What did Tom do to deserve this?"

Turning back toward Rev. Hamlin she called out, "Tell me Reverend. What did he do to deserve dying in some horrible God forsaken country that just takes and takes our young men for no good reason? Can you answer that question, can you give me some understanding? All Tom wanted to do was help the men around him, to give them a chance to live, and now God has chosen to take him. Where is the justice in that? Tell me Reverend, tell me, where is the justice?"

Before the officers could move forward, Mac pushed Glenda aside, as she ran into the nursery followed by Christine. Returning, she walked up to the two army officers who had remained silent so far.

"Tell my son why his father is not coming home. Tell him why he'll never meet his father. For God's sake, don't stand there like some stoic non-caring statues. You need to tell me and explain to Sean, why his daddy will be coming home in a damn box!"

Captain Shell took a deep breath. "Mrs. Kenrude, the President of the United States, and the United States Army regret to inform you that your husband, Sergeant Thomas Kenrude, was killed in action while serving in the Republic of South Vietnam. At this point in time, we do not have the specifics as to what caused his death. We want you to know the army will do whatever it can to help you with final arrangements. Your husband's body will be taken to the army mortuary at Tripler Army Hospital in Honolulu, where he will be prepared for burial. We expect his remains to arrive in Minneapolis within a week. We will notify you of the date and time of arrival. Understand, you may apply to have him interred in Arlington National Cemetery, or Fort Snelling National Cemetery here in Minnesota, we will assist you with those choices and arrangements if you prefer them. Please accept the heartfelt condolences of the President, the United States Army, and a grateful nation."

Mackenzie stood motionless for a moment as she came to terms with everything the Captain explained to her. "Captain, did my husband die in vain? I mean, did he die fighting a war we can never win? We have been there since Kennedy was president, and we never appear to be getting closer to winning. Tell me, what did my husband dies for exactly, and do you even care?"

Major Winz stepped forward, as it appeared Captain Shell was somewhat taken back by Mac's last comment.

"Mrs. Kenrude, we have no answers for your questions regarding the war itself. As you know, your husband enlisted to be a combat medic. At this point in time, we presume he died in combat, attempting to save the lives of other young men who needed him desperately. It takes a true hero to do what he did, constantly exposing himself to enemy fire. We owe him a great debt of gratitude. And yes, Mrs. Kenrude, I honestly do care about the loss of your husband, and the loss of every young man that has been killed. Mrs. Kenrude, for what it's worth, my son is currently in a rehabilitation center in Washington, where he's recovering from massive burns over fifty percent of his body. It may be weeks or months before we know if he's going to survive." Major Winz explained, hoping to bring this most uncomfortable discussion to an end.

Just as Mackenzie was about to speak, Rev. Hamlin placed his arm around her shoulders.

"Mac, these men are just the messengers, and believe me they hate every part of this horrible job. You are angry and hurting very badly right now, and rightfully so. For right now, you need the strength of your family, God, and loved ones to work through this sadness, hurt and grief. Don't blame these men, they are just doing a terribly hard job as best they can.

Is there anyone else you want us to contact, anything else I can do for you right now?"

Before another word was spoken, the porch door swung open, as Steve and Karen rushed into the kitchen.

"Tell me it isn't so! Oh dear Lord, tell me my son isn't dead," Karen shrieked, as she pounded her fists into Major Winz's chest. "No, no, please God, no!" Karen screamed as Steve pulled her away from the shaken officer.

Without saying another word, Karen pulled Mackenzie and Sean into her arms as the women wept bitterly.

Steve walked up to Rev. Hamlin, "It might be a good idea if you would take these officers and go. I think their presence here is doing more harm than good right now. We'll talk to you in the next few days as we begin making funeral preparations."

Nodding his head, Rev. Hamlin turned to guide the officers back out the door. Before they could walk out, Glenda approached them.

"Major, believe me, we are very sorry for what happened to your son. Doing what you have to do cannot be easy after dealing with all of that. We'll keep your son and your family in our prayers."

The major nodded his head in acceptance, as a single tear ran down his cheek. "Thank you, I appreciate that very much. Please take care of Mrs. Kenrude, she needs all the help she can get. This will only get more difficult for her." Stepping forward, he gave Glenda a quick hug before turning to leave.

Just as the men were about to enter their car, Steve ran up behind them. Stopping in front of Major Winz, Steve held out his hand.

"Major, I have an important request. There is a Sergeant Major Francis Doogan serving at Binh Thuy with the 632 Combat Support Group. He and I go back to World War Two. I want him to escort my son's remains back home to Glendale."

The Major nodded his head as he shook hands with Steve. "That will not be a problem Mr. Kenrude. I'll get the paper work going, and make some phone calls when I get back to St. Paul. As I told your daughter-in-law, he can be buried in Arlington or Fort Snelling Cemeteries if you wish. Just say the word and it will be done."

Steve looked down toward the ground for a moment. "I know I can speak for the family when I say that we'll want Tom close by, so we can visit without having to make such a long trip. I'm completely sure that both Mackenzie and my wife would want him back home here in Glendale."

Reverend Hamlin stepped forward. "Steve, allow me to work with Fort Snelling. I know a few people down there, I think we can get a burial team to come up here and perform Tom's burial service. They'll do it properly, with true dignity, exactly what Tom deserves."

Before Steve could respond, Major Winz spoke up. "Don't worry Reverend, I'll take care of all the arrangements with Snelling for a burial team. You need not worry about any of that. Just take care of each other."

After watching the blue sedan drive off, Steve walked back toward the house. He observed his daughter Abigail standing alone near a flower bed. As he approached, she turned around throwing her arms around her father.

"Why Dad? Tom was such a gentle soul, such a good man. He taught me how to fish, how to ride my bike, he looked out for me at school, and he would talk to me whenever I needed a shoulder to lean on. Why Daddy? Why my big brother?"

Steve held his daughter tight as she cried and trembled. "Honey, no one can answer that question but God. We cannot understand his ways. But Abby, you know in your heart that Tom died trying to save the lives of men who desperately needed him to even have a chance to survive. He was there for them in their darkest moments, and he made a difference every damn day he was over there."

Abigail looked up at her father. "But Dad, who was there for Tom when he needed a medic? Who was there to bandage his wounds, to start an IV, to get him on an evac chopper? Tell me, who was there for him? Or did he die all alone with no one there to care for him? I want to know!"

Steve shook his head, "Honey, we may never know the answers to those questions, we may never know exactly how he died, but I'll have Franny look into it when he gets here."

Abigail smiled slightly, "Are you going to have Uncle Franny come for the funeral? It would be so nice to have him here, he is such a wonderful part of our family. I know he loved Tom very much, just as if he was real family."

Steve nodded his head as he stroked Abigail's back. "I asked Major Winz to have Franny escort Tom home. He agreed and said he could make it happen. We'll have him stay at our house. I'll call Harry and Marilyn in a bit, to let them know so they can be here also."

Abigail wiped at her tears. "We need to do everything we can to give my brother the best funeral ever. It just hurts so bad to know Sean Thomas will never know what a great guy his father was. And Mac, God the pain she must be feeling. You should have seen her when we came running into the house. That poor thing, what is she going to do, this is all so awful. I want to wake up and realize this is nothing but a bad dream, but I know that's not going to happen anymore. Oh God, it hurts so much!"

Just as Steve was about to lead Abigail back to the house, Bill Bishop pulled into the driveway. He ran up to Steve taking him by the arm. "Don't tell me Tom's gone. Oh dear Lord, that can't be true, that can't be true!"

Steve placed his arm around Mackenzie's father. "Sorry Bill, Tom was killed in combat, we don't know any more than that right now."

Bill ran toward the door, as Steve and Abigail walked up the sidewalk toward the house.

By now Alex and Nancy, along with Mike and his two sons had joined the grieving family. As Steve and Abigail entered the house, Karen walked over to her husband, grabbing onto his shirt tightly.

"My baby's gone, Steve. Our beautiful baby boy is gone. Why did this have to happen? I want Tom back one more time, just to hold him and kiss him and look into his tender eyes. This wasn't supposed to happen. Tom wasn't supposed to die. I can't deal with this, I just want him back in my arms," Karen called out as she threw her arms around her husband's neck and began to weep. Steve held her tightly, knowing it was going to take a long time for his wife to get past their son's death. It would always leave a hole in her heart that nothing would ever be able to fill.

What he began to worry about most, was whether Karen was going to blame Mackenzie for Tom's death. Regrettably, there always appeared to be some tension between the two of them, ever since the day they informed the family of Tom's decision to quit medical school, and enlist in the Army as a medic. Karen and Mac had openly discussed the situation several times, and all appeared to be forgotten, for all intents and purpose. However, he still always felt there was a layer of animosity and this just might bring everything back to the forefront again, at the very worst time.

By nightfall, the news of Tom's death had spread throughout Glendale into the surrounding township. There was a steady stream of friends and relatives making a solemn pilgrimage to Steve and Karen's house, where the family had decided to set up for a long sleepless night. Around seven o'clock, Gloria Bentner drove into the yard. Mackenzie raced from the house to meet her friend before she could get inside. The two young women stood in the yard holding each other as they cried. After several minutes, Gloria looked intently at her best friend.

"Honey, I'm so very sorry. I couldn't believe the news when I heard it. We were just talking about what we were going to do when Tom came home, and now none of it matters. What are you going to do?"

Mackenzie fought hard to talk as she held onto Gloria. "I don't know. I can't think, I can hardly breathe. Why did this have to happen?"

Realizing there was nothing she could do to comfort her best friend, Gloria took Mackenzie by the hand, and led her back into the house.

As things began to calm down, Steve found a few moments to slip away to the office, to call Harry and Marilyn Jenson down in Iowa to give them the news. Harry took the news very hard, as he recalled a happier time when Tom was christened. Marilyn had an extremely tough time consoling Harry, before he was able to get back on the phone with his closest friend.

After the call ended, Harry looked at his grieving wife. Sweetheart, we need to make this right, we need to have Tom's funeral stand for something. It just can't end this way. Steve and I have been through so much, he and Karen need a tremendous amount of support. First thing in the morning, I'm going to call the guys from our World War Two days, and get them up here for the funeral."

With everyone asleep, Steve walked out onto the back porch. He looked up at the cloudy sky shaking his head. He remembered Harry's words when they returned from Korea, "*I think the Kenrude's and Jensen's have used up all the luck any men can have in war. It's time to live in peace.*"

But where was the peace. Tonight as his son lay in a morgue in Hawaii, men were still dying on the battlefield. Franny was still in Vietnam, after seeing combat in World War Two and Korea. Larry Woodward had committed suicide, and eighty-eight men he trained and knew so well, all died in a snow covered valley in North Korea for no reason. Right now he wished he could speak to Father O'Heally, he always had words of comfort and wisdom no matter the crisis. But he too was dead, killed by an assassin's bullet in Korea. As Steve sat down in a chair on the porch, he thought back to the funeral in Cincinnati for Fr. O'Heally. It had been a moving ceremony he would never forget. He was glad he had taken Karen and the kids to visit the priest's resting place several years ago.

As Steve stood up to return to the house, something caught his attention. There appeared to be someone walking up the driveway toward the house. As he stepped off the porch he called out,

"Who's there, can I help you?" There was no answer but the person appeared to have stopped. Steve attempted to walk down the driveway, but his legs would not move. He was completely transfixed on the figure as it slowly began to approach him. When they were about thirty feet apart Steve called out, "Father O'Heally, is it really you, or is my mind playing tricks on me? Please give me some of your wisdom this night, I need your comforting words."

There was no answer, but he watched intently as the figure bent over, placing something on the ground before returning upright. Steve felt a slight wind blow over him as the moon suddenly appeared brilliantly from behind the dark clouds. At that moment Steve was able to recognize that it was in fact Fr. O'Heally. With a broad smile on his face, Fr. O'Heally nodded his head before making the sign of the cross with his right arm. Then, as if he had never been there, he was gone. Finally, Steve was able to move his legs and began walking forward to where Fr. O'Heally had stood. Reaching down, he found a small wooden cross with the word *'Peace'* etched into it. Steve looked around in every direction as he called out, "Father, come back, I really need to talk with you."

To his regret there was no response. But the small cross he held in his hand was all the proof he needed that Fr. O'Heally had in fact visited him on this awful night. As he walked back to the house, he felt a sense of peace he had never known before, but felt it best not to tell anyone what had happened. He wasn't sure how Karen or anyone else would react to the story. But he did realize that this had been an extraordinary visit from a special man, intended to bring him peace.

Five days later a cardboard box arrived from Vietnam with Tom's personal effects. Mackenzie refused to deal with it at this time and delivered it to Steve, asking him to hold it for her until she was ready. Steve agreed to hold it for her, but Karen became angered at the site of the container, refusing to allow it in the house. So Steve cleared a spot in a cabinet in the garage to store the precious belongings until Mackenzie requested them.

Seven days after the family had been informed of Tom's death, Captain Shell called Steve to inform the family that Franny, Fr. John Neederman, and the casket bearing Tom's remains would be arriving at the Minnesota Air National Guard Base, at the Minneapolis Airport at 1400hrs. on Wednesday.

Under a cloudless azure blue sky, the large crowd that had gathered in front of the National Guard hangar in Minneapolis, watched the massive green Army C-130 Hercules, lumbering across the taxiway. After it came to a stop, and the four powerful engines were turned off, the ramp at the rear of the plane began to open. Six soldiers gently lifted the flag draped steel military casket from the floor of the plane. In perfect unison, they began their slow descent down the ramp. Two men in military uniforms walked slowly behind the casket. One was Sergeant Major Francis Martin Doogan, the other was Captain John Neederman, the Chaplain from Binh Thuy, who had also served in Korea with Steve. As the men reached the bottom of the ramp, the Glendale High School Band began playing a slow funeral march.

As the six men moved forward, a deep voice called out, "Present Arms!" Immediately the color guard and all the military officials took up their proper positions, as the slow procession made their way toward the open door of the black Cadillac from the Glendale Funeral Home.

Steve held on to Karen and Mackenzie, as Mike held onto Glenda and Christine. Mackenzie attempted to pull away from Steve, so she could run out to the casket. It took every ounce of energy he could muster to hold on to his grieving daughter-in-law. Arriving at the hearse, the soldiers gently placed the end of the casket on the floor before sliding it forward in perfect cadence. As the six soldiers backed away, Sergeant Major Doogan, reached down, adjusting the corner of the flag on the casket. As he backed away the deep voice called out, "Parade Rest!" Once again all the military staff moved with precision.

As the door to the hearse was closed, the Chaplain from Fort Snelling stepped forward to a microphone. After a short invocation he turned to face the family. "There is no way for me to fully understand the individual grief all of you are feeling today. We all mourn in our own ways, and surely none of us will ever understand why God decided to take Tom from this world at this time. He was a good soldier and medic, a loving husband and father, and dedicated son. We do know that today Tom is with his Savior Jesus Christ in heaven, where he is getting his just rewards for what he accomplished during his short years on this earth. I can also tell you that today there are many soldiers who are thankful for Tom's willingness to brave the dangers of the battlefield to help them survive during their darkest moments. Tom's spirit will live on in each of those men who survived their injuries because of the selfless acts of bravery Tom performed each and every day. May God bless you all."

After the Chaplain had completed his words, Reverend Hamlin informed the crowd that the funeral would be Saturday at 11:00am at the Glendale High School Gym, and all were welcome. He closed with a prayer before shaking hands with the Chaplain and Master Sergeant Doogan.

The entire family walked over to hug and shake hands with Franny, who was having a hard time as tears rolled down his rough face. Grabbing on to Steve, Franny whispered.

"Tom was the bravest son-of-a-bitch in Vietnam, Stevie boy. You can be proud as hell of him. He was Kenrude through and through. There was none better at what he did."

Steve smiled as he looked at his war buddy. "Thanks Franny, that means a whole lot coming from you. I'm so honored and thankful that you brought my boy home. You and Darcy will be staying with us. Karen and I will not hear a word of argument about it. Harry and Marilyn will be here tomorrow. When will Darcy be arriving?"

"She decided to take the train. She will be in Willmar tomorrow morning around 0830. She wishes this could be on better terms," Franny explained as everyone made their way to their cars.

That evening after everyone had something to eat and exchanged a few stories, Steve and Franny walked outside for a breath of fresh air. "You got such a nice place here, Steve, and a great family all around. I was talking to

Peter for a while earlier tonight. He says he wants to go to the Naval Academy and then learn to fly fighters. Karen just can't be too good with that after what happened with Tom. Have you guys spoken about that? I know it's none of my business, but that boy of yours is Kenrude determined, and I don't think there is anything anyone can say to change his mind."

Steve smiled as he put his arm around Franny's shoulders. "No, we have not had time to think about that yet. But there's no doubt Karen will be attempting to withdraw the blessing she gave him a while back. I guess we'll cross that bridge when we get to it, old friend."

Franny nodded his head before continuing. "Have Tom's belongings arrived yet?"

"Yeah, they're in the garage for now. Mac didn't want to go through them just yet, and Karen didn't want the box in the house. Why?" Steve inquired.

Franny took a deep breath. "When Tom was on that island in the delta, there was a battle. A young Vietnamese girl was killed in the fight. Tom took it real bad, and it hung with him for some time, and maybe still did when he died, but he'd quit talking about it. Before she died, she handed him a Buddhist medallion. He always felt bad he couldn't do more to save her, especially since it might have been his bullet that killed her. He told me if he didn't make it, he wanted that medallion to be buried with him, so maybe she could be at peace. Do you think Mac would mind if we opened the box to see if it's there? I would like to honor Tom's wishes if possible."

After removing the box from the cabinet, Steve cut open the tape. Going right toward the bottom of the box, Steve brought out an envelope containing the medallion. Steve read Tom's hand writing, "*This belonged to Minh Pham, a soldier with the Viet Cong. She gave it to me before passing away. Her memory must always be honored as she was a young, brave, frightened, soldier-child as we all were. God bless her soul.*"

"I think it should be left in the envelope with Tom's request," Steve commented as he handed the envelope to Franny.

"I think you're right. If you don't mind, I'll slip it down beside Tom when no one is watching. That will keep people from asking a lot of questions," Franny responded.

Steve looked at the envelope for a moment. "I think Mac should know about it. I think it's something that might make her feel better about his time over there. Maybe she would like to place it in the casket herself. I think maybe we should give her the option."

Franny nodded his head in agreement. "Yeah, it might help give her a bit of closure. We can talk to her about it before the service."

The following morning when Harry and Marilyn arrived, it was once again a very tearful reunion. Harry explained to Steve about the calls he had made to their former military buddies. He explained that quite a few of them said they were going to attend.

Over the next day and a half, men from Charlie and Alpha Companies began arriving in Glendale. They included Col. Fontaine, Mike Anderson, Gus Rider, Israel Sanchez, Phil Brant, Karl Drussing, Oscar Joblanski, Mitch Hagen, Eddie Schrider, Dave Taggard and Rabbi Ben Rabinowitz. Steve, Karen and Mackenzie were overwhelmed at the outpouring of love and sympathy these brave combat soldiers brought to their family.

That night, Ben Rabinowitz recounted to everyone the story of his saddest day in World War Two, when they came across a concentration camp. He explained how he attempted to take on a German Soldier in a knife fight, hoping to kill the man and get revenge for what they had done to his Jewish people. It was Steve that later convinced him revenge would just add on more hate and sorrow, something he might never have overcome. He told Steve that awful day he decided to become a Rabbi after the war. The men hugged as Steve cried, remembering all that had happened when they liberated the camp.

Before the gathering broke up, Harry took Steve outside to get some fresh air. As he peered into the starry sky he took a deep breath. Turning back toward Steve he said, "Stevie boy, I'm being haunted by those words

I spoke to you when we returned from Korea. I just can't get past it. I told you how the Kenrude's and Jensen's had used up all their luck in war. Those words have been stuck in my throat since we received the call about Tom. I wish to hell I had never said them. It was like I was jinxing everything that would happen in the future. I'm so sorry, Steve, I don't know what I can say or do to make things right. It just gnaws at my soul. The last thing I would ever want to do is hurt you and Karen."

Steve smiled as he walked over toward Harry. "You never jinxed anything, my friend. Sadly, what you said was probably a hundred percent accurate. We went through a lot of hell together, took a lot of crazy chances, and looked death in the face more times than I care to think about. I have thought of those words many times, even before Tom was killed. I guess I knew in my heart you were completely right, bit I didn't want to accept the truth. There has not been a day since Tom left that I haven't been scared out of my mind for him. But Harry, none of that was your fault, no one could have predicted it, and yes, I think the odds were going to catch up with us eventually."

Harry smiled a bit as he looked at his best friend. "Thanks for telling me about your feelings. That really helps a lot. It's just so sad that Sean will never know his daddy, and Mac will have to rebuild her life. I never thought about it much after Europe, although we mourned for a lot of good men. But since Korea and now Vietnam, I'm beginning to wonder if war is ever worth the price that is paid in blood."

Steve nodded his head as he looked down at the ground. After a moment of silence he looked back at Harry.

"Thanks for being here old friend, I'll need your strength to get through the service and all."

Harry placed his hand on Steve's shoulder. "We have both depended on each other many times. I know you'll always be there for me, as I am here for you now."

CHAPTER 25
A SOLEMN GOOD BYE

Friday night, crowds of mourners passed through the Glendale High School Gym at a steady pace, to pay their last respects to one of their own. The family was relieved when they were told the casket could be open for viewing. Everyone was surprised when U.S. Senator Stan Henry and Congressman Art Black arrived. After speaking with the family, Sen. Henry took Peter aside for several minutes, regarding his work to get an appointment to Annapolis for him. Peter was excited to hear everything was in place pending his graduation. He knew Tom would be very proud of him for following his footsteps, although it might be totally different with his mother.

As the crowds were thinning out, Steve and Franny took Mackenzie aside, explaining about Minh Pham on the island in the delta, and the medallion inside the envelope. Steve inquired as to whether or not she wanted the envelope opened so she might see it. After a moment of thought she replied.

"My Thomas placed it in that envelope with his own hands and sealed it. It was as if he was closing the book on her life, so it should never be opened. I'm grateful that Tom and Cal brought her back to the base for burial. It would have been wrong to leave that poor child lying dead on the beach, or to be buried where no one would ever know about her. All of that proves even more to me, what a special guy my Tom was." Taking the envelope from Franny, she boldly walked up to Tom's casket. After kissing the envelope, she slid it inside his uniform jacket. "Your wish has been fulfilled, Thomas. I'm so proud of you. I'll raise Sean the best I can, and never let him forget what a brave, kind loving man you were, and he too will know the story of Minh, so she may also live on. Rest in peace, my love."

Saturday morning the sun was just starting to break through the thick cloud layer that blanketed the eastern horizon, as Steve peered out the kitchen window. Heavy drops of dew that clung to every blade of grass, began sparkling like diamonds, as the first rays of the morning sun beamed down from the heavens. Off in the distance a large hawk screamed as it dove down out of the sky on some small unsuspecting prey. It was the cycle of life. A small rodent would need to die, so the hawk could continue ruling the skies above the Kenrude farm.

Today, the cycle of Tom's short life would also come to an end in a few hours, as his mortal body would be laid to rest in the Glendale cemetery. It was a life cut way too short, in a war that was becoming more unpopular in America, as the long bloody months dragged on.

As he took a sip of coffee he smiled, hearing Sean Thomas raising a fuss, giving his young mother a bad time so early on this day. Thankfully, Tom had been able to leave the Kenrude family a precious gift, in the form of a sweet baby boy that would carry on his lineage. So for the Kenrude family, the cycle of life in Tom's name was getting a fresh new start.

Karen stepped up to her husband. "What are you thinking over here all by yourself. You've been pretty quiet this morning."

Placing his arm around his wife Steve shook his head. "The cycle of life, I suppose. I'm sure Rabbi Ben or Fr. Neederman would be able to explain it better. It's quite a mystery none of us will ever be able to fully explain, or understand."

Karen gently laid her head against her husband's strong shoulder. "So, how are you dealing with it today? My heart feels weak, and my mind is still a jumble of emotions I can't begin to sort out. I ask why, and there's no answer. I ask why Tom couldn't have been just wounded and come home, and there's no answer. I ask God how I'm going to get past all this hurt and anger, and there does not appear to be an answer for that either. What am I doing wrong, why can't God answer me?"

Steve squeezed Karen a bit tighter. "I used to stand down by the lake and attempt to bargain with God, and try to force an answer out of him, but in the end, all I had was silence. I never understood why God would not send a sign or some type of answer. In all reality he always did, I just never understood his answers or realized they existed. He sent me Harry and Franny, he gave me you to raise our children while I was away. He gave me Mike to look after you and the folks, and in both wars he brought me home. I realize now, sometimes the answers show up little at a time, we just have to wait for them. However this time, it's all so hard and it hurts so bad. I guess we can live on through Sean, his presence will require it, even on the hardest of days, and time will heal itself. That's my best guess."

Karen kissed her husband on the cheek. "I really married a very smart man. I know I can thank God for that. I guess we better start getting ready for the day."

Before Karen could turn to walk away, Steve pulled her back. "How are you dealing with Mac? Are you blaming her for Tom's death, can you come to terms with it? Last night it appeared there was friction between the two of you."

Karen nodded her head. "I don't blame her at all. I know Tom was doing what he wanted to do, and he would have talked Mac into it eventually. I think she is still angry with me regarding everything that happened when they told us of his decision. I really unloaded on them, and I said things I should not have said. I can't ever take them back, especially from Tom, and that hurts me the most. But no, I don't blame that poor wounded girl. We have talked several times, but I don't think she has been able to really get past it. I'm praying on that issue also."

Never in the history of Glendale, had such a huge funeral taken place.

By 10:00am most of the High School Gym was already filled. Military flags of all types stood by the north wall where the service was going to take place. Captain Shell and Major Winz busied themselves making sure every preparation had been completed, and that everyone understood where they were supposed to be, and what their tasks were. True to form, Col. Fontaine went behind them, double checking every step to assure all was good and proper.

At the Glendale Funeral Home, family and close friends gathered for the final prayers before the casket was closed. Mackenzie stepped up to the casket holding their son. Turning him in her arms so he could look down at Tom she whispered. "Sean Thomas, meet your daddy. He was a very special person, a man I loved with my whole heart and soul. I know he's looking down upon us from heaven right now, and smiling at what a beautiful boy you are. No matter what you do in this life, know that your daddy will always be there to look out for you. He loved you so very much."

As she began to weep, Sean reached his tiny arm forward toward the casket. Franny stepped forward taking Sean from Mac's arms. As he lowered Sean toward the casket, he reached out once more touching his father's arm and smiled. The room was totally quiet as everyone present watched what was happening. As Franny handed Sean back to his mother, she kissed Franny on the cheek as she whispered, "Thank you so much, I didn't have the strength to do that. I'll never forget this, and Sean will never be allowed to forget his Uncle Franny. Please stay in our lives."

Franny placed his hand on Mac's shoulder and smiled as a tear rolled down his cheek. "I would be honored to be a part of Sean's life. He has a lot to learn about his daddy."

About a half hour later, the funeral procession arrived in front of the school. As the rear door of the hearse was opened, a voice called out. "Present Arms!" Immediately the Color Guard and all the assembled military dignitaries saluted, as the high school band began playing 'America the Beautiful.'

As Franny slowly led the casket into the packed gymnasium, the voice called out, "Parade Rest!" When they reached the front of the gym the casket was turned facing east to west, with a military honor guard standing on both sides. Everyone remained standing as the band played the National anthem.

Once everyone was seated, Rev. Hamlin began the service although he had a very hard time talking during his short homily. When he was finished, Fr. John Neederman walked to the casket. After placing both hands on the flag, he made his way to the microphone.

"My name is Fr. John Neederman. I served in Korea with Steven and the other veterans you see gathered here today. Steven and I were close friends, he shared many letters from home with me, and often spoke about Tom and Abigail. He was proud of how his family was handling everything while he was over in Korea. He was just as proud of the men he led into combat every day, and it showed. You see Steven didn't just lead men, he cared for them, he loved them, and each life was precious to him. So I knew Steve and Karen would raise their son to be a good, honest and caring man. And everything Tom accomplished reflects that they did just that.

Although Tom was not a Catholic, he came to many of my services, and spoke with me often, knowing I had experienced war as a soldier in Korea. He was open and honest about his fears, and how he wondered if he was doing enough for the men that needed him. He was not afraid, nor was he willing to shirk his responsibilities. As St. John says in chapter fifteen, verse thirteen of the Holy Bible, "*Greater love has no one than this: that he lay down his life for his friends.*" That is exactly what Thomas was doing the day he left this earth, and went home to his maker. We will never know his last thoughts, his last fears, or his last words. But we'll always know our Savior was at his side, as he was doing God's work, and he was honoring his fellow man as he did it. Although we can accept that much, finding comfort and peace in our human frailty is a much tougher task. If we reach out to God, he'll hear us and heal us, but it will take time. No doubt, there will always be questions as to why, there will be questions concerning God's decision to take Thomas, when he had a beautiful son to raise, a son he had not yet held in his arms. But in time, God's mercy and kindness heals all wounds. As we go forward today, let us remember Thomas, and try to live the kind of life he exemplified to the scared and wounded men he served each day with compassion. I offer my sincerest condolences to Mackenzie, Sean Thomas, Steve, Karen, all the Kenrude family, and the extended family of fellow veterans and friends that have gathered here today."

As the service ended, Franny once more took the lead, rolling the casket back out of the gym toward the hearse, as the School Band played 'Rock of Ages.'

Just as Franny arrived at the door of the hearse he stopped as a voice called out. "Present Arms!"

As the crowd became silent, the band began playing 'God Bless America.'

When the band was finished the voice called out, "Parade Rest!" Franny turned and stepped aside as the military pall bearers slowly loaded Tom's casket into the long black Cadillac for the short drive to the cemetery.

At the cemetery, the military pall bearers once more slowly unloaded the bronze casket from the hearse, carrying it to the grave site. After Rev. Hamlin read his last prayers, the honor guard slowly removed the flag from the top of the casket and gently folded it into a tight triangle.

Slowly, the sergeant in charge of the burial detail walked over to Mackenzie, holding out the flag saying, "On behalf of the President of the United States, the Army, and a grateful nation, please accept this flag as a symbol of our appreciation for Tom's honorable and faithful service."

As Mackenzie accepted the flag, the sergeant stood erect and saluted. As he turned to take up his position, the seven man ceremonial firing squad from Fort Snelling fired three volleys. As they finished, a bugler blew taps over the quiet cemetery, each plaintive note echoing back from the woods at the far end of the field.

After the honor guard marched off, people began to walk back toward their cars. Steve talked with Harry and Franny for a few moments before turning back toward Mackenzie, Karen, Glenda and Christine, who had all remained seated under the white canopy.

As there was a vacant seat next to Mackenzie, Steve sat down, placing his arm around his daughter-in-law. Mackenzie smiled as she handed the flag to Steve, so she could take Sean back from Glenda. As Steve took the flag he looked down at Mackenzie's hands. He noticed she was clutching a small wooden cross, like the one he found on the road after seeing the apparition of Fr. O'Heally. Quickly Steve stood up and looked around the cemetery. "Mac, where did you get that cross?" he anxiously inquired.

"As we were walking out of the gym, a priest near the door said, 'Bless you my child,' and handed it to me," Mackenzie responded, as she shuffled Sean in her arms.

Taking the cross from Mackenzie, he noticed the same inscription of *Peace* on the front of it.

"Sweetheart, did you see where the priest went, did you see him here at the cemetery?" Steve inquired as he continued scanning the area.

Mackenzie shook her head. "No, I just smiled and thanked him and then turned back toward the hearse. I can't say that I saw him here, I really don't know. Why is it important, is he a friend of yours?"

Steve nodded his head. "Yes, yes he is. I would like to talk with him. He's a very special person. I'm going to take a look around."

After Steve returned, Karen looked strangely at him. "Where did you go, what were you looking for? Are you alright? You actually look a little pale."

Steve took one more look around the cemetery before looking at his wife, who was standing beside Harry and Franny.

"I'll talk to you about it sometime, but not now, it just doesn't make any sense to me. It just can't be real. Trust me, sweetheart!"

Karen and Harry looked at Steve, wondering what was going on when

Mackenzie walked up to them. "I'm not sure what's happening either, Karen, but it started when he saw this cross in my hand, and asked me where I got it."

Harry reached over to take the cross from Mackenzie. After studying it for a moment he looked up at Steve.

"This is identical to the cross Fr. O'Heally used to wear around his neck. I would know it anywhere. Where did you get this Mac?"

Before she could answer Steve replied, "Fr. O'Heally gave it to her when she left the gym. I know that for a fact, because I have one also." Everyone stood there quietly, not sure what to say as Steve retrieved the small wooden cross from his pocket. "I wasn't going to ever tell anyone this, but the night you were all at the house, I stepped outside to get some fresh air. I saw a man walking up the driveway, but I couldn't tell who it was. I couldn't move, it was as if my legs were stuck in concrete. As the figure approached me, I could see an aura around him. He stopped about thirty feet from me, placing this cross on the ground. Then there was a gust of wind, the moon came out from behind the clouds and I could see plain as day that it was Fr. O'Heally. He smiled, made the sign of the cross, and then he vanished as if he had never been there. When I walked over where he had been, I found this cross."

Harry stepped forward, taking the cross from Steve. He turned the crosses around, examining them carefully. "They are identical as anything can be. That is one heck of a story." Handing the cross back to Mackenzie, Harry inquired, "You actually saw the priest close up and he spoke with you? What did he look like?"

In a nervous voice, she explained what the man was wearing and gave a perfect description of Fr. O'Heally, right down to the identical cross around his neck. There was no doubt in their minds that it had been the kindly priest that the men had come to know, love and depend upon so much during the war.

Slowly they began walking toward their cars not saying a word. Just before Steve entered their car, he gave one long last look around the now quiet cemetery. The only people he could see, were the men from the cemetery who were going to finish the grave site once all the mourners were gone. Taking a deep breath, Steve looked up toward the sky for a moment, as a slight gust of cool wind blew over his face. He clearly understood he was not alone in dealing with the loss of his son.

About two months after Tom's death, Mackenzie received a letter from the Department of Defense. It was to notify her that Thomas S. Kenrude was going to be awarded the Distinguished Service Cross, the second highest medal for bravery awarded by the United States Army, for bravery and courage under fire during the battle for Hill 843, during Operation Texas Star.

She immediately grabbed Sean and drove to Steve and Karen's house. She ran in the house to find Karen working on paper work for the farm.

"Karen, you have to see this, I can't believe it. Here, read this!" Mac was yelling as she held out the documents."

Karen swiveled her chair around to face Mackenzie. "What is it, honey," Karen inquired as she took the documents from her daughter-in-law's hand. Tears flowed down her cheeks as she slowly read the documents. "My God, I can't believe this, what did that son of mine do, we have to get this over to Steve right away. He's over at his folk's place."

Mackenzie and Karen drove quickly to the Kenrude homestead where Steve and Mike were repairing one of their combines. The car had barely stopped before Karen threw open the door and was calling for her husband.

Steve and Mike walked over toward the car, meeting Karen half way. "Look at this, Tom is being awarded a medal for bravery."

After wiping his hands off, Steve took the documents from Karen and read them. "Wow, Tom is being awarded The Distinguished Service Cross. I wonder what the hell that kid did."

Three weeks later, the army sent a small bus to the Kenrude farm to pick up family members for the award ceremony at the State Capital in St.

Paul. Arriving in the Governor's reception room, Mackenzie was amazed to see U.S. Senator Stan Henry, Congressman Artimus Black, several State Legislators and a host of military officers. Each one of them came forward to greet her and the family, congratulating them on Tom's award.

At 1100, the Governor walked into the room. After making a few remarks he turned the podium over to Lt. General Arthur Boldrum from the pentagon.

After opening a blue folder, he looked around the room before stopping to meet Mackenzie's eyes. He then began reading from the file.

"*The President of the United States wishes to award Specialist Fourth Class Thomas S. Kenrude, The Distinguished Service Cross, for his selfless Bravery and Heroism in combat. While under heavy fire in the battle for Hill 843, during Operation Texas Star, on 10 May, 1970, Specialist Kenrude, although severely injured himself, continued treating wounded men and delivering them to evacuation choppers. When it appeared Hill 843 was about to be over run, Specialist Kenrude conspicuously placed himself in the line of fire. Despite being wounded numerous times, he attempted to drag wounded men to cover, while fighting off the enemy. After being critically wounded by an enemy mortar round that took his left arm out of use, he laid on the ground, supporting a rifle on his left leg, and continued firing, in order to save the life of a fellow crew member, still attempting to load wounded men. Specialist Kenrude fought valiantly until the last evacuation chopper was able to depart the hill.*

Specialist Kenrude exemplified the true meaning of bravery in the long standing tradition of the United State Army. Specialist Thomas S. Kenrude has brought credit upon himself, the United States Army, and his family. A grateful nation owes him a sincere debt of gratitude."

After the General was finished reading, he motioned for Mackenzie to come forward. After handing her the file, he gently pinned the ribbon to Sean's blanket. He then leaned over toward her and whispered. "If there is anything we can do for you Mrs. Kenrude, my card is inside this file. Never hesitate to call."

As the service came to an end, General Boldrum led two young men forward. "Folks, I would like you to meet Medic Specialist Fourth Class Geno Sarducci and Flight Mechanic Specialist Fourth Class Calvin Dozier. They both served with Tom's squadron, and both were wounded during the battle for Hill 843. You are free to ask them anything you want, they volunteered to be here today."

When just the family was left in the room, Karen looked seriously at the men and asked.

"Did either of you see Thomas get killed? I need to know what happened to my son!"

After swallowing hard, Cal nodded his head. "Yes, Mrs. Kenrude, I did. He died a hero, he died trying to help a lot of good men. All I will tell you is this, the Viet Cong that killed him, have also died and been sent to hell. I feel it's best we just leave it right there."

Before Karen could say another word, Steve and Mackenzie walked forward. Steve placed his arm around Karen's waist. "The man is right, honey. You don't need to know exactly what happened to Tom. In fact, it may only make matters worse for you. Don't put these soldiers through the pain of explaining and reliving things they would rather somehow forget."

Mackenzie placed her hand on Karen's arm. "Steve is right. We don't need to know the grizzly details, I for one do not wish to hear them, I don't want to hear anything more than I heard today. I'm not sure I was ready to hear what the General read from this file. It has made me sick, thinking about what Tom's last few moments in this world were like. I don't want to hear any more."

Karen nodded her head. "I think you both may be right. Let's just go home, I've had enough."

After Mackenzie shook hands with the men, Cal spoke up. "Mrs. Kenrude, it's a pleasure to have met you. Tom and I were good friends, I loved playing jokes on him. We had fun when we could. I was in a really bad place when Minh was killed, and I acted very badly. Through it all, Tom forgave me for my stupidity and lack of dignity. He was a tremendous individual with a very generous heart. I'll miss him forever, and thank you for stepping in. I really didn't want to get into it, especially not with his family. Like his father said, I would rather forget it, although I'm afraid I never will because I would not be here today, if not for Tom."

When Cal was finished speaking, Geno walked up to give Mackenzie a kiss on the cheek. As tears rolled down his face he said, "Mrs. Kenrude, your husband was my best friend. I'll never forget him, and I will always honor him. Everyone that served with him walked away a better person, he was just that kind of guy. You can take this home with you, there are a lot of men who owe their lives to your husband's skill, bravery and caring heart. He'll live on in each of them, Tom's legacy will never pass away."

Mackenzie gave both men a big hug. "Thank you for being here today. Some day as Sean gets older, I would like to have him talk to you, so he gets a better understanding of what his father was all about. Would you be willing to do that for me? Also, would you guys keep in touch with me, at least at Christmas time, weddings and other occasions? I want to be part of your families as Sean Thomas will always be part of yours."

Both men had tears in their eyes, as Christine walked forward handing Sean back to his mother.

"You can count on both of us, we'll keep in touch. After all, we owe that little guy that much," Geno replied.

After exchanging addresses, Mackenzie joined the family for the long drive back to Glendale.

Arriving home, Mackenzie felt lost, it felt as if the entire world had suddenly turned over, and left her hanging upside down, all by herself. Her husband was gone, her dreams and hopes had been dashed forever, and there was nothing anyone could do to change any of it.

With Sean sound asleep and her parents watching television, Mackenzie walked through the evening twilight toward the cemetery. The streets of Glendale were mostly quiet this late in the day, making her feel all the more alone.

Arriving at the cemetery, she walked slowly up to Tom's grave. She stood quiet, as she contemplated all that had occurred over the past three months. In some respects, it still felt as if it had all been a bad dream, but the marble stone in front of her, assured her it was entirely true.

Kneeling down by the stone, Mackenzie ran her fingers across Tom's name as tears streamed down her face.

"I love you Tom Kenrude, and nothing will ever change that. Dear God, why did you have to take him from me? He was my life, my love, my very reason for living. I don't know if I will ever understand your reasons." Placing a blanket on the ground she had carried with her, Mackenzie laid down on top of Tom's grave and closed her eyes. Fractured dreams of Tom and Sean raced through her subconscious, as if memories from a life well lived passed in procession.

As dusk settled over south central Minnesota that evening, it was as if the entire universe was focused on that small plot of land in the Glendale Cemetery, by that marble stone and the sobbing woman whose heart and soul would never be whole again. She laid a single rose in front of the stone as she ran her fingers over her husband's name.

"Thomas, we'll never have the mud hut, nor any other place to call our own, and raise our son, and we won't have the playmate we wanted for Sean. Sweetheart, we never planned on this, and I don't know what to do, I don't know how to start over, or if I really want to."

Looking skyward she shook her head, "Where are you my love, can you see me? Because I can't see you, I want to feel your touch, your kiss, I need to have your strength to raise our son. Oh God, why did I have to agree with your idea of joining the army? Sometimes I get so angry with you, and sometimes I don't know what to feel. I know how you died, you were doing what you wanted to do, helping others that could not do for themselves, and I'm so proud of you. But in the end sweetheart, you are gone and I'm here so alone, so scared, so much in love with you, yet I have no way to give it to you. I never have felt such horrible pain like this ever before."

Opening her purse, she took out the tattered photo she had sent Tom of her and Sean, the one he always carried in his flak jacket. "You knew what was waiting for you back home, why couldn't you come back to be with us. We need you, honey, we need you so bad."

As darkness over took the quiet cemetery, the city of Glendale and the entire world was oblivious to the painful cries of a young woman who clutched a tattered photo as she lay in a fetal position upon the grave of her heroic husband.

EPILOGUE

In the fall of 1999, Sean and his family, along with Mackenzie, Cal Dozier and Geno Sarducci, traveled to Vietnam to visit the site where Tom was killed. They were all amazed to see the burned, rusted skeletons of the destroyed choppers sitting silently, as if they were sentinels guarding the sacred battlefield. Cal led them to the remains of the chopper Tom had lain against, after the last mortar exploded. Sean and Mackenzie pushed an eighteen inch white cross, with a replica of Tom's dog tag into the sodden ground where he died. After saying a few prayers, Sean and Cal used a Swiss Army Knife to shear off four pieces of brittle metal from the outer skin of the chopper.

When they returned home, Sean placed two pieces of the metal into glass frames, giving one to Mackenzie. In 2005, when Sean's oldest daughter Hannah was 12, she came down with a rare type of leukemia. Doctors at the University of Minnesota were not able to find medications to deal with it, and she became progressively worse. One evening Mackenzie brought her glass frame to the hospital. She told everyone that Tom used to say he was going to find a cure for cancer when he became a doctor. Sean placed it on the night stand next to Hannah's bed, but before Mackenzie left for the night, she slid it under Hannah's pillow, along with the wooden cross she had been given by Fr. O'Heally, while giving instructions to the nursing staff to leave it there. Over the next four weeks, Hannah began making a remarkable recovery. After six weeks, the doctors were not able to find a trace of the disease anywhere in her body. Today, Hannah is twenty-six years old and in perfect health with a child of her own, and the disease has never returned.

Many veterans from Alpha Company have reported seeing Fr. Timothy O'Heally during times of grief and emotional hardships. Several other men have reported receiving the small crucifix in different ways. He is buried in the cemetery belonging to St. Cecelia's Parish in Cincinnati, Ohio.

"The Veterans and Family"

*Romey Eliot, Killed in action near Binh Thuy. Buried in Grand Island, Nebraska.
*Walt Kopplemann, Killed in action on night insertion. Buried in Hoboken, New Jersey.
*Warrant Officer Two Chuck Johnson, Lost his hand during the battle for the A Shau Valley. He returned home to Calhoun, Tennessee where he struggled with PTSD and chemical dependency for many years before committing suicide in November of 1977.
*Medic Moe Ashton, killed in the battled of the A Shau Valley. He was awarded the Bronze star he was promised by Capt. Holloway during the Cambodia raid.. He is buried in the Cemetery of the Pacific in Hawaii, near his grandfather who was killed in World War Two.
*Lt. Col. Fargo, killed in the battle of the A Shau Valley is buried in Arlington National Cemetery.
*Medic Everett Tomlin, killed in the battle of the A Shau Valley is buried in Kingston, Ohio.
*Lt. Arthur Mapes, retired from the Army after thirty-three years with the rank of Lt. Colonel. He sold Real Estate for ten years in Macon Georgia before retiring. He is still alive as of this writing.

*Tim Stewart flight mechanic, killed in the Mekong Delta. He is buried in Lake City, Michigan.

*Warrant Officer Rick Palmero, helicopter pilot, killed in the Mekong Delta. The crash site was investigated in 2004. No remains were ever recovered. He remains listed as Missing in Action.

*Medic Frank Ridzik, killed at Binh Thuy. He is buried in Greenville, Alabama.

*Medic Mark Grissom, killed at Binh Thuy. He is buried in San Bernadino, California.

*Medic Orlando Martinez, killed at Binh Thuy. He is buried at Fort Logan National Cemetery, Denver, Colorado.

*Medic Geno Sarducci survived his wounds from the chopper crash. He returned home to Long Island, New York, where he married his high school sweetheart, and went to school to become a registered nurse. He worked in several hospitals before retiring in 2006.

*Crew Chief Cal Dozier, eventually settled in Houston Texas, where he worked on helicopters for several large oil companies, flying crews and supplies to oil rigs in the Gulf of Mexico. He is still alive as of this writing.

*Medic Bill Boulder, killed during the battle in the central highlands. He is buried in Paragould, Arkansas.

*Medic Andre Flinn, returned home to join his father's contracting business. He is alive as of this writing, living in Amarillo, Texas

*Lt. Mark Jurgins, retired from the Army after 30 years in 1995, with the rank of Major. He became a radio talk show host in Twin Falls, Idaho where he still lives today.

*Capt. John Trajillio retired from the Army after 33 years in 1990, with the rank of Lt. Colonel. He went on to serve ten years in The House of Representative for the state of North Carolina. He passed away in 2009 and is buried in Arlington National Cemetery.

*Col. Andre Hernandez retired from the Army after 36 years in 1985.

He went on to work as a stock broker until his death in 2008. He is buried in Phoenix, Arizona.

*Warrant Officer Two Sy Cumberland killed during the battle for Hill 843, when his helicopter was hit by a mortar while landing. He is buried in Woodlawn National Cemetery near Elmira, New York.

*Warrant Officer Two Darnel Franks killed during the battle for Hill 843, when his helicopter was hit by a mortar while landing. He is buried in Alton National Cemetery, Alton, Ill.

*Combat Nurse Roxy Procter, returned home to Akron, Ohio after her second tour of duty. She went to work in the Akron Children's Hospital. A year later she married Dr. Phil Scarborough and had two daughters. She traveled to Glendale in 1980 to meet Mackenzie and Sean. They have remained good friends. Roxy and her husband are both retired and continue to live in Akron.

*Captain Walter Holloway did receive his promotion to Major after leaving Vietnam. He served in many positions before retiring in 2000 with 35 years of service. He lives in Annapolis, Maryland.

*Sergeant Edward Mecklenburg retired from the Army in 1988 at the rank of Sgt. Major. He passed away in 1998.

*Johnnie Semz returned home after losing his arm, but could not adjust to the changes. He was arrested for robbing a bank in 1972 where two people were killed. Johnnie was sentenced to two life sentences in prison. He is alive as of this writing still in prison.

*Chaplain Fr. John Neederman, served two tours in Vietnam before turning to his Parish in Omaha Nebraska. He was killed by a Hamas snipers bullet while visiting Israel in 1995.

*Harry Jensen, he and his wife Marilyn spent many hours visiting Steve and Karen before Harry passed away in 2011 while touring war sites in France and Germany.

*Sergeant Major Francis Martin Doogan the third (Franny) Retired from the army in 1981 at the rank of Command Sergeant Major after forty years of service. He and Darcy moved permanently to Florida where he served two terms in the Florida legislature before retiring to write. He wrote two novels and one book on his war memories. He passed away in 2009.

*Alex Kenrude, Tom's grandfather passed away in 1972.

*Nancy Kenrude, Tom's grandmother passed away in 1974.

*Christine (Kenrude) Simmons, Tom's aunt, worked as a nurse and married an attorney. They live in the Minneapolis, Minnesota area where they raised four children. She and Mackenzie still visit quite often when she gets back to Glendale. She is still alive as of this writing.

*Peter Kenrude, Tom's younger brother did attend Annapolis. He became a naval pilot and served in the First Gulf War flying carrier missions into Afghanistan. He retired from the navy in 2005. He and his wife Mary had two children, and decided to retire in San Diego, California so they could be close to the navy they came to love.

*Mike Kenrude, Tom's uncle, continued working on the farm with his two sons Matt and Greg, and his brother Steve. He passed away in 2011.

*Glenda (Ramsdale) Kenrude, Tom's aunt, moved off the farm shortly after her husband Mike passed away. She lived in Willmar with her daughter Anna until she passed away in 2016.

*Karen (Donnelly) Kenrude, Tom's mother, was never really able to get past Tom's death. It haunted her until she passed in 2017.

*Steve Kenrude and his brother Mike continued building the farm operation their father began. Steve passed away in 2012 while sitting on the back porch of his home reading the newspaper.

*Mackenzie (Bishop) Kenrude spent the rest of her life in the Willmar, Glendale area, working as a nurse in the hospital. She never remarried, choosing to live a rather quiet life enjoying her grandchildren and their families, while donating much of her free time to charitable causes. She is still alive as of this writing.

*Sean Kenrude joined the army after high school, serving as a military police officer, seeing action in the first Gulf War. After the army he returned to Glendale where he joined the Kandiyohi County Sheriff's Department. He married Jackie Swanson, his high school sweetheart. Together they had three children, Hannah, Catherine and Thomas. Sean and Jackie still live in the Glendale area.

AUTHOR'S NOTES

The incident in the barber shop during basic training with the recruit having long hair being referred to as Jesus, happened to a man in my basic training platoon in 1969.

The incident where the men were marched outside in the rain in their underwear, also happened to my basic training platoon in 1969.

The basic training unit Tom was assigned to, A-5-2, was my basic training company.

The incident where Tom was told to act like a cow and eat grass also is factual. It happened to one of the men in my company.

The incident involving Cpl. Edmonds hand being broken while searching for weapons during bivouac actually happened. I knew the man who did the dirty deed.

The incident regarding abuse of a trainee by a D.I. actually happened. We were marching back from the firing range when a man was out of step and could not keep up. When he was ordered to do 50 push-ups, the instructor kicked him in the ribs several times. When the injured man could not continue, the instructor kicked him again and no other instructor came forward to stop it. The explanation of how Pvt. Sid Young, a fictitious name, stepped forward was accurate. When he was challenged by several instructors, he told them of his father's position in the pentagon. He did in fact call his father regarding the incident and the drill instructor was reprimanded.

Having men assigned to work projects on base while in the reception center was normal back in the sixties. I spent one entire day stocking shelves in the commissary, and another half day, filling and stacking sand bags.

The story regarding the attempt to napalm the dog in St. Cloud did in fact take place. The incident received very little press coverage. I met one of the men involved in rescuing the dog about ten years after the incident.

This will be the last book in the Kenrude Family series. I need to move on to other stories in order to help attract a publishing consultant. I hope you have enjoyed these three books, and will continue to follow my future writings, where ever my spirit and God may lead me.

~ Gerry Feld

FACTS ABOUT THE VIETNAM MEMORIAL WALL IN WASHINGTON D.C.

There are 58,267 names on the wall, 39,996 were just 22 or younger, 8,283 were 19, while 33,103 were 18, additionally 12 were 17 years old, and 5 were just 16.

There are 3 sets of fathers and sons on the wall, while 31 sets of parents lost 2 of their sons.

There were 997 killed on their first day in country, 1,448 were killed on their last day. Eight women are on the wall, all nurses. There were 244 soldiers awarded the Congressional Medal of Honor during the war, 153 of them are on the wall.

Vietnam; Honor and Sacrifice

www.ingramcontent.com/pod-product-compliance
Lightning Source LLC
Chambersburg PA
CBHW021350290426
44108CB00010B/184